Leading Ladies of the White House

Communication, Media, and Politics

Series Editor
Robert E. Denton, Jr., Virginia Tech

This series features a broad range of work dealing with the role and function of communication in the realm of politics, broadly defined. Including general academic books, monographs, and texts for use in graduate and advanced undergraduate courses, the series encompasses humanistic, critical, historical, and empirical studies in political communication in the United States. Primary subject areas include campaigns and elections, media, and political institutions. *Communication, Media, and Politics* books will be of interest to students, teachers, and scholars of political communication from the disciplines of communication, rhetorical studies, political science, journalism, and political sociology.

Titles in the Series

The Millennium Election: Communication in the 2000 Campaign
    Edited by Lynda Lee Kaid, John C. Tedesco, Dianne G. Bystrom, and Mitchell McKinney
Strategic Political Communication: Rethinking Social Influence, Persuasion, and Propaganda
    Karen S. Johnson-Cartee and Gary A. Copeland
Campaign 2000: A Functional Analysis of Presidential Campaign Discourse
    William L. Benoit, John P. McHale, Glenn J. Hansen, P. M. Pier, and John P. McGuire
Inventing a Voice: The Rhetoric of American First Ladies of the Twentieth Century
    Edited by Molly Meijer Wertheimer
Communicating for Change: Strategies of Social and Political Advocates
    John P. McHale
Political Campaign Communication: Principles and Practices, Fifth Edition
    Judith S. Trent and Robert V. Friedenberg
The Rhetoric of Redemption: Kenneth Burk's Redemption Drama and Martin Luther King, Jr.'s "I Have a Dream" Speech
    David A. Bobbitt
Reelpolitik II: Political Ideologies in '50s and '60s Films
    Beverly Merrill Kelley
New Frontiers in International Communication Theory
    Edited by Mehdi Semati

Forthcoming

Entertaining Politics: New Political Television and Civic Culture
    Jeffrey P. Jones
Women's Political Discourse
    Molly A. Mayhead and Brenda DeVore Marshall
The 2004 Presidential Campaign
    Edited by Robert E. Denton, Jr.
Politeness and Political Debate
    Edward A. Hinck, Shelly S. Hinck, and William O. Dailey
Media and the Staging of American Politics
    Gary C. Woodward

Leading Ladies of the White House

Communication Strategies of Notable Twentieth-Century First Ladies

Edited by Molly Meijer Wertheimer

ROWMAN & LITTLEFIELD PUBLISHERS, INC.
Lanham • Boulder • New York • Toronto • Oxford

ROWMAN & LITTLEFIELD PUBLISHERS, INC.

Published in the United States of America
by Rowman & Littlefield Publishers, Inc.
A wholly owned subsidary of The Rowman & Littlefield Publishing Group, Inc.
4501 Forbes Boulevard, Suite 200, Lanham, MD 20706
www.rowmanlittlefield.com

P.O. Box 317, Oxford OX2 9RU, UK

British Library Cataloguing in Publication Information Available

Library of Congress Cataloging-in-Publication Data

Leading ladies of the White House : communication strategies of notable twentieth-century First Ladies / edited by Molly Meijer Wertheimer.
     p.   cm. — (Communication, media, and politics)
     Includes bibliographical references and index.
     ISBN 0-7425-3672-6 (pbk. : alk. paper)
     1. Presidents' spouses—United States—History—20th century. 2. Presidents' spouses—United States—Language. 3. Communication—Political aspects—United States. 4. Rhetoric—Political aspects—United States. I. Wertheimer, Molly Meijer. II. Series.
     E176.2.C66   2005
     973'.09'9—dc22

                                                                2004015929

Printed in the United States of America

⊗™ The paper used in this publication meets the minimum requirements of American National Standard for Information Sciences—Permanence of Paper for Printed Library Materials, ANSI/NISO Z39.48-1992.

Contents

Acknowledgments

Serendipity probably plays a larger role in instigating scholarship than any of us would care to admit. That is certainly true in the case of this work, which sprang from a chain of events beginning with an assignment given to my son when he was in third grade. As an antidote for the late-January blahs, his class was asked to read a book, and then come to class as one of the characters. Since he had a Ninja warrior costume which he insisted on wearing, we had to find a book to justify his outfit. A trip to the library produced *The Magic Fan*—all we needed was a fan to use as a prop. Our local Dollar Store didn't have a fan, but it did have remaindered copies of Barbara Bush's *A Memoir*. Blessed with snow the next day, I curled up in front of the fireplace to read about Mrs. Bush's experiences. Another coincidence set the stage for this book. Nola Heidelbaugh phoned to invite me to participate on an ECA roundtable panel on the rhetorical uses of motherhood. Inspired by Mrs. Bush's *A Memoir*, I proposed a paper exploring her uses of motherhood. At the conference, all of the panelists agreed on the need for a book examining the rhetoric of first ladies. Through a call placed on CRT-NET and in other ways, we located chapter authors. The result was *Inventing a Voice: The Rhetoric of American First Ladies of the Twentieth Century*, which was the inspiration for this book.

Although these books began amidst a great deal of fluidity and coincidence, finishing them was a different story, involving a great deal of deliberate and painstaking work—by the authors of these chapters, the archivists at many of the presidential libraries who helped us locate materials, and by colleagues at our institutions who helped us find funds for travel and released time.

In the chapters to follow, the authors acknowledge the help they received in the "notes" sections of their chapters. As editor of this volume, I would like to offer my appreciation to several individuals. Robert Denton was an early supporter, who waited patiently for us to finish the manuscript of *Inventing a Voice*, then recommended it to Brenda Hadenfeldt, Acquisitions Editor in Communication and Journalism at Rowman & Littlefield Publishers. Much appreciation goes to her as well for helping us move that project to completion and for helping me put this volume together.

I would also like to acknowledge the support of two colleagues from the Hazleton Campus of the Pennsylvania State University. Deidre Jago, Assistant Director of Academic Affairs and John Madden, CEO. Thank you, too, to Dr. Sandy Gleason, Associate Dean of Faculty and Research at the University Park Campus, who approved a grant to help defray publication costs.

Special gratitude goes to my son Aaron who, during the completion of this manuscript, has grown from being a little Ninja warrior to a second degree brown belt at a local dojo. His sunny temperament and antics have kept me lighthearted through all phases of this project.

Molly Meijer Wertheimer
Hazleton, PA

Editor's Introduction
First Ladies' Fundamental Rhetorical Choices: When to Speak? What to Say? When to Remain Silent?

Molly Meijer Wertheimer

> I have been so used to freedom of sentiment that I know not how to place so many guards about me, as will be indispensable, to look at every word before I utter it, and to impose a silence upon myself, when I talk.
>
> —Abigail Adams

Used to the freedom of speech afforded by private life, Abigail Adams agreed with a friend who called the "ladyship" a "splendid misery." When to speak, what to say, when to remain silent—all must be newly considered. The construction of a public persona must have been difficult for Mrs. Adams because the Constitution was silent about the duties of the president's wife, and Abigail had only one role model upon which to base her actions—Martha Custis Washington, a woman of decidedly different temperament and personality. As different as they were as individuals, however, they shared a common feeling; Mrs. Washington felt just as "fettered by political considerations" as did Mrs. Adams (Brady 2001, 13). Writing to Fannie Bassett Washington, one of her friends, Martha Washington lamented the set "boundaries . . . I must not depart from" (Anthony 1990, 42). Years later, Grace Coolidge expressed similar sentiments when she wrote in her memoirs after leaving office: "this was I and yet not I, this was the wife of the President of the United States and she took precedence over me" (Coolidge 1992, 62).

Other twentieth-century first ladies have felt every bit as constrained; for example, Pat Nixon, described as "privately spontaneous and lively," controlled her public image so much that she came across as "stiff and wooden" (Mayo 1996, 240). Recently, Sheila Tate, George Bush's press secretary, described Barbara

Bush as "irrepressible," but Barbara admitted to "muzzling" herself "ever since her husband was first elected to public office" (Grimes 1990, 296). Before that, when Nancy Reagan's promptings of her husband were caught on camera, they sparked negative commentary, showing how vigilant the press and public are to any lapses.

The difficulty of learning how to funnel one's spontaneous verbalizations and actions into a form appropriate to the public role is illustrated well by the candidates' wives during Campaign 2000 for the presidency. Although first-ladies-to-be serve sometimes long political apprenticeships as their husbands move up the ladder of public service, often they have not practiced enough to cope with the demands placed upon them as public communicators. For example, the demand to remain silent and in rapt attention requires much concentration. Realizing how uncomfortable Laura Bush must have become as her husband answered several questions, interviewer Judy Woodruff apologized to Mrs. Bush for putting her in such an awkward position. Mrs. Bush was gracious as she listened to her husband's answers, all of which she must have heard countless times before. She was far more controlled than Ernestine Bradley, who goofed while on stage. As her husband conceded to Al Gore in the Democratic primaries, Ernestine wiggled in her chair, rubbed her eyes, looked up at the ceiling and down at the floor; she blurted out an answer to a question that was asked of her husband. When she realized what she had done—spoken at a time when she should have remained silent—she became embarrassed. In contrast, when John McCain conceded to George W. Bush, Cindy McCain stood absolutely motionless, a serene smile on her face (Auster 2000, 3G).

Silence and measured speech are requirements of being a first lady; some first ladies err because they speak "too much" or not in the right way, while others err because they speak "too little." In fact, the rhetorical demands of the position can be so tricky to enact, as I shall discuss below, that no first lady has ever received unanimous acclaim for her performance as a first lady. On the whole, however, first ladies have helped their husbands win public support, which is their fundamental rhetorical exigency. They have also accomplished much more, even becoming a critical part of the United States presidency. As first lady scholar Robert P. Watson writes, "It is no longer a bold statement to suggest that the office of the first lady has shaped the course of U.S. history. . . . [A] new view of the first lady as an activist political partner is beginning to emerge as we recognize the power that has been operating behind the throne" (2000, 205). First ladies exercise considerable power, and they do so both in private and in public through the effective use of rhetorical communication.

First Ladyship: A Position of Constraints and Opportunities

In many ways, the position of first lady is more difficult to perform than the position of United States president. Like Ginger Rogers dancing with Fred Astaire, she must follow his lead, doing whatever he does only backwards and in high heels. While the president is elected and his duties are spelled out in the Constitution, the first lady is neither elected nor given any constitutional or legal guidelines to follow.[1] For better or worse, the basis of her service is her marriage, although she may turn to the precedents established by her predecessors for guidance. Calling the role "undefined," Margaret Truman, daughter of First Lady Bess Truman, stresses the unique obligation that each first lady has to invent the role for herself (Truman 1995, 4–5); the same point is made in a different way by Mary Hoyt: each first lady is "given 'a magic wand' . . . with no instructions on its use—each woman . . . [must] figure that out for herself" (quoted in Caroli 1995, xxii). The difficult part is that she must invent a public persona while onstage, amid much public scrutiny and criticism. No matter how much experience she has had with audiences and the media, this cannot be an easy task.

The public has always been interested in the wife of the president, beginning with Mrs. Washington. In her biography, *Martha Washington: First Lady of Liberty*, Helen Bryan writes that from the time of Martha's arrival in New York (then the nation's capital), she "remained under constant public scrutiny." Although she was treated well by the press, "had Martha put a foot wrong, George's critics and political opponents would surely have pounced on her" (2002, 294). Her successors have experienced the same degree of evaluative attention, leading first lady scholar Robert P. Watson to claim that a first lady is the "most scrutinized lady in the world and must watch her every step" (2000, 39).

Since Martha Washington's day, newspaper coverage has expanded to include magazine, radio, television, and now electronic commentary. Life under such scrutiny has prompted Margaret Truman to say that the American people tend to treat the first family like "public property, like the White House itself" (1995, 8). With the public's sense of ownership have inevitably come expectations of what a first lady can and cannot say and do (10–11). These expectations transcend the individuals who hold the office, that is, the office itself carries a heavy symbolic burden.

Every first lady faces the same dilemma. She is an individual, but she becomes more than that when she assumes the office of first lady. As we have seen, Grace Coolidge early acknowledged the public's demand on her identity when she wrote, "this was the wife of the President of the United States and she took precedence over me; my personal likes and dislikes must be subordinated to the consideration of those things which were required of her." Like Mrs. Coolidge, all first ladies become symbols of American womanhood and as such they are expected to conform to the public's image of "the ideal woman" of their times. The problem is that those "constantly change as the public's view of women evolves and develops" (Gould 1996, xv). Karlyn Kohrs Campbell puts the problem this way, "presidential wives face insuperable obstacles arising out of expectations that they are to represent what we pretend is a single, universally accepted ideal for U.S. womanhood" (1996, 191). In reality, no single standard does, nor ever will, exist.

Although the American public cannot articulate with one voice what they want from a first lady, many are quick to point out what they as individuals do not want once she performs that action. Of course, the public learns about her actions and words through the filter of press coverage, which is governed by cultural "news norms." According to Campbell, "news norms" "affect the kind of coverage the First Lady receives." Today's journalists, she contends, focus especially on whatever is "deviant, dramatic, and controversial" (1996, 190–91). They tend to ignore conservative words and actions, witness the dearth of press coverage of Laura Bush in her first six months as first lady. By exaggerating the unusual and discounting the ordinary, they set the stage for much criticism; "the variety and scope" of which, writes Watson, "seems endless" (2000, 35). Betty Boyd Caroli makes a similar point when she writes:

> First Ladies [have] never lacked detractors . . . [who] pointed to their extravagance (Mary Lincoln), coarseness (Margaret Taylor), casual entertaining (Dolley Madison), elitism (Elizabeth Monroe), prudishness (Lucy Hayes), gaiety (Harriet Lane), excessive grief (Jane Pierce), advanced age (Martha Washington), and youth (Julia Taylor). (Caroli 1995, xxi)

The public has been especially critical of first ladies who have seemed to exert power over their husbands' decisions. The offenders have been "charged with exercising 'petticoat government' (Edith Wilson), running their husbands' careers (Florence Harding), putting words into the president's mouth (Eleanor Roosevelt), 'getting people fired' (Nancy Reagan), and making her husband look like a wimp (Hillary Rodham Clinton)" (Caroli 1995, xxi). These kinds of comments made in the media, according to Campbell, "make it far more difficult for a presidential wife to modify or enlarge her role" (1996, 190–91).

Although press coverage and public criticism challenge the first lady, at the same time they propel her to a position of great visibility on the national and international stages, thereby providing her with an opportunity to exert enormous influence. Edith P. Mayo writes, "even though the first ladies of the twentieth century have felt the burden of intense media coverage, many have used the power of the media to their advantage" (1996, 155) Edith Roosevelt, for example, took control of the first family's image by screening photographers and choosing the journals in which she would place the photographs. She even "selected the authors she thought would place her husband and family in the best light" (Mayo 2001, 34). Lou Hoover delivered radio addresses to further her own agenda, while Jackie Kennedy used the medium of television to present a tour of the White House to the American people. Both Hillary Clinton and Laura Bush have made effective use of the White House website to carry texts of their speeches and official press releases. Indeed, today's "First Lady of the United States," writes Myra Gutin, "has one of the most influential podiums in the world at her disposal" (2001, 57–58). The public has grown so eager for news about the first family and expects some degree of public activism from her that it is "virtually impossible for a first lady to remain incommunicado in the White House" (1989, 177). Besides, a first lady has little choice but to use her rhetorical platform since, as we have seen, with no mandate from the Constitution, the legal statutes, or the public via election to office, the first lady "is required to rely al-most exclusively on her ability as a public communicator" (Watson 2000, 126).

Rhetoric and the Performance of Her Political Role

Ever since first ladies have become aware of their power to influence, increas-ingly have they used that power rhetorically to advance their husbands' and their own agendas. This conclusion is obvious to anyone who has visited the first lady exhibit, "Political Role and Public Image," at the Smithsonian Institute's Na-tional Museum of American History. The duties curators use to organize the ex-hibit's texts and artifacts are: "The Nation's Hostess," "Advocate for Social Causes," "The President's Political Partner," "Political Campaigner," and "Wid-owhood and National Mourning." As I walked through the exhibit the first time and read through the accompanying book afterwards (Mayo and Meringolo 1994), it occurred to me that all of the duties identified as part of the first lady's "political role," at the same time identified "rhetorical processes." All required the use of rhetorical discourse or communication as the means by which they could be achieved. Robert Denton Jr., has argued this point about presidential communication in many forums: "that the essence of politics is 'talk' or human interaction" (1996, xi).[2] There is no reason why the claim would not be just as true when applied to the political role played by first ladies.

In *The Presidents' Wives: Reassessing the Office of First Lady*, Watson expands the number of duties first ladies perform to eleven,[3] including wife and mother, public figure and celebrity, nation's social hostess, symbol of American woman-hood, White House manager and preservationist, campaigner, social advocate and champion of social causes, presidential spokesperson, presidential and po-litical party booster, diplomat, and political/presidential partner (2000, 71–93). These duties, he argues, are "functions of the office" that have developed through custom or necessity rather than being just the "preferences . . . of indi-vidual first ladies per se" (2000, 71). Indeed, a major contribution of Lewis L. Gould's work *American First Ladies: Their Lives and Legacy* (1996) is his focus on the institution of first lady. After two hundred years, the office has developed a "true institutional apparatus," as first ladies introduced innovations and used each others' achievements as precedents (xiii–xix). Still, not every first lady will perform all of the duties available to her. External factors such as a war or the economy as well as internal factors such as her personality or interests may constrain her. Myra Gutin points to other factors that may modify whether and how actively a first lady performs these duties, including her health, world view, experience, and social considerations such as her relationship with her husband, how they view women, and whether she has access to presidential decision-making (1989, 175–78). First ladies also prioritize the duties they perform, de-voting more time to those most meaningful to them. The hierarchy of duties and the pattern of choices a first lady makes cannot be reduced to formula or stereotype. One mistake made in the "media, public, and scholarly literature," writes Watson, "is to see the first lady as either traditional or modern. The of-fice is much more complex and multidimensional" (2000, 24–25).

Regardless of the subset of duties a first lady performs, she must invariably use strategic communication—that is rhetorical communication—to perform them. Her communication activities may vary in that some are "formal or informal, verbal or nonverbal, public or private" (Denton 1996, xi); the kinds of media used may vary as well. In the chapters to follow, authors present an abundance of examples to demonstrate how first ladies have used rhetorical communication or discourse to perform their "political role." Many of them have practiced a rheto-ric of actions more than a rhetoric of words.

With regard to the duty of "hostess," for example, Edith Mayo contends that the social role the first lady plays is "far from being mere 'cultural fluff.'" "A woman who is socially adept and politically savvy," she writes, "can promote her husband's political agenda, and structure the style and image of her husband's presidential administration" (2001, 31–32). On social occasions, first ladies use what Allgor calls "unofficial space" to achieve political goals. These sorts of sit-uations are flexible enough to allow the successful transaction of business; good food, drink, and other distractions provide "an atmosphere of sociability to pro-pose, to probe, to negotiate, and to compromise," as well as to change the sub-ject or to "withdraw if the situation warrants it" (2001, 22). For example, many first ladies have expended great efforts on orchestrating state dinners to stimu-late productive conversations among their guests. Lou Hoover employed an elab-orate set of hand gestures to coordinate the pace of courses served during dinners, while Jackie Kennedy planned seating arrangements by literally spreading out charts on the floor. In the chapters to follow, authors suggest or detail many of the ways in which the first ladies have helped their husbands achieve political goals by demonstrating brilliant rhetorical invention on an interpersonal level and by practicing a "sociable" rhetoric—what Kari Anderson, adapting Robert Hariman's work,[4] identifies as a "social style."

The political duty of "campaigner" also requires significant rhetorical activity for its performance. At the end of the nineteenth and continuing throughout the twentieth centuries, first ladies have helped their husbands campaign for politi-cal office (Mayo 1996, 237–39). Even Ida McKinley, an invalid, helped her hus-band during his 1896 bid against William Jennings Bryan, with whose wife, Mary, a lawyer, she was often compared. She was made the subject of a campaign brochure, and her husband's managers used her image as a campaign symbol; she developed a following of her own (Mayo 1996, 145; Mayo and Meringolo, 38). Other early-twentieth-century political wives have helped their husbands via front porch campaigns, which are interesting because the front porch marks a bridge between the private life inside the home and the public life in the streets. Florence Harding, for example, organized "photo opportunities" during her hus-band's front porch campaign, which were viewed with interest by the public, in-cluding women, who had just gotten the vote. Others candidates' wives have joined their husbands' whistle-stop campaigns, such as Bess Truman and Mamie

Eisenhower. Their participation was "visual"; mostly they smiled and waved, giving rise to Bess Truman's quip: "A woman's place in public is to sit beside her husband, be silent, and be sure her hat is on straight" (1986, 132).

During the 1950s, when women began to vote in equal numbers with men, the political parties used the wives of candidates as a way to appeal to women voters. Artifacts, such as pink nylon stockings embroidered with "I like Ike," were worn by female campaign workers. Lady Bird Johnson went further than her predecessors, when she traveled solo on her own whistle-stop train across the South (Mayo 1996, 239). Of course, she was preceded by Eleanor Roosevelt, who had already presented campaign speeches for her husband, including one at the 1940 Democratic National Convention (Blair 2000). Today, writes Mayo, campaigning is "an integral part of every modern race for the White House." The first lady "must be able to speak well and be persuasive and informed on the issues" (1996, 239).

Maintaining a working relationship with members of the press, another duty of the first lady's political role, requires a great deal of rhetorical acumen. Although press relations have been challenging since the inception of the office (Brady 2001, 11), the challenges have increased with the growth and development of the media. As we have seen, media scrutiny has been pervasive, and news norms have changed over time. The press, for example, was relatively silent about the nature of Ida McKinley's illness, but went into elaborate detail when Betty Ford was diagnosed with breast cancer. Many first lady scholars detail the historical relationship between the first lady and the press, tracing the development of different forms of media used to cover the first lady as well as the kinds of stories covered.[5] One generalization stands out—as the media grew in popularity, so did the public's interest in stories about the first lady. In fact, the public became interested in the entire first family, including the presidents' parents, siblings, children, and even their pets.[6] Today, writes Myra Gutin, "the press plays a critical role in transmitting both the image and the substance of a First Lady" (1989, 176), so much so that the first lady's office now has a specialized staff to handle press relations, including "a press office, press secretary, pollsters, speech writers, communications directors, and media advisors whose job it is to ensure favorable coverage of the president and first lady" (Watson 2000, 151). Her office also "actively attempts to guide or manipulate public opinion . . . by controlling media coverage, seeking favorable coverage, staging and timing public appearances, and the like" (151).

Interestingly, journalism professor Betty H. Winfield, University of Missouri, advises First Lady Laura Bush to become proactive when it comes to press relations. Although a first lady has a great deal of potential influence, Winfield contends, she can only wield it if she can control her image, including her photographic and video images, as well as written and electronic statements. Winfield advises the first lady to select a top-notch staff, plan a coherent strategy concerning the image she wants to project as she performs her many duties—as wife, mother, advocate, and so on—and stick with it by reinforcing aspects of it on a daily basis (2001,

45–51). Years before this advice was written, Eleanor Roosevelt held press conferences with women journalists that became productive, collaborative strategy sessions. The importance of the staff in the first lady's office is further underscored when archivist Nancy Kegan Smith offers Mrs. Bush advice on how to maintain office records and personal papers. She provides a fascinating discussion of the history and usefulness of first lady papers to scholars (2001).

I have touched only briefly on three of the eleven duties Robert Watson presents in *The Presidents' Wives*. From what I have suggested, it must be obvious how much first ladies rely on rhetorical communication to perform those roles. Yet, as important as rhetorical communication is and has been especially to modern American first ladies, unfortunately, they have not been much studied from that perspective. In fact, study of the first lady is a relatively new area of research.

Researching the First Lady

"The first lady remains one of the most fascinating and unexplored facets of the American presidency and the history of women in the United States" (1989, viii), writes Don W. Wilson, former national archivist. He credits the growth of the presidential library system in the 1970s and 1980s with stimulating research on this neglected area of scholarship. Like a treasure trove, presidential libraries from Herbert Hoover through George Bush contain the Social Files of First Ladies, which he says include "thousands of boxes of documents and letters" (vii).[7] Cataloguing these materials is a painstaking, time-consuming process by libraries that are largely understaffed. Increasingly, however, more material is becoming available; some libraries are putting their finding guides online. The papers of first ladies before Lou Hoover are much more difficult to access. What exists is mostly in private hands. Scattered documentation of twentieth-century first ladies from McKinley to Coolidge may be found in the Library of Congress.[8] A resource that continues to increase in usefulness since its incorporation in 1997, is the National First Ladies' Library in Canton, Ohio, which is committed to becoming "a research facility and educational center for scholars of all ages" (Krider 2001, 93). One of their primary goals is: "To update each year a complete, annotated bibliography developed on First Ladies from Martha Custis Washington to Hillary Rodham Clinton" and beyond (94).[9]

With increased availability of first lady material comes increased scholarly output in the forms of conference sessions, journal articles, and published books.[10] In the late 1980s, works such as Betty Boyd Caroli's *First Ladies* (1987) and Myra Gutin's *The President's Partner: The First Lady in the Twentieth Century* (1989) appeared. More popular treatments—anecdotal in nature—appeared as well, such as James. S. Rosebush's *First Lady, Public Wife: A Behind-the-Scenes History of the Evolving Role of the First Ladies in American Political Life* (1987) and Paul F. Boller Jr.'s *Presidential Wives: An Anecdotal History* (1988). In the 1990s, other significant scholarly works appeared, such as Carl S. Anthony's *First Ladies: The Saga of the Presidents' Wives and Their Power* (1990–1991) and Lewis L.

Gould's *American First Ladies: Their Lives and Their Legacy* (1996). Important books of a less scholarly nature were published, such as Margaret Truman's *First Ladies: An Intimate Group Portrait of White House Wives* (1996) and Gil Troy's *Affairs of State: The Rise and Rejection of the Presidential Couple since World War II* (1997). Recent scholarship—directed to both the academic and popular communities—stresses the presidential partnership, such as Robert P. Watson's *The Presidents' Wives: Reassessing the Office of the First Lady* (2000) and Kati Marton's *Hidden Power: Presidential Marriages That Shaped Our Recent History* (2001). *Laura Bush: The Report to the First Lady* (Watson 2001) is an essay collection written by first lady scholars from several disciplines; it was prepared for Laura Bush when she began her tenure as first lady.

Research on first ladies in the disciplines of rhetoric and communication has been limited, but is increasing. To date, there are only two book-length treatments of first ladies written from the perspective of rhetoric and communication. One is Myra Gutin's groundbreaking study: *The President's Partner: The First Lady in the Twentieth Century* (1989).[11] Based on her dissertation, Gutin's argument is that by studying "the speeches, radio and television broadcasts, interviews, press conferences, and magazine and newspaper articles written by the First Lady . . . one is best able to understand and appreciate the changes [in the office] that have taken place over sixty years," the time frame of her study, 1920–1988 (2). Gutin places each of the first ladies from Harding through Carter in one of the following categories: "White Housekeepers: Social Hostesses and Ceremonial Presences" (Harding, Coolidge, Truman, and Eisenhower), "Emerging Spokeswomen" (Hoover, Kennedy, and Nixon), and "Political Surrogates and Independent Advocates" (Roosevelt, Johnson, Ford, and Carter). Her study ends with Nancy Reagan, who, Gutin admits, "defies pigeonholing," shuffling instead between "these classifications as her role has evolved during the Reagan administration" (165).[12] Within each chapter, Gutin traces the forms of communication each first lady uses as well as some of the factors that constrain her, including the quality of the marital relationship and the president's view of what his wife should do as a first lady. Molly Meijer Wertheimer's *Inventing a Voice: The Rhetoric of American First Ladies of the Twentieth Century* (2004) was the origin and inspiration for this book. Studies of first ladies from Ida McKinley through Laura Bush are included in this essay collection. Chapter authors describe in detail each first lady's biography, her rhetorical activities while in office, and her legacy. Students who are interested in twentieth-century first ladies not covered in *Leading Ladies* may want to consult *Inventing a Voice.*

Two significant studies of first ladies from a rhetorical perspective are by Karlyn Kohrs Campbell: "The Rhetorical Presidency: A Two Person Career" (1996) and "The Discursive Performance of Femininity: Hating Hillary" (1998). Both studies provide a framework for understanding why the office of the first lady is "a vital part of the presidency" as well as a difficult ("impossible")—damned if you do, damned if you don't—rhetorical role to play. In the earlier article, Campbell inserts the first lady into the "presidential corporation" of cabinet members, advisors, speechwriters and others. She identifies the blurring of public and private aspects of her office as one of the factors that contributes to the difficulty of its performance as well as a source of public criticism. Summarizing the "factors that make the role so difficult" from a slightly different perspective taken in her later article, Campbell highlights "the ill-defined character of an ambiguous role," the public expectation that she "personify an idealized vision of women when one no longer exists," her function as a "lightning rod for hostile feelings about her husband," and the public demand that women who perform professional roles in public "discursively enact their femininity" (1998, 15). Although these are general problems of the office of first lady, Campbell contends, in the case of Hillary Rodham Clinton they are "writ large." Mrs. Clinton's inability to "feminize her rhetorical style, to perform a culturally defined feminine role publicly" made it difficult for her to achieve her rhetorical goals. Campbell laments the public's "failure to appreciate" the argumentative skills of talented women like Mrs. Clinton and, more broadly, the rejection of educated, potentially contributive women like her: "If we reject all those who lack the feminizing skills of an Elizabeth Hanford Dole, we shall deprive ourselves of a vast array of talent" (15).

The conclusions reached by Shawn J. Parry-Giles and Diane M. Blair are consistent with Campbell's.[13] In "The Rise of the Rhetorical First Lady: Politics, Gender Ideology, and Women's Voice, 1789–2002," they trace "the rise of the *rhetorical first lady* from Martha Washington through Laura Bush." The first lady, they argue, occupies a "contested space" because she functions both as a site "for the performance of archetypal femininity that privileges the ideal republican mother" and also as a site of "feminist advancement that challenges gender stereotypes, expanding women's political space." Their argument, though developed differently, reaches conclusions similar to those put forward by Karrin Vasby Anderson's "The First Lady as a Site of 'American Womanhood,'" which is included in this volume. Anderson further argues for viewing each first lady as a site of heterogeneity and paradox; she stresses the multifaceted nature of identity and advises scholars not to reduce the complexity of first ladies by using a dichotomous logic.

Some other published works that focus in whole or in part on a particular first lady include Barbara C. Burrell's *Public Opinion, the First Ladyship, and Hillary Rodham Clinton* (2001), Diane M. Blair's, "No Ordinary Time: Eleanor Roosevelt's Address to the 1940 Democratic National Convention" (2000), and Karrin Vasby Anderson's, "From Spouses to Candidates: Hillary Rodham Clinton, Elizabeth Dole, and the Gendered Office of U.S. President" (2002). Fortunately, at the time of this writing, faculty and graduate students in rhetoric and communication continue to present conference papers, complete dissertations, and prepare master's theses.[14] Many faculty members are also designing courses on the rhetoric of first ladies, and others are including units on first ladies in their political and/or presidential rhetoric and communication courses.[15] Materials to teach these courses are also forthcoming.[16] All indicate continued and increasing interest in studying the president's spouse from a rhetorical perspective.

Plan of the Book

The authors of the chapters in this volume write with several purposes: one of the most significant is to inform students of the important role first ladies play in American presidential politics and to show how the first ladies studied used rhetorical communication to achieve their goals. For students unfamiliar with "rhetoric" as an area of scholarship, Aristotle's definition of rhetoric as "the faculty of discovering in any given case all of the available means of persuasion" (Cooper 1932) is foundational, although there are countless other definitions from the history of rhetoric, including contemporary rhetorical theory, readily available.[17] Those who study rhetoric and communication professionally focus on different kinds of situations, among them dyads, small groups, public speaking events; they examine oral, written, mass-mediated, and electronic forms of communication, including verbal and nonverbal (pictorial) symbols. Combining the variability of definition with the alternatives of focus produces a veritable kaleidoscope of potential perspectives from which scholars may select and interpret material. As editor of this work, I welcomed the differences, encouraging each author to choose the most striking ideas about her first lady from the material available.

The essays in this work focus on popular and influential United States first ladies all of whom served in the latter half of the twentieth century, with the exception of Eleanor Roosevelt who served as first lady from March 1933 through April 1945. We also include a chapter on the first twenty-first-century first lady, Laura Bush. With the exception of chapter one, all of the authors use the same general headings: Biography, Rhetorical Activities as First Lady, and Legacy. What material to include under each heading and how to organize it were the choices of each author. Consequently, this book is systematic, but only to a certain extent. The headings provide the only preconceived set of topics used; definitions of rhetoric, rhetorical perspectives, the interests, training, and personality of the authors all intersected to determine the content selected. The first ladies themselves also "contributed" to what was written about them. For example, as the author of two of the chapters, I was not always able to write about the same activities largely because these two first ladies are so different and the materials available about them differ widely.

The time for constructing a definitive set of concepts to use to study the rhetorical activities of first ladies is not yet here. Campbell's framework, stressing both the importance of the first lady to the presidential corporation as well as the difficulties involved in performing her ambiguous position, maps out the general terrain, while the duties identified by Watson add the key landmarks. Neither scholar, however, identifies the rhetorical processes in operation. Gutin identifies some of these processes, but the chief strength of her work—her systematic method of analysis—gives rise to its chief weakness—the rhetorical activities and processes that did not fit easily into her categories largely slipped through her analytical net. As editor of this work, my hope is that the freedom of method afforded the authors—their use of conceptual nets that made sense to them—will generate new insights and stimulate future research.

One central theme does emerge from the crisscrossing mesh of our research and that is the theme suggested at the beginning of this introduction by the quotation from Abigail Adams: her realization that her conversation as a first lady could no longer be spontaneous but had to be constrained. For better or worse, a first lady cannot *not* communicate. Whatever she says or does not say and whatever she does or does not do reflect upon her husband and herself. It is the ethos of the presidential couple in the public mind that defines the president's administration. We hope our essays contribute to an awareness of the central part the first lady plays in the American presidency. She is a key player in the presidential administration who must use rhetorical discourse to help advance her own and her husband's agendas.

Questions for Discussion

1. Why are the rhetorical demands of the first lady position so difficult to enact?
2. Do you think the American public has a set of expectations for first ladies? What might they be? What happens when a prospective first lady violates public expectations?
3. Does the American first lady have to use rhetorical communication to achieve her goals? Why or why not?
4. During his reelection campaign, one of George W. Bush's television ads pictured Laura Bush looking over his shoulder, and her voice was heard throughout the commercial. Why do you think the campaign featured Laura Bush?

Internet Resources

http://www.firstladies.org/
This is one of the most complete and useful websites for studying the first lady of the United States. It is sponsored by the National First Ladies Library in Canton, Ohio. Here you can find biographical sketches of every first lady as well as bibliographies of articles and books both by first ladies and about them. Also, you can find source guides to manuscript collections and for material in other media such as video and film.

http://www.whitehouse.gov/firstlady/
This website is a wonderful resource for the current first lady. On the site, you can find texts of speeches given by the first lady and press releases issued by her office. There are descriptions of the first lady's main initiatives and photos taken at representative events. By clicking on "Presidents and First Ladies" and then "First Ladies," you can find a chronology of first ladies and their biographies.

http://www.archives.gov/presidential_libraries/addresses/addresses.html
The National Archives and Records Administration has a page devoted to presidential libraries. By clicking on her husband's library, you can find photos and materials of a particular first lady.

Notes

1. That she can't be appointed to any official position seems covered under the "Bobby Kennedy Rule," which states that "immediate members of the president's family can no longer be appointed to positions in the federal government" (Watson 2000, 69).

2. Robert Denton Jr., *The Symbolic Dimensions of the American Presidency*; Robert Denton Jr. and Gary Woodward, *Political Communication in America*; Robert Denton Jr. and Dan Hahn, *Presidential Communication*; and Robert Denton Jr., *The Primetime Presidency of Ronald Reagan*.

3. To arrive at his list, Watson summarized the attempts of other first lady scholars to categorize these duties.

4. Robert Hariman, *Political Style: The Artistry of Power* (1995).

5. For example, see Gutin (1989, 3–4) and Watson (2000, 150–51).

6. For example, see Bonnie Angelo, *First Mothers: The Women Who Shaped the Presidents* (2000); Harold I. Gullen, *Faith of Our Mothers: The Stories of Presidential Mothers from Mary Washington to Barbara Bush* (2001); Roy Rowan and Brooke Janis, *First Dogs: American Presidents and Their Best Friends* (1997); and Margaret Truman, *White House Pets* (1969).

7. Temporarily, the Clintons' papers are housed in a presidential "Project" and will be turned over to the United States Archivist once the Clinton Library is constructed (Smith 2001, 80).

8. A succinct overview of the way first lady papers have been handled historically is Nancy Kegan Smith's "Advice to the Incoming First Lady on Her Records and Establishing Files That Successfully Reflect Her Role" (2001, 79–83). Myra Gutin's "Biographical Notes" provides a starting point for using primary material on the first ladies she studied (1989, 179–184). Another work worth consulting is Nancy Kegan Smith and Mary C. Ryan's (1989) *Modern First Ladies: Their Documentary Legacy*. A bibliography of resources on first ladies, including guides to locate their papers may be found in Elizabeth Lorelei Thacker-Estrada's "Presidential Wives, the White House, and Washington, D.C.: Recommended Readings and Resources for the First Lady" (2001, 92).

9. This material may be accessed at www.firstladies.org.

10. A good review of the literature on first ladies (biographical, anecdotal, and scholarly) may be found in Elizabeth Lorelei Thacker-Estrada's "Presidential Wives, the White House, and Washington, D.C.: Recommended Readings and Resources for the First Lady" (2001, 85–92). My summary of the literature here follows Robert Watson's work (2000).

11. Burrell's *Public Opinion, the First Ladyship, and Hilary Rodham Clinton* (2001) is on a particular first lady from a mass communication perspective.

12. In all fairness, Gutin had little access to primary materials on Nancy Reagan who was just finishing her term as first lady when Gutin was preparing her manuscript (1989, 165).

13. See also: Janis L. Edwards and Huey Rong Chen. "The First Lady/First Wife in Editorial Cartoons: Rhetorical Visions through Gendered Lenses" in *Women's Studies in Communication*.

14. On August 19, 2002, I placed a request on CRTNET, a widely circulated listserv sponsored by the National Communication Association, to hear from scholars who were engaged in research on first ladies. Several scholars e-mailed me, sending the titles of papers which they have presented or are scheduled for presentation at national and regional conferences. In addition, two graduate students e-mailed me the titles and brief descriptions of their dissertations: Lisa M. Burns, University of Maryland, "Presidential Wives and the Press: News Framing and the Construction of the First Lady Institution in the Twentieth Century"; and Misty L. Knight, University of Southern Mississippi, "In Defense of First Ladies Rhetoric: A Case for a Critical Genre." Other graduate students informed me of their completed research and interest in writing their master's theses on first ladies. Although information to include in this note and the next was not collected systematically, for my purposes, it is sufficient to indicate the interest of scholars in the fields of rhetoric and communication on first ladies.

15. Several authors of chapters in this collection teach courses on the rhetoric of American first ladies including: Beth M. Waggenspack (Virginia Polytechnic Institute and State University) and Linda Hobgood (University of Richmond). Other faculty members teach courses devoted in part to first ladies such as Diana B. Carlin (University of Kansas), Janis L. Edwards (University of Alabama), and Shawn J. Parry-Giles (University of Maryland). Faculty members other than authors of chapters in this book also offer similar courses such as Myra Gutin (Rider University) and Barbara Garvey (Hanover College in Indiana). Doubtless, this list just scratches the surface of the graduate and undergraduate courses in the United States that devote a substantial amount of class time to first ladies as rhetoricians.

16. Paula Wilson Youra sent me an e-mail message to announce the release of a videotape produced by the Educational Video Group/Alistair Press, Greenwood, Indiana. The videotape contains speeches by Barbara Bush, Hillary Clinton, Elizabeth Dole, Tipper Gore, Hadassah Lieberman, and Laura Bush. They were given at different Democratic and Republican national conventions and they are all speeches of nomination.

17. For definitions drawn from the history of rhetoric, see for example: www.stanford.edu/dept/english/courses/sites/lunsford/pages/defs.htm; www.stanford.edu/www.hf.ntnu.no/engelsk/shakespeare/defs.htm; www.missouri.edu/~engjnc/rhetoric/defining_main.html. In addition, there are rhetorical scholars who argue against defining rhetoric and those who object to the idea of needing a foundation for rhetoric (Scott 1973). For a summary of the variety of scholarship produced by those who "profess rhetoric at the end of the twentieth century," see Antczak, Coggins, and Klinger (2002, ix).

References

Allgor, Catherine. 2000. *Parlor Politics: In Which the Ladies of Washington Help Build a City and a Government*. Charlottesville, Va.: University of Virginia Press.

Anderson, Karrin Vasby. 2002. From Spouses to Candidates: Hillary Rodham Clinton, Elizabeth Dole, and the Gendered Office of U.S. President. *Rhetoric and Public Affairs*, 5:1, 105–32.

Angelo, Bonnie. 2000. *First Mothers: The Women Who Shaped the Presidents*. New York: HarperCollins.

Antczak, Frederick J., Vinda Coggins, and Geoffrey D. Klinger. 2002. *Professing Rhetoric: Selected Papers from the 2000 Rhetoric Society of America Conference*. Mahwah, N.J.: Lawrence Erlbaum Associates.

Anthony, Carl Sferrazza. 1990. *First Ladies: The Saga of the Presidents' Wives and Their Power 1789–1961*, Vol. 1. New York: William Morrow.

Auster, Elizabeth. 2000. Political Wives, Smiling, Stoic, Silent Partners. *Plain Dealer* (Cleveland), 12 March, 3G.

Blair, Diane. 2000. No Ordinary Time: Eleanor Roosevelt's Address to the 1940 Democratic National Convention. *Rhetoric and Public Affairs*, 4:2, 203–22.

Brady, Patricia, 2001. Martha Washington: The Lady Who First Created the Role. In *Laura Bush: The Report to the First Lady*, ed. Robert P. Watson, 11–15. Huntington, New York: Nova History Publications.

Bryan, Helen. 2002. *Martha Washington: First Lady of Liberty*. New York: John Wiley & Sons.

Burrell, Barbara C. 2001. *Public Opinion, the First Ladyship, and Hillary Rodham Clinton*, rev. ed. New York: Garland.

Campbell, Karlyn Kohrs. 1996. The Rhetorical Presidency: A Two Person Career. In *Beyond the Rhetorical Presidency*, ed. Martin J. Medhurst, 179–95. College Station, Tex.: Texas A & M University Press.

———. 1998. The Discursive Performance of Femininity: Hating Hillary. *Rhetoric and Public Affairs*, 5:1, 1–19.

Caroli, Betty Boyd. 1995. *First Ladies*, expanded edition. New York: Oxford University Press.

Coolidge, Grace Goodhue. 1992. *Grace Coolidge: An Autobiography*. Ed. Lawrence E. Wikander and Robert H. Ferrell. Worland, Wyo.: High Plains Publishing Company, Inc.

Cooper, Lane, trans. 1932. *The Rhetoric of Aristotle*. New York: Appleton Century Crofts.

Denton, Robert E., Jr. 1982. *The Symbolic Dimensions of the American Presidency*. Prospect Heights, Ill.: Waveland.

———. 1988. *The Primetime Presidency of Ronald Reagan*. New York: Praeger.

———. 1996. Series Introduction. In *From the Margins to the Center: Contemporary Women and Political Communication*, ed. Patricia A. Sullivan and Lynn H. Turner, xi–xiii. New York: Praeger.

Denton, Robert E., Jr., and Dan Hahn. 1986. *Presidential Communication*. New York: Praeger.

Denton, Robert E., Jr., and Gary Woodward. 1990. *Political Communication in America*, 2nd ed. New York: Praeger.

Edwards, Janis L., and Huey Rong Chen. 2000. The First Lady/First Wife in Editorial Cartoons: Rhetorical Visions through Gendered Lenses. *Women's Studies in Communication*, 23:3, 367–91.

Gould, Lewis. 1996. The First Lady as Symbol and Institution. In *American First Ladies*, ed. Lewis L. Gould, xiii–xx. New York: Garland.

Grimes, Ann. 1990. *Running Mates: The Making of a First Lady*. New York: William Marrow & Co.

Gullen, Harold I. 2001. *Faith of Our Mothers: The Stories of Presidential Mothers from Martha Washington to Barbara Bush*. Grand Rapids, Mich.: William B. Eerdmans.

Gutin, Myra. 1989. *The President's Partner: The First Lady in the Twentieth Century*. New York: Greenwood.

———. 2001. Public Discourse and the American First Lady in the 20th Century. In *Laura Bush: The Report to the First Lady*, ed. Robert P. Watson, 53–63. Huntington, N.Y.: Nova History Publications.

Hariman, Robert. 1995. *Political Style: The Artistry of Power*. Chicago: University of Chicago Press.

Krider, Pat. 2001. National First Ladies' Library. In *Laura Bush: The Report to the First Lady*, ed. Robert P. Watson, 93–96. Huntington, N.Y.: Nova History Publications.

Mayo, Edith P., ed. 1996. *Smithsonian Book of the First Ladies: Their Lives, Times, and Issues*. New York: Henry Holt and Co.

Mayo, Edith P. 2001. "Party Politics": The Social Role of the First Lady and its Political Influence. In *Laura Bush: The Report to the First Lady*, ed. Robert P. Watson, 31–35. Huntington, New York: Nova History Publications.

Mayo, Edith P., and Denise D. Meringolo. 1994. *First Ladies: Political Role and Public Image*. Washington, D.C.: Smithsonian Institution.

Parry-Giles, Shawn J., and Diane M. Blair. 2002. The Rise of the Rhetorical First Lady: Politics, Gender Ideology, and Women's Voice, 1789–2002. *Rhetoric and Public Affairs*, 6:5, 565–600.

Rowan, Roy, and Janis Brooke. 1997. *First Dogs: American Presidents and Their Best Friends*. Chapel Hill, N.C.: Algonquin Books.

Scott, Robert. 1973. On *Not* Defining "Rhetoric." *Philosophy and Rhetoric*, 6:2, 81–96.

Smith, Nancy Kegan. 2001. Advice to the Incoming First Lady on Her Records and Establishing Files That Successfully Reflect Her New Role. In *Laura Bush: The Report to the First Lady*, ed. Robert P. Watson, 79–83. Huntington, N.Y.: Nova History Publications.

Smith, Nancy Kegan, and Mary C. Ryan. 1989. *Modern First Ladies: Their Documentary Legacy*. Washington, D.C.: National Archives and Records Administration.

Thacker-Estrada, Elizabeth Lorelei. 2001. Presidential Wives, the White House, and Washington, D.C.: Recommended Readings and Resources for the First Lady. In *Laura Bush: The Report to the First Lady*, ed. Robert P. Watson, 85–92. Huntington, N.Y.: Nova History Publications.

Troy, Gil. 1997. *Affairs of State: The Rise and Rejection of the Presidential Couple since World War II*. New York: The Free Press.

Truman, Margaret. 1969. *White House Pets*. New York: David McKay Company.

———. 1986. *Bess W. Truman*. New York: Macmillan.

———. 1995. *First Ladies: An Intimate Group Portrait of White House Wives*. New York: Fawcett Columbine.

Watson, Robert P. 2000. *The Presidents' Wives: Reassessing the Office of First Lady*. Boulder, Colo.: Lynne Reinner Publishers.

———, ed. 2001. *Laura Bush: The Report to the First Lady*. Huntington, N.Y.: Nova History Publications.

Wilson, Donald W. 1989. Foreword to *Modern First Ladies: Their Documentary Legacy*, ed. Nancy Kegan Smith, vii–viii. Washington, D.C.: National Archives and Records Administration.

Winfield, Betty H. 2001. The First Lady's Relations with the Mass Media. In *Laura Bush: The Report to the First Lady*, ed. Robert P. Watson, 45–51. Huntington, N.Y.: Nova History Publications.

CHAPTER ONE

The First Lady
A Site of "American Womanhood"

Karrin Vasby Anderson

The way that she fulfills her role as First Lady marks a real "departure." Her husband consults her on political policy and trusts her as his closest adviser. An unelected force in the White House, she is highly controversial. She may even draft legislation. Hillary Rodham Clinton? No. "She" is Nellie Taft, Florence Harding, Edith Bolling Wilson, Eleanor Roosevelt and Rosalynn Carter.

—Edith P. Mayo

During the 1992 presidential campaign, Hillary Rodham Clinton was asked about a potential conflict of interest between her duties as a lawyer and her status as the wife of the governor of Arkansas. Her reply revealed an attempt to balance career and family obligations in an effort "to have an independent life and to make a difference." At the conclusion of her explanation she quipped, "I suppose I could have stayed home and baked cookies and had teas but what I decided to do was fulfill my profession which I entered before my husband was in public life" (Jamieson 1995, 27). That offhand remark came to be known as "one of [Rodham Clinton's] most serious gaffes in primary season," (Sullivan and Levin 1995, 277) and it sparked commentary both in scholarly and popular circles (Barone 1992, Caroli 1995, Jamieson 1995, Sullivan and Levin 1995). Rodham Clinton's remark was cited as an indication of her choice to depart from the traditional roles played by United States first ladies, in favor of more activist roles. Rather than being the product of twentieth-century feminism, however, her remark echoed sentiments uttered nearly 150 years earlier by one of her predecessors, Sarah Polk. When the wife of Henry Clay, James Polk's opponent in the 1844 presidential election, was heralded for her domesticity, she countered, "If I get to the White House, I expect to live on $25,000 a year and I will

1

neither keep house nor make butter" (Caroli 1995, 62). As Polk's retort suggests, first ladies have been challenging norms and churning up controversy ever since the inception of the role.

Historically, first ladies have functioned as "symbols" of traditional white middle- to upper-class femininity in America, a condition that has both constrained and empowered them (Mayo and Meringolo 1994). Critics who have reflected on how first ladies have performed their roles often comment on the nature and extent of their power within presidential administrations. While that is a significant question, it is not the only one to study. My argument in this chapter is that first ladies also influence conceptions of "American womanhood," and how they do that has broad implications for all women. Indeed, by virtue of their husbands' elections, first ladies become "sites" for the symbolic negotiation of female identity. Discourses by and about first ladies function culturally to shape notions of femininity and so both foster and constrain women's agency. Thus, the study of first ladies is important not only for a historical appreciation of some of the "great women" who have contributed to that institution, but also as a critique of how "American womanhood" has been and continues to be inscribed, negotiated, and contested in the United States. On the one hand, first ladies are viewed as reflections of traditional femininity, notions of which have been disciplined by long-standing cultural metaphors—such as the metaphor of containment. Yet, even corralled within this cultural milieu, first ladies have also been able to develop "social styles" that are rhetorically responsive to the political situations they (and their husbands) face. Moreover, many have been able to confound the ambiguities latent in gender dichotomies by deploying paradox in ways that deconstruct female identity and open possibilities for political agency, thereby proving liberating for women. Before this more progressive view of the U.S. first ladyship can be explored, however, one must examine how the role developed within the cultural milieu of containment.

Containment and U.S. Identity

First ladies became icons of American femininity partly because their role was undefined and partly because their role was constructed within the larger culture of "containment," a metaphor that has influenced American culture, identity, and practice since colonial times.[1] David Campbell explains that America, as an imagined community, used the dichotomy between "civilized" and "barbarian" to justify its colonization of the New World (1992, 116). The impulse to colonize was further legitimated by the myth of American exceptionalism, which originated with the Puritans and suggested that the "American self was the product of divine intent" (121). These two discourses combined to foster a culture that strove to contain "barbarism" wherever it was found (127). Campbell explicates the ways in which containment metaphors surfaced in Puritan doctrines of civility (the need to contain the internal barbarian), in frontier structures designed to keep Native Americans out of settled areas (the need to contain the pagan barbarian), and in colonial slave codes (the need to contain the racialized barbarian). He argues that fear of the Other is inscribed into U.S. identity, and the strategy of containment historically has been the mode of operation for combating that fear.

Like other containment rhetorics, sexual containment has roots in early American discourse. Most notably, containment metaphors emerged in the debates over women's suffrage, with opponents of suffrage arguing that women should remain cloistered in the private sphere (Campbell 1989, Zaeske 1995). Not only did they object to women voting, they deemed any woman who spoke to "promiscuous" audiences composed of women and men to be "masculine, unwomanly, aggressive, and cold" (Campbell 1989, 12). Sexual containment, therefore, was enacted through nineteenth-century attempts to label women's power as unnatural, desexed, and threatening.

Sexual containment strategies did not disappear after U.S. women won the vote in 1920. The fear of outspoken, politically active women has informed much of popular culture and political discourse throughout the twentieth century. In fact, the discursive strategies of nineteenth-century antisuffragists reemerged during the debate over women's liberation and the Equal Rights Amendment (ERA) in the 1970s. Susan Douglas notes the ways in which "radical feminists" at this time were castigated in the media as "ugly, humorless, disorderly man-haters in desperate need of some Nair" (1994, 189). The image of the desexed woman's rights advocate was subsumed into popular culture and political discourse almost as easily in the late twentieth century as it had been one hundred years earlier.

Like other women, U.S first ladies have felt the impact of containment rhetoric. In fact, they have developed as symbols of "American womanhood" within this long-standing containment milieu. For example, Mamie Eisenhower's preoccupation with pink and her prowess as a presidential hostess exemplified the domestic ideal that governed the Cold War era.[2] Yet first ladies have been held up as icons of traditional femininity long before the Eisenhowers' tenure in the White House, and contemporary first ladies like Hillary Rodham Clinton are castigated for supposed breaches of tradition. Today, the tension between the traditional role of first ladies and the modern roles they can play remains.

The First Lady: A Site of Traditional Femininity

The term "first lady" appeared in journalistic references to the president's wife as early as 1870, although its use hearkened back to 1789 when "crowds accustomed to the pomp of royal persons heralded the wife of their new president as 'Lady Washington'" (Caroli 1995, xv). During the nineteenth century, it was assumed that the first lady would occupy a position "at the head of the female society of the United States" (Caroli 1995, 38). Today, although phrases like "female society" sound arcane, the first lady continues to stand as a symbol of American womanhood, reflecting, as Betty Boyd Caroli states, "the status of American women of their time while helping shape expectations of what women can properly do" (1995, xxi).

The United States historically has "expected first ladies to reflect ideals of home, family and womanhood," with the term "lady" connoting "middle-and upper-class respectability and suggest[ing] a certain kind of demeanor" (Mayo and Meringolo 1994, 8). Margaret Carlson calls the first ladyship "the most tradition-bound and antiquated model of American womanhood" (1992, 28), while Germaine Greer concurs, quipping that the first lady "is the archetypal lipstick-skirt-high-heels beside the archetypal suit" (1995, 20). Caroli explains that norms of femininity were inscribed into the role of first lady in the eighteenth century, since the majority of early first ladies "acquiesced in limiting themselves to a supportive role reflecting the predominant attitude about femininity" (1995, 32). This standard continued through the mid-nineteenth century, when "[y]outhful surrogates [as first ladies] became a tradition because they evidently fit in with prevailing ideas about femininity—womanliness could be exemplified in obsequious, smiling mannequins who showed little evidence of thinking for themselves" (Caroli 1995, 57).

Certainly, not every early first lady reacted to cultural norms of femininity by declining to think for herself. Abigail Adams, Sarah Polk, and Mary Lincoln each were vocal, independent presidential spouses. Mayo notes, however, that "virtually every First Lady who has used her influence has been either ridiculed or vilified as deviating from women's proper role or has been feared as emasculating" (1993, A52). Historian Simon Schama attributes America's resistance to assertiveness in the first lady, in part, to cultural *mythos*, stating:

> Haunting the West is the ancient myth of women as swallowers of virile men. In the White House, the choice is to be a dutiful reflection of the husband's virtue or to devour the husband's strength. And this Delilah image is so deeply rooted that it's incredibly difficult to transcend. (Kornbluth 1995, 34)

This cultural fear of feminine strength is complicated by the expectations of masculinity tied to the presidency (Daughton 1994; Kimmel 1996, 36–38). Assertive presidential wives may fare better if their husbands are viewed as strong and effective (i.e., as the "man in charge"), whereas presidents lacking overtones of masculinity and strength can be perceived as too easily swayed by the opinions of politically involved wives. Caroli asks, for example, "[c]ould Eleanor Roosevelt have broken so many precedents if Franklin had accomplished less? Did Rosalynn Carter's determination make Jimmy look less decisive?" (1995, 65). Even in the face of FDR's popularity, many contemporary journalists derided Eleanor Roosevelt's political activism. After criticizing her propensity for travel, which resulted from her taking on the role of FDR's "eyes and ears," journalist Malcolm Bingay advised the first lady to "light somewhere and keep quiet" (quoted in Beasley 1987, 103). Former President Richard Nixon echoed Bingay's admonition, warning: "[i]f the wife comes through as being too strong and too intelligent it makes the husband look like a wimp" (Steele 1992, 43).

Journalist Michael Barone charged that Hillary Rodham Clinton "makes [President Bill Clinton] appear weak" (1994, 32), and his observation was borne out by several cultural examples. *Time* magazine described the caption under a photo of Rodham Clinton, which hung in a Pentagon briefing room as "the Commander in Chief" (Farley 1993, 7). A caption in the same article under-scored this perspective by stating, "Five-star first lady: Ms. Rodham Clinton's real boss, according to Pentagon wags" (Farley 1993, 7). This same perception was fostered during the health-care reform campaign, at which time, "[a]fter Clinton signaled a willingness to compromise on health care, a highly placed Democrat reports, one senator said, 'Wait, he hasn't checked with Mama yet'" (Barone 1994, 32).

This cultural prohibition against assertive and independent first ladies has in-fluenced many of them to play up their own femininity. For example, Mamie Eisenhower "exemplified the supportive wife who immersed herself in her hus-band's life and career—an ideal of femininity strongly promoted in the 1950s" (Mayo and Meringolo 1994, 22). Pat Nixon emphasized "her domesticity" and once confided to reporters that whenever she had a free evening, she took down her husband's suits and pressed them. Rather than talking about what she read or her views on national issues, she shared her thoughts on sewing dresses for her daughters and stitching up draperies on her home machine. Her husband em-phasized the same helpmate quality in Pat when in the famous "Checkers" speech, he referred to her as a "wonderful stenographer" (Caroli 1995, 247). Richard Nixon's later statement about the proper comportment for a political wife suggests that Pat Nixon's domestic persona was a strategic rhetorical move designed to facilitate a political goal. Barbara Bush, similarly, cast herself in "the role of national grandmother," a persona that garnered her consistently favorable approval ratings (Walsh 1992, 36; Truman 1995, 313–19).

This preference for domestic first ladies stems, in part, from cultural interpre-tations of women's roles. Although "for the past 20 years more wives have worked [outside the home] than have not," "[t]hree-quarters of married couples say that mothers should make a full-time job of bringing up their children, if money allows it" ("Merry Wives" 1992, 26). Cultural attitudes toward working women in the public and private spheres suggest that "Ozzie and Harriett, the mythical television couple of the 1950s, are still alive in spirit, if not always in fact" ("Merry Wives" 1992, 26). Many critics agree that the angst over the first lady goes beyond expectations for domesticity inscribed into this traditionally feminine role. The controversies that run "throughout our history" also are about "America's continuing, deep-seated ambivalence, even hostility, toward power in the hands of women" (Mayo 1993, A52). Journalist Susan Riley asks:

> Why does society insist on an archetypal wife, an Everywife, a figurehead with no political power but potent symbolic performance? What is the political wife saying about women, about marriage, about the way power is distributed in our society? It sounds as if she is saying that women are status symbols, possessions, and mirrors for the men they live with. But aren't those days gone? (1987, 3–4)

In response to Riley's question, Ann Grimes concludes, "[e]vidently not. The public behavior of political wives—and of the first lady—and the public acceptance and expectations of their largely ceremonial, symbolic role say a lot" (1990, 318).

Since the inception of the role of first lady, it has come to signify traditional femininity and domesticity, operating to constrain the actions and speech of the women who occupy that role. The implications of this culture, however, reach beyond the office of the first lady. Since first ladies are taken as signifiers of American womanhood, the constraints that affect them will, in turn, impact all women to some extent. To view the role as only a reification of traditional femininity, however, is to oversimplify the rhetoric of the first ladyship. In the next section of this essay, I explore the ways in which United States first ladies have achieved political agency within presidential administrations and have fostered that agency on a broader scale through the development of a strategic social style. Some used social style to promote their husbands' political agendas, while others used it to promote their own political and personal goals.

The First Lady: A Site of Women's Agency

Although the duties and responsibilities of the first lady are not prescribed in the Constitution, presidents' wives have always had to assume a visible position in American politics, due, in part, to the unique nature of the American presidency. Caroli points out that the office of the president combines two jobs which typically are distinct in other governmental systems: "a head of state who presides over ceremonial functions, and a head of government who makes major appointments and takes a decisive role in legislation" (1995, xviii). Because the president is occupied with responsibilities as the head of government, presidential spouses often have assumed many of the ceremonial functions performed by the head of state, placing them in the limelight on the national and international stage. Furthermore, Caroli notes the ways in which the president's "living arrangements" foster the involvement of first ladies in national governance, since private and public spaces coalesce in the White House (1995, xviii).[3] Finally, Caroli highlights the fact that the election process, particularly the heightened involvement of candidates' wives in political campaigns during the twentieth century, expands the role and significance of political spouses (1995, xix).

Even without "a constitutional directive or formal portfolio," the majority of first ladies have "exercised authority . . . by virtue of marriage," insofar as most have "support[ed] a two-person/one career White House" (Winfield 1994, 59, 61). Some first ladies have achieved political agency without violating norms of femininity by cultivating what I term a "social" political style. Since the inception of the role, first ladies have been expected to perform social and ceremonial functions. The political power that inhered in this social role historically has been occluded, but even a brief examination of the actions of first ladies reveals the impact of social style. The exemplar for first ladies' social style is Dolley

Madison, a presidential spouse typically remembered for "throwing great parties" (and wrongly credited with introducing the United States to ice cream). Madison's "parties," however, were strategically orchestrated political events designed to facilitate the political aims that she shared with her husband, James Madison. Mayo and Meringolo cite one example of her social style as follows:

> She invited James Madison's enemies in Congress to dinner, and with her warmth and gregariousness won support for him before the 1812 election. So charming and hospitable was she at these gatherings that Congressman Jonathan Roberts observed, "You cannot discover who [are] her husband's friends or foes." Her sixteen years as a leader of Washington society established Dolley Madison as the most dominant force in the social life of the early republic. (1994, 16–17)

Not only did Madison's social prowess earn her the reputation as a "dominant force in the social life of the early republic," it also promoted her and her husband politically. Caroli observes that Madison's dinner for members of Congress during the 1812 campaign led politician James Blaine to "credi[t] Dolley with a large share in her husband's 1812 victory" (1995, 15).

This version of social style is based upon Robert Hariman's (1995) theory of political style, which posits that style is connected to power in intimate and fundamental ways. He defines political style as "a coherent repertoire of rhetorical conventions depending on aesthetic reactions for political effect," and identifies four styles prominent in male-dominated political spheres: realist, republican, courtly, and bureaucratic (13). According to Hariman, political style operates through rules for speech, interaction, and performance. It functions to shape identity, generate consensus, and distribute power. For example, the realist style is exemplified in Machiavelli and instantiates the political actor as strategist. Speech is devalued in the realist style, artlessness is professed, and text is sublimated for a focus on "unencumbered experience" (13–49). Conversely, the republican style, which is premised on the Ciceronian citizen-orator, privileges rhetoric, operates from consensus, and draws power from heroic *mythos* (95–140). In the courtly style, roles of decorum are sovereign, attention is focused on the body, and speech is suppressed (51–94). The bureaucratic style, drawing on the work of Franz Kafka, catalogues the "set of communicative conventions uniquely constitutive of office culture" (142) and examines the power of assimilation (141–76).

Hariman presents his four political styles as androgynous, equally employable by women and men. Yet, the archetypes used to generate each style (Machiavelli, Kapuscinski, Kafka) are male and the gendered nature of political power is not a question tackled by Hariman. He does suggest, however, that his typology is just a beginning, and he urges other scholars to explore additional versions of political style. The analyses in this book respond in part to that call by suggesting a social style derived from the first lady's role as hostess and social partner of her husband.

Dolley Madison was not the first presidential spouse to enact the social style. Social obligations of first ladies began to be defined earlier at the turn of the nineteenth century, when Louisa Adams "traveled around Washington, calling on as many as twenty-five women in a single day from a list her husband drew up for her" (Mayo and Meringolo 1994, 18). The fact that John Quincy Adams took the time to prescribe an itinerary for his wife testifies to the political import of social interactions.

The political nature of private sphere activities routinely is downplayed, particularly in reference to the activities of political wives. For example, when First Lady Edith Roosevelt held weekly meetings with wives of cabinet members, presidential aide Archibald Butt assumed that the women did little more than "take tea and compare crochet patterns." Helen Taft, wife of the secretary of war, also referred to these gatherings as social affairs, and her assertion shows an understanding of "social affairs" as innocuous and apolitical (Caroli 1995, 121–22). From another perspective, however, Roosevelt's gatherings were every bit as much an enactment of a social style that fostered the accomplishment of political goals.

Grace Coolidge facilitated her husband's political achievements by using social style to temper Calvin Coolidge's interpersonal uneasiness. Caroli notes that "[a]t official receptions, the president curtly nodded to the people and quickly passed from one obligatory handshake to the next while Grace's exceptional memory for names and her genuine concern for guests' comfort made them feel at ease" (1995, 168). Mamie Eisenhower also achieved political advancement for Ike by embodying hospitality. Mayo and Meringolo explain that "[t]hroughout the nation's history, advancing a husband's career through social entertainment has been a traditional female role, and Mamie saw her primary duty as first lady as that of a successful White House hostess" (1994, 21). Similarly, Lady Bird Johnson fulfilled the "responsibilities" of a "political wife" early in her marriage to Lyndon Johnson by accommodating "any of Lyndon's political friends," as well as "those he hoped to bring into that category," whom he frequently brought home unannounced (Caroli 1995, 232–33). Barbara Bush testifies in her autobiography about George Bush's propensity to bring home guests with virtually no notice, both before and after their arrival in the White House (1994).

These examples illustrate how the social style of first ladies functions to support the political achievements of United States presidents, deflating the myth that politics historically has been transacted only by men in the public sphere. As early as the eighteenth century, women participated in politics through their social interactions. One assumption underlying this social style is that political power is rooted not just in the public sphere but also in private interactions. Consequently, one implication of defining political power in this manner is the collapse (or, at least, intermingling) of public and private spheres.

Abigail McCarthy notes that political wives contribute to their husbands' careers by providing "status maintenance, intellectual contributions, and public performance" (1984, 215). Social style, however, has not been used exclusively to further the political agendas of male politicians. Some first ladies have also employed the social style in service of their own political or personal goals. Florence Harding garnered favorable journalistic coverage by "invit[ing] newspaperwomen to cruise down the Potomac with her on the presidential yacht" (Caroli 1995, 162). Eleanor Roosevelt invited young African American women from the National Training School for Girls to a White House garden party, using a feminine medium of entertaining to make a progressive statement about race (Beasley 1987, 101–2). Mayo and Meringolo note that many first ladies extended their role as the "nation's hostess" in order to act "as diplomats," identifying Eleanor Roosevelt, Jacqueline Kennedy, Pat Nixon, and Nancy Reagan as examples of first ladies who used the social style in this manner (1994, 23).

Each of these anecdotes begins to suggest a typology for social style. First, social style is gendered feminine and power resides in the ceremonial presence. As such, it challenges the masculinized forms of public, political power that dominate most critical discussions. Second, the social style brings together components of Hariman's (1995) courtly and republican styles. From the courtly style it draws a focus on decorum, minimization of speech, and attention to the body. Since first ladies have always been quasi royalty in America, their style is likely to dovetail in some respects with the courtly style (Campbell 1996, 188). From the republican style the social style garners an emphasis on consensus, efforts to foster a constituent base, and the standard of civic virtue. Although first ladies have been America's royals, they also are expected to be "regular citizens." First ladies like Nancy Reagan who have embraced the royal air too enthusiastically are harshly criticized. Like their presidential counterparts, republican first ladies must exude the air of civic virtue and embody American patriotism and spirit, an aspect of social style at which Barbara Bush was especially adept.

The social style has developed, in part, as a response to the double bind that casts first ladies as simultaneously courtly and republican. They are caught between styles that sublimate and privilege speech, and attend (alternately) to the body and the mind. Consequently, a third component of the social style is that it enacts political power while disguising its nature as political. In this way, the social style invokes the realist style's artistry disguised by professed artlessness. First ladies have been forced to disguise their political power by professing apoliticism. Some of the most political first ladies such as Barbara Bush have been the most insistent about their disconnection from political matters (Sullivan 1992, 42). Finally, the social style is defined by the constraint of conforming to norms of femininity while, at the same time, developing a tacit ability to employ femininity in order to achieve political agency.

First ladies have generated limited political agency by strategically employing social style and outwardly conforming to norms of traditional femininity. Yet, the first ladyship remains a controversial role because so many first ladies transgressed expectations that they would "stay out" of politics, involving themselves explicitly in national governance. Some first ladies acted as gatekeepers, influencing governance by monitoring communication exchanges. Abigail Adams "kept [John Adams] informed of political sentiment" in Massachusetts while he was away (Caroli 1995, 11). Eleanor Roosevelt left notes for FDR beside his bedside at night so he would attend to matters she deemed important, and she "brought individuals to meet the president and steered the conversations into fields of her own interest (Beasley 1987, 103).[4] After Woodrow Wilson had his stroke in 1919, Edith Wilson began to monitor correspondence so that "[a]ny communication that reached the president went first to the president's wife" (Caroli 1995, 149). Caroli reports that "[r]equests to the president frequently began 'Dear Mrs. Wilson,' indicating that the writers recognized her as controlling access to the president." Some first ladies downplayed the significance of their influence by tying their actions to their "wifely" duty to care for their husbands. Roosevelt garnered the reputation as FDR's "eyes and ears," promoting her activist outings as actions of a devoted wife (Beasley 1987, 104). Sarah Polk justified her involvement in James Polk's political activities by claiming that she was "assisting her husband in order to protect his health" (Caroli 1995, 63). After James Polk became fatigued due to the late hours he kept reading papers, Sarah Polk began to read them for him, marking "those portions she thought deserving of his attention" (Caroli 1995, 63).

In addition to garnering political agency by serving as gatekeepers for their spouses, many first ladies have participated explicitly in political decision-making. Caroli explains that while "an NBC special on [First Lady Nancy Reagan], broadcast in June 1985, showed her laughingly dismissing accounts of her political expertise and interest," only "the naive believed," since "high White House sources . . . described her as 'indispensable,' 'a savvy adviser,' and important on political matters, such as 'getting the Russians to a summit,' personnel decisions, such as removing Alexander Haig from the cabinet, and procedures, such as preparing her husband for debates against Walter Mondale during the 1984 campaign" (1995, 277). Sarah Polk, one of Reagan's nineteenth-century predecessors, achieved political agency by developing "her own supporters— people who valued her abilities and judgment apart from her husband's. In that respect, she foreshadows a later development that saw its culmination in the campaign buttons, 'Betty's husband for President'" (Caroli 1995, 62).

This history of involvement by first ladies in presidential administrations has resulted in widespread recognition of the influence of first ladies in American politics. Caroli notes that "[b]oth outspoken Eleanor Roosevelt and reticent Bess Truman were named during their husbands' administrations as among the 'most powerful people in Washington,' while the vice-presidents were conspicuously absent from such lists" (1995, xvii). Of course, such influence is not always well received. Opponents of first ladies' power have disparagingly used such terms as "Madame President" for Abigail Adams (Winfield 1994, 61), "petticoat government," referring to the Wilson administration (Caroli 1995, 149), and "Lady Macbeth in a headband" in reference to Hillary Rodham Clinton (Miller 1992, 280; Sullivan and Levin 1995, 279). But scholars of the first ladyship agree that while derogatory labels are often applied to so-called "exceptional" first ladies such as Adams, Roosevelt, and Rodham Clinton, the vast majority of first ladies have used their position to enact political power. Caroli and Winfield (1994, 66) note that Rodham Clinton received unusual attention because she was particularly candid about her involvement in administration activities; Caroli underscores that "[t]he candor—not the power—was new" (1995, 307).

In order to further women's agency in the political sphere, the "overt, not covert, power" of first ladies must be recognized (Grimes 1990, 328). Although the "private influence" of first ladies through the employment of "pillow talk" is widely acknowledged and accepted, their public participation in administration business is deemed improper. Pierre Saint-Amand explains the ramifications of that bias for women, claiming:

> Influence is perceived as a form of hysterical persuasion, the incessant effort on the part of the woman to meddle in male discourse or performance. But at the same time influence condemns the woman to illegitimacy; it is a sort of enunciator who is revealed only in the utterance of the other, the one vested with authority of discourse and action. Influence, in the end, always exposes a woman in her impotence. (1994, 385)

Thus, although first ladies may achieve legitimate political agency through private influence, if that is the only type of agency sanctioned by the culture, political discourse and action are reified as male activity. Some locate concern over the first lady's power in her status as a "behind the scenes" operator or as an unelected official, but both of those concerns prove to be disingenuous. First, if critics truly were more concerned about covert influence, they would have been more deeply troubled by, for example, Barbara Bush or Nancy Reagan than Hillary Rodham Clinton. The outcry over Rodham Clinton's appointment to head the task force on health-care reform demonstrated that the public experienced greater consternation over a first lady who exercised her power in public, perhaps because in order to assess Rodham Clinton's use of political power, everyone had to acknowledge it. That acknowledgment countered the cultural narrative that casts the first lady as an embodiment of domestic femininity, and undermines the ways in which American womanhood has been defined. With reference to the second charge, that first ladies' political power is improper because they are not elected, Katha Pollitt rightly points out that "no one who serves in a presidential administration is elected except the Vice President" (1993, 657). Moreover, those who impugn the political involvement of first ladies in their husbands' administrations routinely trade on sexist stereotypes, illustrating the misogynistic assumptions that guide the ways in which first ladies often are perceived. Uncovering sexist assumptions in the discourses surrounding the first ladyship facilitates a broader recognition of the ways in which stereotypes constrain all women in the public sphere and operate as rhetorics of containment.

The first ladyship in the United States can be conceived of as a site of women's agency because of the pragmatic and creative strategies employed by first ladies who found themselves situated within cultural narratives of containment and expected to fulfill norms of traditional femininity. Historically, first ladies have balanced personal desires to facilitate the political goals of the presidential administrations they supported with impulses to achieve political agency for themselves. Although presidential spouses exhibit a variety of responses to the rhetorical situations they face, many have helped create a political style premised on the power of ceremonial, social, and private exchanges. In so doing, first ladies challenge the legitimacy of drawing distinctions between social and political spheres. An even more important contribution of U.S. first ladies to the project of promoting women's political agency, however, is the implicit challenge many have posed to understanding identity as discrete and uniform. Insofar as the rhetoric of the first ladyship exhibits paradox and heterogeneity, it offers potential correctives to the double binds faced by all women. In the concluding section of this essay, I argue that by enacting rhetorical strategies that employ paradox, U.S. first ladies have challenged the double bind and modeled the ways in which political women can develop more complex public personae.

The First Lady: A Site of Heterogeneity and Paradox

One characteristic of the public personae of many first ladies is heterogeneity, and this characteristic, perhaps above all others, has the potential to liberate women insofar as it helps to confound the double binds that constrain women. Diane Shoos theorized the "heterogeneity of the individual female subject," underscoring the complex, multifaceted nature of identity and challenging the dichotomous logic that curtails women's agency (1992, 225). For example, Abigail Adams's heterogeneity is illustrated in a description provided by her grandson, Charles Francis Adams, who wrote that she was "a farmer cultivating the land and discussing the weather and the crops; a merchant reporting prices current and the rates of exchange and directing the making up of invoices; a politician speculating upon the probabilities of war, and a mother . . . and in all she appears equally well" (Caroli 1995, 27).

The potential of heterogeneous individual identities to liberate women lies not in the mere recognition of the multiple roles played by each person, but rather is located in the notion that identity is complex. Tamara K. Hareven observes that "between the two extreme images of Eleanor Roosevelt—that of the shallow busybody first lady and that of the humanitarian reformer and consummate politician—stands a complex figure full of contradictions and paradoxes, a social reformer who could not be easily stereotyped" (1984, 201). Many, in particular the mass media, reinforce dichotomous thinking because it helps to order complicated social narratives and makes political actors more easily identifiable as "heroes" or "villains." The January 15, 1996, cover of *Newsweek* magazine that labeled Hillary Rodham Clinton "Saint or Sinner?" oversimplified a complex public persona, fostered vilification and scapegoating, and ignored the evolutionary nature of human identity. Identity is best conceived of as a process characterized by contradiction and paradox. Mayo and Meringolo observe that Mamie Eisenhower was noted both for her traditional femininity and for a "spine of steel" that made it appear "as if it were she who had been a five-star general" (1994, 22). Similarly, Caroli notes that Caroline Harrison is remembered for two very "different achievements—starting the White House china collection and helping make one of the country's major medical schools [Johns Hopkins] coeducational" (1995, 108). As these examples suggest, to label any first lady "feminine" or "feminist," "activist" or "reticent," "influential" or "marginal," ignores the nuances of first ladies' political identities.

This book examines modern U.S. first ladies from a rhetorical perspective. Each chapter augments the standard portraits with an appreciation of the symbolic—the persuasive power of the words and visual images of first ladies, the rhetorical use of first ladies as symbols, and the complexity of identity as it is constructed symbolically.

Questions for Discussion

1. Author Karrin Vasby Anderson claims that first ladies influence conceptions of American womanhood by functioning as sites for the "symbolic negotiation of female identity." What does she mean?
2. In what ways is the position of first lady a site of traditional femininity?
3. Do you agree with Anderson's claim that there is a cultural bias toward traditional first ladies as well as a cultural prohibition against modern first ladies?
4. In what ways is the position of first lady a site of women's agency? Include "social style" as part of your answer.
5. Anderson claims that the best way to understand the position of first lady is to see it as a site of heterogeneity and paradox. What does she mean and what reasons does she give for her position?

Internet Resources

http://womenshistory.about.com/cs/firstladies/
This website provides links to other sites on historical first ladies, first ladies from other countries, and first ladies of state officials. A cross-cultural perspective provides the opportunity to discover what is unique about American first ladies, especially of the latter twentieth century.

http://www.pbs.org/newshour/bb/white_house/first_lady_1-15.html
Hillary Clinton was a controversial first lady because she was outspoken and activist. This website provides a discussion of Clinton, putting her activities into historical perspective. Discussants include presidential historians Doris Kearns Goodwin and Michael Beschloss; first lady scholar Carl S. Anthony; and journalist Jim Lehrer.

http://news.bbc.co.uk/2/hi/americas/3404405.stm
During Campaign 2004, many newspapers and magazine articles appeared about the wives of the presidential candidates. This website carries a discussion of the

candidates' wives in terms of their lifestyles, personalities, and what they might bring to the office of first lady. Use this article as a beginning point for a discussion on public expectations of first ladies. What do we expect from prospective first ladies? Are these expectations fair?

http://gos.sbc.edu and http://www.americanrhetoric.com
Both websites have texts of speeches by first ladies such as Hillary Rodham Clinton, Barbara Bush, Laura Bush, Rosalynn Carter, Eleanor Roosevelt, and so on.

Notes

1. My analysis regarding containment and U.S. culture first appeared in Karrin Vasby Anderson, "'Rhymes with Rich': 'Bitch' as a Tool of Containment in Contemporary American Politics" (1999, 599–623).

2. For elaboration of the argument that domesticity was a governing ideology of the Cold War era see, for example, Kozol (1996, 231–50).

3. For an excellent illustration of the ways in which public business gets transacted in the private spaces of the White House, see Doris Kearns Goodwin (1994).

4. Also see Goodwin (1994, 15) for references to "the Eleanor basket—in which the first lady regularly left memoranda, communications, and reports for the president to read."

References

Anderson, Karrin Vasby. 1999. "Rhymes with Rich": "Bitch" as a Tool of Containment in Contemporary American Politics. *Rhetoric & Public Affairs*, 2, 599–623.

Barone, Michael. 1992. Entering the Combat Zone. *U.S. News & World Report*, 30 March, 39. [Online] *Expanded Academic ASAP*, accessed 29 March 1995.

———. 1994. Bad News for Boomer Liberals. *U.S. News & World Report*, 29 August, 32. [Online] *Expanded Academic ASAP*, accessed 27 October 1995.

Beasley, Maurine H. 1987. *Eleanor Roosevelt and the Media: A Public Quest for Self-Fulfillment*. Urbana, Ill.: University of Illinois Press.

Bush, Barbara. 1994. *A Memoir*. New York: St. Martin's Press.

Campbell, David. 1992. *Writing Security: United States Foreign Policy and the Politics of Identity*. Minneapolis, Minn.: University of Minnesota Press.

Campbell, Karlyn Kohrs. 1989. *Man Cannot Speak for Her*, Vol. 1. New York: Greenwood.

———. 1996. The Rhetorical Presidency: A Two-Person Career. In *Beyond the Rhetorical Presidency*, ed. Martin J. Medhurst, 179–95. College Station, Tex.: A & M University Press.

Carlson, Margaret. 1992. All Eyes on Hillary. *Time*, 14 September, 28. [Online] *Expanded Academic ASAP*, accessed 27 October 1995.

Caroli, Betty Boyd. 1995. *First Ladies*, expanded edition. New York: Oxford University Press.

Daughton, Suzanne M. 1994. Women's Issues, Women's Place: Gender-Related Problems in Presidential Campaigns. *Communication Quarterly*, 42, 106–19.

Douglass, Susan J. 1994. *Where the Girls Are: Growing Up Female with the Mass Media*. New York: Random House.

Farley, Christopher John. 1993. Commander Hillary. *Time*, 26 April, 7, [Online] *Expanded Academic ASAP*, accessed 27 October 1995.

Goodwin, Doris Kearns. 1994. *No Ordinary Time: Franklin and Eleanor Roosevelt: The Home Front in World War II*. New York: Simon & Schuster.

Greer, Germaine. 1995. Abolish Her: The Feminist Case against First Ladies. *New Republic*, 26 June, 20–26, [Online] *Expanded Academic ASAP*, accessed 27 October 1995.

Grimes, Ann. 1990. *Running Mates: The Making of a First Lady*. New York: William Morrow.

Hareven, Tamara K. 1984. ER and Reform. In *Without Precedent: The Life and Career of Eleanor Roosevelt*, ed. Joan Hoff-Wilson and Marjorie Lightman, 201–13. Bloomington, Ind.: Indiana University Press.

Hariman, Robert. 1995. *Political Style: The Artistry of Power*. Chicago: University of Chicago Press.

Jamieson, Kathleen Hall. 1995. *Beyond the Double Bind: Women and Leadership*. New York: Oxford University Press.

Kimmel, Michael. 1996. *Manhood in America: A Cultural History*. New York: Free Press.

Kornbluth, Jesse. 1995. Free Advice: Five Historians Comment on Hillary's Dilemma. *New Yorker*, 30 January, 34.

Kozol, Wendy. 1996. Good Americans. In *Bonds of Affection*, ed. John Bodnar, 231–50. Princeton, N.J.: Princeton University Press.

May, Elaine Tyler. 1988. *Homeward Bound: American Families in the Cold War Era*. New York: Basic Books.

Mayo, Edith P. 1993. The Influence and Power of First Ladies. *Chronicle of Higher Education*, 15, A52.

Mayo, Edith P., and Denise D. Meringolo. 1994. *First Ladies: Political Role and Public Image*. Washington, D.C.: Smithsonian Institution.

McCarthy, Abigail Q. 1984. ER as First Lady. In *Without Precedent: The Life and Career of Eleanor Roosevelt*, ed. Joan Hoff-Wilson and Marjorie Lightman, 214–25. Bloomington, Ind.: Indiana University Press.

The Merry Wives of Washington. 1992. *Economist*, 8 August, 26.

Miller, Judith. 1992. The Cookie-Cutter Wives of Politics. *Vogue*, November, 280–83.

Pollitt, Katha. 1993. The Male Media's Hillary Problem: First Lady Bashing. *The Nation*, 17 May, 657. [Online] *Expanded Academic ASAP*, accessed 27 October 1995.

Riley, Susan. 1987. *Political Wives: The Lives of the Saints*. Toronto: Deneau.

Saint-Amand, Pierre. 1994. Terrorizing Marie Antoinette. *Critical Inquiry*, 20, 379–400.

Shoos, Diane. 1992. The Female Subject of Popular Culture. *Hypatia*, 7, 215–26.

Steele, Scott. 1992. A Man of Hope (Ark.). *Maclean's*, 16 November, 43.

Sullivan, Andrew. 1992. Sacred Cow. *New Republic*, 22 June, 42.

Sullivan, Patricia A., and Carole Levin. 1995. Women and Political Communication: From the Margins to the Center. In *Political Rhetoric, Power, and Renaissance Women*, ed. Carole Levin and Patricia A. Sullivan, 275–82. New York: State University of New York Press.

Truman, Margaret. 1995. *First Ladies: An Intimate Group Portrait of White House Wives*. New York: Fawcett Columbine.

Walsh, Kenneth T. 1992. Barbara Bush's Subtle and Significant Campaign Role. *U.S. News & World Report*, 27 April, 36.

Winfield, Betty Houchin. 1994. "Madame President": Understanding a New Kind of First Lady. *Media Studies Journal*, 8, 59–71.

Zaeske, Susan. 1995. The "Promiscuous Audience" Controversy and the Emergence of the Early Woman's Rights Movements. *Quarterly Journal of Speech*, 81, 191–207.

CHAPTER TWO

Eleanor Roosevelt
A Rhetorical Reconstruction of First Ladydom

Lisa R. Barry

I am in a position where I can do the most good to help the most people.

Women, whether subtly or vociferously, have always been a tremendous power in the destiny of the world and with so many of them now holding important positions and receiving recognition and earning the respect of the men as well as the members of their own sex, it seems more than ever that in this crisis, *It's Up to the Women!*

—Eleanor Roosevelt

Eleanor Roosevelt was a prolific speaker and writer. Thousands of speech transcripts, writings, and articles are housed in the Franklin Delano Roosevelt Library, the Franklin and Eleanor Roosevelt Institute, the Library of Congress, and in books and periodicals. Many scholars have dedicated their careers to examining Mrs. Roosevelt's activities and legacy as a first lady.[1] Rather than recreate their studies, this chapter focuses on the ways in which Mrs. Roosevelt used both oral and written rhetoric to educate women who were recently enfranchised.

Mrs. Roosevelt's rhetorical strategies took many forms. At times, she spoke only to women, such as during her three hundred press conferences that were open only to female reporters. This rhetorical action helped at least some women gain meaningful careers. She also spoke directly to women through a variety of columns such as *My Day* and *If You Ask Me*, which provided Mrs. Roosevelt a means of educating women about civic responsibility. Her press conferences help us understand how she supported women's work outside of the home, while her other writings, collected in book form as *It's Up to the Women*, help us understand her belief that women are necessary for a healthy public sphere.

Eleanor Roosevelt took her role as first lady seriously, turning it into a position with long-term effects. According to presidential historian Doris Kearns Goodwin, "She was the first president's wife to hold—and lose—a government job, the first to testify before a congressional committee, the first to hold press conferences, to speak before a national party convention, to write a syndicated column, to be a radio commentator, to earn money as a lecturer" (1994, 10). She effectively changed the role of the first lady from a predominantly social hostess role to a social activist. Indeed, "She shattered the ceremonial mold in which the role of the first lady had traditionally been fashioned, and reshaped it around her own skills and commitments to social reform" (Goodwin 1994, 10).

Mrs. Roosevelt's many speeches and articles often addressed women's special ability to recognize social issues such as racism and working conditions and their capacity to solve these problems.[2] Because cameras were often focused on her, Mrs. Roosevelt worked hard to ensure that she was surrounded by women. Thus, in many photographs she is shown meeting with women of all races, classes, and professions. Together, these artifacts speak to the special emphasis she placed on the importance of women in the public sphere and demonstrate her commitment to social feminism. Ultimately, she worked to educate the nation about its immense potential made possible only through the inclusion of women and the recognition that all individuals in a society are important to its health, happiness, and success.

Eleanor Roosevelt's personal investment in the success of the individual drove her rhetoric, which was neither as polished nor as smooth as her husband's. She was an ordinary person speaking to and with ordinary people.[3] A close analysis of *It's Up to the Women*, one of her key monographs, demonstrates how Mrs. Roosevelt achieved a balance between the personal and political that made her such a viable and important first lady. She used neither speechwriters nor ghostwriters, so a close analysis of her edited compilation of speeches and columns provides insight into her stance on key issues and her rhetorical skill in articulating them. My analysis illuminates the rhetorical strategies she used to construct an identity consistent with, but separate from, her husband's. This identity encompassed many elements, including the traditional roles of wife, mother, and especially educator. Importantly, she taught school before embarking on what was to become a respected political career.

Eleanor Roosevelt has garnered much scholarly attention, however, scholars have not interpreted her many writings, interviews, and speeches as a rhetorical attempt to educate the nation. Most scholars agree that she was more involved in politics and in her husband's decisions than any first lady before her.[4] This chapter seeks to demonstrate that Mrs. Roosevelt's political involvement not only fulfilled her personally, as Maurine Beasley (1987) claims, but also enabled her to educate the nation about the importance of all its people—women, minorities, the underprivileged, the ill—in the development of a peaceful and equitable society. *It's Up to the Women* is a particularly useful text for illuminating how she incorporated her beliefs into all that she wrote and said and, in so doing, became the nation's teacher. The analysis of her book provides an opportunity to explore how Mrs. Roosevelt rhetorically reconstructed the role of first lady as she negotiated her public and private personae.

Biography

Born Anna Eleanor Roosevelt on October 11, 1884, Eleanor Roosevelt was the only daughter of an alcoholic father and a beautiful, but often aloof, socialite mother who publicly criticized her daughter's homely and unattractive appearance. Eleanor was insecure about her appearance and her future, especially whether she would be able to achieve the social status of her mother. Her home life was somewhat unstable as her father frequently traveled for business or attended medical facilities because of his alcoholism. Despite this, Eleanor and her father were emotionally very close. When her mother died in 1892, Eleanor and her siblings went to live with their grandmother who was better able to care for them. Her father died two years later, and her grandmother, Mary Hall, became her guardian (Gould 1996, 424). Because of her father's death, Eleanor felt empty, alone, and unsure about her grandmother's ability to guide her. However, her grandmother sent her to London's Allenswood Academy in 1899, a school that proved extremely influential in setting her future course.

Eleanor studied under Mademoiselle Marie Souvestra, "a bold, articulate woman whose commitment to liberal causes and detailed study of history played a key role in shaping Eleanor's social and political development" (Gould 1996, 424). Eleanor considered the three years spent at Allenswood the happiest of her adolescence; she formed close friendships that lasted throughout her life, studied subjects such as language and history, "learned to state her opinions on controversial political events clearly and concisely" (Gould 1996, 424), and gained confidence and independence. When Eleanor returned to New York, she joined the National Consumers League and became active in other social movements. Her devotion, enthusiasm, and commitment to these political activities garnered her a reputation in New York reform circles as an asset to their causes. These activities also gave her practical political experience and helped refine her political beliefs.

Eleanor was reacquainted with her cousin Franklin Delano Roosevelt (FDR) during the summer of 1902, and, after a year of secret meetings, the two announced their engagement on November 22, 1903. Franklin's mother disapproved and attempted to separate the couple, but they married on March 17, 1905. President Theodore Roosevelt, Eleanor's uncle, gave her away in the ceremony. She spent the next eleven years as a dutiful wife during which she bore six children, one of whom died in infancy. She admitted that she had not been prepared for nor had she understood what being a loving wife and mother entailed, but she dutifully attended to both. Her marriage was not ideal, though, and when she mistakenly opened a letter to her husband that revealed his romantic affair with her former social secretary Lucy Mercer (in whose arms he later died), she offered to divorce him. He refused, and their relationship became a formal one that took on the characteristics of a business partnership. This proved to be advantageous for both; FDR had a trusted confidante and Mrs. Roosevelt had the opportunity to pursue her own political and professional interests.

Although she had placed her political career on hold while she raised her children, Mrs. Roosevelt resumed it when FDR served in the New York senate, 1911–1913. During her husband's tenure as assistant secretary of the navy, she continued to hone her political skills. When he was paralyzed with polio in 1921, she became active in the women's division of the State Democratic Committee; her purpose was to maintain *his* political interests by becoming an integral member of a powerful political team.

Mrs. Roosevelt shocked the nation when she said that she would not leave her job if her husband were elected to the presidency. "During [FDR's] four years in the Albany statehouse, Eleanor had traveled down to New York City to teach three days a week at her school on East Sixty-fifth Street, and she saw no reason why his transfer to Washington should alter her schedule or stop her from doing what she 'enjoyed more than anything I have ever done'" (Caroli 1987, 185). Prior to her husband's election, she had formed two business partnerships with other women: "one to operate a school in New York City and the other to manufacture furniture at Hyde Park" (Caroli 1995, 189).

FDR was elected to the presidency in 1933, and, because of his physical condition and her political and social knowledge, she became his eyes and ears. During World War II, Mrs. Roosevelt traveled the world and reported to her husband. Her travels resulted in widespread public admiration for a woman who truly cared about the American people. The many photographs taken during her travels demonstrate her commitment to people; she was often seen with people of color and with women.

Mrs. Roosevelt delivered many speeches, wrote daily columns that appeared in newspapers and magazines, wrote several books, and compiled her speech transcripts and columns into other books. She held regular press conferences, as we have seen, limiting attendance to female journalists in an effort to help them gain entry into an otherwise male-dominated industry. These rhetorical activities provided an opportunity for her to speak out against racism, segregation, and sexism. She was particularly vocal about her opposition to Jim Crow and her support of women's rights. When she equated American racism with fascism and argued that segregation would lead to Aryanism, J. Edgar Hoover—then director of the Federal Bureau of Investigation—attempted to silence her. She was not silent, however, and continued to educate American citizens about the plight of marginalized groups in the United States. Part of this effort included capitalizing on photo opportunities by surrounding herself with women and people of color.[5] Mrs. Roosevelt was not always popular; her opposition to racism and her support of social advancement and education for colored people earned her many enemies.

Although Mrs. Roosevelt spoke publicly about her opposition to existing social and political practices, she was careful not to publicly challenge her husband's

New Deal policies. She was very influential during his presidency, and some reporters speculated about whether she ran the White House instead of her husband.

As mentioned earlier, Mrs. Roosevelt engaged in a variety of rhetorical activities, many of which she compiled into books. For purposes of clarity, this analysis focuses on her press conferences and her book *It's Up to the Women*. Rather than examining specific press conferences, I will discuss their general themes and show how she used the press conference as a rhetorical tool. I will also offer a close analysis of *It's Up to the Women*, because she selected the contents carefully to represent her political and philosophical beliefs.[6]

Rhetorical Activities as First Lady

Despite her childhood insecurities, Eleanor Roosevelt became a confident woman concerned with the rights of all people regardless of race, creed, religion, class, or gender. She learned a considerable amount from her political activities when her husband was senator of New York and assistant secretary of the navy. Her friendship with reporter Louis McHenry Howe and later with Lorena Hickok also enabled her to attain the skills she needed to address audiences as well as the knowledge that fueled her activism. When she entered the White House in 1933, she was prepared to embark on a personally fulfilling public political career.[7]

Women's rights was a key issue that Mrs. Roosevelt tackled during her years in the White House. As first lady, she held approximately 300 press conferences, restricting attendance to female reporters. She knew that news organizations would have to hire women in order to gain access to her. Other issues she addressed include the rights of African Americans, subsistence farmsteads, and World War II. She also campaigned on behalf of her husband's New Deal and sought ways to improve the quality of life for the less fortunate; the letters she received from her constituents influenced her deeply. She addressed these issues in approximately 1400 speeches, lectures, radio broadcasts, and short statements that she delivered between 1933 and 1945, as well as in magazine and newspaper articles, books, and autobiographies (Gutin 1989, 97). She also "wrote, without a ghost writer, four autobiographies, seven monographs, seven children's books, and more than 550 articles. . . . In February 1933, she began a monthly column, which existed in a variety of forms until her death in November 1962. On December 30, 1935, she began 'My Day,' a 500-word column published five days a week, which ran continuously until September 27, 1962" (Black 1999, 2). As we have seen, she condensed what she believed were the most telling aspects of her speeches and columns (many of which were also collected in other book-length manuscripts) in *It's Up to the Women*. All of these texts may be viewed as distinct rhetorical artifacts that demonstrate Mrs. Roosevelt's abiding interest in social issues and her passion for teaching—persuading—all Americans to understand their importance.

She believed her projects could resolve social issues and was thus able to convey a sincerity that her audiences readily perceived. Because many of the issues she cared about fell comfortably under the purview of women's concerns (nurture, domesticity, peace), she furthered feminist causes while she simultaneously presented herself as the country's matriarch and the nation's educator. Beasley acknowledges that Mrs. Roosevelt "assumed the role of an instructor for American women on various social topics during [her] press conferences." Her skill at "disguising" her politics enabled her to "[establish] herself at the center of a network of those involved in women's causes" even "if governmental action or policy changes did not result from the issues discussed" (Beasley 1987, 59). She was a feminist fighting for feminist causes years before doing so was fashionable.[8]

Press Conferences

As a first lady who refused the traditional constraints associated with the role of first lady, Eleanor Roosevelt made certain that her public activities were newsworthy and used them as an opportunity to educate her constituency. Mrs. Roosevelt's press conferences helped to establish female reporters as worthy of more than social news. Media historian Maurine Beasley states, "many of the thirty-five women reporters who assembled for Mrs. Roosevelt's first press conference had struggled against the handicap of their sex to attain journalistic careers" (1987, 38). Mrs. Roosevelt limited attendance at her press conferences to only one female reporter from each of the Washington newspapers (Beasley 1987, 41). As a result, many Washington newspapers scrambled to hire female reporters so they could gain access to the first lady. They hoped she would reveal insights about her husband's political agenda, but they believed that she would also contribute information that readers of the social columns would find interesting. Many male reporters believed the press conferences would be social gatherings and disregarded them entirely.

Commonly referred to as "newspaper girls," Mrs. Roosevelt attempted to alter the inequities that many of the thirty-five reporters in attendance faced. They were not allowed membership in the National Press Club where prominent figures often appeared, so they created their own professional group, the Women's National Press Club. However, they still had difficulty gaining access to prominent figures and were often consigned to soft news stories such as social functions. Because Mrs. Roosevelt limited attendance at her press conferences to women, she attempted to provide them the same opportunities afforded to their male counterparts.

Beasley claims that the publication of a well-known photograph taken at the second press conference, March 13, 1933, prompted resentment and contempt by male reporters who perceived the conferences as social gatherings disguised as political meetings. This photograph showed Mrs. Roosevelt with the female reporters gathered around her—some standing, some sitting on the floor near her feet.[9] Although the photograph was intended to promote the legitimacy of women's work and the value of female reporters, "The pose prompted masculine competitors to dub the group 'the incense burners,' and gave them an excuse to scoff at the gatherings, which they initially had scorned" (Beasley 1987, 47).

Although the press conferences appeared to be entirely social, they were not, nor were they simply for show. Mrs. Roosevelt agreed to have weekly personal contact with reporters, which broke all precedents for a first lady's press relations, and her reasons for doing so had significant implications. At the first press conference, held March 6, 1933, Mrs. Roosevelt was nervous, unsure as to how much she should play the role of hostess, the traditional role most first ladies had enacted. She was, however, clear about her purpose: she wanted the reporters to use their articles for educative purposes to teach the American public—especially women—how the government worked. At that meeting, Mrs. Roosevelt labeled female reporters "interpreters to the women of the country as to what goes on politically in the legislative national life and also what the social and personal life is at the White House" (Beasley 1987, 38). Mrs. Roosevelt recognized the value of these reporters as a means to communicate directly to U.S. women; she claimed that a female reporter's job was, "to make her impressions go to leading the women in the country to form a general attitude of mind and thought" (Beasley 1987, 38).

Clearly, Mrs. Roosevelt saw herself as a teacher charged with educating U.S. women about civic responsibility, and the reporters were the means by which she distributed her lessons. At one conference, Mrs. Roosevelt taught women how to read a newspaper properly and encouraged them to read three newspapers with opposing viewpoints on a daily basis, so they could form their own opinions and reach their own conclusions about social and political issues. Personally, she feared she would lose her political identity as the result of her husband's election, so she used the press conferences to construct a public persona, one related to, but separate from, the president's.

Mrs. Roosevelt worked to "disguise" her political involvement during press conferences, hoping to maintain what Beasley (1987, 61) classifies as, "the conventional fiction that a president's wife should remain aloof from politics." Yet, by the time her husband was elected, she already had a well-established political career. Not only had she raised a family, taught school, and managed a business, she had also, "coordinated statewide and national political campaigns, chaired investigative committees and statewide reform organizations, became a respected lobbyist, launched a career as a journalist, and . . . developed a reputation in her own right as a skilled politician who refused to abandon her commitment to democratic ideals" (Black 1999, 2). She did not want to abandon these activities to become merely a social hostess. Doing otherwise, however, would too obviously challenge established beliefs about the proper role and activities of a first lady. The press conferences offered her the opportunity to act politically while at the same time appearing to adhere to the constraints of first ladydom.

Because she limited attendance to female reporters, male reporters and editors dismissed the conferences as soft news, social gossip, and so on. Under this disguise, Mrs. Roosevelt championed women's right to work, to do so with equal pay, and women's role in politics, among other political and social issues. According to historian Allida Black (1999, 2), "Although other first ladies had been active behind the scenes, they had concealed their influence from the public, leaving [Mrs. Roosevelt] no overt precedent to follow for public activism on behalf of social change and public policy." Mrs. Roosevelt saw herself as a teacher and the press conferences as "classes" of a sort, and so her activities were consistent with those in women's traditional sphere of teaching. Thus, she was able to perform a traditionally feminine activity while she simultaneously challenged and enlarged the role of the first lady. She was able to balance the feminine and the feminist in ways that often went unchallenged.

Presidents traditionally hold press conferences, but Mrs. Roosevelt was the first first lady to make herself available to the press on a regular basis. She was encouraged by her husband and his advisors to discuss only social issues such as parties and gatherings, but Mrs. Roosevelt refused. She did mention social events occasionally, but only if they provided a means by which to approach other more political issues. Clearly, her press conferences were the first attempt at political communication by a first lady, and as the conferences progressed, Mrs. Roosevelt became increasingly skilled as a rhetor.

The press conferences benefited both Mrs. Roosevelt and the journalists who became her close friends. Often the reporters gave her advice about how to conduct the conferences, and in time several helped her plan them to ensure they would have news to report that would impress their male counterparts. Sometimes, "they planted questions, proposed topics, and coached on the wording of statements. Sometimes Mrs. Roosevelt accepted their advice; other times she did not" (Beasley 1987, 51). Together, they worked to educate women of the country about politics, human rights, civic responsibility, and at times, about Mrs. Roosevelt's personal life.

Mrs. Roosevelt's press conferences were an effective rhetorical tool for teaching the country about certain issues, but they did not neatly present the entirety of her political and philosophical beliefs. Moreover, reporters sometimes edited or characterized her comments in ways Mrs. Roosevelt did not always agree with. As a result, her press conferences alone do not adequately represent her efforts to educate the nation's women. Therefore, it is necessary to examine her personal writings; in particular, her 1933 book, It's Up to the Women, which she presented as a tool for women to use as they worked to establish new roles and identities. It covered much of the same material as her press conferences, but in a more succinct manner. Because Mrs. Roosevelt authored and compiled the book, we can assume that it accurately reflects her personal philosophy on life, love, and politics in ways her press conferences could not.

It's Up to the Women
"Rushed into print in November 1933, the book contained a compilation of Mrs. Roosevelt's speeches and articles urging women to sacrifice, volunteer and become politically active to make the best of hard times" (Beasley 1987, 72). Although it

might be argued that all of Mrs. Roosevelt's speeches, columns, letters, and articles sought to educate the citizens of this country, this monograph in particular reads like an educational tool and is consistent with her early attempts to appear as if she were adhering to conventional feminine activities.

Because she had successfully raised a family and cared for a sick husband, she possessed an identity consistent with societal norms and expectations for women. She fulfilled her roles as mother and wife, only then did she turn to projects that enabled her to fulfill her own needs and desires. Her work enabled her to create a separate identity that was consistent with her own personality; at heart, she was an activist and educator as well as a mother and wife. Importantly, as a teacher she chose to focus her lessons on issues that were consistent with society's beliefs about women and women's concerns. Thus, she was able to further a feminist agenda by encouraging women to read and think while simultaneously "disguising" that agenda through her choice of subjects and her persona as the country's matriarch.

It's Up to the Women covers many of Mrs. Roosevelt's beliefs, especially her strong belief in the role that women must play to help the country survive the Great Depression. She attributes that belief to historical precedent, that is, the role women have already played in helping the pilgrims survive starvation and our fledgling forces overcome the British during the Revolutionary War. She argues that the first winter in New England was devastating, "a real battle in which many women and children paid with their lives for their heroism" (viii). Although she admits that the Great Depression is different from other crises faced by the United States, she insists that women can pull the United States out of its current crisis, and her book is dedicated to that purpose: "Perhaps we need again a little of the stern stuff our ancestors were made of. In any case, it will do us no harm to look at ourselves somewhat critically in relation to some of the problems that confront us to-day [sic]" (x).

Mrs. Roosevelt suggests many ways that women might contribute to the country's success, not the least of which is to discuss women in relation to various jobs. Yet she recognizes that the only way for women to gain and retain a job outside the home is to maintain their duties inside the home (this double bind persists today). Mrs. Roosevelt argues that women are fully capable of doing both.

The book offers twenty chapters that deal with various concerns women have and the challenges they face, including budgets, time management, recreation, and health. Of particular importance for this analysis are those chapters that address women and jobs, education, family life, working conditions, and peace. These chapters will be discussed in the order they appear in her book.

In the first chapter, "To-day's Challenge to Women," Mrs. Roosevelt establishes a matriarchal identity, offering motherly advice in a way that not only makes sense, but also comforts us. In an attempt to reinforce an identity that audiences would be comfortable with, she focuses on what was known about her; she relies on her reputation as a devoted mother and wife. She draws upon that as she uses the book to counsel women to look beyond a man's earning power and focus on his qualities as a person when choosing a spouse.

The Great Depression factors heavily in this discourse, but Mrs. Roosevelt is able to convey motherly concern and wisdom as she encourages all people to focus on their roles as spouse, parent, neighbor, and citizen. At the same time, she sets the stage for commentary about women's work and their ability to contribute to the family income. Thus, she uses a rhetorical strategy whereby she conforms to societal expectations, but, at the same time, works to develop a constituency of women who will be motivated to take action on their own behalf and on behalf of others. Mrs. Roosevelt also invites the audience, both men and women, to perceive themselves as able to contribute to the country's well-being, regardless of their economic status. She offers the kind of faith in our potential that is typical of motherly and teacherly advice, and we embrace it.

The next chapter of interest in the book is chapter 8, "Modern Family Conditions." In it, Mrs. Roosevelt addresses family composition and divorce. She recognizes that the increasing number of women holding professional jobs is changing traditional expectations and understandings of the family. She does not advocate divorce, but counsels acceptance when it is the best course of action. Making marriage more difficult to enter into, she claims, might be the answer: "I personally think that probably it would be wiser if marriage were made far more difficult" (124). Here she might be reflecting her own marital unhappiness, hoping that the younger generation will not marry out of necessity or tradition, but rather for reasons far more meaningful. In this chapter, she also recognizes the need for society to understand and accept men in general and women's work. In fact, she claims that she *expects* women to work; this point she makes in the chapter's last sentence when she says that women are now more likely to hold jobs outside the home.

Mrs. Roosevelt uses her position as first lady as a platform for advocating women's rights, just as she uses her matriarchal persona to discuss the family with regard to marriage and divorce. She advocates tolerance of societal changes, but she insists that the family will persist. She counteracts the nation's concerns with a discussion of Russia, where a movement occurred in which children were to grow up in professional homes and the family was to become obsolete. Even there, she claims, the family persisted and the movement died. Knowing that U.S. society holds the family in high regard, she argues that women's ability to hold jobs outside the home need not necessarily compromise the family and, with a little tolerance and acceptance, the family will persist. Mrs. Roosevelt thus "camouflages" a political issue—women's rights—with a discussion grounded in the family, nurture, and tradition. She does not call attention to her discussion as political, but works toward political ends. She constructs an identity that appears concerned with life, love, happiness, and trust—a persona befitting the country's matriarch. At the same time, she constructs an identity that demonstrates knowledge and wisdom, and offers guidance and counsel—a persona befitting the nation's educator.

Of particular importance in the book is the chapter that discusses types of positions women should pursue and subtly restates her views on women's work.

Chapter 11, "Women and Jobs," begins with a tacit acknowledgment of societal concerns, "Nowadays there is a great deal of agitation as to whether married women should work or not and in order to consider the question, I think we should go back a little bit further and consider whether women should work at all" (142). Mrs. Roosevelt neatly articulates the issue and uses it as a starting point for a discussion of women's "proper" role in society, societal assumptions, equity, and women's rights. She writes about a time when very few women worked outside the home, when society paid little attention to them, when their work was taken for granted, and when they received only food and lodging as compensation. She contends that women have advanced from this condition, but only as they have gained economic independence for themselves and, in turn, provided financial help in their homes. She thus claims that society must consider the question of whether or not women should work "not as an academic question, but as an actual situation which is with us to stay in the industrial world and in the average family" (143–44).

Mrs. Roosevelt claims that, although society may believe that single women work so they can be wasteful and indulgent, many work to help support their families. She maintains that single women must have the opportunity to work, so they can support their families (parents, siblings) and/or themselves. Of more importance, though, is her belief that married women should be given equal opportunity to work outside the home. She attempts, through her writing, to demonstrate the possibility of balancing family and career. She argues that family and career need not be oppositional. We recognize in this chapter that her commentary is based on her own experiences as a devoted mother and wife, who also assumed a "career" as first lady when her husband was elected president. She invites her readers to recognize their own special talents, needs, and desires, and to consider that just as men must sacrifice certain aspects of their lives when they get married, so must women. This statement of equality—Mrs. Roosevelt's belief that women are in most respects just like men—establishes her as a political activist and feminist. Interestingly, although she advocates women's rights, she also recognizes love and marriage, and a woman's interest in and duty to her family. She therefore balances the personal and political in a way that does not call attention to her discourse as political.

Later in this chapter, Mrs. Roosevelt defines the work women have done historically, and demonstrates that this work is similar to the work being done by contemporary women. She attempts to link home and work, family and career, by demonstrating that today we purchase many items that women made previously in their homes. Thus, she invites her readers to support and encourage women's desire to do the same kind of work outside their homes. In addition, Mrs. Roosevelt argues that by working outside the home, women become more interesting to their families:

> The very best thing that comes to a woman with a job is the fact that she has to use her brains in order to find the time for both her job and her home duties. This keeps her brain from stagnating. She has something new to talk to her husband

about and he never will get the feeling that she is just like the old chair, which he has always sat in—comfortable, but thoroughly familiar and never very interesting in consequence. (148–49)

Clearly, Mrs. Roosevelt seeks to improve women's status both inside and outside the home. Some women, she insists, may not be very good at performing some caretaker roles: "There is no use in closing your eyes to the fact that women do not become satisfactory nurses and governesses simply because they have brought children into the world" (152). On the other hand, some women with children might be better suited to work outside the home, and we should give women the opportunity to discover their true talents. She invites the audience to perceive themselves as players in the drama she presents and, in so doing, to accept her views. In this way, she adheres to traditional standards of womanhood, while attempting to extend them.

Chapter 12 presents "Various Occupations for Women." Although Mrs. Roosevelt discusses only two in detail, she begins with a list of those occupations available to women that she believes are worthwhile. She writes, "We can be librarians, secretaries, stenographers, newspaper reporters, photographers, hostesses on planes; in the professions we can be lawyers, doctors, scientists of various kinds, and in the arts women have excelled as sculptors and we have good women poets, writers, painters, playwrights" (153). Notably, she does not restrict the list to those traditional occupations that seem well suited for women. Instead, she expands it to include not only the more traditional roles of secretaries, librarians, and hostesses, but also newspaper reporters, lawyers, doctors, scientists, and artists. However, Mrs. Roosevelt limits her extended discussion to follow to two vocations that she believes are particularly important: teaching and nursing. She discusses the specialized fields of nursing that require advanced education and training, but cautions, "I do not believe that any one who does not really care about alleviating the suffering of humanity can become a good nurse" (168). She thus links nursing with the more traditional roles of women, which include nurturing and caring for others. She argues that women can find complete and utter satisfaction as nurses, but acknowledges that the physical and emotional rigors of that occupation can wear a woman out. She urges women to set money aside for their later years, when they will no longer be able to sustain the demands of that career.

The vocation to which Mrs. Roosevelt devotes most of the chapter is teaching, and it is here that she truly establishes her identity as the nation's educator. She begins by stating that historically, "Women became teachers long before they entered any other gainful employment because it was the one occupation which tied in with the life of the home closely" (154). She states that many enter the profession without any real aptitude, "because we who constitute the public have given so little thought to what we wish to produce in our teachers and to what we expect from our private and public education" (154). She then turns to a discussion of what distinguishes great teachers from others. According to Mrs. Roosevelt, "The quality which makes men or women great teachers is the ability to inspire with curiosity the youthful mind" (156). She subtly argues that women are well suited for careers in teaching because, traditionally, they have concerned themselves with children's lives and well-being. In this way, she placates those who might object to women teachers by framing such outside work as consistent with women's traditional roles.

Mrs. Roosevelt compares European models of education and declares the English model to be best because of its focus on culture. She claims that our country should follow the English model and argues that doing so will help to prevent another world war, which would surely wipe out our civilization. She maintains that women are superior teachers, not only because we are better able to understand and inspire children, but also because we are more concerned with peace, self-preservation, and the betterment of humanity. Therefore, for the sake of world peace, her argument goes, women should be teachers, and beliefs that prevent women from working outside the home as teachers must be changed. Mrs. Roosevelt thus disguises the political nature of her comments by building on traditional assumptions that women are not only concerned with nurturing children, but also peace and the preservation of humanity.

Mrs. Roosevelt champions equal pay for equal work in her discussion of teaching. She claims:

> Year by year, however, what with sports and college and coeducational courses, girls are finding themselves less and less handicapped and I believe for that reason that the day will come when places will be filled by people who are capable of filling them quite regardless of their sex. This is the goal for which every woman who is now working should be striving, for no one wants special privileges these days, but an equal chance, and for equal work, equal wages should be paid. (166–67)

Mrs. Roosevelt therefore demonstrates her belief in the value of an education that will enable women to perform well in their places of employment. Rather than receiving "special privileges" because of their gender, she believes women can take their part in the workforce and should be paid equally for doing so. Her position seems progressive—to be very much ahead of its time.

In chapter 14, "Women and the Vote," Mrs. Roosevelt addresses political issues and does so directly. She reviews the benefits accorded women with the passage of the Nineteenth Amendment and the responsibilities associated with it. Because Mrs. Roosevelt believes in the importance of civic action, she champions the right to vote for all people regardless of gender, race, or class. She works to educate everyone about the benefits of following politics and voting. In this chapter, she claims that the right to vote provides direct power for women—something they had not previously possessed—and acknowledges those individuals who worked to provide women with that right. She references key figures of the suffrage movement and emphasizes the unselfish devotion that is considered traditionally feminine. She insists that unselfish devotion to a cause is noble and encourages us to devote ourselves not only to our families (if we have them), but also to other social and political issues that affect humanity.

Although the power of the vote provides women with the opportunity to act unselfishly toward the betterment of humanity, Mrs. Roosevelt is forced to consider what women have achieved with the power they have been given. She does not disguise her politics; rather, she recognizes that women have not accomplished all that the suffrage movement hoped they would. She then muses about what might be possible if women exercise their right to vote. In this way, she emphasizes civic virtue and works to develop a constituency that will enact civic duty. Clearly, her position as first lady enables her to address what might otherwise be considered a touchy subject, but does so by celebrating the efforts of those who came before her and by using an educational perspective to encourage her audience to read the works of those individuals who fought publicly and politically to secure women's right to vote.

Mrs. Roosevelt then turns to a discussion of the responsibilities of citizenship. She claims that women may think they have little time for anything but to earn a living. However, for the men and women of this country, "Their good citizenship consists in leading their lives so as to make them as productive of good for all around them as they can be, and their public duty is expressed by using their vote as intelligently as possible" (191). While the only intelligent vote is a knowledgeable vote, Mrs. Roosevelt claims that women often vote according to what others tell them. She encourages women to seek out the information that will help them become more informed and to compare a candidate's agenda with his or her personal needs and experiences. She also claims that party affiliation should not be the result of family tradition, but of careful consideration of the platforms and issues associated with candidates. She then provides the names of agencies (such as the League of Women Voters) that offer a means for women to obtain the knowledge they need to be responsible, intelligent voters. This endorsement politicizes Mrs. Roosevelt's discourse differently from earlier chapters. However, since she claims only to want to educate women, this politicization is minimized.

Mrs. Roosevelt wants her readers to become informed voters. Unfortunately, she admits that many people are not interested in casting their votes intelligently: "The vast majority of women," she laments, "remain as indifferent to the vote and how they use it as are the vast majority of men" (192). In this respect, Mrs. Roosevelt maintains women are not inferior, but rather are as indifferent about politics as men are. The problem, she claims, is that we are all happy to let others think for us. She does mention a few women who worked to educate themselves about politics and who entered the political realm, and she expresses a hope that others will follow. She also mentions her efforts to educate women about how political decisions affect every facet of our lives. She recognizes, though, that women have as yet made no significant changes in politics.

Although women have not yet acted on their right to vote, Mrs. Roosevelt still believes they are at least thinking about voting and about issues. She predicts that women will run for office despite the fact that "many women have dreaded the give and take of a campaign, they have dreaded the public criticism, they have not learned to discount the attacks of the opposition; but business and professional life is paving the way and this reason will not deter them much longer" (199). By articulating some of the challenges of politics and the difficulties involved in running for political office, Mrs. Roosevelt attempts to educate her audience about them and to encourage women to rise to the challenge.

Mrs. Roosevelt then turns her attention to the future and reemphasizes civic virtue by envisioning a democracy that offers more than material compensation to its citizens. Again, she incorporates "social problems" into her discussion, which realigns her comments with traditional expectations about women. She argues that women have to work together first and foremost. This focus on constituency and consensus is political, while her focus on social issues is traditional. Thus, she balances the personal and political through her carefully constructed arguments. At the same time, she reveals the political nature of her comments as she incorporates the New Deal into her discussion, a political issue to which she was as devoted as her husband. Once again, although her comments are political, they are in line with traditional expectations of the president's wife and as an advocate of her husband's agenda.

Mrs. Roosevelt also offers a discussion of a political nature in chapter 15, "Women in Public Life." Throughout the chapter, she discusses the need for women to educate themselves about the various public positions they might obtain by starting at the bottom and working their way up. In this way, women will be able to learn about all aspects of a position, so they will understand that political life is, at times, sordid, and "that human beings are disappointing" (211). This is essential for a complete understanding and acceptance of the responsibilities associated with public life.

Mrs. Roosevelt then turns to a discussion of another political issue—the presidency. This discussion is complex and filled with text and subtext. On the surface, she acknowledges that women will be unable to hold the office of president until sex is no longer an issue; she also implies that some men who hold the office will be unworthy, but they will be less scrutinized than women would be in the same position. She contends that the sex of a candidate should not matter, but because it does, she encourages women not to run for the presidency or for any other office until they have gained the experience necessary to succeed. This includes education of the sort that she addressed in earlier chapters such as voting, learning about issues and candidates, and working their way up from the bottom to higher positions.

The subtext is even more political than the text. For instance, although Mrs. Roosevelt claims that a woman will not be president until a worthy candidate appears, she also implies that when a woman does run for president she will likely be a more worthy candidate than the man she runs against. This stems from her belief that women are more concerned with humanity and that such concern necessarily makes them more capable of holding positions that have the power to affect society on a grand scale. She may also have in mind her own experiences in the political arena, experiences that afforded her the opportunity to see the underside of politics. Mrs. Roosevelt also implies that women will be judged more harshly than men, and that any woman who might consider running for political office should be sure she is capable of filling it. Women must thus be more intelligent, articulate, responsible, civic-minded, and willing to suffer the sneers and judgment of those who will oppose their candidacies. This implication relates to her earlier discussion about the importance of education. It reinforces Mrs. Roosevelt's persona as educator, because all that she says in *It's Up to the Women* is designed to educate women for life—civic and economic.

Mrs. Roosevelt closes this chapter with an editorial on civic virtue that emerges, if we read the subtext, from her personal experience. Mrs. Roosevelt was not popular when she began to speak publicly about political issues. Many around her, including her husband and the FBI, attempted to silence her or at least convince her to speak about issues traditionally befitting a first lady and social hostess. She persisted, however, and her success as a politically involved first lady resulted from her ability to disguise the nature of her discourse as political. In this discussion, Mrs. Roosevelt seems to draw on her experience as she recognizes that people who enter public life are open to criticism and accusation, but encourages them to make up their own minds and stand firm in their positions. Ultimately, their convictions will prevail and, although they may not win friends, they will win respect. It was her strong convictions that eventually won her the respect and admiration she deserved. At times, her convictions may have benefited not only her, but her husband's administration as well.

Another chapter worth examining is chapter 17, "Women and Working Conditions." In this chapter, Mrs. Roosevelt devotes attention to working conditions generally, and the discrimination that women who work outside the home face. Again, she supports equal pay for equal work. She also provides evidence for her claim that women deserve equal pay when she insists that machinery has enabled everyone to accomplish the work that must be done. More important, however, is her tacit support for women's work outside the home; she discusses it as if it is an unquestionable fact. Again, Mrs. Roosevelt balances the scales by demonstrating that women are equal to men in the work they do. Although not explicit, she argues that women should be afforded the right to pursue work outside the home, to expect equal pay, and to have the opportunity to pursue their interests. At the same time, she addresses a very dangerous topic—unions and unionization.

Mrs. Roosevelt does not champion existing male-dominated and male-run unions for women; rather, she encourages women to create women's trade unions designed to protect their special needs. She placates those who might object by focusing on the differences between men and women. Although she worked throughout this book to demonstrate the many ways in which women are equal to men, here she differentiates women to provide special protections based on their physical abilities. In addition to better working conditions, she argues that women deserve equal pay, a minimum "living" wage, and time off for childbirth. This appears to be an important and notable precursor to the contemporary

Medical and Family Leave Act championed by Hillary Rodham Clinton, one that recognizes women's unique ability to bear children. By demonstrating the need for such accommodations, Mrs. Roosevelt appeals to traditional societal expectations and, in subtle ways, disguises the political nature of her discourse. At the same time, she challenges the legitimacy of male-dominated unions—a move that was dangerous for her husband's administration—by arguing that they do not provide the special protections women need. While she addresses explicitly political issues, however, she works to foster a constituency that, if educated about social issues and motivated to vote responsibly, could ultimately have benefited the Roosevelt administration.

A final chapter worth examining is chapter 18 in which Mrs. Roosevelt addresses "Women and Peace." In a move that appears designed to return to traditional expectations and assumptions about women, she discusses the many ways women can work to maintain peace both at home and abroad. Mrs. Roosevelt claims, "One of the things in which women are vitally interested to-day [sic] is the abolition of war as a means of settling disputes between nations, and I feel that this is particularly a question which is up to the women" (237). As she did at the beginning of the book, Mrs. Roosevelt contends that women are particularly concerned about the preservation of humanity and that women are uniquely able to address these issues. In another move designed to disguise the political nature of her comments, Mrs. Roosevelt demonstrates the way women can work toward peace when she states, "As I see it there are two things which women must do. One is to create a *will to peace* in all things and the other is to make adventurous some other things in life besides war. The will to peace will have to start with women and they will have to want peace sufficiently to be crusaders on the subject" (238).

The will to peace that Mrs. Roosevelt describes can only be achieved through education, the type of education that women are expected to provide—a mother's education. Women have the unique ability to affect children's lives and attitudes by virtue of bringing them into the world and assuming the role of primary caretaker. Because she champions motherhood as much as she champions women's rights, it makes sense that she would return to the virtues of motherhood—explicitly or implicitly—at book's end. It makes more sense that she would allude to the special power mothers have to instill a will to peace in their children, just as they might instill a will to succeed. Importantly, Mrs. Roosevelt encourages women to become crusaders on the subject. This politicizes her discussion, but only subtly, as it nevertheless focuses on womanhood traditionally conceived. She then turns to a brief discussion of Joan of Arc who, although a peasant, possessed a vision of freedom, and she encourages U.S. women to possess a similar vision of world peace.

Mrs. Roosevelt continues by acknowledging the thrill of adventure and argues that war appeals to youth because the sacrifice and patriotism associated with it are exciting. Her solution is the excitement of working to organize a new social order based on democracy. "This challenge to organize a new social order not in one place, but all over the world, has possibilities of adventure and excitement, a society which of itself should take the place of the old glamour surrounding war. Only the women and the youth of any country can initiate this change" (246–47). Motherhood, then, provides the means by which women can affect change by instilling certain values in their children. Thus, motherhood is politicized, and the personal becomes political. However, because it appears to adhere to the constraints of tradition, its politicization is disguised and its threat to tradition is diminished.

In chapter 20, her conclusion, Mrs. Roosevelt oscillates between contemporary issues and established tradition. She discusses from where women have come and where women might go. She shares a hope that women will embrace her words and act responsibly in the world. After recounting a story about her grandmother who expected her to be more thoughtful and sensible than her brothers, she claims that women of that generation accomplished a great many things "by working through the men when they hardly knew they were being influenced" (262–263). She closes the book with a challenge to women wherein she contends, "women, whether subtly or vociferously, have always been a tremendous power in the destiny of the world and with so many of them now holding important positions and receiving recognition and earning the respect of the men as well as the members of their own sex, it seems more than ever that in this crisis, 'It's Up to the Women!'" (263). In this final statement, Mrs. Roosevelt marries the personal and the political. She claims that women have always had power and the ability to affect the world around them. She challenges women to use their power. She does so, however, by remembering traditional expectations and arguing that even within the constraints of tradition women have had power. She thus challenges women to act both within and outside societal constraints to change the world.

It's Up to the Women was written during the Great Depression and dealt with many of the issues facing both men and women. Throughout, however, Mrs. Roosevelt maintains the belief that only women have the power to help the United States overcome the crisis. How they can do it is the impetus for the book, and Mrs. Roosevelt cleverly oscillates between the virtues of womanhood and the virtues of feminism. In sum, the book argues that womanhood provides a power not available to men, a power that can change the current social order in the United States and in the world. By discussing feminist power as an element of traditional womanhood, however, Mrs. Roosevelt disguises the political nature of her arguments, thereby enacting a rhetorical persona best understood in terms of social style. By focusing on education—as a vocation and as a means to demonstrate women's power—and on womanhood, especially, motherhood, she both celebrates and enacts an identity consistent with societal expectations. As a result, her rhetorical identity is strategically social in that it is not explicitly political (except in a few instances), and it relies for its validity on her position as the president's wife. Her role as first lady gives her a voice, but limits its power because of traditional assumptions about wifedom. Clearly, this book was a balanced political endeavor, as were most of Mrs. Roosevelt's rhetorical activities.

Legacy

When Franklin Delano Roosevelt died on April 12, 1945, Mrs. Roosevelt was prepared to move forward with her political career, although she did not intend this kind of future. After her husband's death, she told a reporter, "The story is over" (quoted in Anthony 1990, 513). Within a week of his death, she coordinated his funeral and moved out of the White House. She also hosted a farewell reception for the women's press corps, where she answered questions about her political and journalistic career, which she implied would end.

Mrs. Roosevelt's political career did not end with the death of her husband, however. In fact, "Over the next decade and a half, she continued to be the most effective woman in American politics" (Chafe 1980, xvi). She was appointed to the first American delegation to the United Nations where, as the U.S. representative to the Social, Humanitarian, and Cultural Committee of the General Assembly, she helped draft the Universal Declaration of Human Rights (Black 1999, 10). Mrs. Roosevelt considered this document to be her greatest achievement, both personally and politically. In many respects, it serves as the most articulate statement of her beliefs and vision of the world. Her rhetorical activities during her husband's presidency were less conspicuous than those after his death. Although she publicly disagreed with her husband often, she nevertheless felt obliged to support his political agenda. She therefore limited her disagreements to those issues that did not directly challenge his New Deal policies. After his death, she more clearly articulated her own beliefs, and texts such as the Universal Declaration of Human Rights are indicative of them.

Mrs. Roosevelt's rhetorical activities as first lady helped reshape the way the public thought about this important, if unelected, role. Moreover, she helped pave the way for first ladies who followed by demonstrating that they could be politically active. She did so, however, without appearing to be political. As her husband's eyes and ears, she fulfilled traditional expectations by functioning as a devoted wife, while at the same time promoting her political beliefs and agenda, that is, educating the nation about the importance of all its people, and laying the foundation for what was to be a long and satisfying political career.

Eleanor Roosevelt championed many causes during her lifetime, especially during her tenure in the White House, but none seems as important as the role of women in society. Although not politically popular during the Roosevelt administration, she believed in the rights of all people regardless of race, class, and gender. Underneath her many causes was a personal drive to succeed that manifested itself in the form of a feminist perspective that still resonates with those who read her works today.

It's Up to the Women is particularly interesting because it enables Mrs. Roosevelt to educate her audience, in a concise and articulate manner, about issues of concern to her. The monograph outlines many issues of concern to Americans during the depression, and argues throughout that women are uniquely able to solve the problems she addresses. She arranges her arguments in a manner that enables her to "disguise" her feminist perspective by using traditionally feminine images. Thus, her argument that women should be encouraged to work outside the home appears as an editorial about how such work might enhance a marriage by providing conversation that is lively and new. Similarly, she bases her argument on behalf of women's involvement in politics on the ability of women to recognize social ills and to work for the betterment of humanity.

Not only did her monograph support women's rights, so did her presence both within and outside of the White House. Indeed, when the United States was involved in World War II, Mrs. Roosevelt "insisted that the struggle would not be worth winning if the old order of things prevailed" (Goodwin 1994, 10). Her argument that women should receive equal pay for equal work eventually led to commentary about how women accepted the challenge to support the war effort. This was supported by a variety of photographs in which she was surrounded by women. These were not idle women, though; they were photographed at their places of employment. As Goodwin notes, "Ultimately, 350,000 women would serve as members of the Women's Army Corps and the WAVES (Women Accepted for Voluntary Emergency Service in the Navy)" (1994, 415). Mrs. Roosevelt celebrated the women who rose to the challenge by visiting with them and describing her visits in her many columns and articles. This seems to have been a way for her to celebrate women's work outside the home and to demonstrate that the "lessons" presented in her books, columns, press conferences, and speeches were worthwhile and valuable.

According to Allida Black, Mrs. Roosevelt's "legacy as first lady, delegate to the United Nations, Democratic Party leader, humanitarian, and social activist made her an icon to millions, many of whom would agree on nothing other than their respect for her" (1999, 1). Her husband's death enabled her to speak her mind about issues that were important to her, including Democratic domestic policies. She also began to address more vigorously international issues with which she disagreed such as human rights issues. She believes these were not confined only to the free world, but also existed in communist countries such as the Soviet Union and China. Her humanitarian interests resulted in her appointment to the first American delegation to the United Nations by Harry Truman.

Mrs. Roosevelt strongly believed that this was the most important position of her life—more important than that of first lady—and she dedicated much of the rest of her life to promoting and defending the United Nations and its policies. She guided the writing of the Universal Declaration of Human Rights and worked for its adoption as the U.S. representative to the Social, Humanitarian, and Cultural Committee of the General Assembly (Committee III). This was no easy task, as the committee consisted of delegates with diverging political agendas. However, her grace and determination resulted in a unanimously supported document. Although she admitted that there was no official recourse for countries who failed to uphold the Declaration's principles, she believed that its completion and adoption was her finest achievement.

As with her time in the White House, Mrs. Roosevelt was not always popular. In fact, J. Edgar Hoover continued to monitor her activities, believing her to be a communist sympathizer. Her FBI file indicates that the agency closely monitored her columns as well as articles written about her for signs or clues that she was spreading communist propaganda. She eventually was one of the most outspoken opponents of Senator McCarthy's communist witch-hunt that was the Red Scare. She was particularly outspoken in her speeches and her columns about the practices of the House Un-American Activities Committee (HUAC). She claimed that Senator McCarthy was engaging in the very same politics of fear in which he accused the communists of engaging. In addition to her opposition to Senator McCarthy's tactics, Mrs. Roosevelt outraged southern politicians when she publicly supported *Brown v. Board of Education* and the Civil Rights Acts of 1957 and 1960. "[A]s she became more familiar with the unique problems African Americans faced, [Mrs. Roosevelt] abandoned her position as a defender of equal treatment to become a staunch advocate of integration and nonviolent protest. She had joined the board of directors of the National Association for the Advancement of Colored People (NAACP) in 1945" (Black 1999, 13). She continued to agitate for the right to vote, fair housing, quality education, and the right to organize in protest against discriminatory practices. When students, both African American and white, were attacked on the Freedom Rides, she was outraged and likened the actions of the white mobs to those of the Nazis against the Jews during World War II.

Mrs. Roosevelt was outspoken and dedicated to her causes, but continued to foster a matriarchal persona in the media. Beasley agrees that, "She herself continued to present to the public an image of a gracious, dignified lady with a motherly concern for oppressed peoples everywhere" (1987, 167). This reinforced and strengthened public support for her and her causes, which the media regularly monitored. Most of the mainstream media delighted in praising her, often implying that she was able to retain her womanly attributes while matching wits with men. In 1948, *Time* called her "perhaps the best known woman in the world" (Beasley 1987, 177). *The Saturday Review of Literature* in 1951 named her both the "greatest living American woman" and "the greatest woman in the world" (quoted in Beasley 1987, 177). She did not adhere to traditional societal expectations for women, though, and was often censured. This included criticism from those who believed she was responsible for her children's string of unsuccessful marriages. Yet, she continued to provide a role model for women who wanted to combine feminine qualities with the type of power and influence usually attributed to men. Her grace and dignity, combined with her dedication to her causes and her determination to fight for human rights made her a role model that many women (Hillary Rodham Clinton, for example) admire today.

Published late in her life, *You Learn by Living* is a monograph that articulates her philosophy of life. In it, she claims that women are uniquely well equipped to adjust to new situations because they are constantly forced to adjust to the lives of their husbands and children. This book is evidence that Mrs. Roosevelt refused to give in to her old age and her ailments. Her appointment as a visiting lecturer at Brandeis University is further evidence that she intended to remain active. This appointment also reflects her passion for teaching, something that was evident throughout her life. She thus embodies the most feminine qualities at the same time she uses them with a cunning that only the most successful men to that time had exhibited.

Mrs. Roosevelt created an identity separate from her husband. According to Beasley "Heywood Broun, a popular columnist, compared Mrs. Roosevelt to Nora, the heroine of Ibsen's play, A Doll's House, who sought to be a human being rather than a plastic creation of her husband. He contended, 'Neither marriage nor the last national election can obliterate the fact that Eleanor Roosevelt is an individual.'" She was perceived as the country's matriarch whose family was the entire country. She emerged as the nation's educator and believed, "Teachers are more important than anything except parents in the lives of children" (quoted in Hershan 1993, 140).

Eleanor Roosevelt expanded the political possibilities for first ladies by speaking out on issues, asserting her right to earn money independently, and developing a journalistic career with journalistic admirers who, as a result, treated her fairly in news reports about her. She did so within the constraints of a patriarchal society that defined what was and was not acceptable for women—especially the first lady. The preceding analysis has helped to illuminate how Eleanor Roosevelt created an identity that simultaneously championed women's rights and placated patriarchal unease. Admittedly, much of what she did and many of her causes are considered philanthropic and therefore appropriate for upper-class women. "What was revolutionary about Mrs. Roosevelt was . . . [her] ability as first lady to inspire the public with a message that reinforced traditional values at the same time it enlarged them" (Beasley 1987, 81). Democracy, she believed, relied for its success on the participation of all individuals in a society. She was passionately devoted to democratic principles, even when those around her appeared not to be. Democracy was—and is—the basis for all social change. Ultimately, Mrs. Roosevelt believed that social change was up to the women. And it still is.

Eleanor Roosevelt died from a rare form of tuberculosis on November 7, 1962. She was seventy-eight years old. She left a legacy that is unique among first ladies.

Questions for Discussion

1. Eleanor Roosevelt played many roles when she was first lady. What are some of them?
2. How did the public view Mrs. Roosevelt as a first lady? Did they perceive her as a traditional first lady, as an activist first lady, or in some other way?

3. Eleanor Roosevelt held weekly press conferences with women journalists when she was first lady. What did she want to accomplish? Why were the press conferences significant?
4. Do you consider Mrs. Roosevelt a feminist? Why or why not?
5. In your view, what are Mrs. Roosevelt's most provocative ideas in *It's Up to the Women*? From what you have read about it, does it seem to address contemporary readers?

Internet Resources

http://www.gwu.edu/~erpapers/
This website provides access to the Eleanor Roosevelt Papers. The website is sponsored by a research center associated with the Department of History at George Washington University. Many of Eleanor Roosevelt's writings are available online and can be accessed for free by students, teachers, and the research community. You can find copies of the Universal Declaration of Human Rights in eleven languages.

http://www.ervk.org/
The Eleanor Roosevelt Center at Val Kill in New York sponsors this website. Visit the site to see what programs are going forward today in Mrs. Roosevelt's name.

http://www.cr.nps.gov/museum/exhibits/elro/index.html
Sponsored by the National Park Service of the United States Department of Interior, this website presents Eleanor Roosevelt as an American visionary. You can access texts and photographs on Mrs. Roosevelt's family, political allies, office, and more.

http://www.fdrlibrary.marist.edu/
The Franklin D. Roosevelt Library and Museum contains many documents and photographs of Mrs. Roosevelt. Use the finding aids to locate material.

Notes

1. Some of the most prominent scholars are Black (1996), Cook (1992) and Beasley (1987). Presidential scholars such as Goodwin (1994) and first lady scholars such as Gutin (1989) have devoted a great deal of attention to Mrs. Roosevelt's influence during her husband's tenure as president.
2. Scholars such as Black (1995, 1996, 1999), Chadakoff (1989) and Roosevelt (1946) among others support this claim. Often considered the preeminent Eleanor Roosevelt scholar, Black has compiled many of Eleanor Roosevelt's essential speeches and writings. I have used her compilations and insights throughout this essay as a springboard for many of my own arguments.

3. Beasley (1987) claims, "Admirers accepted the triteness of her comments, both written and spoken, as her way of identifying with ordinary people" (74). However, Mrs. Roosevelt claimed (and Beasley agrees) that she addressed people the only way she knew how. Later in her career—both during her White House years and afterward—Lorena Hickok acted as Mrs. Roosevelt's editor and helped her refine her prose.

4. See, for instance, Beasley (1987), Black (1995, 1996, 1999), Chafe (1980), Eaton (1956), Goodwin (1994), Gould (1996) and Youngs (1999). In their introductions or biographical narratives, all of these scholars acknowledge that Eleanor Roosevelt acted politically and publicly. In addition, most agree that this was the result of Franklin Delano Roosevelt's paralysis. Regardless, all acknowledge that Mrs. Roosevelt changed the role of the first lady through her actions and her willingness to champion issues important to her.

5. Many well-known books such as Goodwin (1987) and Beasley (1987) include press photos in which Mrs. Roosevelt is surrounded by women and people of color. The Franklin D. Roosevelt Library website also includes a page of copyright-free photographs, which present Mrs. Roosevelt with dignitaries, her husband, women (many in their places of employment such as pilots and nurses at military hospitals during the war), and children (such as those at a "Negro Nursery"). Other photographs include Mrs. Roosevelt surrounded by her close friends (such as Lorena Hickok). All photographs of Mrs. Roosevelt appear to demonstrate the lessons she distributed in her writings.

6. Eleanor Roosevelt was a rhetor in the most traditional sense, and her rhetoric encompasses a range of activities of the sort studied by rhetorical scholars. However, it is not enough to study only her speeches and press conferences, or her letters and columns. A careful critic must also examine her autobiographies and monographs, which she filled with insights, hopes, and convictions so strong that they demand sustained meditation. Indeed, many scholars study a variety of her texts from different perspectives; to date, however, no sustained examination of her monographs exists. It seems to me that her monographs offer the most focused statements of her political beliefs and, as such, deserve critical attention. This kind of study is outside the scope of my present essay.

7. The use of "public" in this statement is specific and intentional. Although other first ladies engaged in political activities behind the scenes, mostly influencing their husbands during private conversations, Eleanor Roosevelt chose to make her activities public and, in so doing, radically changed the way the public saw the first lady and her importance to what Karlyn Kohrs Campbell calls "the presidential corporation" (1996).

8. This argument is based on a belief that the fight for women's suffrage was not fashionable; moreover, it recognizes that the suffrage movement was made up of different constituencies, each with their own ideas about methods and goals. For more about the women's rights movement, see Flexner and Fitzpatrick (1996).

9. This photo is published in several scholarly books, including Beasley (1987) and more popular works, including Mayo (1996).

References

Anthony, Carl Sferrazza. 1990. *First Ladies: The Saga of the Presidents' Wives and Their Power 1789–1961*, Vol. 1. New York: William Morrow.

Beasley, Maurine H. 1987. *Eleanor Roosevelt and the Media: A Public Quest for Self-Fulfillment.* Urbana, Ill.: University of Illinois Press.

Black, Allida, ed. 1995. *What I Hope to Leave Behind: The Essential Essays of Eleanor Roosevelt.* Brooklyn, N.Y.: Carlson.

———. 1996. *Casting Her Own Shadow: Eleanor Roosevelt and the Shaping of Postwar Liberalism*. New York: Columbia University Press.

———, ed. 1999. *Courage in a Dangerous World: The Political Writings of Eleanor Roosevelt*. New York: Columbia University Press.

Campbell, Karlyn Kohrs. 1996. The Rhetorical Presidency: A Two Person Career. In *Beyond the Rhetorical Presidency*, ed. Martin J. Medhurst, 179–95. College Station, Tex.: Texas A & M University Press.

Caroli, Betty Boyd. 1995. *First Ladies: An Intimate Look at How 38 Women Handled What May Be the Most Demanding, Unpaid, Unelected Job in America*. New York: Oxford University Press.

Chadakoff, Rochelle, ed. 1989. *Eleanor Roosevelt's "My Day": Her Acclaimed Columns 1936–1945*. New York: Pharos.

Chafe, William H. 1980. Roosevelt, Anna Eleanor. In *Notable American Women, the Modern Period: A Biographical Dictionary*. Cambridge, Mass.: Belknap-Harvard University Press,

Cook, Blanche Wiesen. 1992. *Eleanor Roosevelt: A Life*, Vol. 1. New York: Viking.

Eaton, Janette. 1956. *The Story of Eleanor Roosevelt*. New York: William Morrow.

Edens, John A. 1994. *Eleanor Roosevelt: A Comprehensive Bibliography*. Westport, Connecticut: Greenwood.

First Ladies. 2000. www.firstladies.org/anna_roosevelt.

Flexner, Eleanor, and Ellen Fitzpatrick. 1996. *Century of Struggle: The Woman's Rights Movement in the United States*. Cambridge, Mass.: Harvard University Press.

Goodwin, Doris Kearns. 1994. *No Ordinary Time. Franklin and Eleanor Roosevelt: The Home Front in World War II*. New York: Simon & Schuster.

Gould, Lewis L. 1996. *American First Ladies: Their Lives and Their Legacies*. New York: Garland.

Gutin, Myra. 1989. *The President's Partner*. Westport, Conn.: Greenwood.

Hershan, Stella K. 1993. *The Candles She Lit: The Legacy of Eleanor Roosevelt*. Westport, Conn.: Praeger.

Mayo, Edith P., ed. 1996. *The Smithsonian Book of the First Ladies: Their Lives, Times, and Issues*. New York: Henry Holt & Co.

Roosevelt, Eleanor. 1946. *If You Ask Me*. New York: Curtis.

———. 1933. *It's Up to the Women*. New York: Frederick A. Stokes.

Scott, Anne Firor, and William H. Chafe, eds. 1986. *The Papers of Eleanor Roosevelt, 1933–1945*. Frederick, Md.: University Publications of America.

Youngs, J. William T. 1999. *Eleanor Roosevelt: A Personal and Public Life*. New York: Longman.

CHAPTER THREE

Jacqueline Kennedy
The Rhetorical Construction of Camelot

Elizabeth J. Natalle

If you fail your husband and your children . . . that really is the role that means the most to me. I am an old fashioned wife.

The first lady should preserve the traditions and enhance [the White House] and leave something of herself there.

There will never be Camelot[1] again.

—Jacqueline Bouvier Kennedy

Jacqueline Kennedy, wife of thirty-fifth president John Fitzgerald Kennedy, was the thirty-ninth woman to serve in the role of first lady or its equivalent in the United States. Although she occupied this role for only one thousand days from January 20, 1961, to November 22, 1963, Mrs. Kennedy left an enduring legacy that indisputably ranks her as one of the most popular first ladies both at home and abroad. She has, in fact, achieved iconic status among the American people, in popular culture, and in artistic and fashion circles. Known for her regal beauty, her fierce protection of her family's privacy, and her stunning sense of aesthetics, Mrs. Kennedy was also a behind-the-scenes influence on diplomatic protocol and foreign policy through her interpersonal and letter-writing skills.

Veteran UPI correspondent Helen Thomas credits Mrs. Kennedy with changing the way first ladies were covered by the press corps: "In large measure, she made our coverage hit the front pages more often than not, and she set the tone for full-time coverage of first ladies that persists to this day" (1999, 244). Several factors contributed to this change in coverage, but the power of televised media was the most important during the Kennedy administration. Mrs. Kennedy was quickly catapulted to the most photographed woman in the world, to be surpassed only by Princess Diana in the 1990s. Thus, visual imagery is a central tenet in the overall iconography of Jacqueline Kennedy and calls for semiotic consideration. This is a significant departure from traditional approaches to first lady scholarship, which tend to be more text-based rhetorical analyses.[2]

Mrs. Kennedy's skillful rhetorical-semiotic construction of what became known as Camelot will be the focus of this chapter. Through her strategic choice of causes, primarily the White House restoration project and the infusion of new cultural standards for the executive branch, Mrs. Kennedy influenced American life as no other contemporary first lady. Her courageous demeanor throughout her husband's funeral cemented her place in the heart of the American public and influenced the interpretation of President Kennedy's legacy as well. The challenge in analyzing Mrs. Kennedy's rhetorical role as first lady lies in the fact that she gave no substantial personal interviews during her residency in the White House, nor did she release during her lifetime a memoir or personal reflections on her role.[3] This chapter seeks to understand the juxtaposition of public and private persona in Mrs. Kennedy's role as first lady as the key to her rhetorical impact. This analysis also affords the opportunity to explore the intersection of rhetorical and semiotic analysis in the understanding and effect of public icons.

Biography

Jacqueline Lee Bouvier Kennedy Onassis, was born to the aristocratic parentage of Janet Norton Lee Bouvier (Auchincloss) and John Vernou "Black Jack" Bouvier III on July 28, 1929, in Southampton, Long Island.[4] She died from non-Hodgkin's lymphoma on May 19, 1994, in New York City. Jacqueline grew up surrounded by wealth, horses, fashion, and the privilege of a high society education including study at The Chapin School in New York and Miss Porter's School in Farmington, Connecticut. Her life revolved around society activities in New York, Newport, and suburban Washington, D.C. She was named Debutant of the Year by the *New York Times* in 1947, attended Vassar from 1947–1949 as a literature major, studied during her junior year in Paris, and graduated from George Washington University in 1951. Although she won the *Vogue* Prix de Paris prize in 1951, she chose not to accept the prize of becoming a *Vogue* junior editor. Clearly, up to this point, Jacqueline's introduction to art, literature, poetry, fashion, and French culture provided a framework for her to develop an aesthetic perspective that would guide her decision-making as both first lady and as a private citizen. The year in Paris and her three-month European trip with her sister in 1951[5] stand out as the single most important influence from which she crafted an integrated sense of American and French ideals in her personal aesthetic. In fact, she wrote in her self-portrait for the *Vogue* prize competition what would prophesy her life:

> Last winter I took my Junior Year in Paris and spent the vacations in Austria and Spain. I loved it more than any year of my life. Being away from home gave me the chance to look at myself with a jaundiced eye. I learned not to be ashamed of a real

hunger for knowledge, something I always tried to hide, and I came home glad to start in here again but with a love for Europe that I am afraid will never leave me. (quoted in Brenner 1994, 253)

While still living with her parents, Jacqueline enjoyed a brief stint with the *Washington Times-Herald* as a photographer, where she met Senator John Fitzgerald Kennedy of Massachusetts when interviewing him for her column entitled "Inquiring Camera Girl." Jacqueline married Jack on September 12, 1953. For the next seven years, Mrs. Kennedy played the role of senator's wife, entertaining in their Georgetown home and concentrating on her preferred role throughout her adult life: mother. She had difficult pregnancies. A daughter was stillborn in 1956, Caroline Kennedy was born in 1957, and John Jr. in 1960. In spite of her pregnancy, Jackie campaigned during her husband's 1960 bid for the presidency, and they entered the White House two months after John Jr.'s birth. A son named Patrick died several days after birth in 1963.

During the three years (1960–1963) that the Kennedys occupied the White House, Jackie Kennedy rose to iconic status in the eyes of both the American public and the world at large. Although she did not engage a public speaking schedule to promote causes as first lady, Mrs. Kennedy's personal plan and fundraising effort to restore the White House launched a national agenda to see the White House and the presidency take on near-royal status. Through the adept use of television, strategic interviews, and personal correspondence, Jackie Kennedy established an aesthetic ideal for the pure art of living. The overwhelming success of the televised tour of the restored White House in February 1962, along with her fashionable appearances at official functions and international visits catapulted Mrs. Kennedy into a global spotlight that continued until her death.

Jacqueline Kennedy considered her primary roles in the following order: mother, wife, and public figure. Shunning the title of first lady, she preferred to be called "Mrs. Kennedy" and made every effort not to make the role of first lady a series of public appearances to greet visitors to the White House. Ironically, her White House restoration project, her stunning Oleg Cassini wardrobe, her ability to charm political dignitaries with her skill in French, Italian, and Spanish, her wit and intelligence, and her choice of artistic entertainment fascinated the American public to the extent that she became the most public of contemporary first ladies.

On November 22, 1963, President Kennedy was assassinated in Dallas, Texas, and Jackie, widowed at age thirty-four, orchestrated one of history's most famous funerals, which she patterned after the protocol established at President Lincoln's funeral. It was in the 1963 interview with *Life* correspondent Theodore White that the legacy of the Kennedy presidency was named with Jackie's reference to her husband's favorite musical, *Camelot*.

Five years after President Kennedy's assassination, Jacqueline married Greek shipping magnate Aristotle Onassis, which dismayed the American public. Her popularity, however, never waned, and her period as fashion icon and jet-setter from 1968–1975 reinforced her image as an international star. Mrs. Onassis did not remarry after the death of her husband; she returned permanently to her Fifth Avenue apartment in New York, and worked as a book editor for Viking and, subsequently, Doubleday Press. Her children, John Jr. and Caroline, remained close by, and she spent time in the company of financial advisor and diamond dealer Maurice Tempelsman. In addition to her work as an editor, patron of the arts, and advocate for public landmarks such as Grand Central Terminal, Mrs. Onassis concentrated on the pleasures of mothering and grandmothering, thus retaining a role that she always considered a primary responsibility.

Jacqueline Kennedy Onassis's death in May 1994 brought an unexpected, yet not surprising, reaction from the public. She is the only former first lady to have complete television coverage of her funeral, and fittingly, she had chosen to be buried in Arlington National Cemetery with John F. Kennedy and their two children, the unnamed baby girl, and Patrick Bouvier Kennedy. John F. Kennedy Jr., who was killed in a plane crash in July 1999, was buried at sea rather than at the Kennedy gravesite in Arlington.

The Sotheby's auction of personal items selected for sale by her children in April 1996 drew a record $34.5 million (Gray 1996), and is yet another indicator of the literal "craze" that the American people continue to have for Jacqueline Kennedy Onassis. Many of these items were from the Kennedy White House or the Georgetown home occupied during John Kennedy's years as senator, including an oak rocking chair, golf clubs, the Louis XVI mahogany desk on which JFK signed the Nuclear Test Ban Treaty in 1963, and a three-strand pearl necklace that Jackie wore in a famous photograph with John Jr. *USA Today* dubbed the auction "Camelot for Sale" (Williams 1996), and a recurring theme among the media throughout the period of the auction was the desire of the American public to literally own a piece of Camelot. In some sense, the auction was the largest public revelation ever of a private life that Jacqueline Kennedy Onassis sought to protect throughout her lifetime. To date, the copyright and sealed protection that are in effect regarding her personal papers hamper the Kennedy Library from systematically offering materials to the academic community. Each year more personal papers are released by the Kennedy Library for public access, but Mrs. Kennedy's wish to protect her own and her family's privacy while retaining the status of a very public icon continues to be a theme.

Rhetorical Activities as First Lady

Jacqueline Kennedy's rhetorical activities as first lady have been described as "emerging" by communication scholar Myra Gutin (1989, 41). That is to say, Mrs. Kennedy was the first "television" first lady, which meant increased coverage and scrutiny of her daily activities; she was the first to appoint her own press secretary; she staged elaborate state dinners and cultural entertainment; and she traveled officially overseas as first lady unaccompanied by her husband. Yet, she spent much time avoiding the press in an attempt to protect the privacy of her family, and she set no formal agenda to engage in political or social activities to change the lives of ordinary American citizens. Her public speaking was limited to extemporaneous, ceremonial remarks, for example, brief speeches in India and Latin America. Most of her time as first lady revolved around two agenda items: caring for her family as wife and mother and, according to documentary filmmaker Suzanne Bauman (1999), using art to elevate politics. In other words, Jacqueline Kennedy rhetorically constructed the ideal aesthetic presidency that would become known as Camelot to satisfy her own belief that art and politics are intertwined. Perhaps the best example of this was the fact that she persuaded French minister of culture, André Malraux, to bring the *Mona Lisa* to the United States in 1963, as a gesture of friendship. This was the first time the *Mona Lisa* officially had left French soil since da Vinci brought it to France in 1516 (Folliard 1963); therefore, the gesture represents a significant rhetorical statement regarding the political relationship between France and the United States at that time. The loan of the *Mona Lisa* also serves as the exemplar of how Mrs. Kennedy engaged communication as a visual, that is, semiotic form of persuasion. It is the ultimate cultural statement to be made about the mutual taste of the United States and its allies.

In this chapter, Mrs. Kennedy's rhetorical activities are divided topically, yet each type of activity is based on an aesthetic form, and each is a component of Camelot. The analysis that follows includes fashion as persuasion, the White House restoration project, White House entertainment, the orchestration of President Kennedy's funeral, and interpersonal diplomacy. The least important type of rhetorical activity was public speaking, therefore, only brief remarks will be included regarding Mrs. Kennedy as a formal public speaker.

Fashion as Persuasion

Before Mrs. Kennedy even entered the White House as first lady, the press and the public began what became known as "Jackie Watching." Much of the gaze was turned on her clothing and hair, and she and her personal couturier, Oleg Cassini, created what became known as "The Jackie Look" (Cassini 1995, 22). Jacqueline Kennedy herself was the rhetorical object, and her ability to heighten the ethos of the Kennedy administration through her personal presentation is unmatched by any other first lady. Although other first ladies, such as Ida McKinley, enjoyed beautiful and expensive clothes, it is Mrs. Kennedy who elevates the iconography of fashion (Barthes 1990) to its central position in relationship to how first ladies present themselves and are received by the American public. Fashion is not whimsical or trivial, indeed, as the Smithsonian Institution exhibition on first ladies demonstrates. When curators redesigned the Smithsonian First Ladies exhibition from its focus on inaugural ball gowns to a wider ranging exploration of "political role and public image" (Mayo and Meringolo 1994), there was a public backlash against the fact that so many of the first ladies' gowns were removed from the public view. I have visited the first ladies exhibition several times in its new format, and the ball gowns still draw the largest groups of people who spend more of their time viewing the dresses than other artifacts on display. One need only remember the public's view of Rosalynn Carter as dowdy, and their subsequent praise of Nancy Reagan for returning the look of the first lady to designer clothes, to know that the appearance of the first lady is largely a rhetorical act that influences the perception of the presidency.

In the exhibition showing in 2001–2002, entitled "Jacqueline Kennedy: The White House Years," the Kennedy Library has collaborated with the Costume Institute of the Metropolitan Museum of Art to renew the public's knowledge and interest in Mrs. Kennedy as *the* icon of twentieth-century American style and fashion. In this stunning exhibition commemorating the fortieth year since she became first lady, over eighty ensembles are displayed within the contexts of the 1960 presidential campaign, the inauguration, White House style, and travel. Hats and riding habits are also on display along with other artifacts such as videos of both the president's and Mrs. Kennedy's public speaking. Metropolitan director, Philippe de Montebello, appropriately described the impact of the exhibition as I witnessed it: "Thus, in our galleries, these garments held by the Kennedy Library, and valued in that context for their historical associations, have the expanded implications of an aesthetic response to the highly public and ceremonial role of first lady" (Bowles 2001, vi).

Mrs. Kennedy's rhetorical action could literally be termed "fashion diplomacy." Over 300 dresses were hand sewn for her during the time she occupied the White House, including more than 100 dresses during the first year. Unlike the previous several first ladies, thrity-one-year-old Jackie was five feet seven inches tall, slender, and carried herself with perfect posture. Her dark hair, striking eyes, long neckline, and beautiful collarbone structure were physical attributes that Cassini capitalized on as he created a personal wardrobe for Mrs. Kennedy that rivaled and copied the haute couture creations of European designers such as Givenchy, who designed a strikingly similar wardrobe for film star Audrey Hepburn. In fact, there is evidence that Mrs. Kennedy would have preferred to wear Givenchy designs, which she did at her discretion (Bowles 2001). As an American first lady, however, she was under pressure to wear "American" couture.

Cassini reports that he had a particular philosophy that governed the "Kennedy Look":

> For the daytime, there is a bit of the military and menswear approach to the clothes—slightly severe but comfortable. For evening, the Egyptian theme predominated because of the strength of Jackie's shoulders. Often her chiffon dresses were inspired by hieroglyphics. I saw Jackie as a geometric goddess. (1995, 33)

Cassini's "architectural" concept of minimalism consisted of A-line cuts, sheaths, one-shouldered or strapless gowns, deep cut backs with a "covered look" for the front bodice, and sumptuous fabrics such as dupioni silk, silk peau d'ange, silk gazar, Swiss double satin, chiffon, silk velvet, silk brocade, and silk crepe de chine. In addition to the Egyptian leitmotif, many of Mrs. Kennedy's ensembles echoed military themes with the use of double rows of large buttons, fringed or tasseled decoration, cockades, and piping. Evening clothes were sometimes decorated with beading, but very few patterns were evident overall. Most often, a single bow provided accent, and she often wore a triple strand of pearls. Monochromatic color and geometric lines prevailed. Her choice of colors reflected her knowledge and interest in painting and history, according to Cassini. Although she preferred white and black, Veronese green, Nattier blue, "old master" yellows, pinks, reds, greens, and blues were also favorites. Finally, Mrs. Kennedy was one of the last first ladies to regularly wear hats, and her famous pillbox style sitting back on her bouffant styled hair was, according to Cassini's interpretation (1995), inspired by images of Nefertiti of Egypt.

Cassini's aim was to orchestrate glamour through clothing that would allow Mrs. Kennedy to stand out from everyone else in the room. He aimed at a royal look, and he succeeded from the first outfit he designed for Mrs. Kennedy. The white Swiss double satin gown she wore to the inaugural gala was so stunning that it is reported President-elect Kennedy wanted the lights turned on in the limousine as they rode through the city "so they can see Jackie" (Thayer 1971, 62). Cassini correctly analyzed that "nobody suspected back then, not even the President, that Jackie was to become his best public relations tool" (1995, 33). Starting with the first trip abroad in May of 1961, where Mrs. Kennedy was photographed with Royal Canadian Mounted Police in a red wool suit that complemented their uniforms, to the Givenchy-designed gown for an evening with President de Gaulle at Versailles, to the chiffon gown she wore for the unveiling of the *Mona Lisa* at the National Gallery of Art in 1963, she epitomized the American version of royalty. The public was mesmerized, and as Cassini flatly states, "There was nobody to touch Jackie in using style as a political tool" (1995, 178).

From a visual perspective, Jackie Kennedy became what David Halberstam (1979) would call part of the supporting cast in her husband's recognition that television conflated theatre with politics. In an astute analysis of the influence of media on the presidency, Halberstam argues that Kennedy was the man with the appropriate instincts to exploit media coverage so that "style became in some ways as important as substance, and on occasion *more* important" (1979, 389). The star power of President Kennedy included the constellation of family, particularly Jackie, as both a glamorous first lady in haute couture, but also as a mother photographed with the adorable Caroline and John. Much of the visual imagery was an attempt to control the tension between public access and the protection of privacy,[6] but there is absolutely no doubt when looking at the dazzling array of photographs from 1961 to 1963 that Mrs. Kennedy was at her best in evening gown entertaining heads of state, artists, and other important people.

In both popular and academic measure, only Princess Diana of Wales comes close to matching Jacqueline Kennedy's status as fashion icon. In her analysis of American fashion, entitled *Looking for Jackie*, Kathleen Craughwell-Varda classifies a fashion icon as a woman with a personal style whose imitated look across class lines "permanently [alters] the American cultural landscape" (1999, 9). She sees first ladies as a clear category of icon and Jacqueline Kennedy Onassis as the epitome of the phenomenon:

> Despite the current ubiquity of fashion-conscious celebrities, it is safe to say that no single figure has emerged in the last forty years who can rival the appeal and impact of Jacqueline Kennedy. That no contemporary woman has taken Jackie's place in the public consciousness is perhaps a reflection of our unwillingness to find a replacement for her; to do so would mean relinquishing the mythical appeal of the golden era of Camelot. (1999, 198)

In the popular press, Jackie Kennedy has remained, even after her death, as one of America's most admired fashion icons of the twentieth century (Collins 1994; Keogh 2001; Pogoda 1996; *Vogue* 1999). Academic analysis of women's magazines (Wang 1987) also documents Mrs. Kennedy, along with Princess Diana, as fashion leaders of their times.

White House Restoration

Nonverbal communication scholars who study impression management (Leathers 1992) often argue that one's personal body and, by extension, one's home are the two sites where individuals have control over the image they wish to present to the public, therefore influencing the outcome of the communication situation. Mrs. Kennedy, indeed, presented herself and the White House as aesthetic aspects of the Kennedy administration, with the result that the American public has consistently rated the Kennedys and the Kennedy White House years as one of the most popular and effective presidencies ("American Opinion" 1999; Gallup 2000; Watson 2000, 179–95). The single most cited agenda item of Mrs. Kennedy's is undoubtedly her White House restoration project. The Smithsonian First Ladies exhibit posts a placard which reads: "Jacqueline Kennedy marked a pivotal transition in the role—after her, first ladies would be expected to have significant agendas of their own." The agenda in question pertains to her restoration project and the subsequent congressional legislation she saw passed that insured the preservation and protection of White House artifacts. Mrs. Kennedy's greatest contribution to American history is the transformation of the White House itself to a museum quality building that represents an accurate portrayal of presidential life, including authentic artifacts and furniture representing some of our most important presidents. Although presidential libraries convey historical pictures of individual presidents, it is the White House itself that provides the larger context for the life of the president and first family in regard to both private living and state entertainment. Mrs. Kennedy's knowledge of history, art and antiques, and her aesthetic sense in general converged as she set her agenda to make the White House an American rival to European houses such as Versailles.

Mrs. Kennedy unveiled the restoration project in some detail to *Life* magazine correspondent Hugh Sidey in an interview accompanied by seven photographs published in September of 1961. Two important things are established in this interview. First, Mrs. Kennedy's academic approach to the restoration was clear when she stated, "Everything in the White House . . . must have a reason for being there. It would be sacrilege merely to 'redecorate' it—a word I hate. It must be *restored*—and that has nothing to do with decoration. That is a question of scholarship" (Sidey 1961, 57). More importantly, in this interview Mrs. Kennedy reveals the restoration project as a long-term vision she brought with her to the White House. In other words, she came with an agenda that would give the Kennedy administration a place in history:

> I knew the White House would be one of my main projects if he won . . . How could I help wanting to do it? she asks. I don't know . . . is it a reverence for beauty or for history? I guess both. I've always cared. My best friends are people who care. I don't know . . . when you read Proust or listen to Jack talk about history or go to Mount Vernon, you understand. I feel strongly about the children who come here. When I think about our son and how to make him turn out like his father, I think of Jack's great sense of history.[7] (Sidey 1961, 62)

To achieve the restoration, Mrs. Kennedy created a White House Fine Arts Committee to advise her and assist with the work. Membership included David Finley, chair of the National Commission of Fine Arts and Henry Francis Dupont of the Winterthur Museum. Lorraine Pearce became the first curator of the White House. Jacqueline Kennedy established a permanent association between the White House and the Smithsonian by persuading her husband to support legislation she had introduced to Congress by Representative J. T. Rutherford and Senator Clinton Anderson. The legislation proposed that the Smithsonian store all White House objects not in use at any given time and provide a permanent curator for the White House. Behind the scenes she used the advice of French interior designer Stephane Boudin, although there is some evidence that his presence was a source of controversy regarding the amount of French influence needed for an American design project (Klein 1996; Truman 1995).

Mrs. Kennedy further established the White House Historical Association (JFK Library website; Salinger Papers) as a body that would raise funds for the restoration through donations and the publication of the first White House guidebook. She wrote the introduction, approved the text, selected photographs, and designed layout for *The White House: An Historic Guide*, which was published in 1962, and became a success with visitors. This editorial endeavor was a precursor to Jacqueline Kennedy Onassis's career as an editor from 1975 until her death in 1994. The restoration project itself was the first of a number of restoration projects she became involved in during her lifetime, including redesign of the Rose Garden, saving historic homes on Lafayette Square from demolition, saving the War, State, and Navy Building from demolition to be remodeled and renamed as the Old Executive Building, and, as Helen Thomas reports (1999), she assisted with the redesign of Air Force One by enlisting the help of designer

Raymond Loewy. Again, these activities foreshadowed her lifelong interest in historic preservation. In later years, she campaigned to save Grand Central Station and preserve portions of Central Park, and she assisted with the establishment of the Costume Institute at the Metropolitan Museum of Art.

In addition to bringing historic preservation to the attention of the American people, Mrs. Kennedy chose to present the restored White House through a one-hour televised tour on February 14, 1962. It is one of two events in which she spent a sustained period of time communicating with the American public. (The other event was the funeral of President Kennedy, where her communication was entirely nonverbal.) Several sources document the tour, including the CBS copy of the program itself, a summary of the tour linked to the JKF Library website, and a fascinating book entitled A Tour of the White House with Mrs. John F. Kennedy by Perry Wolff in conjunction with CBS. Wolff sums up the essence of the rhetorical situation: "A woman spoke for an hour and the White House once more became the central symbol of America" (1962, 10). Camelot was visually and firmly established for America as a result of the tour. The number of viewers who saw the tour[8] runs from one-third of a nation (Wolff 1962, 9) to 48 million (Thomas 1999, 245) to 50 million (JFK Library website) to 80 million (www.geocities.com/~newgeneration/tour.htm). The Nielsen rating was 28.3 million homes (Thayer 1971, 330), so calculations vary based on number of people estimated per home. Whatever the actual number, it is the most significant public speaking Mrs. Kennedy did as first lady.

Wolff (1962) reported that CBS shot the tour over a three-day period in January. Mrs. Kennedy was on set about seven hours to produce a one-hour documentary comprised of approximately 100,000 electronic images. Correspondent Charles Collingwood served as the interviewer, but much of the final footage is Mrs. Kennedy herself explaining the purpose of various rooms and the historic significance of the furniture and artifacts in each room.

Several features characterize Mrs. Kennedy as a public speaker. Most noticeable visually is Jacqueline Kennedy as a "perfect model of American manners," to use a description offered by Arthur Schlesinger Jr. (1999). She appears impeccably dressed in a two-piece wool suit with a bouffant hairstyle, and her posture is absolutely perfect throughout the broadcast. She is poised and polite to Mr. Collingwood, and she confidently leads the way through the White House without ever erring in direction or control. In reality, the tour is a videotape with 190 splices in the master tape, that is, about 95 scenes were inserted (Wolff 1962, 243). However, few retakes were needed for the live taping. Wolff reported, "It was obvious that her intensity about the White House and her work was communicable" (248). When President Kennedy makes a brief appearance, his commentary appears to flow in tone and content with the rest of the tour. In reality, the president's appearance was taped twice since he did not like the impact of his words on the first take, according to Wolff (1962, 233).

Vocally, Mrs. Kennedy had a high-pitched, breathy style of speaking that, by today's standards, would be considered detrimental to a woman's public speaking impact. Her vocal quality has been described in various ways: "softly in a whispery voice" (Gutin 1989, 58), "little girl whisper" (Klein 1996, 5), and by her sisters-in-law she was jokingly referred to as "Babykin, a popular talking doll" (Klein 1996, 124). The *London Observer*, however, called her voice "a phantom intimacy" (quoted in Anthony 1991, 72), which was clearly meant as a compliment. For the 1960s, Mrs. Kennedy's voice was not a liability overall; rather, it epitomized her femininity while masking the interior strength and control that she needed as first lady. To further enhance her natural movement and voice, she was fitted with a hidden microphone under her suit jacket. Her spontaneity appeared flawless.[9]

Finally, Mrs. Kennedy spoke on camera from memory. The level of detail she mastered regarding historical fact was rather incredible and greatly impressed the American public. It certainly enhanced her ethos and proved that she was not only physically attractive, but highly intelligent as well. This was a winning combination for the Kennedy administration. *The White House Tour* was a sensation. It was broadcast in Europe and Asia and received an Emmy Award. A reported 10,000 letters came into the White House after the initial broadcast, and tourists increased between one-third and one-half from the previous year (Thayer 1971). *The Guide*, selling for one dollar, appears to have financed much of the restoration project. After the televised tour, Camelot was firmly entrenched in the American public's visual memory. The White House was seen as a kind of American royal palace or "national shrine" (UPI 1964, 70). This is an important distinction because the White House and the Capitol vie with the Statue of Liberty as perhaps the most important icons of democracy in the world.

White House Entertainment

During the tour of the White House, CBS correspondent Charles Collingwood has the following exchange with Mrs. Kennedy:

> CC: Mrs. Kennedy, this administration has shown a particular affinity for artists, musicians, writers, poets. Is this because you and your husband just feel that way or do you think that there's a relationship between the government and the arts?
>
> JK: That's so complicated. I don't know. I just think that everything in the White House should be the best—the entertainment that's given here and, if it's an American company that you can help, I like to do that. If it's not, just as long as it's the best. (Wolff 1962, 78–79)

The evasiveness of the remark is not genuine. Mrs. Kennedy knew very well that she wanted a relationship between the government and the arts in a manner that emulated her observations of French culture and government. First ladies scholar Carl Anthony (1991, 27–43) offers a marvelous analysis of her cultural agenda, and he gives her credit for her intelligence regarding her reasoning for a government agency to promote the arts and for a Washington National Cultural Center patterned after Lincoln Center in New York. The Johnson administration would follow through with the National Endowment for the Arts and the National Endowment for the Humanities. The Kennedy Center opened in her lifetime, but during her service as first lady, the arts flourished inside the White House. Interestingly, Mrs. Kennedy's first caller at the White House was George Balanchine, choreographer and director of the New York City Ballet, while one of President Kennedy's first callers was poet Robert Frost (Thayer 1971). Literally, the stage was set for what would come in the next three years.

Immediately upon JFK's election to the presidency, Jacqueline assembled members of a team who would assist her to literally transform White House style in entertaining. Letitia Baldrige, an old friend from Vassar and an experienced mistress of etiquette, was appointed social secretary. Shortly after, Pamela Turnure was hired as Mrs. Kennedy's press secretary (although her title was Assistant Social Secretary for the Press) and Oleg Cassini as her couturier, J. B. West was already in place as the chief usher of the White House, Providencia Parades served as Mrs. Kennedy's maid, and George Thomas was the president's valet. After an initial disastrous dinner party, French chef Rene Verdon was hired to bring truly good food to all White House guests. In a delightful book entitled *In the Kennedy Style* (1998), Letitia Baldrige describes six of the most memorable state dinners from the Kennedy administration, and Rene Verdon includes menus and recipes for each event. Ms. Baldrige's observations, however, run deep regarding the rhetorical-semiotic effects of the first lady's decisions. The total sensual appeal of sight, fragrance, taste, and sound made White House galas communication extravagances that boosted everyone's ethos. As novelist William Styron noted on one occasion, "even Republicans were gaga" (Baldrige 1998, 90).

Given how badly the White House needed to be restored, it is not surprising that the public rooms, particularly the State Dining Room, were not conducive to entertaining. The lighting was poor, the colors and furniture were unsightly and uncomfortable, and the general feeling was cold and dismal. Mrs. Kennedy was already a seasoned hostess and knew social protocol. She told Letitia Baldrige, "The entertaining is going to be very important to us . . . There are many things that can be done to make it [the White House] warmer, more gracious, more distinguished" (1998, 21). Indeed, Mrs. Kennedy made several strategic choices that changed the entire nature of the communication during a White House event. According to Baldrige, round tables seating eight or ten replaced horseshoe or rectangular tables. Walls painted white or yellow and pale blue tablecloths lightened the rooms and the mood. Flemish style flower arrangements were plentiful and of low height to provide fragrance (to mask the smells of cigarettes and cigars) and color without obscuring sightlines. Intimate and lively conversation was now possible. Given the age of the Kennedys, it is not surprising to know that one aim of their entertaining was to have fun. Dancing, alcohol, and smoking were permitted.

Communicatively, Mrs. Kennedy used seating charts and room arrangements to enliven the possibilities for conversation. At large dinners, two dining rooms were necessary. She presided in one while her husband hosted in the other. Husbands and wives were separated (a break in tradition) by room and tables so that each could meet different people and have something to talk about after the party. Guests of honor were usually seated at the president and Mrs. Kennedy's tables, but the guest lists were so innovative that each table seated interesting people. Pierre Salinger (1966) reported that Mrs. Kennedy would literally spread out the seating charts on the floor of her sitting room and plan seating. For a dinner of 120 guests, typically forty people would be seated based on government protocol, and she would decide where to seat the other eighty. The Kennedy's were a glamorous couple, and they invited glamorous people to mingle with heads of state and government officials. Depending upon the events of the evening, the Kennedys often had guests of honor to their family quarters before or after dinner for private conversation.

The White House truly took on the persona of Camelot a short time into the Kennedy administration. Mrs. Kennedy wore her Cassini gowns, sometimes accented with a tiara or sunburst brooch, and the president greeted dignitaries in formal white tie. Three entertainments are well known for their extravagance or innovation regarding the celebration of arts and culture. The most ambitious event ever undertaken was an outdoor dinner for 132 guests staged at Mount Vernon to honor the president of Pakistan on July 11, 1961. The president and his guests sailed down the Potomac River to Mount Vernon and dined under a gigantic tent. For Mrs. Kennedy, the dinner was reminiscent of the evening when she and the president were entertained at Versailles by President de Gaulle. Mount Vernon represented a historic monument that the American people could show to their guests, and the site truly represents a consistent theme with the Kennedys: history is important because it is the story of the United States. Again, Mrs. Kennedy selected a visual icon, Mount Vernon, as the symbolic presentation of America to the president of Pakistan.

The most remembered artistic evening in the White House was November 13, 1961, when Pablo Casals gave a concert after a dinner for 155 guests. It was a stunning coup to persuade Casals to come dine and entertain the president. At a time when an invitation to the White House catapulted the recipient to unequaled social status (Baldrige 1998, 67), Casals declined the first invitation to come because he continued to boycott U.S. support of Francisco Franco during the Spanish civil war. In the end, Casals did perform in the United States for the first time since 1928 in the company of the governor of Puerto Rico and composers such as Samuel Barber and Leonard Bernstein. Casals' worldwide fame as a cellist boded well for the Kennedys. After a thirty-three-year hiatus from performing in the United States, Mrs. Kennedy is credited with renewing our country's relationship with one of the world's most gifted musicians.

Finally, there was the party for "the brains," which was Ms. Baldrige's code name for the dinner honoring the American Nobel Laureates on April 20, 1962. This was the evening where, among the 175 guests, Linus Pauling waltzed impromptu after marching on the White House earlier in the day to advocate banning the atom bomb. The evening with the American intelligentsia highlights the focus on intellect that the Kennedys were known for, but also adds to the list of "firsts" for White House entertaining, among them poetry readings, opera, ballet performances, youth concerts, and the first reception ever for Congressional Medal of Honor recipients (Baldrige 1998, 87). The rhetorical impact of these events was not lost on the rest of the world. Like the great European palaces, the United States could now boast that we, too, appreciated music, art, intellect, and politics as part of our great traditions. The presence of such important people in the White House symbolically demonstrated the value of American culture and succeeded in elevating the history and the passion of this country. Mrs. Kennedy's strategy endures as art and politics continue to mix at the White House.

Orchestration of President Kennedy's Funeral

On November 21, 1963, Mrs. Kennedy traveled to Texas with her husband as part of a strategy to strengthen Democratic allegiance to the president. It was her first trip since suffering the loss of Patrick, a son born in August who died within three days of a premature birth. Most analysts agree that the Kennedys were at a turning point in their personal relationship and looked forward to a stronger marriage as a result of their family loss. Mrs. Kennedy's popularity was as strong as ever, marked by the comments President Kennedy made when she arrived fashionably late to a breakfast in Forth Worth on the morning of November 22. He quipped that "nobody wonders what Lyndon and I wear" (Office of the Federal Register 1964, 888), when she entered the dining room in a Cassini pink suit and matching pillbox hat. Approximately four hours later President Kennedy was assassinated in Dallas, presumably by Lee Harvey Oswald. To this day, one of the most enduring images of November 22, 1963, is Jacqueline Kennedy wearing the blood-splattered pink suit as Lyndon Johnson took the oath of office on Air Force One and, later, as she descended from the plane to accompany the coffin to Bethesda Naval Hospital. Most astonishing, however, is the calm dignity with which thirty-four-year-old Mrs. Kennedy carried herself from November 22 until the close of the funeral on November 25. Upon reflection, *Look* correspondent Laura Bergquist wrote, "Last November she showed her quality. It was her toughness and discipline that carried a nation through the trauma with a transcendent dignity" (1964, 36).

Margaret Truman's analysis may be most accurate:

> Aristocrats also have a sense of their own stature, as well as life's depths. They have been trained to speak and behave in a style that fits the occasion, no matter what their private feelings may be. Jackie's previous three years, in which, behind her various masks, she had forged her own unique identity as First Lady, became a resource on which she drew to sustain not only herself but the American people in this tragic ordeal. . . . Jackie's dignity, her sense of history, enabled the nation to focus on its grief. (1995, 44)

Mrs. Kennedy had the presence of mind to think rhetorically even as she returned to Washington, D.C., aboard Air Force One sitting next to her husband's coffin (Smith 1964, 33). Instructions were given to research the details of President Lincoln's funeral, and by the next morning, the iconography of the Kennedy funeral began to reflect the formality of a national protocol inclusive of several presidential funerals, most notably Lincoln's, but also laden with military imagery reflecting the superpower status of the United States. The extensive television coverage allowed the American people, as well as citizens around the globe, a constant image bathed in black against the sound of muffled drums. This message lasted from Saturday through Monday, during which time Mrs. Kennedy did not speak publicly, yet appeared as the symbol of our national grief. Not once did she lose control in front of a television camera.

Several rhetorical gestures characterize President Kennedy's funeral. Black bunting in the East Room, where the president lay in state on Saturday, was similar to the Lincoln funeral (UPI 1964, 45). In the Capitol rotunda, Kennedy's coffin laid on the same catafalque that held the coffins of Presidents Lincoln, McKinley, and Garfield. During the eulogy in the Capitol on Saturday, Mrs. Kennedy and her daughter Caroline approached the flag-draped coffin and kneeled down, Jacqueline kissing the flag and Caroline touching the coffin. This was a poignant moment of grief for families everywhere. On Monday, the day of the funeral, John F. Kennedy Jr., on his third birthday, saluted his father's coffin as it came down the steps of St. Matthew's Cathedral. The photograph is, perhaps, the most well known and enduring of the funeral itself, and it was his mother who prompted John to salute. The funeral procession included six horses drawing the caisson, three of them riderless, and behind the coffin, a black riderless horse with boots inserted into the stirrups backwards as the symbol of a lost leader (UPI 1964). Finally, Mrs. Kennedy selected an eternal flame to grace the graveside in Arlington National Cemetery, where she chose to have President Kennedy buried (rather than in his home state of Massachusetts) because she reasoned "he belongs to the country" (UPI 1964, 99). The eternal flame was an extremely important choice because it symbolically continues the Kennedy legacy forward in history. For those of us who witnessed the events of November 1963, the flame is both a reminder of tragedy, but also a symbol of endurance and hope.[10] President Kennedy will not be forgotten, and Jacqueline Kennedy's orchestration of his funeral was the final rhetorical act of the Kennedy administration.

Interpersonal Diplomacy

Although Mrs. Kennedy did not speak in public as part of her role as first lady, other than ceremonial remarks, it is clear in hindsight that she engaged a kind of interpersonal diplomacy that is fitting to her view of politics. I want to argue here that she had a keen sense of interpersonal relationships and how to maneuver within the constraints of the patriarchal social protocol of the 1950s and 1960s. It has been said (Gutin, 1989) that Jacqueline Kennedy had no interest in politics, that, in fact, politics bored her and that she did not care to participate in politics.[11] I do not believe this to be entirely true, and there is evidence that, for example, during the Cuban Missile Crisis Mrs. Kennedy was present during some of the conversations of the president's inner circle (Anthony 1991, 81). Further, Margaret Truman (1995) reports that Mrs. Kennedy used her intelligence and good judgment to smooth the relationships between President Kennedy, Indian prime minister Nehru, and U.N. Ambassador Adlai Stevenson. She also sent political observations from her trips to India and Italy in personal letters to her husband.

No first lady can divorce herself from politics since it is at the core of White House life. Mrs. Kennedy was an intelligent, well-read woman who shared with her husband a keen sense of history (Sidey 1961; White 1963). They discussed history often, she made mention of history in public remarks, and she knew that the relationship of the president to the American public was one of the most documented relationships in American history. Although she may not have been interested in discussing publicly particular policy issues, there is no doubt that she was very aware of politics and a role that she might play as a first lady. Historian Carl Anthony (1990; 1991) documents Mrs. Kennedy's role as campaigner, speech advisor, listener, sounding board, debate partner, and historical consultant to her husband from his senator years until his death. However, it is clear that Mrs. Kennedy chose to exercise her knowledge and power behind the scenes in terms of President Kennedy's formal political agenda.

She clearly was not an Eleanor Roosevelt regarding an activist agenda, nor was she the housewifely Mamie Eisenhower. For the public record, Mrs. Kennedy claimed the following in a written interview with journalist Helen Thomas: "When I asked her what was the best thing about living in the White House she responded, 'Seeing my husband be a great president,' but politics, to her, took a backseat to being a mother to her children. 'The official side of my life takes me away from my children a great deal,' she said. 'If I were to add political duties, I would have practically no time with my children and they are my first responsibility. My husband agrees with me'" (1999, 58–59). Mrs. Kennedy, however, understood the value of politics, as evidenced by this response in a televised interview:

I think politics is one of the most rewarding lives any woman can have—to be married to a politician. I think every woman wants to feel needed, and in politics you are—so much more than in other areas. You're always living in a state of crisis. You're always being demanded to meet a challenge, and when you meet it, it's a great satisfaction to you. (The World of Jacqueline Kennedy 1962)

She did find a way to engage politics, even if she did not set an official political agenda.

Specifically, Mrs. Kennedy used three rhetorical strategies to aid her husband's presidency: first, her fashion diplomacy was a calculated persuasive strategy to present the best face of the presidency. Her iconic beauty and sophisticated interpersonal style particularly paid off in smoothing the relationships between President Kennedy and French president Charles de Gaulle, and more importantly, President Kennedy and Russian president Nikita Khrushchev. Her skills in French allowed her to serve as the translator between de Gaulle and her husband on their 1961 trip to Paris, which was a highly unusual position for a first lady, but which solidified Mrs. Kennedy's position as the pivot on which French–American relations were strengthened. One of President Kennedy's most quoted lines is, of course, the statement he made to a press luncheon after the first two days of their visit: "I do not think it altogether inappropriate to introduce myself to this audience. I am the man who accompanied Jacqueline Kennedy to Paris, and I have enjoyed it" (Blair 1961, 1). In 1962, she journeyed to India on a highly successful state visit to bolster her husband's credibility and U.S. influence over India's foreign policies regarding Pakistan, Portugal, and China. President Kennedy and Prime Minister Nehru had not seemed compatible when Nehru visited the United States, yet Kennedy was very interested in supporting India as a pivotal site of Asian interest (Schlesinger 1965). Mrs. Kennedy's diplomacy accomplished the goal.

Her second persuasive strategy concerned protocol. By redesigning the staging for state dinners, White House cultural entertainment, and informal parties, Mrs. Kennedy was able to widen the number of people who came into contact with the president, bring people together for behind-the-scenes politicking while enjoying highbrow cultural entertainment, and she solidified the inner circle of influence by hosting frequent private lunches and parties for both friends and key political figures whose company the president and first lady desired. Even on the day of her husband's funeral, Mrs. Kennedy had the poise to host a receiving line in the Red Room of the White House for international heads of state (Baldrige 1998), and over 200 people were members of this group (UPI & *American Heritage Magazine* 1964).

Mrs. Kennedy's third persuasive strategy was her use of handwritten, personal letters and notes. She is, in fact, known for her handwritten memos to staff on yellow legal pad paper and her colorful handwritten notes to friends and family, in which she often included drawings and lines of poetry (Salinger 1966). Although she very often used such notes as follow-ups for a job well done by her personal staff, she also wrote to heads of state and other important people, including her own husband. Biographer Margaret Thayer reported that whenever Mrs. Kennedy traveled, her personal maid hand carried a briefcase that contained "writing paper; information about places on the itinerary; and list after list, with brief profiles attached, of the important and interesting people Mrs. Kennedy would meet" (1971, 277). She was never out of touch with people and used her letter-writing skills as a preferred form of communication.

Given the tense nature of American–Russian diplomacy during the Kennedy administration, it is worth noting that Jacqueline Kennedy may have served to restrain not only the personal awkwardness between President Kennedy and Mr. Khrushchev (as was evident in Vienna in 1961), but she also may have aided in restraining the diplomatic animosity between the two countries. It is evident that Mr. Khrushchev was quite fond of Mrs. Kennedy, and it is clear that she saw the importance of preserving a civil relationship between the United States and the Soviet Union.

In June 1999, President Boris Yeltsin released approximately forty declassified documents to President Clinton, one of which is a copy of a top secret cipher telegram from Russian ambassador Anatoly Dobrynin dated December 4, 1963 (U.S. Dept. of State, LS no. 0692061-27). In this document, Ambassador Dobrynin sends to the Kremlin the contents of a personal letter from Jacqueline Kennedy to Nikita Khrushchev. Dobrynin explains that the letter is handwritten ("considered here [the United States] to be a sign of particular respect for the addressee") on small pages with the stamp of the White House. The text of the letter contains 367 words in which she thanks Mr. Khrushchev for sending a representative to President Kennedy's funeral and then writes an extremely personal and political message which reads in part:

> I am sending it [this letter] only because I know how much my husband was concerned about peace and how important the relations between you and him were to him in this concern. He often cited your words in his speeches: "In the next war, the survivors will envy the dead."
>
> You and he were adversaries, but you were also allies in your determination not to let the world be blown up. You respected each other and could have dealings with each other. I know that President Johnson will make every effort to establish the same relations with you. The danger troubling my husband was that war could be started not so much by major figures as by minor ones.
>
> Whereas major figures understand the need for self-control and restraint, minor ones are sometimes moved rather by fear and pride. If only in the future major figures could still force minor ones to sit down at the negotiating table before they begin to fight.
>
> I know that President Johnson will continue the policy my husband believed in so deeply—the policy of self-control and restraint—and he will need your help. I am sending you this letter because I am so deeply mindful of the importance of the relations that existed between you and my husband, and also because you and Mrs. Khrushchev were so kind in Vienna.

Mrs. Kennedy's political savvy is astute. According to the telegram, even President Johnson and Secretary of State Dean Rusk were not aware of the contents of this letter, yet Mrs. Kennedy sets the stage for the Johnson administration to enter into American–Russian diplomacy on a positive note. Further, her ability to show interpersonal consideration for Mr. Khrushchev and his wife is a strategic stroke of genius given that, by all accounts, beginning with the 1961 meeting in Vienna, Kennedy and Khrushchev did not personally get along. Khrushchev, however, was smitten with Mrs. Kennedy as evidenced by a *Life* magazine (1994) photograph in which he adoringly smiles at Jackie. She probably also knew about the secret correspondence between her husband and Khrushchev that served as a means to negotiate within the tense context of nuclear threats during this phase of American–Soviet relations (Salinger 1966).

Jacqueline Kennedy's interpersonal skills also intervened to soften the relationship between President Kennedy and his own vice president, Lyndon Johnson. Katharine Graham reports in her autobiography (1997) that right from the 1960 Democratic Convention, when Johnson was selected as Kennedy's vice-presidential running mate, there was tension between Johnson and the Kennedy family as a whole. Johnson is reported to have said that Jacqueline Kennedy was the only person from the Kennedy clan who was nice to him, and she speaks highly of him in her oral history for the LBJ Library (Onassis 1974). Apparently, she was genuinely kind to him throughout the Kennedy administration, even when she was delegating unwanted public appearances as first lady to Mrs. Johnson (Anthony 1991; Truman 1995). In a recent release of telephone tapes from the LBJ Library (Tape No. WH6409.02), the American public was astonished with the fact that President Johnson asked Mrs. Kennedy if she would serve as ambassador to Mexico for the Johnson administration. She graciously declined the offer. Pierre Salinger reported (1995) that President Johnson asked him to carry a personal message to Mrs. Kennedy in 1964 requesting her acceptance of an ambassadorship to France; however, she declined once again. Clearly, Mrs. Kennedy's diplomatic skill and her facility in Spanish and French impressed Lyndon Johnson, however inappropriate an invitation to become ambassador might be for the new widow of a former president.

Although much of the public's perception of Mrs. Kennedy's achievements as first lady was contained in images that reflect her use of fashion diplomacy and protocol, the written and oral forms of communication she employed are less known. Her public imagery as mother and fashion icon are a subtle form of political influence and, perhaps, should even be characterized as social-cultural influence on the shaping of American life. But, a look behind the photographs indicates that, like other first ladies, Mrs. Kennedy exercised considerable political power through her strategic use of silence and discretion. Mrs. Kennedy's private persona, called the most "complex" of recent first ladies by White House usher J. B. West (Anthony 1991), balanced the public image of glamour that the press insisted on creating during the Kennedy administration. Ironically, Anthony notes that the public's "adulation was often insulting to her intelligence. Her celebrity intruded on her privacy, and consequently her ironclad limitations on her role began to serve as refuge from the intensity of global fame" (1991, 44). It is not surprisingly, then, that first ladies scholars have not been able to ascertain fully how politically influential Mrs. Kennedy actually was given that her husband's assassination cut short her role as first lady and that the press coverage insisted on glamour images whenever possible. Since she was the first "television" first lady, the true tension between public and private in a first lady's life may be epitomized by Jacqueline Kennedy. The fact that she chose to remain an enigma for the rest of her life only increases the ambiguity of her personal politics.

Mrs. Kennedy as Public Speaker

Contrary to the usual starting point for analyses of first lady rhetoric, I selected to privilege visual forms of communication over public speaking in regard to Mrs. Kennedy. I do so because Mrs. Kennedy herself did not shape her role as first lady through her public speaking. In fact, she chose to shun the public platform once in the White House. It is clear from those close to the Kennedy Senate and presidential campaigns (O'Donnell and Powers 1970; Salinger 1966) that Jacqueline Kennedy was very good at campaigning. She retained good cheer, was genuine to people whom she met, listened to what voters had to say, and spoke with enthusiasm when asked to take the stage on her husband's behalf. Kennedy confidants Ken O'Donnell and Dave Powers even tell an amusing story in which Jackie Kennedy borrowed the manager's microphone in a supermarket to tell people about her husband during the 1960 presidential campaign. She also wrote a column entitled "Campaign Wife," distributed by the Democratic National Committee (Anthony 1990). In this column she covered a range of observations about her husband as a presidential candidate out on the trail, but also offered her point of view on such serious issues as education and medical care for senior citizens ("Jacqueline Kennedy: The White House Years" 2001).

We do know that Mrs. Kennedy assisted her husband with his speech writing, primarily by suggesting quotations or discussing books with him. It is reported that she even translated French books on Indochina and read passages from de Gaulle's *Memoires* that later influenced her husband's thinking (Schlesinger 1965, 103).

Mrs. Kennedy's low priority for her own public speaking is also reflected in the fact that there is no systematic documentation for a "speaking schedule" or speech texts. During the White House years, she spoke rarely and always on ceremonial occasions. Her speeches were short and extemporaneous. The videotape archive at the JFK Library contains the best documentation of her public speaking, although the occasions are not always dated or places cited. The arts, for example, were one of her priorities as first lady, and she spoke on several occasions to support art patronage (e.g., *Accent* 1961). However, most interesting is Mrs. Kennedy's preference to give speeches in French or Spanish, or to speak in front of an international audience. Anthony (1990) documents the radio tapes and brief remarks she made in Spanish to voters of Latin, Hispanic, and Spanish descent during the 1960 presidential campaign. She continued this trend while in the White House.

I have documented (translated on occasion) thirty public speeches/press interviews by Mrs. Kennedy,[12] but this must be considered incomplete as it is the first attempt to piece together a chronology. One of the highlights is her taped interview in French that aired on French television the night before she and President Kennedy arrived in Paris in May 1961. In the interview she is remarkably charming, even coy, as she speaks to Monsieur Crenesse about the history of the White House, including some links to France through artifacts such as a Cezanne painting in the Green Room. She also discusses her role as a mother, the importance of family, and the way the Kennedys relax by listening to music. This interview was a highly successful public relations strategy (Salinger 1966). Helen Thomas (1999) reported that while in France, Mrs. Kennedy snubbed American reporters, but obligingly spoke in French to French reporters.

On the Latin American state visit in 1961, she spoke briefly in Spanish in Venezuela, concluding: "You know my husband's profound desire to help those who need help. I am sure that with your collaboration, he will be successful." In Mexico, she spoke at a luncheon honoring President and Mrs. Mateos on June 30, 1962. The text (Moreno, n.d.) contains 177 words and carries a message in which she tells the Mexican people to retain their culture and spirit even as they gain material progress: "Your profound faith in the dignity of man has been expressed in your art and literature over the centuries. . . . The ancient spirit of Mexico has not changed. . . . material progress can make a change without destroying the values of the heart and the human mind."

Even on the trip to Texas, she delivered a seventy-three-word speech in Spanish to the League of United Latin American Citizens in Houston (Thayer 1971). Her most unusual speech, other than a badly done interview she conducted with the captain of the U.S. Olympic Equestrian Team in 1963, was delivered in December of 1962 at the Orange Bowl in Miami to the brigade of rebels left from the Bay of Pigs (Schlesinger 1965). In an odd political statement that links the bravery of the rebels to teaching her son the story of the Bay of Pigs, she compliments the rebels in Spanish for their courageous fight for democracy.

Film footage from her trip to India and Pakistan in 1962 shows her speaking comfortably—in English—from a balcony overlooking Shalimar Gardens in which she makes the following speech:

> I must say I am profoundly impressed by the reverence which you in Pakistan have for your art and your culture and for the use which you make of it now. My own countrymen, too, have a pride in their traditions. So, I think, as I stand in these gardens, which were built long before my country was born, that that's one more thing that binds us together and always will. (Invitation to Pakistan, 1962)

Note that Mrs. Kennedy was predisposed to short greetings or compliments that contained references to culture, particularly art and literature. She always tried to link the audience to her husband or the United States to show a positive and mutual relationship.

Altogether it is not unfair to say that Jacqueline Kennedy enjoyed the ethos of first lady most often when projecting the presidency to audiences who were not American born, and for this reason, she could be called our most "international" first lady. At the 1963 reception for the three branches of government, Speaker of the House John McCormack toasted Mrs. Kennedy as "a great diplomat and a great Ambassador—who has given an image of America which has made the world smile again" (quoted in Thayer 1971, 190). After three years in the role of first lady and official trips to Canada, France, Austria, England, Latin America, Italy, India, and Pakistan, Mrs. Kennedy earned such high praise from Speaker McCormack, and it is no wonder that President Johnson sought to honor Jacqueline Kennedy as an ambassador. As much as she celebrated the best of the United States, Mrs. Kennedy's public persona is international in scope, particularly when analyzed from the perspective of the public speaking she engaged in as first lady.

Legacy

At his mother's funeral on May 23, 1994, John F. Kennedy Jr. told the mourners that he and Caroline had discussed three themes that had influenced his mother's life: "love of words, emphasis on family, and desire for adventure" (Gould 1996, 494). Clearly, Jacqueline Kennedy's love of words is a chief theme in her life, but it is a personal more than a public theme. She read voraciously and in several languages. She wrote poetry, memos, and letters virtually every day. She edited books. She spoke often and with a great sense of intelligence and wit in private conversation. For public consumption, little is recorded to give a coherent view of this complex first lady. Rather, the public thrived on the imagery of a beautiful woman who brought to the White House a sense of modern style that was copied the world over and continues to influence fashion and popular culture.

Jacqueline Kennedy's emphasis on family translated into the primary tension she had to negotiate while living in the White House, that is, how to protect her family from the overzealous press. Helen Thomas summed it up, "Jackie was more elusive, due I think to her shyness, and as time went on her antipathy to the press grew in proportion to her fear of a loss of privacy" (1999, 58). Mrs. Kennedy was known as a woman of many masks. She had two children under the age of five when she entered the White House, and she had a husband who came from one of the most patriarchal clans in the country. Her priority was to protect her family even when it cost her on a personal basis. One of her strategies was to employ her own press secretary. Pamela Turnure described her duty as "to help preserve Mrs. Kennedy's privacy and not to create publicity" (quoted in Thayer 1971, 32). This is an odd position for a press secretary, and it worked only partially. As the first modern press secretary appointed to a first lady, Ms. Turnure was really under the direction of Pierre Salinger, President Kennedy's press secretary, even though Mrs. Kennedy outlined an extended plan in her initial memo regarding policies. Mr. Salinger was really the one to deal with the public–private tension on Mrs. Kennedy's behalf, but he did stay true to her wishes: "minimum information with maximum politeness" (Thayer 1971, 34). Mrs. Kennedy was, indeed, an expert at avoidance strategies, or as she termed it "the polite brush-off."[13]

What first lady does not have at least a small desire for adventure? Jacqueline Kennedy may have had more than the average woman, but she was born and lived in material circumstances that allowed her to fulfill her dreams. Her love of travel, language, history, art, and culture motivated her to seek adventure as far away as Cambodia, but during the White House years she was the first modern first lady to represent the United States to the pope and the prime minister of India without her husband by her side. This signaled the beginning of a new strategy for first ladies to become international ambassadors on behalf of the United States. But, beyond adventure or ambassadorship, Mrs. Kennedy translated her ability to connect nations on a cultural level into tremendous influence on her husband. In an exhibit entitled "Jacqueline Kennedy Travels Abroad"

(2000) at the JFK Library, it was astounding to see a three-page memorandum she wrote to JFK outlining a complete plan to save the temples of Abu Simbel during the time that Egypt was struggling financially to create the Aswan Dam and preserve its monuments. The United States was a ten-million-dollar contributor to the preservation project. This type of power was simply not known to the public. Nevertheless, Mrs. Kennedy paved the way for other first ladies, such as Rosalynn Carter and Hillary Rodham Clinton, to engage in international "goodwill tours" as an appropriate domain for first ladies.

It is difficult to draw a single conclusion about a first lady as complicated as Jacqueline Kennedy. It is easy to overstate her case as the ultimate female American icon of the late twentieth century. The dialectical tensions between public and private, imagery and silence, modesty and stardom, intelligence and restraint all characterize this first lady. Her communication choices were extremely difficult given the media fishbowl that surrounded her at a young age. Had she not come from an aristocratic family, she may not have survived the White House years, particularly the assassination of her husband, with the dignity that she demonstrated. Perhaps her most effective communication choice was the strategic use of silence. She used image rather than words to convey messages that allowed public satisfaction while preserving her privacy as an individual. She thus became the female archetype, or idealized self, that every woman aspires to (Brenner 1994).

In this chapter I have argued that Jacqueline Kennedy executed a rhetorical-semiotic series of strategies to construct the legacy of Camelot. These strategies included what I have termed "fashion diplomacy," the restoration of the White House as a symbol of the presidency and a site for all pilgrims of democracy, a restructuring of entertainment protocol, and interpersonal diplomacy. Earlier in this volume, Kari Anderson argues that several first ladies have achieved political agency without violating norms of femininity by cultivating what she calls a "social political style." Like Dolley Madison, Jackie Kennedy knew how to throw a good party and, likewise, she did translate the role of hostess into diplomat. In fact, the placard at the JFK Library that leads visitors into the exhibit entitled Ceremonial and State Events reads: "They used social and diplomatic occasions at home and abroad to express important national values; to celebrate American history, culture, and achievement; and to enhance the role of the arts in national life."

But, I want to resist Anderson's frame of containment rhetoric in regard to Jacqueline Kennedy. Anderson argues that first ladies used social style as a political strategy against cultural constraints (i.e., containment) to liberate themselves and exercise power. Although her argument is noble, political agency was *not* Mrs. Kennedy's primary goal. Unlike Eleanor Roosevelt and Hillary Rodham Clinton, who clearly articulated political agendas, Jacqueline Kennedy's agenda was a more complicated mix of personal achievement and political participation. Mrs. Kennedy did not need the role of first lady to achieve her life goals. Her stature and position in society would have allowed her to create a life of social and cultural contribution with or without politics. She was not interested in a formal political agenda, so she did not need to circumvent the kind of containment described by Anderson. I would argue that Mrs. Kennedy's training placed her in a "comfortable" position regarding her goals as first lady. Her difficulties were based much more in the relentless invasion of her privacy from the press and the overt sexism from the Kennedy family that often left her in compromising or humiliating personal circumstances. If, however, first ladies represent a unique rhetorical strategy that conflates social and political style, then Jacqueline Kennedy is the epitome of such a strategy, but *not* because she used it to achieve a political agenda. Her strategy was based more on class and gender within the context of the historical period in which she lived. No other modern first lady has come from such an aristocratic background. As such, it places Jacqueline Kennedy in a unique position and may account for the public's fascination and willingness to see the Kennedy administration as the myth of Camelot.

Questions for Discussion

1. What experiences in Jacqueline Bouvier's early life predicted the kind of first lady she would become?
2. Chapter author Elizabeth J. Natalle claims that Mrs. Kennedy's relationship with the press allowed her to achieve "iconic status" both at home and abroad. What is "iconic status"? Do you think Mrs. Kennedy's press coverage allowed her to achieve it?
3. In this chapter you learn that Jackie Kennedy used rhetoric to create a "Camelot," meaning she used aesthetic ideals to create her rhetorical role as first lady. In what ways did Mrs. Kennedy use art to elevate politics?
4. Chapter author Natalle used the phrase "fashion diplomacy" to describe Mrs. Kennedy's rhetorical use of her clothing. How did she achieve "rhetorical action" through her wardrobe?
5. What were Mrs. Kennedy's characteristics as a public speaker?
6. In what ways did Mrs. Kennedy exercise "interpersonal diplomacy?"

Internet Resources

http://www.jfklibrary.org/jbkmenu.htm
The John F. Kennedy Presidential Library and Museum has material available on Jackie Kennedy. Because of Mrs. Kennedy's desire to maintain privacy for her children and their families, her papers are only slowly becoming available to students and scholars. The website above provides a beginning point for exploring pages on Mrs. Kennedy's biography, her wedding, and years in the White House.

http://www.metmuseum.org/special/se_event.asp?OccurrenceId=%7BACBF8E1 2-B196-11D4-93B6-00902786BF44%7D
In 2001, the Metropolitan Museum of Art's Costume Institute and the John F. Kennedy Presidential Library and Museum collaborated to bring to the public

80 of Mrs. Kennedy's iconic fashion statements. On exhibit were outfits Mrs. Kennedy wore on the campaign trail, to the inauguration, in the White House, and on international diplomatic missions. This website provides images from the exhibit, from her travel albums, and from her work on the White House restoration.

http://www.usatoday.com/life/special/jackie/ljack000.htm
This fascinating website sponsored by *USA Today* describes the auction in 1996 of artifacts belonging to Jackie and John Kennedy. You can explore items that were auctioned off and the prices they fetched. The site also contains links to interesting articles covering the auction.

Notes

1. Making the choice to frame Mrs. Kennedy's rhetorical activities as Camelot was a difficult point of scholarship. Pierre Salinger, press secretary to JFK and close friend of Jacqueline Kennedy throughout her life, claims (1995) that the media was guilty of *Camelotization*, which was not reflective of Mrs. Kennedy's view. Nevertheless, it *was* Mrs. Kennedy who evoked the name in her interview with Theodore White in 1963. (It is very clear in White's notes from the interview that she wanted *Camelot* to be known to the public.) After the word *Camelot* appeared in White's two-page remembrance in *Life* magazine, it became the synonym that the public has consistently used to describe the Kennedy White House years. At this time in history, it is more than a name; it evokes a clear mythology and symbolism about the Kennedy presidency and the role Jacqueline Kennedy played during those years. Because rhetorical activities of first ladies are judged by the public, I have selected the public perspective as the primary mode for analyzing Jacqueline Kennedy.

2. For those readers who are not familiar with semiotic analytical techniques or vocabulary, I will argue here that it is a necessary expansion of traditional rhetorical analysis. Because Mrs. Kennedy does not allow for a straightforward text-based analysis of her words, it is crucial to see her as a visual sign who actually signifies Camelot. She stands for, or signifies, the cultural aspects of Camelot. Additionally, as a cultural icon, she is the object that the general population attempts to simulate with regard to style and fashion. Semiotics is the study of signs, hence I will analyze Jacqueline Kennedy as a sign (icon) with communication value when considering the very idea of a first lady. *See* Wendy Leeds-Hurwitz's *Semiotics and Communication* (1993) for an excellent introduction to semiotic methodology.

3. Both the JFK Library and the Oral History Archive at the LBJ Library contain written and spoken materials from Mrs. Kennedy. Interestingly, the LBJ Library interview is available, while much of the oral material at the Kennedy Library is designated to be released to the public at various times, for example, some will not be unsealed until sixty years after her death in 2054. The oral history at the LBJ Library, a copy of which is also available at the JFK Library, is confined to comments about the relationships of the Johnsons and Kennedys. Lewis Gould (1996) reports that Mrs. Kennedy kept no diary. Pierre Salinger quotes Jackie Kennedy Onassis as saying, "I want to live my life, not record it," when asked why she hadn't written a personal memoir (1995, 209).

4. The following biographical sketch is a compilation of cross-checked references from at least eight biographies on Jacqueline Kennedy, including Anthony (1991), Boller

(1998), Caroli (1996), Gould (1996), Gutin (1989), Mills (1999), Thayer (1971), and Truman (1995). Although there are several dozen biographies of Mrs. Kennedy, which vary from the academic to the tawdry, only the works of M.V.R. Thayer and Carl S. Anthony claim cooperation from Mrs. Kennedy.

5. In 1974, Jacqueline (Onassis) and Lee Bouvier published a delightful memoir of their trip entitled *One Special Summer*. It is actually the exact journal that the two of them constructed as a gift to their mother. Jackie created the drawings, poems, and narratives on Rome and Spain, while Lee wrote the journal entries describing the boat trip on the *Queen Elizabeth* and their activities in London, Paris, Venice, Rome, and Florence. This book is a microcosm of the Bouvier style and, importantly, captures the personal style that Jacqueline used throughout her adult life. Prose and poetry are mixed together in witty, highly personal expression. The handwriting is large and dramatic, and drawings are crammed into any free space.

6. The issue of releasing photographs was a difficult one for Mrs. Kennedy. The public adored her children and wanted to see or take photographs. She had press secretary Pierre Salinger schedule photography sessions in the private quarters of the White House to appease the public and control the imagery of the first family.

7. In my view, this quotation sums up the essence of Jacqueline Kennedy. It contains references to all of the things she consistently cared about throughout her life: beauty, history, French literature, her husband, and the legacies left to children.

8. Although CBS was the official network, the program was simultaneously broadcast on CBS and ABC, according to Wolff (1962). Thayer (1971) reports that CBS broadcast the tour on February 14 followed by both NBC and ABC on February 18.

9. At least two people disagree with this assessment of Mrs. Kennedy's performance. Communication professor Mary Ann Watson charges that "any observer with a modicum of objectivity could not deny that she seemed awkward and stilted" (1987, 124). The other cynic, Norman Mailer, whose criticism of Mrs. Kennedy was published in his unkind essay in *Esquire* of July 1962, labeled her a "royal phony." Arthur Schlesinger (1965) reported that Mrs. Kennedy took no offense at Mailer's comments and probably agreed with him!

10. In October of 1997, I flew out of Washington National (now Ronald Reagan International) Airport just as darkness set in. As the plane rose, I looked out of my window and was taken aback to see below me the blackness of Arlington National Cemetery. In the center of the blackness was the eternal flame burning on Kennedy's grave. I spontaneously cried at the sight, remembering clearly the events of 1963, but also recognizing the hopeful symbolism of the flame. I will never forget that image as something that *is* contemporary America.

11. There is also ample evidence that Mrs. Kennedy did a good job as a campaigner during her husband's Senate race in 1958 and again during the presidential bid in 1960. Although she probably would not have put campaigning high on a list of favorite activities, she could do it and may even have enjoyed small doses of campaign activities ("Kennedy's Wife" 1960).

12. No major speeches given. Chronology for ceremonial remarks and interviews that follows was compiled from documentary evidence at the JFK Library and cross-referenced with *The New York Times*.

July 14, 1960　　　　　Press Conference, Hyannis Port, Massachusetts
March 16, 1961　　　　Televised Remarks on National Gallery of Art 20th Birthday

April 11, 1961	Remarks at White House Women's Press Luncheon
May 5, 1961	Opening of Annual Flower Mart, Washington, D.C.
May 10, 1961	Interview with French Television Journalist, M. Crenesse (in French)
June 1, 1961	Press Interview and Receiving Line at U.S. Embassy in Paris
June 20, 1961	National Women's Press Club Dinner, Washington, D.C.
October 27, 1961	Presentation of President's Cup at Washington International Horse Show
December 16, 1961	Greetings at La Morita Agrarian Reform Project, Caracas, Venezuela (in Spanish)
December 17, 1961	Dinner Speech at San Carlos Palace, Bogota, Colombia (in Spanish)
February 14, 1962	Televised White House Tour
March 15, 1962	Presentation of Children's Art Carnival Gift to Indira Ghandi, India
March 21, 1962	Remarks for All-India Radio
March 22, 1962	Shalimar Gardens Speech, Pakistan
March 26, 1962	Farewell Message from Karachi, Pakistan
May 8, 1962	Christening of Submarine U.S.S. Lafayette, Groton, Connecticut
June 21, 1962	Opening of White House Library
June 28, 1962	Opening of White House Treaty Room
June 28, 1962	Ceremony Marking Publication of White House *Guide*
June 30, 1962	Luncheon Address at the Hotel Maria Isabel, Mexico City (in Spanish)
August 23, 1962	Message of Sympathy to Earthquake Victims, Ravello, Italy (broadcast in Italian)
September 11, 1962	Presentation of National Culture Center Model, Newport, Rhode Island
November 29, 1962	Closed-Circuit Broadcast of National Culture Center Benefit, Washington, D.C.
December 29, 1962	Cuban Brigade Speech, Orange Bowl, Miami, Florida (in Spanish)
June 20, 1963	Jacqueline Kennedy Interviews Captain of U.S. Olympic Equestrian Team Recorded at the White House
November 21, 1963	Dinner Speech to League of United Latin American Citizens in Houston, Texas (in Spanish)
January 14, 1964	Televised Thank-You Speech to the Nation Broadcast from Attorney General RFK's Office, Washington, D.C.
May 29, 1964	JFK Memorial Telecast, Hyannis Port, Massachusetts
June 5, 1964	Testimony to Warren Commission
November 17, 1964	Memoir of JFK for *Look* Magazine

13. Although the public wanted to hear all about family and children, the press releases in Pierre Salinger's Papers on file at the JFK Library are all geared toward the White House restoration project and formal White House entertainments such as dinners, teas, concerts, and theatre events. Interestingly, the restoration project press releases were most numerous and are highly detailed regarding expenditures, committee membership, acquisition of pieces, identification of donors, etc. Entertainment press

releases always contained menu, guest list, entertainment program, and a precise description of the flowers in the table arrangements.

References

Accent. 1961. 20th Birthday of National Gallery of Art. JFK Audiovisual Archives Code TNC: 57.

American Opinion in the 20th Century. 1999. *USA Today*, 15 December, 8A.

Anthony, Carl S. 1990. *First Ladies: The Saga of the Presidents' Wives and Their Power, 1789–1961*, Vol. 1. New York: Quill/William Morrow.

———. 1991. *First Ladies: The Saga of the Presidents' Wives and Their Power, 1961–1990*, Vol. 2. New York: Quill/William Morrow.

Baldrige, Letitia, with Rene Verdon. 1998. *In the Kennedy Style: Magical Evenings in the Kennedy White House*. New York: Doubleday.

Barthes, Roland. 1990. *The Fashion System*. Translated by Matthew Ward and Richard Howard. Berkeley, Calif.: University of California Press.

Bauman, Suzanne. 1999. *Jackie: Behind the Myth*. PBS Television, 29 November.

Bergquist, Laura. 1964. A Lonely Summer for Jacqueline. *Look*, 17 November, 36–37.

Blair, W. Granger. 1961. Just an Escort, Kennedy Jokes as Wife's Charm Enchants Paris. *New York Times*, 3 June, A1.

Boller, Paul F., Jr. 1998. *Presidential Wives: An Anecdotal History*. 2nd ed. New York: Oxford University Press.

Bouvier, Jacqueline. 1950. Prix de Paris Essay. Rpt. 1994 in *Vogue*, August, 255, 302.

Bouvier, Jacqueline, and Lee Bouvier. 1974. *One Special Summer*. New York: Delacorte Press.

Bowles, Hamish. 2001. *Jacqueline Kennedy: The White House Years—Selections from the John F. Kennedy Library and Museum*. [Exhibition Catalogue]. New York: The Metropolitan Museum of Art/A Bulfinch Press Book/Little, Brown and Company.

Brenner, Marie. 1994. The Unforgettable Jackie. *Vogue*, August, 246–53, 300–302.

Caroli, Betty Boyd. 1996. Jacqueline Kennedy. In *American First Ladies: Their Lives and Their Legacy*, ed. Lewis L. Gould, 476–95. New York: Garland.

Cassini, Oleg. 1995. *A Thousand Days of Magic: Dressing Jacqueline Kennedy for the White House*. New York: Rizzoli.

Collins, Amy Fine. 1994. JKO. *Harper's Bazaar*, August, 148–51.

Craughwell-Varda, K. 1999. *Looking for Jackie: American Fashion Icons*. New York: Hearst Books/Fair Street-Welcome.

First Ladies: Political Role and Public Image. Washington, D.C.: National Museum of American History.

Folliard, Edward T. 1963. Escorting *Mona Lisa* to America. *National Geographic*, June, 838–47.

Gallup Opinion Presidential Poll. 2000. *CNN Headline News*, 21 February.

Gould, Lewis L. 1996. *American First Ladies: Their Lives and Their Legacy*. New York: Garland.

Graham, Katharine. 1997. *Personal History*. New York: Alfred A. Knopf.

Gray, Paul. 1996. What Price Camelot? *Time*, 6 May, 66–73.

Gutin, Myra G. 1989. *The President's Partner: The First Lady in the Twentieth Century*. New York: Greenwood.

Halberstam, David. 1979. *The Powers That Be*. New York: Alfred A. Knopf.

Interview with French Journalist (M. Crenesse). 1961. Film, 10 May. JFK Audiovisual Archive Code FON 10C.

Invitation to India. 1962. USIS Film. Washington, D.C.: JFK Audiovisual Archive Code USG: 1–10.

Invitation to Pakistan. 1962. USIS Film, 15 min. Washington, D.C.: JFK Audiovisual Archive Code USG: 1–14.

JBK Interviews U.S. Olympic Equestrian Team Captain. 1963. Film, 6 min., 20 June. Washington, D.C.: JFK Audiovisual Archive Code IFP: 200.

Jacqueline Kennedy: The White House Years. 2001. Exhibition, May 1–July 29. New York: Metropolitan Museum of Art.

Jacqueline Kennedy Travels Abroad. 2000. Exhibition, May 27–November 1. Columbia Point, Mass.: John F. Kennedy Library and Museum.

John F. Kennedy Library Website. 1998. *Jacqueline Bouvier Kennedy: First Lady.* www.cs.umb.edu/jfklibrary/jbkexhi.htm, accessed 31 December.

———. 1998. *The Wedding of Jacqueline Lee Bouvier and John Fitzgerald Kennedy.* www.cs.umb.edu/jfklibrary/jbkwed.htm, accessed 31 December.

Kennedy's Wife Finds Campaign Exhilarating. 1960. *New York Times,* 20 April, 29.

Keogh, Pamela Clarke. 2001. *Jackie Style.* New York: HarperCollins.

Klein, Edward. 1996. *All Too Human: The Love Story of Jack and Jackie Kennedy.* New York: Pocket Books.

LBJ Library Telephone Tape Collection. Conversation with Pierre Salinger. December 23, 1963. Tape No. K6312.16, Program No. 5.

LBJ Library Telephone Tape Collection. Conversation with George Reedy. September 2, 1964. Tape No. WH6409.02, Program No. 1.

Leathers, Dale M. 1992. *Successful Nonverbal Communication.* 2nd ed. New York: Macmillan.

Leeds-Hurwitz, Wendy. 1993. *Semiotics and Communication: Signs, Codes, Cultures.* Hillsdale, N.J.: Lawrence Erlbaum Associates.

Magic Moments. 1962. USIS Film, 13 min. JFK Audiovisual Archive Code USG: 1-1.

Mailer, Norman. 1962. An Evening with Jackie Kennedy. *Esquire,* July, 57–61.

Mayo, Edith P., and Denise D. Meringolo. 1994. *First Ladies: Political Role and Public Image.* Washington, D.C.: Smithsonian Institution.

Mills, Jean. 1999. *Moments with Jackie.* New York: MetroBooks.

Moreno, Maria Eugenia. 1962. *Jackie, Mexico: 1962.* N. P. Columbia Point, Mass.: JFK Library.

O' Donnell, Kenneth P., and David F. Powers (with Joe McCarthy). 1970. *"Johnny, We Hardly Knew Ye": Memories of John Fitzgerald Kennedy.* Boston: Little, Brown, and Company.

Office of the Federal Register, National Archives. 1964. *Public Papers of the President: 1963.* Washington, D.C.: United States Government Printing Office.

Onassis, Jacqueline Kennedy. 1974. Interview I with Joe B. Frantz for LBJ Library Oral History, January 11. Transcript available, Library, Columbia Point, Mass.: John Fitzgerald Kennedy Library.

Pogoda, Diane. 1996. Who's Got Style. *Women's Wear Daily,* 8 August, B2.

Salinger, Pierre Papers. n.d. Press Releases from the Office of Assistant Social Secretary for the Press. Columbia Point, Mass.: John Fitzgerald Kennedy Library.

———. 1966. *With Kennedy.* Garden City, N.Y.: Doubleday and Company.

———. 1995. *P. S.: A Memoir.* New York: St. Martin's Press.

Schlesinger, Arthur M., Jr. 1965. *A Thousand Days: John F. Kennedy in the White House*. Boston: Houghton Mifflin Company.

———. 1999. Guest Appearance on *Face the Nation*, CBS Television, July 25.

Sidey, Hugh. 1961. "Everything Must Have a Reason for Being There." *Life*, 1 September, 56–57, 62–65.

———. 1994. Introduction. In *Remembering Jackie: A Life in Pictures*. New York: Warner Books.

Smith, Merriman. 1964. Eyewitness Account. In *Four Days: The Historical Record of the Death of President Kennedy*, edited by United Press International & American Heritage Magazine, 32–33. n.p.: American Heritage Publishing Co.

Thayer, Margaret V. R. 1971. *Jacqueline Kennedy: The White House Years*. Boston: Little, Brown and Company.

Thomas, Helen. 1999. *Front Row at the White House: My Life and Times*. New York: Scribner.

Truman, Margaret. 1995. *First Ladies*. New York: Random House.

United Press International & American Heritage Magazine, eds. 1964. *Four Days: The Historical Record of the Death of President Kennedy*, n.p.: American Heritage Publishing Co.

U.S. Department of State. Top Secret Cipher Telegram. [Letter from Jacqueline Kennedy to Nikita Khrushchev.] L.S. no. 0692061-27. Received from National Archives, October 1999.

Valentino. 2001. Introduction. In *Jackie Style* by Pamela Clarke Keogh. New York: HarperCollins.

Vogue supplement. 1999. "The People in *Vogue*." n.p.

Wang, Whei-Fang. 1987. An Investigation of Fashion Leadership of Princess Diana (English 1981–1985) and Mrs. Jacqueline Kennedy Onassis (American 1961–1965) as Shown in Selected Publications. Unpublished Ph.D. diss., University of North Carolina at Greensboro.

Watson, Mary Ann. 1987. An Enduring Fascination: The Papers of Jacqueline Kennedy. *Prologue* 19, 117–25.

Watson, Robert P. 2000. *The Presidents' Wives: Reassessing the Office of First Lady*. Boulder, Colo.: Lynne Rienner Publishers.

White House Website. 1998. *Jacqueline Lee Bouvier Kennedy Onassis, 1929–1994*. www2.whitehouse.gov./wh/glimpse/firstladies/html/jk35.html, accessed 31 December.

———. 1998. White House Tour. .geocities.com/~new/.htm, accessed 31 December.

White, Theodore. 1963. For President Kennedy: An Epilogue. *Life*, 6 December, n.p.

White, Theodore Papers. 1963. The Camelot Documents, item III-A, dated 19, December: Interview with Jacqueline Kennedy on November 29, 1963. Transcription of Notes (carbon copy) from Columbia Point, Mass.: John Fitzgerald Kennedy Library.

Williams, Jeannie. 1996. Camelot for Sale: Auction Catalog Opens a Window on Jackie's Life. *USA Today*, 8 March, D10.

Wolff, Peter. 1962. *A Tour of the White House with Mrs. John F. Kennedy*. Garden City, N.Y.: Doubleday.

The World of Jacqueline Kennedy. 1962. Film, 56 min. JFK Audiovisual Archive Code TNN: 1.

CHAPTER FOUR

Lady Bird Johnson
The Making of a Public First Lady
with Private Influence

Diana B. Carlin

> The Constitution of the United States does not mention the First Lady. She is elected by one man only. The statute books assign her no duties; and yet, when she gets the job, a podium is there if she cares to use it. I did.
>
> —Lady Bird Johnson

Jacqueline Kennedy's tenure as first lady resulted from her husband's triumph at the polls and began amidst the inaugural glamour that ushered in what was called a new Camelot. Her successor, Claudia Alta (Lady Bird) Taylor Johnson, became first lady at a somber swearing-in ceremony that ushered in an era marked by assassinations, racial tensions, an unpopular war, social unrest, and changing social mores.

In the diary she began the day President John F. Kennedy was assassinated (November 22, 1963), Lady Bird Johnson expressed her sentiments during a time of national tragedy: "I feel I am suddenly onstage for a part I never rehearsed" (Johnson 1970, 16). The reality, however, was that her many years in Washington as the wife of a politically active man who served as a congressional aide, member of Congress, Senate majority leader, and vice president, ultimately made her one of the best-prepared presidential partners. She had been a surrogate campaigner for Jackie Kennedy during the 1960 campaign and had filled in for Mrs. Kennedy at numerous functions since Mrs. Kennedy "frequently refused to appear on ceremonial or political occasions" (Caroli 1987, 236).

Added to her Washington savvy was what her daughter Luci described as "a calm soul who smooths [sic] us down, and makes all of us feel closer together" (Boller 1988, 379). During a time of growing unrest, Lady Bird Johnson not only calmed her family and brought them together but she did the same for the country. She weathered the jeers and signs of protesters, who appeared frequently, and she enthusiastically boarded a whistle-stop campaign train to travel through hostile political territory championing her husband's election and causes that she believed were right. The respect she showed to those who opposed her husband enabled her to fulfill her mission and earned her admiring crowds and standing ovations. She even found time in her demanding schedule during difficult times to embrace a cause of her own and in doing so made us all more aware of the fragility of the environment and our need to be good stewards of the earth.

Margaret Truman asked the question, "Has there been a First Lady who did it all—who was a flawless White House hostess, a loving and protective wife, an astute political partner, and an admired public person in her own right?" Truman answered her own question by noting that "a remarkable consensus of historians, reporters, and average Americans[1] seem to agree that there has been one First Lady who came close: Claudia Alta Taylor Johnson, better known to the world as Lady Bird" (Truman 1995, 169).

Lady Bird Johnson was indeed a first lady well suited for the challenges posed by a changing and tumultuous time. The rise of the rhetorical presidency[2] and the increased presence of television brought with it more demands on first ladies as public figures with a rhetorical role as well as a social one. By the time Mrs. Johnson became first lady, it was becoming more difficult for a presidential partner to avoid the limelight. How first ladies approached their rhetorical roles has differed greatly, as this book illustrates. However, after Lady Bird Johnson it would become more difficult for a Bess Truman or Mamie Eisenhower to occupy the White House. While the public would not want a copresident, as Hillary Rodham Clinton learned, it did expect a first lady to be "a reliable sign of the values or underlying beliefs of her husband" (Campbell 1996, 181). Jackie Kennedy's appointment of the first press secretary for a first lady was a signal that presidential wives would have difficulty *not* making news of their own. Lady Bird Johnson's move to expand the role of her press office and take the first lady from the society page to the front page firmly established the rhetorical presidency as what Karlyn Kohrs Campbell called it: "a two-person career" (180).

Viewing the first lady as a partner in a rhetorical presidency forms the basis for this essay on Lady Bird Johnson. To fully understand Mrs. Johnson's rhetorical activities and legacy, both in terms of defining the role and responsibilities of a modern first lady and in projecting a public agenda, it is important to begin with a brief biography of her life. Her background clearly influenced her values, interests, and rhetorical activities as first lady. Those activities included an active campaign agenda, promotion of her husband's issues, development of her own environmental agenda, and private influence on her husband's decisions and rhetorical activities.

Biography

Claudia Alta Taylor was born on December 22, 1912, in the East Texas town of Karnack. Biographers differ as to when she was given the nickname by which the world came to know her, but they agree on who gave it to her. Somewhere between the time she was an infant and two years of age, a nurse, Alice Tittle, claimed that she was "pretty as a ladybird." The name stuck, and the official White House Historical Society biography of the first ladies notes that, "perhaps the name was prophetic, as there has seldom been a First Lady so attuned to nature and the importance of conserving the environment" (Klapthor 1989, 80).

Her father, Thomas Jefferson Taylor, was a successful and wealthy businessman who operated a general store. Her mother, Minnie Pattillo Taylor, was a native of Alabama who died as the result of an accident when Lady Bird was five. Her mother's unmarried and somewhat sickly sister, Effie, was enlisted to move to Karnack and assist Mr. Taylor and the servants in raising her. Aunt Effie "initiated her niece into the pleasures of literature and nature, [but] she left other areas untouched. 'She never taught me how to dress or dance,' Lady Bird remembered, and her weakness and frailty presented a model of what to avoid, rather than what to attempt" (Caroli 1987, 231). Thus, Lady Bird's father, who showed physical strength and business acumen, became her role model.

Most biographical accounts of her early years indicate that her childhood was lonely and caused her to retreat to nature. According to one biographer, "Her father's money and her mother's absence made her an outsider, the subject of both envy and pity by her friends" (Russell 1999, 68). She came to enjoy quiet, solitary time on Caddo Lake or in fields of flowers.

She was an excellent student throughout elementary school and high school. When the time came for graduation from Marshall High School in 1928, she realized that if she finished in the top two in her class, which she surely would, she would have to give a speech—something she feared greatly. She also thought she might risk the loss of one of her closest friends, Emma Boehringer, who was also in contention for a top spot. She purposely let her grades slip and "prayed if she came in first or second in her class that she would be struck by smallpox" (Russell 1999, 69). Her plan to lower her class ranking did succeed, and she finished in third place by half a point behind Emma and another girl.

Having graduated from high school at the age of fifteen, she was considered by her family to be too young to leave for college. Her goal to leave Karnack, however, took her to her mother's family in Alabama where she enrolled in summer school at the University of Alabama. She missed Texas and her friends, so she decided to return home. The brief stint in Tuscaloosa, however, was something she would use to establish identification with the people of Alabama when she visited the state and university as first lady. When she returned to Karnack she asked to be allowed to accompany another friend to Dallas for two years of junior college at a boarding school, St. Mary's Episcopal School for Girls. Although her father and uncle both opposed the move—her father because it was an unlikely place for her to find a husband and her uncle because he failed to see the value of a college education—she was firm in her decision (Russell 1999, 70). Her father finally agreed and sent her to Dallas in a car of her own with a monthly allowance and charge accounts.

She compiled an excellent academic record at St. Mary's and began working on her shyness in public by playing small roles in the school's theatrical productions. It was during her time at St. Mary's that she converted to the Episcopal faith.

At the conclusion of her junior college years she enrolled at the University of Texas. She received a bachelor of arts degree, majoring in history, in 1933. She took an additional year to earn a journalism degree in 1934, and "perfected her typing and stenographic skills" (Caroli 1987, 231). She aspired to be a newspaper reporter but also had made sure that she had the necessary courses for a teaching certificate. She was prepared for a multitude of possibilities and opportunities. However, the opportunity that presented itself almost immediately after she graduated was marriage.

In September 1934, she met Lyndon Johnson and married him on November 17, 1934, after a whirlwind courtship of seven weeks. The courtship was conducted primarily long distance through mail and phone calls. Lyndon Baines Johnson, four years her senior, was secretary to Congressman Richard Kleberg. A friend introduced Johnson to Lady Bird during one of Johnson's trips back to Texas. Their first date took place at breakfast the day after they were introduced. Johnson, who had decided immediately upon meeting her that Lady Bird was special, used the breakfast to tell his life's story—including his financial status down to the size of his life insurance policy. Lady Bird told an interviewer when she was first lady that the encounter left her knowing "I had met something remarkable, but I didn't know quite what" (Janeway 1964, 64). When Johnson returned to Texas intent on leaving only with Lady Bird beside him as his wife, he had support from her father and eventually a willing bride.

After a brief honeymoon, Lady Bird found herself in Washington embarking on a fast-track political education that would serve her for the rest of her life. Her life centered on Lyndon and his political friends, who showed up at their apartment usually unannounced and expecting a meal. She learned how to cook and to budget his salary to cover their expenses and save money as well. And while she attended to the domestic sphere, she learned the intricacies of politics by listening and observing.

Three years after their marriage, a congressional seat opened in Texas when a congressman died. Lyndon decided to run. Lady Bird entered the fray with him and exhibited for the first time the political savvy and quiet, behind-the-scenes influence that would be instrumental in Johnson's successful political career. She visited Alvin Wirtz, a former state senator, attorney, and political insider, for advice. She wanted to know what Lyndon's chances were for winning and what it would take to lodge a successful campaign.

Wirtz gave her an honest assessment and a dollar amount that would help launch a campaign to create the necessary name recognition he needed. She then called her father and asked for a $10,000 campaign loan from her inheritance from her mother. Her father, who did not like politics and thought the amount was too much, finally consented. The money was in the bank the next day, and Johnson was the first to announce in the special election. Johnson campaigned tirelessly, and while Lady Bird "criticized herself for being too timid to get out and campaign with him" (an activity that was not expected of wives at the time), she "pushed herself to work harder behind the scenes" (Russell 1999, 131). When

Johnson had an emergency appendectomy two days before the election, Lady Bird was with him, but she spent election day making phone calls to get out the vote. He won the election, and their political partnership was firmly launched.

The role that Lady Bird played in the partnership grew with the start of World War II. Johnson volunteered for active duty in the navy immediately after the attack on Pearl Harbor. For the eight months her husband was on active duty, Lady Bird managed his congressional office without compensation. He wanted her in charge instead of one of his aides because she had "the authority of his name" (Russell 1999, 135). Such recognition of the surrogate role a political wife could play was atypical. This was an era in which wives usually remained in the background of everyday politics or at best at their husbands' sides smiling, waving, and saying little.

The experience of running the congressional office gave Lady Bird a firsthand view of what was expected of an officeholder and an appreciation for the need to be at the service of constituents. The experience caused her to become more involved in meeting with constituents, talking with them, and taking them on tours of Washington sites. In the process, she gained valuable information for her husband about what was happening back home.

Lady Bird learned the ways of Washington and Capitol Hill society early on as a congressional wife. She participated in a ritual of the times that required congressional wives to make official calls on other wives. Mrs. Johnson described the practice as being "like a business" in which the wife was equipped with her personal calling cards and those of her husband.

> On Mondays, she called on the wives of the Supreme Court justices. On Tuesdays, she went to visit other congressional wives. Wednesdays were reserved for cabinet wives. Thursdays for the Senate wives, and Fridays for the Diplomatic Corps. She went to the White House whenever invited. (Russell 1999, 134)

She did this because it was expected, but her shyness caused her, as she indicated in interviews later, to hope the women weren't in so that all she had to do was leave her calling card for the wife and Johnson's for the husband (Russell 1999, 134).

Her tenure in Johnson's office, however, gave her confidence that she could do things on her own, and made her aware of the need for income beyond a congressional salary to advance LBJ's career. She looked for a way to invest the inheritance from her mother and uncle to secure their financial and political futures. In late 1942, using part of her resources and an additional loan, Lady Bird bought a bankrupt Austin radio station. It became the foundation for a family broadcasting business that made her a multimillionaire. Neither the initial purchase nor the expansion of the business into television came without controversy, however. There was a political battle for the license that included a conservative Austin newspaper owner who was a vocal opponent of President Roosevelt. FCC Chairman James Fly, a fellow Texan and FDR supporter, blocked the application and opened the way for Lady Bird's successful rival bid. Including only Lady Bird's name on the licenses finessed conflict of interest charges, but, understandably, questions were raised. When Lady Bird applied for a license for a television station in Austin several years later, she was the only applicant. This fact raised some eyebrows over the years, but biographers and observers point to no clear evidence that federal agencies favored the Johnsons. The best explanation that was given for the lack of competition was simply that when word got out that the senator's wife was applying, no one else decided to challenge (Caroli 1987, 234).

After the purchase of the radio station, Lady Bird spent time in Texas hiring a staff and overseeing daily operations. She maintained oversight through close communication with the staff and visits to Austin. She also claimed that LBJ took an active interest in the business and that she did not build the empire alone. Giving recognition to her husband was important for Lady Bird. According to biographer Russell, "Lady Bird invested her time and money in helping to create a grand persona for LBJ. She helped build his reputation as a great man, a Texas rancher, a wealthy businessman, as well as a member of Congress—someone worthy of the whole nation's leadership" (1999, 143).

Although much went well for the Johnsons, their lives were not without setbacks, disappointments, rumors, and challenges. In 1941, Lyndon waged an unsuccessful race for a Senate seat. Lady Bird suffered a series of miscarriages before finally giving birth to their first child, Lynda Bird in 1944, and Lucy (later changed to Luci) Baines in 1947. When Johnson suffered a heart attack while serving as majority leader in the Senate in 1955, Lady Bird once again found herself overseeing the office until his return. The heart attack was a reminder to Johnson of his mortality and also made him realize how important Lady Bird was to him. The significance of the role she played in being by his side during recovery and also overseeing his office again was made greater by the fact that rumors of his unfaithfulness were prevalent throughout much of their marriage.

Lyndon was a demanding husband who was known to criticize his wife's clothes or makeup in public and even to embarrass her with his often-crude manner. She tolerated the negative side of his personality with dignity publicly and showed devotion and loyalty to him both publicly and privately. Her behavior spoke volumes about her shared vision of the significant and historical role he could and would play as a public official and her own view of a wife's duty. In an interview in *American Heritage*, she acknowledged that her traditional view of a wife might have been unacceptable to some, but she adopted a traditional role because "I really wanted to serve my husband and serve the country, and if that sounds—geesy, well . . ." (Klaw 1980, 7).

Lady Bird balanced dedication to her husband, children, and country as LBJ's career continued its ascent in 1948, during his successful campaign for the U.S. Senate. Even with small children to care for and a broadcasting business to run, Lady Bird was determined to find ways to extend her role in Johnson's campaign and do more than she had in 1941. She found someone to help with management of the business and worked from her home to organize a women's division for the campaign. She sat in on strategy sessions and made her first campaign speeches. She worked the main streets of towns throughout Texas. "She enlisted the services of friends and former high school and college classmates, arranged teas for her husband in the little towns they visited together, went over speeches with him and suggested phrases to use in them" (Boller 1988, 384). As she had done in his first campaign in 1937, she also organized the get out the vote activities in the waning hours of the campaign.

Initial vote counts had Johnson's opponent, former Texas governor Coke Stevenson, ahead by a slight margin. Johnson eventually won the election by a highly suspicious eighty-seven-vote margin achieved from one ballot box in South Texas. The count was challenged by his opponent but was upheld in the courts.

Johnson's election to the Senate and his growing prominence later as majority leader set him up for a presidential race in 1960. While he had given some thought to retiring from political life after his Senate term ended, he decided to make a run for the ultimate political office and challenge. When LBJ failed to get the nomination and then accepted the second position on the ballot with John F. Kennedy, Lady Bird's political life took another major step.

Although she had taken a more public role in LBJ's Senate campaigns, most of her work was still confined to a support function. In 1960, she knew she would have to expand her public role. Because Jackie Kennedy was pregnant with John F. Kennedy Jr. and had to restrict her campaign activities, Lady Bird was called upon both to campaign as the vice presidential candidate's spouse and to assist the Kennedy women in organizing and waging their own campaign. She introduced the president's mother, sister Eunice, and sister-in-law Ethel to Texas politics at a tea in Houston. Given the importance of Texas and the Kennedy's East Coast roots and Catholic faith, Lady Bird's efforts were instrumental in helping to win over Texas women's votes. She also worked with the Kennedy campaign to fill in for Jackie when needed.

Soon after the Los Angeles nominating convention and at the age of 48, she decided to take a speech course to help her meet the demands of the campaign. It was a wise decision. During the campaign she traveled 35,000 miles. She made 16 campaign appearances in 11 states on her own and accompanied her husband on 150 stops. She traveled a total of 35,000 miles in two months.

Her second wise decision was to hire Liz Carpenter, a Texan who co-owned a Texas newspaper chain and a Washington news bureau, to assist her with the press and her part of the campaign. Carpenter would later serve as Mrs. Johnson's press secretary and chief of staff in the White House. It was Carpenter's advice two weeks after Lady Bird became first lady that helped her create the rapport with the media that enabled her to succeed in getting the media's coverage and cooperation to promote her causes. Carpenter advised Mrs. Johnson that the media's request in her dealings with them was simple: "'Be Available' and 'Never Lie—tell us you can't tell us, but never lie'" (Johnson 1970, 15). She followed the advice assiduously, and the results quickly became apparent as she garnered her own political coverage and compliments from the Washington press corps.

During the vice presidential years, Lady Bird was often called on to pinch-hit for Jackie Kennedy who disdained most aspects of political life. Anything Jackie Kennedy did not want to do would be given to her social secretary, Letitia Baldrige, with the instructions: "Give them to Lady Bird" (Russell 1999, 210). In her first year as second lady, Lady Bird substituted for Mrs. Kennedy at fifty official events along with keeping her own schedule.

When the Kennedy assassination thrust the position of first lady upon her, Lady Bird instinctively knew what to do even as she expressed doubts about her preparation. The entry for November 23, 1963, in A White House Diary shows a woman whose primary concern was "the million and one things to be done—just the simple things that are part of going on living, if one is among those who are going to go on living. Lyndon will be wrestling with the very big business of making the country go on living" (Johnson 1970, 8).

As first lady, Mrs. Johnson also followed the advice former president Harry Truman gave her when the two of them attended the funeral for King Paul of Greece. She asked him, "What is the best thing a wife can do for her husband in the White House?" to which Truman replied, "Protect him. Don't let people use you. If people bring you some sort of proposition they want you to talk to the President about, it's all right to tell him, but if you have doubts about them be sure and tell him that" (Johnson 1970, 83).

Lady Bird did not hesitate to voice her opinion about any issue her husband addressed, as is evident in her diary, papers, and biographies of her life. Perhaps her adherence to Truman's advice was best seen in her taking charge of a highly volatile situation during the 1964 campaign. Johnson's longtime friend and aide, Walter Jenkins, was arrested on a morals charge. As the incident became public, LBJ listened to advisors who told him to ask for Jenkins' resignation and distance himself from him. Johnson was in New York where he had a full schedule of speeches when he learned of the problem. He consulted his advisors and mulled over his options. He orchestrated what needed to be done to bring about Jenkins' resignation; he removed his personal and business files that were in Jenkins' keeping, and he helped create a new position in Texas for Jenkins.

Lady Bird, however, disagreed with the advice to put politics above loyalty to friends and expose Jenkins to more public embarrassment and scrutiny than she thought was necessary. She swung into action to diffuse the potentially explosive political and personal situation. She and Liz Carpenter penned a three-sentence statement supporting Jenkins and delivered it to the media—a group that included many Jenkins supporters. The statement read: "My heart is aching today for someone who has reached the point of exhaustion in dedicated service to his country. Walter Jenkins has been carrying incredible hours and burdens since President Kennedy's assassination. He is now receiving the medical attention he needs" (Russell 1999, 268). The approach worked and the story died quickly with no damage to the president and his campaign.

Throughout the entire diary one finds evidence of a woman who balanced concerns about her husband's health—physical, emotional, and political—and her desire for the family to live as normal a life as possible with the demands of her multifaceted position. She saw her official role as contributing to what it took for everyone to go on living, and "living" required her to be a "participant in 718 different ceremonial activities [that comprised an estimated] . . . 75 percent or more of her time on official duties" (Gutin 1989, 118–19).

Nancy Kegan Smith who worked as an archivist at the Johnson Library and dealt with Mrs. Johnson's papers best summarizes the extent of her activities as first lady:

> She gave over 164 speeches. She founded and chaired the First Lady's Committee for a More Beautiful Nation's Capital, served as the honorary chairman of the Project Head Start program, was a member of the Committee for the Preservation of the White House, and acted as the president's representative on the committee responsible for the planning and building of the Johnson Library. She established and hosted the Women Doer Luncheons [a series of 16 luncheons to highlight women's achievements] and presided over countless White House dinners, teas, luncheons, receptions, tours, and presentations. To highlight President Johnson's "See the U.S.A." program and while accompanying her husband on foreign visits, she traveled hundreds of thousands of miles. (1989, 111)

After leaving the White House in 1969, the Johnsons returned to Texas. Lady Bird worked on her book, A *White House Diary*, which was published in 1970. She continued to assist her husband in his postpresidential pursuits until his death in 1973. She was instrumental in helping plan the Lyndon Baines Johnson Library in Austin. She founded the National Wildflower Research Center in 1982, and served as a trustee on the board of the National Geographic Society. She also returned to active involvement in the family business from which she retired in 1996, giving way to daughter Luci's management. At the turn of the century and the start of a new millennium, she was nearing ninety. She continued to live on the family ranch where LBJ is buried and to devote time to her family and to the environmental causes that were born out of her youthful need to embrace nature as a way to go on living.

Rhetorical Activities as First Lady

The increased attention to the role of first lady in recent years has resulted in numerous books about the evolution and current status of the position.[3] In reading any of these books, one point becomes immediately clear: since Martha Washington, every first lady has, in her own way, exerted influence on both the position of first lady and on the man to whom she was married. There is no denying that occupants of the White House share a unique kind of partnership, with some first ladies in the background as silent partners influencing the president quietly or concentrating on the hostess role. Others are seen as independent spokeswomen for their own causes, as openly influencing their husbands, or as making their own views on issues publicly known whether they are in concert with his or not.

Karlyn Kohrs Campbell (citing the work of sociologist Hanna Papanek on careers that place "institutional demands on a married couple") argued that the presidency epitomizes a "two-person career" or one that "precludes a traditional public–private spousal division of labor and requires their cooperative efforts if it is to be pursued successfully." As such, Campbell claimed that "the First Ladyship is a vital part of the presidency," worthy of study by presidential scholars, and that first ladies' rhetoric provides insight into how their enactment of the role contributes to the institution of the presidency (1996, 180).

Historian Carl Anthony noted that soon after becoming first lady, Lady Bird's staff "sent out a statement of her 'duties' and though 'hostess' was first, it listed a primary one as 'advancement of the President's programs'" (1991, 110). Mrs. Johnson told Liz Carpenter when she hired her as press secretary for the 1960 campaign that she wanted to be a "doer" not a "talker" (Russell 1999, 191), and she reaffirmed that commitment as first lady. However, doers require talk or rhetoric to accomplish what they want to do, and the act of "doing" itself has symbolic power. Lady Bird Johnson knew that better than most. Thus, her tenure as first lady was marked, as noted previously, by a heavy speaking schedule, committee work, travel with and on behalf of her husband, and social events with a political purpose. Her "doings," which included activities such as visiting poverty-stricken parts of the country to highlight her husband's War on Poverty or Head Start program were also intended to open the eyes and minds of Americans about the problems facing the country so that they would act also (Anthony 1991, 110). The rhetorical nature of her "doings" is indisputable, as is their direct relationship to her husband's goals.

Based on an acceptance of the argument that the presidency is a two-person career and that a study of a first lady's rhetoric provides insights into a presidency, Lady Bird Johnson's rhetorical activities are examined to determine how they enhanced Lyndon Johnson's presidency and furthered the development of the role of first lady. Terlip (1986) identified seven criteria that are commonly used by critics and the public to evaluate a wife's effectiveness as a political partner. They are: (1) she conveys support of her husband's positions and activities, but also demonstrates independence and strength; (2) she influences her husband, but doesn't actually affect his policies or positions; (3) she addresses issues, especially "women's issues," but not in a way that makes her more expert than he is; (4) she is both a traditional and a modern woman; (5) she selects an appropriate cause; (6) she has a good relationship with the press; and (7) she is careful about discussing personal problems. These criteria are considered in analyzing Mrs. Johnson's rhetoric and legacy.

Given the extent of Lady Bird's rhetorical activities, it is impossible in a single chapter to do justice to the length and breadth of her achievements as first lady. As a means of providing representative examples of how her rhetoric enhanced her husband's presidency, this section examines her campaign rhetoric during the 1964 whistle-stop tour, her beautification campaign, and her behind-the-scenes influence on her husband's rhetoric.

The 1964 Whistle-Stop Campaign

Abigail McCarthy, who was married to Senator Eugene McCarthy, reflected on her campaign experiences and noted, "A candidate's wife making a speech is, by the very nature of things, at a terrible disadvantage. . . . It is only a very dull woman who is unaware of the speculative curiosity mixed with hostility with which her every platform appearance is greeted" (McCarthy 1972, 5). Lady Bird Johnson was anything but a dull woman and knew that she could be an asset to her husband if she took risks to break out of the traditional role of observer and take to the platform. As noted previously, Lady Bird learned to control her fear of public speaking and began taking an active part as a campaigner in the 1948 Senate campaign. After the 1960 campaign, she was a seasoned veteran who was ready to face both the cheers and jeers that greeted both her and her husband during a tumultuous period of American history.

A political wife giving a speech does face a difficult rhetorical situation, as McCarthy observed. The wife simultaneously creates an identity for both herself and her husband. She asks audiences to identify with her as a means of identifying with her husband. Her credibility is affected by her husband's, and she, in turn, can enhance or hurt his. In essence, "her every word is scrutinized in the belief that she is a reliable sign of the values or underlying beliefs of her husband. Accordingly, she becomes a lightning rod for discontent with his administration or opposition to its stands on particular issues" (Campbell 1996, 181).

Given these realities, the task that Lady Bird Johnson undertook in the 1964 campaign was one of the most difficult assigned to any first lady—her own whistle-stop campaign tour. In a memorandum to President Johnson on August 18, 1964, presidential staffer, Douglass Cater, commented on Mrs. Johnson's appearances in several western states and provided the arguments for having her campaign independently:

> Mrs. Johnson represents a political asset for the campaign, which is unique in Presidential history. She is highly appealing and effective on the platform. She comes across as intelligent and knowledgeable and *unlike* Eleanor Roosevelt thoroughly feminine. She maintains grace under the most hectic conditions. Politicians and reporters alike felt she would be more sought after than the Vice Presidential nominee for many occasions. The consensus was that she should make a number of treks apart from you—that she could give extra push in critical states, visiting communities that lie outside the Presidential circuit. (Cater 1964, 1)

Of all the country, the one region that was eventually determined to be outside the presidential circuit was the South. Passage of the 1964 Civil Rights Act under the leadership of a Democrat president from the South, made it nearly impossible for either Lyndon Johnson or his running mate, Hubert Humphrey to visit the South and "get in and out . . . with their hide on—or they couldn't take the time to visit because it was a lost cause" (Carpenter 1970, 145). The South, however, could not be ignored and holding ground was a crucial part of the strategy. In the end, half of the South held for the Johnson–Humphrey ticket, and Lady Bird's whistle-stop campaign was credited with helping.

Between October 6 and October 9, the nineteen-car Lady Bird Special carried 300 passengers including media, staff, supporters, Southern political wives, and the Johnson daughters. It traveled 1682 miles with 47 stops and 4 "slow downs." The trip was carefully planned with input from the president and first lady regarding the stops. Topics were suggested by staffers, including one that would associate her with an issue that was commonly considered a "women's issue" but held the key to the South's future—education. The memo noted, "She would be a natural talking about education . . . TVA was FDR's dream for the South. Education can be the new dream and the ingredients are already at hand" ("Whistle-Stop" 1964, 1)

Mrs. Johnson personally called southern governors and members of Congress to invite them to be on the train with her when she arrived in their states. Many of them provided feeble excuses, such as a hunting trip that could not be canceled, to avoid being seen with anyone close to the administration. She persevered, however, and found enough high-profile supporters to lend credibility to her message.

From the first stop in Alexandria, Virginia, to the last stop in New Orleans, Lady Bird gave speeches that showed pride in her southern roots, acknowledged her locale, recalled great southerners and their accomplishments, called on her audiences to find those things that unify Americans, and asked her fellow southerners to accept the new law and their responsibility in ensuring equal rights for all of us.

The words were largely hers and represented what she called "a journey of the heart." In notes she dictated while preparing for the trip, she acknowledged that her feelings "may not always be politic or wise ones. Some thread of this, however, will have to bind together whatever I say . . . or else it won't be natural" ("Whistle-Stop" 1964, Folder 3). Many of the random thoughts in her memorandum appeared almost verbatim in each of the speeches to explain why she was there and what she expected of all Americans. This excerpt from the first stop in Alexandria set the tone and the theme:

> I want to tell you from Alexandria to New Orleans that to this President and his wife the South is a respected and valued and beloved part of the country. I know that many of you do not agree with the Civil Rights Bill or the President's support of it, but I do know the South respects candor and courage and I believe he has shown both. It would be a bottomless tragedy for our country to be racially divided and here I want to say emphatically, this is not a challenge only in the South. It is a national challenge—in the big cities of the North as in the South. (Smith 1989, 115)

With those words she sought to identify with her audience and to show that their values were her husband's. She showed support for her husband but also demonstrated her own convictions by taking on a challenge that was even too big for the president. She assuaged any feelings southerners might have that they were being singled out for blame by identifying the racial divide as a national problem, not a southern one.

At every stop she made a comment about the locale and local politicians and related personal connections to the location to establish identification. This opening in Valdosta, Georgia, illustrates her strategy:

> I understand from Mrs. Sanders, the wife of your governor, that this is a fisherman's paradise. I just hope I can come back some leisurely time and try it.
>
> This is a campaign visit, but it is also a sentimental journey. From the time I was six until I was twenty-one, my summer times were spent in Alabama with side trips to Georgia. Georgia strains run strong in my family and my husband's family—his great grandfather, Jesse Johnson, came from Oglethorpe County. (Johnson 1964b, 1)

In developing the substance of the speeches, Mrs. Johnson did not attempt to show her expertise on the issues of race, education, or other localized topics. She accomplished her goal of representing her husband and not influencing him or representing her own views by framing the issues within a value system representative of the South and her husband. This allowed her to make a subtle argument that LBJ's positions were a natural outgrowth of him as a person—a southerner who had his home region's needs and best interests at heart.

Later in her speeches, she attempted to transcend the issue of the legislation itself by looking at the larger issue of the nation, its future, and the important role the South would play:

> I'm even more proud of the new South, the spirit of growth, advances in the economy and progress in education, and I share the irritation when unthinking people make snide jokes about us. None of this is right. None of this is good for the future of our country. We must search for the ties that bind us together, not settle for the tensions that tend to divide us. (Carpenter 1970, 156)

Throughout the four days, the spirit of the South was exhibited in one small town after another. High school bands played, signs waved, crowds cheered, as plastic train whistles, paper engineer hats, and saltwater taffy were distributed from the train to the crowds that grew larger with each stop. The media coverage intensified interest in the campaign and helped demonstrate the strength of a soft-spoken daughter of the South when some crowds inevitably turned ugly.

In Columbia, South Carolina, a group of hecklers yelled out "We Want Barry! We Want Barry!" as soon as the governor finished his introduction of Lady Bird. She waited, then she calmly raised a hand and said, "My friends, in this country we are entitled to many viewpoints. You are entitled to yours. But right now, I'm entitled to mine" (Carpenter 1970, 162). That quieted the crowd, and the film of the incident that aired on the evening news caused the Goldwater camp to denounce the tactics. The belief that it would be difficult to attack a southern woman in the South where women are respected, if not revered, proved correct. Southern chivalry was not dead and was evidenced as more male political leaders joined the train and praised Lady Bird and Lyndon.

The steel magnolia, who showed courage under fire and respect for a dissenting opinion, found a way to make the crowds listen and the message did get through. A reporter asked one man at a stop in Charleston, South Carolina, about his candidate preference, and he replied, "Johnson, because I'd rather stand beside a Negro in a factory than stand behind a white man in the soup line" (Carpenter 1970, 163).

At the final stop of the tour, a buoyant Mrs. Johnson expressed her belief that the trip had been a success:

> Eight states, sixteen hundred miles, and 47 speeches ago, when we left Alexandria, I said that this was a journey of the heart. And truly it has been that. . . . This was, however, not only a sentimental journey, but also a political trip. I came because I wanted to say that for this President and his wife, we appreciate you, and we care about you, and we have faith in you.
>
> We have too much respect for the South to take it for granted and too much closeness to it to ignore it.
>
> I am aware that there are those who would exploit its past troubles to their own advantage. But I do not believe that the majority of the South wants any part of the old bitterness. And the more I have seen these past few days, the more I know that is true. (Johnson 1964c, 1)

By the time the Lady Bird Special reached its final stop in New Orleans, to be joined by the president, the atmosphere was such that Lyndon Johnson could build on what his wife had done and give a speech from his heart as well to end the journey. In a departure from his prepared text, Johnson hit the race issue head-on and redefined civil rights into something other than a "Negro" issue. In a folksy manner reminiscent of his early campaigns, he rolled up his sleeves and told a story about a southern politician at the end of his career who bemoaned:

> I wish I felt a little better. I would like to go back home and make 'em one more Democratic speech. I feel like I have just one more in me. The poor old state. They haven't heard a Democratic speech in thirty years. All they ever hear at election time is nigger, nigger, nigger!
>
> After gasps and then applause led by the Blacks in the crowd, Johnson said in his own voice: "There is only one real problem that faces you. It isn't an economic problem. It isn't a Negro problem. It's whether you're going to live or die!" (Carpenter 1970, 170)

Without Lady Bird leading the way, Johnson would not have been in New Orleans to make such a pronouncement. A newspaper story illustrated the partnership that was the whistle-stop tour, the larger campaign, the Johnsons' political lives, and the Johnson presidency: "Together, the President and the First Lady made an assault on the heart and the mind of the South that must be the most remarkable joint campaign effort in American political history" (Carpenter 1970, 170).

The Beautification Campaign

While Lady Bird Johnson's whistle-stop tour during the 1964 campaign signified a major shift in the role a first lady would play in the public sphere, the rhetorical activities for which she is best known are those related to the environment and her beautification program. Given the scope of her environmental advocacy, only a cursory treatment is provided here. Lewis L. Gould's *Lady Bird Johnson and the Environment* (1988) and *Lady Bird Johnson: Our Environmental First Lady* (1999) provide a thorough study of Mrs. Johnson's beautification and environmental activities. Given the availability and extensiveness of Gould's work, this analysis concentrates on the strategies she used in promoting the issues and how they demonstrate the Johnsons' political partnership and complementary agendas.

Lady Bird's decision to adopt a cause was made soon after the 1964 election was over. The choice of the environment and beautification was one that evolved gradually and naturally out of a series of events in which she and the president participated in his early months in office and during the 1964 campaign.[4] Selection of the environment and beautification was strategic rhetorically in and of itself.

It was a comfortable topic for Lady Bird since her affection for wildflowers and nature began during her youth in Texas. Thus, it was not just something that was selected for public relations or publicity purposes. The timing of the choice was also excellent. Lady Bird became first lady when environmental issues were gaining attention through books such as Rachel Carson's 1962, *Silent Spring*, which called attention to the environmental harms of pesticides. It was also a time when the city of Washington needed a major face-lift.

The environment could be viewed as a natural issue for a political wife—it merged the more traditional domestic sphere interests of a political wife with policy initiatives. Gould noted, "When Lady Bird Johnson launched her campaign for natural beauty in 1964–65, she was taking her place among other female advocates of the environment in the United States who had been a positive force in improving the quality of the nation's life since the late nineteenth century" (1988, 1). Among the women Gould discussed in his book were those who led beautification programs of major cities. She could be an advocate in a very public sense without appearing to directly take on a "presidential" issue. Finally, it was an issue of concern to LBJ and one that related to initiatives such as his Great Society program, the "See the USA" tourism promotion to keep U.S. dollars in the country, and the broader environmental agenda that began surfacing soon after he was elected.

The way that Lady Bird developed her campaign demonstrated her adept organizational and rhetorical skills. She wrote in her diary, "How many things are launched in the name of a tea!" (Johnson 1970, 240). Her beautification program began with meetings at the Texas ranch and with teas and social gatherings at the White House designed to enlist the key people she needed to provide the political and financial clout to make her projects work.

She sought advice from many sources on the scope and content of her project. "Lady Bird Johnson rarely limited herself to one set of advisors or to one line of action" with the result being a decision to start with a beautification campaign for Washington, D.C., that would relate to her husband's Great Society goals of improving the overall quality of life. She would chair a committee to give awards for preservation and beautification of cities, and she would promote initiatives to remove unsightly junkyards and billboards from the nation's highways to better highlight the country's natural beauty (Gould 1988, 52–54).

It was also decided that her efforts in Washington, D.C., would combine public and private funds and would involve all interest groups as well as environmental experts. She provided opportunity for input and shared ownership from the beginning. Without widespread support and cooperation, she would not have succeeded. Once all of the decisions were made and her plan was in place, she went public through an interview in *U.S. News and World Report*. The result of her Washington, D.C. project and the national publicity she received was a nationwide campaign to improve the quality of cities and the landscape nationally.

One of the major problems with the campaign was the name itself—"beautification"—which was seen by some as "superficial" and "cosmetic" (Gould 1988, 64). Mrs. Johnson, however, dealt with the criticisms head on. Through her speeches, she defined what she meant, demonstrated the impact of the issue on everyone in a community, provided examples of legal and public policy actions related to her cause, and challenged her listeners—regardless of their professions—to acknowledge the relationship of the environment to their own lives. She elevated the issue of beautification to something that was not cosmetic but had major public policy, economic, and social implications.

A speech at the Yale Political Union in 1967, illustrates how she recast the issue:

> The word "beautification" doesn't really convey the full sweep of the concept. It embraces all of these questions:
>   How can we rebuild the core of our cities?
>   How can we create new towns, pleasant and functional?
>   How can we bring order rather than chaos out of our highways and transit systems?
>   How can we provide parks and open space to let our cities breathe and our people relax?
>   How can we control the waste we pour into our air and water?
>   To me, in sum, "beautification" means our total concern for the physical and human quality of the world we pass on to our children. (Johnson 1967)

While she continued to have her critics and detractors even with clarifications such as these, she had a major impact in Washington, D.C., and nationally.

In Washington, D.C., millions of bulbs, flowering plants, and shrubs were planted. Trees and shrubs were trimmed. Statues were scrubbed, schools were cleaned up, and recreation areas were installed in the inner city. To honor her efforts, her committee arranged to have a million daffodils and twenty-five hundred dogwood trees planted in an area on Colombia Island, on the route to Reagan National Airport. The area was named "Lady Bird Johnson Park" (Anthony 1991, 160), and the results can still be seen today.

Nationally, individuals and organizations embraced the cause. "Civic groups long advocating similar themes hitched themselves to her work. Lady Bird was pitted against "Litter Bug" when—as a tribute to her—Keep America Beautiful, Inc., sent out one thousand informational packages to state and local officials suggesting community programs and role models" (Anthony 1988, 133). Thousands of letters poured into the White House offering support and advice, and she received more speaking invitations throughout the country than her schedule could accommodate. She logged over 100,000 miles on behalf of her cause. Her efforts to promote U.S. tourism, especially in the national parks, resulted in increased numbers of tourists, including a tripling of visitors at Big Bend Park (Anthony 1988, 134).

The public support and interest in the campaign prompted Lady Bird to work with the West Wing to introduce legislation, the Highway Beautification Bill. Through a combination of her charm and her husband's well-honed skills in pushing through legislation, the bill became law. She did incur criticism along the way from Republicans in the Congress, such as Kansas senator Robert Dole, who questioned the appropriateness of Lady Bird's activism (Russell 1999, 279). Opposition also came from many small businesses that relied on billboard advertising, and she even took on the Defense Department's billboards. But she was unrelenting in her advocacy and weathered the political cartoons and other slings and arrows. After the legislative victory, she returned to public appeals for support and refrained from further congressional lobbying.

In the course of promoting her environmental cause, Lady Bird recognized that "the environment, after all, is where we all meet; where we all have a mutual interest; it is one thing that all of us share. It is not only a mirror of ourselves, but a focusing lens on what we can become" (Johnson, 1967, 5). Just as she understood the importance of creating identification during her whistle-stop tour, she also recognized the role identification could play in her advocacy for environmental issues that went far beyond simply planting flowers and cleaning up neighborhoods. She spoke to the need to find answers to questions that "will reveal our quality as a civilization" and that she anticipated would be answered "in the next two decades" (Johnson 1967, 5). Twenty years after Lady Bird embraced the environment as her "cause" she very likely considered herself a success in light of Earth Day celebrations, less litter on highways, community recycling projects, the establishment of an Environmental Protection Agency, and clean air and water legislation. All of these would, most likely, have come into existence without Lady Bird Johnson, but no movement succeeds without some degree of consciousness raising by those who have access to a bully pulpit and know how to use it to motivate others.

Private Influence

According to Margaret Truman, Lady Bird Johnson was "an implementer, an embellisher and translator of her husband's ideas" (Truman 1995, 179). Often those actions occurred outside of the public eye. As a political advisor to LBJ, she furthered her husband's agenda and influenced his decisions and actions. Carl Anthony described her as "her president's political partner" (Anthony 1991, 114) and quoted an academic, Eric Goldman, who was "hired to advise and observe the administration" as indicating that LJB respected the "'judgment of his wife in all matters'" and "'talked politics, all aspects of it, on a basis of equality.'"

The 1964 campaign provides several important representative examples of Lady Bird's role as an advisor and her influence on LBJ throughout his career. In 1964, she played an important role in his decision to run, his acceptance of the nomination, and his handling of a controversy at the convention.

Soon after becoming president, LBJ had to decide if he would run in 1964. Knowing that the years ahead would be difficult, he engaged in serious soul-searching about what was best for the country, his family, and himself. In May, as the president neared a decision, Lady Bird consulted with two physicians who were going to examine the president to determine his physical and emotional readiness for a campaign and a potentially difficult four-year term. While she waited for them to arrive at a friend's home in Virginia where she was visiting, she wrote, "a nine-page analysis of what I thought his situation was. First, in case he definitely decided that he wanted to use it, there was a suggested announcement that he wasn't going to run again. . . . I hope he won't use it—that's that! Then I put down the alternatives" (Johnson 1970, 138). The alternatives included a frank discussion of what they all would face—both the opportunity for triumph and its satisfaction and the pain of failure and hostility. She stated her belief that he would win and made a realistic assessment of a life for him without politics and power. She asked the two physicians to deliver it to him and then met with them to discuss "the possibilities for Lyndon" (Johnson 1970, 140). In drafting the analysis, she exhibited an understanding of what drove Lyndon Johnson and also what demons he had to conquer to continue. Only she could have written such a candid analysis and given him the freedom to make the choice he ultimately made.

Three months later, Lady Bird discovered that her husband was still haunted by self-doubts. After the opening of the 1964 Democratic National Convention on August 25, 1964, Lyndon Johnson considered withdrawing his name as the party's nominee. While he had brought the nation through a difficult period following the Kennedy assassination, he questioned his suitability to lead the country at that point in its history. He drafted a withdrawal statement and shared it with Lady Bird. She responded by writing him a letter telling him that,

> You are as brave a man as Harry Truman—or FDR—or Lincoln. You can go on to find some peace, some achievement amidst all the pain. . . . To step out now would be *wrong* for your country, and I can see nothing but a lonely wasteland for your future. . . . I am not afraid of *Time* and lies or losing money or defeat.

In the final analysis I can't carry any of the burdens you talked of—so I know it's only your choice. But I know you are as brave as any of the thirty-five. (Johnson 1970, 192)

The combination of words that were once again crafted to bolster his confidence, challenge him, and appeal to his sense of duty worked, and "Johnson credited his wife with his decision to stay in the race" (Heckler-Feltz 1997, 88).

That was not the only example of her influence during the convention, however. The president was confronted with a credentials challenge to the all-white delegation from Mississippi. Civil rights leaders wanted the president to support the challengers. When it came time for him to make a decision, he asked Lady Bird to draft something for his consideration. She wrote a statement that supported the elected delegation, but confirmed the president's support of civil rights:

> I believe the legal delegation ought to be seated. I am not going to bend to emotionalism. I don't want this convention to do so either. The election is not worth that.
>
> I am proud of the steady progress that has been made in the area of human and equal rights. In 1957, in 1960, and again in 1964, I was in the leadership to bring equal rights and decent progress to the Negro. I would not change a line of what has been passed or written. So long as I am President I will continue to lead the way within the guidelines of the law and within the framework of justice. (Johnson 1964a)

A compromise made it unnecessary for Johnson to respond publicly, but "the document is important . . . because it shows that President Johnson so valued Mrs. Johnson's advice that he asked for her guidance on a potentially explosive key issue" (Smith 1989, 114).

Throughout Lady Bird's diary and within the thousands of boxes of her papers are additional insights into her influence on her husband's speeches and decisions. She was one of the few around him who could offer candid criticism and constructive advice. One of the most frequently referenced examples of her teacherlike critiques was one captured on tape in the first few months after he became president. Lady Bird took four pages of handwritten notes while watching her husband speak that served later as promptings for the critique of the news conference. At the top of the first page is a bold "B+"—the grade she gave his performance—followed by notes on delivery ("Perhaps slightly fast & not enough change of pace") and content ("De Gaulle answer not really good—Viet Nam answer good—Answer on Lodge good") (Museum Display 1964).

The tape revealed that LBJ welcomed the critique but also became defensive and that Lady Bird knew exactly how far to push him, when to insert flattery, and when to revert to her role as wife. It was this balance of roles that made her effective in her dealings with her husband and in the execution of her duties. This excerpt demonstrates her political insights, political savvy, and agility in dealing with her husband:

> Mrs. Johnson: I thought your answer on Lodge was good. I thought your answer on Vietnam was good. I really didn't like the answer on DeGaulle because I think I've

heard you say, and I believe you actually have said out loud, that you don't believe you ought to go out of the country this year . . .

President Johnson: Uh . . .

Mrs. Johnson: . . . so I don't think you can very well say that you can meet him anytime it's convenient for both people.

President Johnson: Well, when it can be arranged. I'm not goin' out of this country. I didn't say where I'd go. (Long pause) I didn't say I'd go out of the country at all, there . . .

Mrs. Johnson: Uh, no, I guess you . . .

President Johnson: Yes, I reaffirmed that I wouldn't go.

Mrs. Johnson: I see. Uh huh. Well, I didn't hear . . . I didn't get the meaning out of it that everyone else did. I think the outstanding things were that the close ups were excellent. . . .

In general, I'd say it was a good B+. How do you feel about it?

President Johnson: I thought it was much better than last week.

Mrs. Johnson: . . . It will be interesting to hear everybody else's reaction. And we've, uh, got the Thornberrys (sp?) anyhow are wanting a reasonably early dinner with us, and I got my 10 o'clock date and you can do anything you want to about getting another couple or two to eat with us and let me know. I love you very much. (Telephone Conversation 1964)

This taped interaction is useful in providing understanding of their personal relationship and political partnership. The written record is equally helpful in identifying her skills as a rhetorician and strategist for her husband. Speech drafts in the president's files literally show her hand and confirm the comments in her diary about the active role she played in the speech writing and vetting processes. She wrote comments in the margins of drafts, provided analyses on notepaper, and wrote new sentences in cursive or shorthand. The shorthand comments reveal her penchant for taking notes during meetings she attended—something most of her biographers commented on as being necessary because of LBJ's reliance on her to remember names and details.[5]

While she underplayed her role and referred to it as "infiltrating" (Anthony 1991, 114) rather than overtly influencing, the historical record suggests otherwise. She had a powerful influence on the president, his words, and, ultimately, the presidency. She described the ideal first lady as one who could argue issues with her husband but remain quiet in public about those issues (Anthony 1988, 115). Her ability to reach her own definition of ideal is what added to her power behind the scenes.

Legacy

Lady Bird Johnson said of her husband, "Lyndon stretches you. He always expects more of you than you're really mentally or physically capable of putting out" (Truman 1995, 174). It can be said of Lady Bird that she stretched the role of first lady to be a composite of the roles played by her predecessors. Lady Bird Johnson clearly achieved the characteristics of Terlip's effective political wife. She demonstrated that a first lady can be a consummate hostess, wife, and mother who provides the atmosphere a president needs to withstand the rigors of the job while simultaneously pursuing her own policy interests. She recognized that any event that took place in the White House or involved the first lady had potential political and rhetorical implications, and she took advantage of every opportunity to advance her husband's agenda. Her understanding of her husband and her own political instincts made her a valued and valuable advisor.

She built on the legacy of Eleanor Roosevelt and expanded the public role of the first lady into an independent and interdependent position. After Lady Bird Johnson, presidential candidates' wives became more active campaigners. She demonstrated to future political wives how to use their own experiences to build identification with an audience and then transfer that identification to their husbands.

She took on an issue—the environment—in a way that advanced positions expressed in her husband's speeches but also put her own mark on it. Her selection of the environment, while criticized in some circles, proved to be an issue with longevity. Anyone who lives in, works in, or visits Washington, D.C., today benefits from her efforts. She helped raise the national consciousness about the environment—a consciousness that eventually produced Earth Day, legislation, and efforts by average citizens to be good stewards of the earth through recycling and other measures.

Her environmental work also taught a lesson about the importance of language and how things are named. The word "beautification" sounded frivolous and expensive at a time when the nation was embroiled in divisive issues and costly social and wartime pursuits. It produced public criticism and derision of her as a first lady. However, her speeches reflect her understanding of how to address a problem as she redefined the nature of her campaign and linked environmental interests with LBJ's promotion of domestic tourism. These strategies overcame some criticism and demonstrated the advantages of linking a first lady's issues to her husband's.

Finally, Lady Bird Johnson undoubtedly made Lyndon Johnson, the politician, possible. If ever there was a wife who balanced her husband's temperament, supported and challenged him equally, and enabled him to do what he could not do himself, it was Lady Bird Johnson. Whatever the legacy of the administration of Lyndon Baines Johnson, it is a legacy shared with Lady Bird. Initiatives with long-term impact such as the 1964 Civil Rights Act and Head Start were issues she embraced along with her husband.

Although Karlyn Kohrs Campbell did not mention Lady Bird Johnson in her chapter on the presidency as a two-person career, she could have. If there was ever a couple that embodied the concept, it was the Johnsons. If there was a woman who helped shape the modern first ladyship, it was Lady Bird Johnson. Meg Greenfield recognized Lady Bird's reshaping of the office within two years of her becoming first lady. She wrote:

> What Lady Bird Johnson has done is to integrate the traditionally frivolous and
> routine aspects of the East Wing life into the overall purposes of the administration

and to enlist the peculiar assets of First Ladyhood itself in the administration's behalf. They are assets no one fully understood until Mrs. Johnson moved into the White House—or at least no one fully understood their potential political clout. (Greenfield 1965, 29)

Future political wives would be wise to study Lady Bird Johnson's record of her White House years and follow her example.

Questions for Discussion

1. Lady Bird Johnson's education and experience positioned her well to become first lady in 1963 when President John F. Kennedy was assassinated. What activities helped prepare her for the role of first lady?
2. A prospective first lady may face many challenges as she speaks to the public in support of her husband as a candidate for the presidency. What were some of the challenges Lady Bird Johnson faced as she campaigned for her husband during her 1964 Whistle-Stop Campaign? What rhetorical strategies did she use to meet those challenges? What made the Whistle-Stop Campaign unique?
3. Lady Bird Johnson is best known for her environmental initiatives. According to chapter author Diana B. Carlin, Mrs. Johnson's choice of beautification "demonstrate[d] the Johnsons' political partnership and complementary agendas." Describe how beautification meshed with Johnson administration policies. What rhetorical strategies did Lady Bird use to promote beautification nationally?
4. Lady Bird Johnson has been described as an active political partner of her husband, although much of her influence occurred in private. Describe examples of her behind-the-scenes advice as presented by chapter author Diana B. Carlin.
5. Describe how Lady Bird Johnson helped shape the role of the modern first lady. How did she build on the activities of her predecessors to expand what a first lady could do while holding that position? How did she permanently change the role and expectations of first ladies?

Internet Resources

http://www.lbjlib.utexas.edu/
The Lyndon Baines Johnson Presidential Library and Museum contains material on Lady Bird. You can access an extensive list of awards she won and honorary degrees bestowed upon her. The website also contains Mrs. Johnson's papers and photographs of her. You can search for material online, and access some of it over the internet.

http://www.wildflower.org/
The Lady Bird Johnson Wildflower Center was founded by the former first lady in 1982 as the National Wildlife Research Center, and renamed in her honor in

1998. Through this website you can access text and images describing the center's activities as well as Mrs. Johnson's support of them.

Notes

Diana Carlin would like to thank Nancy Kegan Smith for sharing files and insights about Lady Bird Johnson.

1. Numerous polls of primarily presidential scholars ranking both presidents and their spouses rank Lady Bird Johnson among the best. Robert P. Watson (2000, 179, 188–89, 195) in his book *The Presidents' Wives: Reassessing the Office of First Lady* includes several measures that show Mrs. Johnson ranked sixth on two, fourth on another, and seventeenth on a third. A Gallup Poll cited by Watson showed that Lady Bird remained on the list of most admired women through 1974. Betty Boyd Caroli (1987, 385–90) includes earlier surveys in *First Ladies* that rank Mrs. Johnson third among all first ladies and second among twentieth-century first ladies among scholars and first in a public survey.

2. See James W. Ceaser, Glen E. Thurow, Jeffrey K. Tulis, and Joseph M. Bessette, "Rise of the Rhetorical Presidency"; Jeffrey K. Tulis, *The Rhetorical Presidency*; and Martin J. Medhurst, editor, *Beyond the Rhetorical Presidency*.

3. See Carl Sferrazza Anthony, *First Ladies: The Saga of the Presidents' Wives and Their Power 1789–1961*; Betty Boyd Caroli, *First Ladies*; Myra G. Gutin, *The First Lady in the Twentieth Century*; Margaret Truman, *First Ladies*; and Robert P. Watson, *The Presidents' Wives: Reassessing the Office of First Lady*.

4. See Gould (1988, 37–50) for a chronology of speeches given by both President and Mrs. Johnson prior to and during the 1964 campaign that related to the environment and beautification that formed the basis for the selection. According to Gould (39), "The Johnson administration's impulse to promote natural beauty in 1964 was part of a general revival of the conservation movement that had begun in the late 1950s and had gathered momentum during the years of the Kennedy presidency."

5. See Anthony, *First Ladies: The Saga of the Presidents' Wives and Their Power 1961–1990*, Vol. 2., Paul F. Boller Jr., *Presidential Wives*, and Jan Jarboe Russell, *Lady Bird: A Biography of Mrs. Johnson*.

References

Anthony, Carl Sferrazza. 1990. *First Ladies: The Saga of the Presidents' Wives and Their Power 1789–1961*, Vol. 1. New York: William Morrow and Company.

———. 1991. *First Ladies: The Saga of the Presidents' Wives and Their Power 1961–1990*, Vol. 2. New York: William Morrow.

Boller, Paul F. 1988. *Presidential Wives*. New York: Oxford University Press.

Campbell, Karlyn Kohrs. 1996. The Rhetorical Presidency: A Two-Person Career. In *Beyond the Rhetorical Presidency*, ed. Martin J. Medhurst, 179–95. College Station, Tex.: Texas A & M University Press.

Caroli, Betty Boyd. 1987. *First Ladies*. New York: Oxford University Press.

Carpenter, Liz. 1970. *Ruffles and Flourishes: The Warm and Tender Story of a Simple Girl Who Found Adventure in the White House*. Garden City, N.Y.: Doubleday & Company.

Cater, Douglass. 1964. Memo: Douglass Cater to Bill Moyers, 18 August. EX PP5/son, Lady Bird 7/15/64–10/l/64. Box 62, LBJ Library.

Ceaser, James W., Glen E. Thurow, Jeffrey K. Tulis, and Joseph M. Bessette. 1981. Rise of the Rhetorical Presidency. *Presidential Studies Quarterly*, II, 158–71.

Greenfield, Meg. 1965. The Lady in the East Wing. *Reporter*, 15 July, 28.

Gould, Lewis L. 1988. *Lady Bird Johnson and the Environment*. Lawrence, Kans.: University Press of Kansas.

———. 1999. *Lady Bird Johnson: Our Environmental First Lady*. Lawrence, Kans.: University Press of Kansas.

Gutin, Myra G. 1989. *The President's Partner: The First Lady in the Twentieth Century*. New York: Greenwood.

Janeway, Elizabeth. 1964. The First Lady: A Professional at Getting Things Done. *Ladies' Home Journal*, April, 64.

Johnson, Lady Bird. 1964a. Draft Statement by Mrs. Johnson, 31 August, EX PP5/Johnson, Lady Bird. Box 62, WHCF, LBJ Library.

———. 1964b. Press Release: Remarks of Mrs. Lyndon B. Johnson, Valdosta, Ga., 8 October. Mrs. Johnson—Press Release Copies of Mrs. Johnson's Speeches, LBJ Library.

———. 1964c. Press Release: Speech by Mrs. Lyndon B. Johnson, Depot at New Orleans, 9 October. Mrs. Johnson—Press Release Copies of Mrs. Johnson's Speeches, LBJ Library.

———. 1967. Press Release: Remarks by Mrs. Lyndon B. Johnson, Yale Political Union, New Haven, Conn., 9 October. Mrs. Johnson—Press Release Copies of Mrs. Johnson's Speeches, LBJ Library.

———. 1970. *A White House Diary*. New York: Holt, Rinehart and Winston.

Heckler-Feltz, Cheryl. 1997. *Heart and Soul of the Nation: How the Spirituality of Our First Ladies Changed America*. New York: Doubleday.

Klapthor, Margaret Brown. 1989. *The First Ladies*. Washington, D.C.: White House Historical Association.

Klaw, Barbara. 1980. Lady Bird Johnson Remembers. *American Heritage*, 13 December.

McCarthy, Abigail. 1972. *Private Faces/Public Places*. Garden City, New York: Doubleday & Company.

Medhurst, Martin J., ed. 1996. *Beyond the Rhetorical Presidency*. College Station, Tex.: Texas A & M University Press.

Museum Display. 1964. Taken from an Envelope dated 7 March, CTJ Diary Collection, LBJ Library.

Russell, Jan Jarboe. 1999. *Lady Bird: A Biography of Mrs. Johnson*. New York: Scribner.

Smith, Nancy Kegan. 1989. A Journey of the Heart: The Papers of Lady Bird Johnson. In *Modern First Ladies: Their Documentary Legacy*, ed. Nancy Kegan Smith and Mary C. Ryan, 109–20. Washington, D.C.: National Archives and Records Administration.

Telephone Conversation. 1964. Lyndon B. Johnson and Lady Bird Johnson, 7 March, at 4:10 PM, Citation #2395, WH6403.05, PNO 8, LBJ Library.

Terlip, Laura A. 1986. Communicating Ideals: The Role of the Politician's Wife. Conference Paper, Central States Speech Association, Chicago, April.

Tulis, Jeffrey K. 1987. *The Rhetorical Presidency*. Princeton, N.J.: Princeton University Press.

Truman, Margaret. 1995. *First Ladies*. New York: Random House.

Watson, Robert P. 2000. *The Presidents' Wives: Reassessing the Office of First Lady*. Boulder, Colo.: Lynne Rienner Publishers.

Whistle-Stop October 13–16. 1964. Memo, n.d., p.1, Box 11, Liz Carpenter's Subject Files, White House Social Files, LBJ Library.

———. Box 12, Liz Carpenter's Subject Files, White House Social Files, LBJ Library.

CHAPTER FIVE

Pat Nixon
Wisdom to Know the Difference

Linda B. Hobgood

I believe that even when people can't speak your language, they can tell if
you have love in your heart.

—Patricia Nixon

Socrates: Tell me, then: you say, do you not, that in the rightly developed man
the passions ought not to be controlled, but that we should let them grow
to the utmost and somehow or other satisfy them, and that this is a virtue?
Callicles: Yes; I do.
Soc.: Then those who want nothing are not truly said to be happy?
Cal.: No, indeed, for then stones and dead men would be the happiest of all.[1]

Henriette Wyeth Hurd painted the official portrait of Patricia Nixon. The
woman depicted is serene, almost sad. She appears fragile, yet brave. Above all,
the face that gazes from the canvas understands—the wisdom in her eyes reflects
that sense of tribulation bequeathed by experience. Both the painting and the
subject reflect "calm at the center." It is an insightful portrayal of the American
first lady known to the world as "Pat."

As the wife of a man who was by the time he became president one of the
most well-known public figures of the twentieth century, Pat was herself a familiar face. Richard Nixon featured his family in every political contest he entered,
and by 1968, the nation knew the Nixons—even their dog, Checkers. Television, as a medium of news, burst on the scene to coincide with Richard Nixon's
rise in national politics. As the visual medium expanded press coverage, any privacy that political families once may have enjoyed could no longer be presumed.
This explains in part why so many of our memories of Pat are the indelible photographic images of her across more than four decades of American history.

Remarkable for their similarity are the terms used—both complimentary and critical—to describe Pat Nixon. Those who paid tribute to her upon her death praised the same qualities in her character. She seemed to embody all the virtues of Reinhold Niebuhr's familiar prayer, the very qualities revealed in her official portrait: serenity to accept what she could not change, courage to change what she could, and wisdom to know the difference.

What is striking about Pat Nixon's image is that while nearly everyone of her era recognized her familiar face, she remained a mystery. The life beyond the range of the camera's lens was a private one that Pat worked hard to protect. What the public did not know was left to speculation and caricature. Pat's response to such characterizations—even those that were blatantly false—was always a perspicacious silence. Faith that the truth as she knew it would have the final say gave Pat the confidence to refrain from elaboration and sustained her during the most trying times of her life. The temptation to publicly respond to criticism during or after her White House years was something Pat Nixon resolutely resisted.

We often forget that Pat Nixon was a wartime first lady. Undeclared and far away, the Vietnam conflict cast a shadow over the Nixon presidency that never lifted. American lives were sacrificed in the jungles of Southeast Asia for more than thirteen years, five and a half of which comprised the Nixon administration. Entrenched fears of the Cold War, mistrust of the Soviet Union and of its communist rival the People's Republic of China, Soviet aggression in Eastern Europe and the quashing of liberty in Czechoslovakia, heightened tensions between East and West Berlin, and the perilous aftermath of the six-day Arab–Israeli war combined to make Nixon's a more tremulous diplomatic and complex international challenge than the presidency had been since the Second World War.

Discontent with the Vietnam War led to violence at home. The sounds of protest in Lafayette Park across the street were the voices to which Pat Nixon awakened every morning of her White House stay.[2] Increasingly stark ideological differences between the two political parties in Congress were compounded by resentment over the narrow majority by which Richard Nixon won the presidential election of 1968. Finally, there was Watergate and, following an overwhelming victory in 1972, the unprecedented resignation of the president. Through it all there was the quiet calm of Pat Nixon.

Discernment seemed almost inherent in Pat. She had an instinct for what mattered and what, in the long term, did not. This "wisdom to know the difference" was complemented by two additional qualities in her character—a rigidly demanding definition of public service and an unwavering sense of self-discipline. These two qualities may have strengthened her capacity to withstand political battles that would have overwhelmed almost anyone else. At the same time, they gave rise to perceptions hardly compatible with the person friends and family knew her to be. The uncertainty that lingers regarding the stoic figure of so many press photographs reveals a failure of press and public to penetrate her silence to appreciate her sense of duty or share her regard for privacy. Pat's own supposition that these predilections should not need explaining may have contributed to her persona as an enigma. In the vacuum, otherwise implausible portrayals of Pat Nixon in print and film nourished a fungible narrative[3] easier to believe than to question. Lack of inquiry, however, deprives us of an understanding of Pat Nixon's indomitable strength and steadfastness that are hallmarks of her life and legacy as first lady.

Because by choice she gave so few publicly recorded remarks, the informal expressions and the activities of Pat Nixon form the basis of my analysis. If indeed they "speak louder than words," the actions of this first lady are valid assessments of her rhetorical effectiveness. This study begins with a biographical overview that records Pat Nixon's lengthy public career, examining especially the advantages and constraints of its duration and high profile. My study culminates in a critical look at Mrs. Nixon's White House years and the remaining two decades of her life.

Biography

In 1960, *Time* magazine featured the nation's second lady on its cover. In the accompanying story, headlined "The Silent Partner," author Burt Meyers wrote:

> Along with her bottomless energy, Mrs. Nixon has formidable reserves of poise and aplomb, and a notably retentive mind. . . . Since her abrupt debut into public life, there have been many occasions to test her serenity, and she has never failed to meet the test.
>
> Pat Nixon's stamina and courage, her drive and control have made her into one of the U.S.'s most remarkable women—not just a showpiece Second Lady, not merely a part of the best-known team in contemporary politics, but a public figure in her own right.
>
> She earned that right the hard way—in a tough childhood that knew little luxury. (Meyers 1960, 25)

Lessons in self-discipline, explicit and inferential, accompanied the meager circumstances into which Thelma Catherine Ryan was born. Nicknamed "Pat" because her birth came on the eve of St. Patrick's Day 1912, she adopted the name officially to honor her father's memory upon his death. The third child and first daughter born to Will and Kate Ryan, Pat inherited her father's love of reading and adventure. A sailor and then miner, Will moved his family from Ely to Artesia, California, to try his luck at farming when Pat was just a year old. Money was scarce, and Pat learned at an early age to be content with little—to accept the things she could not change.

Before she was in school, she already knew how to suppress her tears and keep her head high. One of her earliest memories is of riding into the little southern California town of Artesia with her farmer father to buy the weekly staples. While Will Ryan shopped, his four-year-old daughter waited patiently, perched on the high seat of the family buggy. "I would never ask for anything," she remembers, "but how I hoped! I'd watch the corner to see if he came back carrying a strawberry cone. That was the big treat." If there was no cone, the little girl understood that her father had no money left for treats, and she stifled her disappointment. "I just waited and hoped" (Meyers 1960, 25).

Pat knew better than to ask for such luxuries. Not wishing to add insult to the injury of Will Ryan's struggle to provide for his family's needs, Pat seemed to dread the thought of causing or adding undue misery even unintentionally. She therefore learned to read not just the printed word, but people as well. She developed an instinct for recognizing others' underlying emotions and responding with sensitivity. Years later, as first lady, Pat's "way with people" was the trait staff and visitors alike recalled best. Susan Porter Rose, who served as Mrs. Nixon's appointments secretary, recalled the White House reception for a group of Appalachian quilters, who were so overwhelmed by actually being at the White House and shy in the presence of the first lady that many began weeping uncontrollably.

> When [Mrs. Nixon] walked into the Diplomatic Reception Room to greet the quilt makers and heard the sobbing, she simply went around the room and wordlessly gave each of her guests a hug. Susan remembers that as the tension eased she was so moved that she felt tears spring into her own eyes. (Eisenhower 1986, 84)

Neither economic circumstance nor age seemed to make any difference in Pat's ability to anticipate and respond to others' needs. As first lady her "way" with children became almost legendary.

> Once, when a little crippled boy came to the White House for a photo opportunity with the First Lady, Pat saw the youngster was terrified and tried everything to help him relax, to no avail. Suddenly, he blurted: "This isn't your house!"
> "Why do you say that?" Pat asked.
> "Because I don't see your washing machine."
> Pat solemnly conducted him to the third floor and showed him the washing machines in the laundry room. He returned to the first floor holding her hand, as contented and cheerful as if he were with his own mother. His awed parent said that it was the first time he had ever been at ease with a stranger. (Truman 1995, 192–93)

Her mother died of Bright's disease and cancer of the liver when Thelma Ryan was thirteen. The details of Kate Ryan's life, her family, her faith, her favorite things, and the advice and hopes she no doubt had for her daughter were never conveyed. Pat recalled: "We were so busy on the farm. It was always a struggle. We didn't have much time to talk. And when you're thirteen you do not ask questions about philosophy or family" (Eisenhower 1986, 27).

In the years that followed, Pat assumed household responsibilities, attended school where she excelled academically, and found time for extracurricular activities such as debate and drama. She put off college to nurse her father through silicosis until he died in 1930. Then the youngest Ryan, who had taken care of her father and brothers since the time of her mother's death, was on her own to pursue an education and her dream to travel. Both necessitated constant employment.

Her degree in merchandising from the University of Southern California, with teaching and office administration certifications, was financed by research assistantships and work as an x-ray technician, jobs that included serving food in the cafeteria, checking books at the library, and performing bit parts as a movie extra. One faculty member commented on Pat Nixon's ubiquity on campus because of her numerous people- or service-oriented occupations. Another professor wrote of Miss Ryan's "splendid attitude towards young people, with her buoyant enthusiasm for life in general." The assessment by the teacher who supervised Pat Ryan's practice teaching is telling: "Her students are very fond of her and she gets good results from them" (quoted in Eisenhower 1986, 48).

The opportunity to travel presented itself when an elderly couple asked Pat if she would chauffeur them in their Packard from California to Connecticut. Such an offer, coming at the onset of the Great Depression, must have seemed especially exciting. She traversed dangerous mountain highways, learned to change flat tires, and reached the East safely in the fall of 1929. Her payment was a bus ticket back to California, but Pat decided to see as much of the East Coast as possible before returning to complete her undergraduate work. She visited relatives she had never met, saw the nation's capital for the first time, and toured the White House. Pat's Aunt Kate, a nun with the Sisters of Charity, worked at Seton Hospital in New York. She offered Pat a position that autumn working with the patients who suffered from tuberculosis. In one of many letters to her brother Bill back in California, Pat wrote: "I love to help others. . . . It's funny but even a cheerful smile uplifts them. . . . Sometimes I feel that I should like to spend my life just working for the afflicted unfortunates—helping them to be more happy. Too, I enjoy hospital work" (Eisenhower 1986, 37).

Pat avoided sharing with her brothers that the Seton patients would soon die of the very disease that had taken Will Ryan's life. Years later, Pat's daughter Julie asked her mother if she had been afraid that she too would contract the illness while caring for these patients, but Pat claimed she had not been afraid. Pat showed the same courage to care for others in difficult conditions when she was first lady. Her first solo mission to a foreign country was to Peru to bring comfort to the many victims of a devastating earthquake. She also visited soldiers wounded in Vietnam, becoming the first president's wife to enter a designated combat zone on foreign soil. Photos of Mrs. Nixon at the bedsides of amputees and wounded servicemen, often on her knees so that they might whisper private messages for her to convey, reveal a woman singularly focused on the face of each of the suffering and completely oblivious to self.

Pat returned to California to complete her studies as the summer of 1934 came to an end. Her brother Tom financed the bus trip home, and to save money Pat shared an apartment with her brothers for the remainder of her college years. Upon graduation, she accepted a teaching position at the local high school in Whittier, California. An earnest sponsor of extracurricular activities, Caroli's biography suggests that Miss Ryan's willingness to support the students' pursuits beyond the classroom was mutually rewarding. She writes:

> Her students found her so lively and likable that they selected her to advise the Pep Committee, organized to arouse school enthusiasm. Robert C. Pierpoint, who later covered the White House as a correspondent for CBS, was a member of the Pep Committee, and he remembered Miss Ryan of his Whittier student days as: "approachable, friendly, and outgoing. She was happy, enthusiastic, sprightly. Her disposition was sunny, not intermittently but all the time. . . . We liked her enormously." (Caroli 1987, 246; David 1978, 40)

Pat also found an opportunity to pursue acting, from high school days a source of enjoyment. The decision to join a local theatre group changed the course of her life. In February 1938, Pat went to a tryout for the Whittier Community Players and met Richard Nixon. Their daughter, Julie Nixon Eisenhower, recounts that for her father it was love at first sight. He actually proposed that evening, in a manner of speaking.

A young attorney in Whittier's Wingert and Bewley law firm, Richard Nixon was highly regarded in the community. Awarded a scholarship to Harvard upon graduation from high school, Nixon had been forced to turn down the offer because his family lacked the money for his travel and boarding expenses. He had instead attended nearby Whittier College where he excelled and was elected president of the student body. His high academic achievements continued at Duke University Law School where Nixon was inducted into the Order of the Coif (the law equivalent of Phi Beta Kappa) and served as president of the Duke Law School Student Bar Association. Back home in Whittier, he was a member and future president of the 20–30 Club (sponsored by the Rotary), an active Kiwanian, and the town's deputy city attorney. But in 1938, his attentions turned to the popular and attractive Miss Ryan. His spontaneous proposal was followed by a courtship that lasted more than two years. Dick and Pat discovered common interests and marked similarities in background beyond their mutual Irish heritage.

In 1940, they were married. Within two years, America was at war. The couple moved to Washington, D.C., where Dick had been hired in the new Office of Price Administration (OPA). Pat volunteered as a secretary for the Red Cross until also finding employment with the OPA. Richard Nixon's service in the navy included duty overseas during which time Pat was employed in a bank in Iowa and then again with OPA as a price analyst in San Francisco. When Dick returned home, his military obligation situated the couple for a brief time in Baltimore. It was there that Richard Nixon received a message from associates in Whittier asking him to return and to consider a congressional candidacy in the upcoming 1946 election against the incumbent House member. Nixon ran and won, against formidable odds.

Pat gave birth to the Nixons' first child in February 1946, just one month after the couple had returned to California. She also managed her husband's campaign office by herself while he stumped across the district to win first the Republican nomination and then the November election. Dick's mother Hannah Nixon cared for their baby Tricia during the day while Pat performed secretarial, accounting, and other campaign duties at the headquarters. In her introduction to campaigns, Pat was exposed to the dark side of politics. A break-in occurred at the Nixon campaign headquarters. Pat, who had sold her small inheritance of land so the couple could afford to produce and distribute campaign pamphlets, reacted with a kind of hurt and disbelief over the loss of all their campaign materials. It was particularly disheartening to her that there was so little press or public outcry, something that, years later, struck her as ironic. It was a sobering lesson. The upset victory, hard fought and hard won, probably overshadowed the loss of political naiveté that accompanied the campaign of 1946. Nixon won reelection two years later, and it was during that campaign that their second daughter Julie was born.

In 1950, Richard Nixon's bid for the U.S. Senate, also viewed as an uphill race, was successful. His unlikely victories in a crucial state, his prominence on the House subcommittee investigating Alger Hiss, and his relative youth made Nixon a popular choice for vice president on the 1952 Republican ticket alongside presidential hopeful Dwight Eisenhower. Their candidacy was a successful one, but charges made in late summer that the vice presidential candidate operated a secret fund for purposes unreported drew sufficient press attention as to demand a response from Nixon. Republicans and Democrats alike called for an explanation, and there were suggestions that Nixon should withdraw from the ticket. For Nixon, this was tantamount to an admission of guilt. Determined to answer charges he viewed as deliberately false, Nixon was granted airtime on national television to give his side of the story. He determined that the only way to fight the fund allegations would be to disclose his finances entirely and to reveal—as no candidate had ever done before—all personal and family expenses, investments, and debts. Naturally a private person, Pat's exposure to three campaigns had only intensified her inclinations toward protecting the family's privacy. That she supported so resolutely the need for her husband to respond to the fund accusations and agreed with the way he chose to respond is an indication of her own hierarchy of values. Only the injustice of the situation as she perceived it permitted such a violation of their personal life. And though Pat did not know exactly what her husband planned to say, she was by his side at the broadcast. Earlier in the day, he had spoken of quitting the race, but Pat insisted that he defend himself and give the American people the truth they deserved.

The Checkers Speech is one of the most remarkable events in the history of American political campaigns. Nixon spoke directly to the camera for thirty plus minutes; he urged his audience to contact the Republican National Committee to voice their opinions as to whether he should be kept on the ticket. He bared his political and financial soul, listing the costs of his car and his mortgage, his assets and his debts. While his wife didn't have a fur coat, but instead wore a "good Republican cloth coat," he unabashedly asserted, "she'd look good in anything."

And he acknowledged that the family had accepted one gift from a supporter in Texas: "It's a dog, a black and white spaniel, and our daughter Tricia named it Checkers and no matter what they say we're going to keep it."

Response was overwhelmingly supportive and Nixon was kept on the ticket. Eisenhower even boasted about his running mate at subsequent campaign rallies. But in the nearly fifty years since the event, those who recall the speech remember that though it was Nixon who spoke so unconventionally and Checkers for whom the event was named, the lasting image is that of a poised Mrs. Nixon. Press accounts at the time described her as cool and collected, but a watching public recalls another Pat. Seated on the stage of the El Capitan Theatre in Los Angeles just a few feet from Nixon she set her unblinking, unflinching gaze on her husband with a somber, tight-lipped smile that barely masked the personal indignation she felt toward what had become politics at its nastiest and most intrusive. The pain in her expression was so palpable that the television viewer could feel it; the camera seemed a heartless trespasser. A half-century later with such supposed sophistication toward the television medium, her image still has that effect on the viewer.[4]

The Checkers Speech would be a key recollection of that 1952 campaign, but another incident, all but forgotten, also left indelible memories. During the Republican National Convention, on the night Richard Nixon accepted the vice presidential nomination, reporters, anxious for a story, brushed past a bewildered baby-sitter in the Nixon home where their daughters were sleeping. They wakened Tricia, six, and Julie, four, making them pose for pictures in a frenzied haste to get the girls' reaction to their father's nomination. The flashbulbs scared the youngsters to tears. The incident was not considered newsworthy, but this was the part of politics neither Pat—nor any mother—could easily forget. It could hardly help but leave a lasting impression regarding the behavior of particular reporters and the press in general.

The 1952 GOP ticket won in a landslide and repeated the victory in 1956. One of the well-known photographs of those years was taken at the 1957 Inaugural Ball. In the picture, the Nixons are smiling and waving to supporters from their box seats, but the new vice president's wife is looking sideways at a yawning daughter Julie. The photo is emblematic of the dual existence that characterized this stage of Pat's life. For the next eight years, Nixon and his wife were put to work on behalf of the administration at home and overseas. Ruth Cowan's feature article on Pat, published at the outset of her husband's vice presidency, is typical of the favorable coverage Mrs. Nixon enjoyed in that era.

> Mrs. Richard Nixon as second lady of the land is beginning an exciting new chapter in a life that already has been as dramatic as any story out of Hollywood in her home state of California. In fact, her life story as a movie could "pack 'em in." The plot is the kind Americans really like—a pot of gold at the end of the rainbow that was reached only after a lot of ups and downs. (Cowan 1953, S3)

During both Eisenhower terms, concern for the president's health limited his activities, and the Nixons assumed diplomatic responsibilities, especially those involving travel to foreign countries. There seems to have been little question but that Mrs. Nixon would accompany her husband, though the decision involved leaving their two young daughters. Her biographers indicate this was a wrenching choice. Nevertheless, response to her activity as an ambassador of goodwill and surrogate on official state occasions was uniformly positive. Members of the media who accompanied the vice president and his wife marveled at Pat's stamina. Julie Eisenhower's biography of her mother, which provides the most comprehensive account of the second lady's travels, includes the impression recounted by Robert Hartmann of the *Los Angeles Times*, following the attack on the vice president's motorcade by violent mobs of communist-inspired insurgents during the couple's 1957 trip to South America:

> At the American Embassy, reporter Bob Hartmann, who had watched the attack from the press truck, was one of the first to talk to my parents and to file a dispatch back to the United States. Part of his report read, "Pat Nixon was magnificent today"; at the end of her ordeal, "she still had a stiff upper lip, but when newsmen cheered her, tears welled in her eyes." (Eisenhower 1986, 176)

In these diplomatic and political duties, Pat Nixon reportedly welcomed opportunities for direct interaction despite the time and energy required. Helen Thomas listened to Richard Nixon describe what became a pattern:

> I remember through all of our campaigns, whether it was a receiving line or whether it was going to a fence at the airport, she was the one that always insisted on shaking that last hand, not simply because she was thinking of that vote, but because she simply could not turn down that last child or that last person. (Thomas 1975, 165)

Support of her husband's political philosophy was by all accounts genuine; Pat appears to have enjoyed demonstrating that support as his traveling partner. Following a press reception in Belgrade, a Yugoslav reporter concluded her story: "I wondered whether I was talking with the wife of a politician or with a woman who is herself a politician. I again remembered the words of Dwight Eisenhower: 'The Nixons are a team'" (Eisenhower 1986, 300). Pat was developing a penchant for informal opportunities.

In all their travels, Pat made it her special purpose to extend goodwill beyond officialdom to citizens of the countries they visited despite age, health, or economic circumstance. Beyond embassy security she came face-to-face with the danger of their ambassadorial role. By far the most dramatic episode occurred in Caracas on the 1957 trip to South America. Communist insurgents had inspired and fomented anti-American sentiment and sympathizers congregated to stimulate protests at points along the planned motorcade routes. The protests quickly became riots and local government officials were unwilling or unable to curb the demonstrators. Hostility greeted the Nixons at every stop, but as the visit progressed the violence increased. Anger culminated at the airport where protocol demanded, despite the danger of the situation, an official departure ceremony. Julie Eisenhower describes the accounts of eyewitnesses:

> When the Venezuelan national anthem was unexpectedly played at the entrance to the terminal, causing my parents to stand immobile in respect for their host country, the screaming crowd on the observation deck directly above them showered them with a sustained rain of spit and some garbage. At first the spit looked like giant snowflakes, but it turned to foul, dark blotches when it hit my mother's red suit and the clothes of those standing with her. Then, with the aid of the Secret Service, my parents walked through a shouting, spitting mob to the motorcade. At the car Don Hughes hurriedly rolled up the windows and then pulled out his handkerchief and wiped the saliva off the seat my mother would occupy. And yet, as Americans read in their newspapers the next day, reporters saw Pat Nixon ignore the final onslaught and stop to hug a child who had given her flowers. They also saw her lean across a barricade to pat the shoulder of a young girl who had just cursed and spit at her. The girl turned away in shame. (Eisenhower 1986, 84)

Secret Service and military channels of communication from Caracas were blocked that day. News of the rioting interrupted regular television programming back in the United States. The president and official Washington obtained their first glimpse of the trouble by tuning in, as did the Nixon daughters, who attended public school in their Washington, D.C., neighborhood and were home for lunch. The TV program the girls were watching was interrupted by film showing the smashed automobiles that had transported their parents through the dangerous streets. Dramatic voice-overs gave no indication as to whether the vice president and his wife had escaped harm. Attempts to reassure the Nixon daughters were, upon returning, their mother's heavy-hearted task.

Pat no doubt gained during these years an acute sense of the strain public service may bring to the families and personal lives of those who serve. That she nevertheless urged active involvement in public service at informal gatherings and the few formal settings in which she spoke belies Pat's fundamental faith in the value of representative democracy. She had, by her mid-forties, observed a sufficient number of alternative forms of government to endorse knowledgeably, even with its flaws, participatory government and the American system.

Domestic travel was as much a part of the Nixons' schedules as were their foreign assignments. While Pat did not go on every campaign swing, she kept a wearying pace in the campaign for reelection in 1956, and accompanied her husband to assist Republican candidates for House and Senate in the non-presidential election years. During one campaign season, Republicans coined a slogan "Let's Make a Clean Sweep," designed to inspire the recapture of a majority in the November election in both houses of Congress. At a scheduled campaign stop in Cleveland, Ohio, the Nixons emerged from their plane and were greeted by an unexpectedly large crowd of supporters. They enthusiastically chanted the clean sweep slogan and waved scores of brooms, the vast quantity of which had been supplied by a member of the Ohio congressional delegation, George Bender. More than a dozen years later, First Lady Pat Nixon was the special guest at a Congressional Club reception in Washington, D.C., at which a replica of her inaugural gown was to be unveiled. Spotting Senator Bender's widow among the invited guests, Pat approached her and exclaimed suddenly "The brooms!" The first lady then clasped Mrs. Bender's shoulders and said earnestly "You cannot imagine how much that reception meant and what those brooms did for our spirits." Taken completely by surprise at this recollection, Mrs. Bender was overwhelmed by Pat's memory and genuine thoughtfulness (Hobgood 2001).

Victorious in five consecutive elections, a proven leader in presiding over the U.S. Senate and in his role as presidential surrogate, and an impressive defender of American values and interests overseas, the vice president was considered a significant asset in assisting GOP candidates for office. He was so visible and influential that columnist Murray Kempton nicknamed the 1950s the "Nixon Decade." It was a foregone conclusion that Richard Nixon would seek to succeed Eisenhower as president; Pat, whom many thought had lost her love of campaigning in the years following the Checkers Speech, summoned her energies and approached the coming contest with customary dedication and enthusiasm. Pat had, by 1959, learned to martial her talent for recollection and her interest in others with so little apparent effort that she could be counted on to recognize former acquaintances as she made new ones. The famous and not-so-famous were treated alike as is demonstrated by one exchange in Idaho that proved typical:

> Danny Kaye stopped to chat for a moment, and Art Linkletter, in a shaggy bearskin serape, got a guffaw from Dick Nixon, and a comment: "Is this man or beast?" Then a stocky man in a blue-and-white Norwegian sweater came by. "I'm Bob Bennett," he said. "I'm sure you don't remember me, but I'd like to shake your hand." Replied Pat, without a moment's hesitation: "Of course I remember you. You were our campaign manager in Tulare County in 1950. After that big meeting we had there, we went to your house. You raise oranges." Muttered Bennett in wonderment as he walked off: "It's been ten years." (Meyers 1960, 24)

At some point in her husband's political career, Pat Nixon deliberately limited the ways in which she would express her political views, at least stateside during a campaign season. According to her daughter Julie, it was during the first congressional campaign in 1946 that Mrs. Nixon determined the extent of her own political activity:

> My mother had an innate sense of what would or would not be politically appropriate for her. She knew that she would never be comfortable with a public speaking role, so she confined her remarks to brief "greetings" in which she thanked the volunteers for their efforts. She felt strongly also that there should be only one voice on issues in the campaign—the candidate's. (Eisenhower 1986, 89)

On one occasion in 1956, when the flu kept Richard Nixon from delivering prepared remarks, Pat filled in with a three-minute speech at a stop in Oklahoma

City. Julie Eisenhower's biography traces the otherwise faithful twenty-eight-year maintenance of this policy and Mrs. Nixon reiteration of it in response to reporters' questions. In one instance, Julie combines her mother's response to one of the many "why no policy pronouncements from the First Lady" with an assertive call by Mrs. Nixon (one of many informal exhortations) to citizen involvement:

> She avoided policy statements, telling Vera Glaser of the North American Newspaper Alliance, "I don't think one person can speak for another. The candidate should speak for himself." Repeatedly, she declared that individuals could make a difference. "Get involved. Instead of complaining, go to work. People should participate in local political groups. Each community has some kind of organization in which it is possible to become active. Work for a candidate whom you believe to be qualified—they are the ones who can take a problem to the top. Indicate interest to your Congressman or Senator." (Eisenhower 1986, 243)

Here is clear indication that Mrs. Nixon's reluctance to speak publicly on issues did not reflect a lack of interest or concern. And according to Julie Eisenhower, "[t]hat philosophy—the individual can change the quality of life—would be the theme of her White House years" (Eisenhower 1986, 243). Nevertheless, this combination of inclinations creates a challenge for a first lady who evidently enjoyed interacting with people in almost any situation but that of making a formal address. As one who held to certain values including the need to support her husband's positions, and who felt that attitudes or beliefs could and should be supported by action, her sense of propriety restricted expression. The rhetorical dilemma for Pat Nixon was, therefore, one of her own making. Having eliminated the option of speaking formally to effect persuasion, she limited the number of available and appropriate rhetorical options by which to exert influence. In the 1960 election, this dilemma called for creative alternatives.

Columnist Ruth Montgomery, writing in her syndicated column, asserted that "for the first time in American history one woman could conceivably swing a presidential election." According to Julie Eisenhower:

> Another reporter evoked historical precedent when she pointed out that Pat Nixon was the first woman around whom a separate campaign was being built. The Republican National Committee's women's division decided to sponsor a Pat Week beginning October 3, during which Mother would attend coffees and mini-rallies in her honor, and precinct workers would canvass the neighborhoods. (Eisenhower 1986, 189)

Pat was reportedly uncomfortable with these efforts and her permission had not been sought in advance. She would not have approved activities that distracted from the candidate himself, and she may not have fully realized the extent to which she herself was viewed as an asset by her husband's campaign organizers.

The 1960 campaign and election proved physically and emotionally draining. Richard Nixon had, by age 47, run for office twice nationally, five times successfully. Any discussion of losing was viewed as tantamount to admitting defeat during the campaign, so between Pat and Dick there was no speculation about this possibility. They maintained a grueling schedule, ignoring illness and strain. The president was judged by First Lady Mamie Eisenhower too ill to stump for Nixon; Ike's absence from the campaign was easily misinterpreted. The first televised debates took place between Kennedy and Nixon; the unprecedented role and impact of the visual medium created exigencies that families and supporters of both candidates had to face abruptly. When it became clear on election night that the outcome was the closest in U.S. history and that Richard Nixon appeared to have lost, Nixon ignored reports of voting fraud incidents and irregularities and made a swift decision to concede. Supporters who jammed the Ambassador Hotel ballroom in Los Angeles, dismayed at his admitting defeat so early, chanted to the Nixons as they entered the room "Don't give up!" "You're still going to win!" As the vice president and his wife stood at the microphones waiting for the applause to subside, Pat Nixon, whose poise had come to be presumed, looked out at the crowd of friends and supporters of fourteen years and more and lost her composure. Again there is the unforgettable photo of Pat whose face bore all the shock and strain and disappointment of months spent exhausting themselves only to face this first defeat.

The Nixons remained in Washington until the summer 1961 when their daughters completed the school term, but it was a difficult time. Julie Eisenhower writes:

> In a sense those months in Washington marked another turning point in my mother's attitude toward politics. Nineteen sixty disillusioned her beyond redemption. She saw a stolen election and could not understand why so many were indifferent. Gradually she resolved to channel her energy into the new life awaiting us in California." (Eisenhower 1986, 204)

It was time to change the things she could.

More likely for reasons of party loyalty and anxiousness to avoid the almost inevitable split that subsequently occurred among California Republicans, Richard Nixon was less than two years later a candidate for governor of his home state. Pat had grave misgivings as to the outcome, and her fears were well founded. In the famous press conference that followed his humiliating defeat, Richard Nixon bade farewell to politics with the bitter promise "You won't have Dick Nixon to kick around anymore." Pat, watching via television, reportedly cheered, counting on this to be a promise kept.

One can therefore hardly comprehend Pat Nixon's thoughts as she came to the realization that she would be returning to the political scene. The family had moved to New York where Richard Nixon practiced law. He traveled extensively for his firm, campaigned for Republican candidates, and addressed the 1964 GOP National Convention, but the family remained close, indulging in long-postponed visits with treasured friends. On at least one of these visits, the notion of a second run for the presidency was discussed. Pat's closest friend Helene Drown recalled for

Julie Eisenhower: "I sensed strongly that Pat still had a deep belief in your father's unique talent. She was sure that he alone was capable of solving some of the problems we were facing in the country then" (Eisenhower 1986, 232). As to her mother's attitude in 1968, Julie reflects: "It took courage to re-enter public life as spiritedly as she did." And she wisely notes: "She had no illusions about campaigns or Washington; no confidence that success lay at the end of the rainbow" (235).

Pat understood the odds. They did not have vast wealth, her husband steered a moderate course, he had been tagged a loser, or a has-been, and they had no way of knowing whether he still had a real political following. At the same time, foreign and domestic crises had reached a critical point. The significance of Julie's observation is that the campaign of 1968 seemed to be an experience Pat thoroughly enjoyed. She appeared buoyant and lighthearted after years away from the limelight. She obliged the demands of campaign protocol in such a way that they seemed second nature, almost fun. She paced herself and her activities. Her happiness did not appear to depend on the election outcome. Her children had reached adulthood, there was a degree of family financial stability and, except for what he considered a minor bout with phlebitis, Dick and Pat Nixon enjoyed extraordinary good health.

The outcome in 1968, was again razor thin, but this time the edge went to Richard Nixon. Acknowledging to supporters that "Winning's a lot more fun," the president-elect and his family prepared for the wedding of daughter Julie to David Eisenhower, and their return to Washington. Daughter Tricia was married to Edward Cox in the White House Rose Garden in June 1971. Nixon was re-elected president in 1972, by the largest landslide to that time. Then, exactly six years and one day following his 1968 acceptance of the Republican presidential nomination, Richard Nixon became the first president in American history to resign from office, under threat of impeachment. The former president and first lady retired to La Casa Pacifica, their home in San Clemente, California, where Pat Nixon suffered a stroke in June 1976, from which she never fully recovered. The Nixons moved back to New York and New Jersey to be near their children and four grandchildren. Pat Nixon died on June 22, 1993, the day following her fifty-third wedding anniversary and was buried on the grounds of the Nixon Library in Yorba Linda, California, next to the home that was her husband's birthplace. Her epitaph[5] reads: "I believe that even when people can't speak your language, they can tell if you have love in your heart."

Rhetorical Activities as First Lady

That Patricia Nixon took living in the White House seriously yet did not take herself too seriously created a blend of character that was recalled fondly by those who helped her perform the duties of first lady. In the brief months that I served on her staff, I asked my coworkers questions on every conceivable subject, but the answer to "What is the event or occasion you remember best?" was always the same: "The POW Dinner." The White House staff, used to entertaining, was less accustomed to planning a gala of this size and scope. Returning from imprisonment in Vietnam, the 591 servicemen were invited along with their families to an evening of supper and entertainment on the South Lawn of the White House in May 1973. Preparations for the event were unprecedented, but what her staff recalled uniformly was that Mrs. Nixon seemed especially moved by the bravery of these men and the fortitude of their families. The suffering they had endured was matched by the gratitude they expressed, and the celebration was carefully designed to honor them in a way they would remember for the rest of their lives.

To combine a dignified reserve with a genuine sense of caring that transcended age, language, and cultural limits is uncommon. My first observation of Mrs. Nixon entertaining a little boy in the White House Library convinced me that the combination of gentleness and encouragement I witnessed was something rare. In greatest detail, the child, who was afflicted with a disease for which there was then no known cure, described losing his tooth the evening before. Mrs. Nixon knelt beside him so that from his seated position he could show her the empty space in his mouth that had so recently housed his tooth. She listened attentively, oblivious to the presence of the others in the room. His spontaneous embrace came as no surprise, and she returned it warmly when it was time for him to leave. Such moments occurred regularly, but nothing about Mrs. Nixon's demeanor on these occasions could be considered routine. Carl Anthony likened her to Grace Coolidge: "As teachers, they focused on children requiring special attention. . . . Children seemed to respond to Pat Nixon as openly as she did to them, embracing, kissing, and leading them by the hand because she felt like it" (Anthony 1991, 165).

As a teacher, Pat was fastidious in all manner of contact with others. Her staff—four key assistants plus their respective teams—was well acquainted with her rules regarding correspondence. In the wording of letters, vagueness, jargon, trite or clichéd terms were to be avoided. She checked every letter she signed for spelling, punctuation, and grammatical errors. It was explained to me that while we might become accustomed to seeing White House letterhead there were citizens worldwide who cherished the only letter from the White House they might receive in a lifetime. Pat had seen letters from the White House framed and hung in homes' most special places. It was considered our responsibility to treat each piece of stationery, funded by the taxpayer, with utmost care.

Pat Nixon did her homework. She spent weeks and months prior to state visits, studying culture and customs, the people and politics with whom she expected to visit. William Safire recalls how well her extensive preparations served her when she was in Moscow for the 1972 summit and was seated next to Aleksei Kosygin at an official dinner. He quizzed her specifics of American government and the number of women holding elective office, inquired as to names of members of the traveling White House press corps, compared views of Russian theatre, and the Moscow subway system versus the one proposed for Washington, D.C. They discussed the Orlov Diamond and the clamor of fire engines outside the Soviet Embassy in New York City. Kosygin wryly suggested that the reason Americans had a grain surplus was because they didn't eat enough bread. Pat Nixon replied to all his jokes and queries. She had noted all the names (present and past) of the places in which he had spent his childhood and asked him to tell her of his youth. He recalled famine and hardship as a young boy and went on at great length because the American first lady seemed somehow to understand. Safire recounts the conversation as evidence "of a First Lady doing her job—nothing dramatic, but a bit of flavor that rarely makes the reporting of great events" (Safire 1975, 609–10). This was just as Pat Nixon would have wanted it.

Every Pat Nixon biographer alludes to the keen sense of duty and dedication maintained throughout her career in public life: "She believed that publicly the First Lady must always be an unquestionable example of high virtue, a symbol of dignity, yet refused to fall prey to the trappings" (Anthony 1991, 165). She had a kind of sixth sense, however, about when to uphold the standards of decorum and when it was actually more appropriate to "be flexible" in ceremony and protocol. Perhaps because of this otherwise strict adherence to appropriateness, it was always a special delight to see Mrs. Nixon "let down her guard." Children, pets, and holidays accommodated perfectly such occasions. So too, did the presence of another first lady, the widowed Mamie Eisenhower, who Pat welcomed into the life of the Nixon family and White House. Mamie lent a kind of "impish" grandmotherly presence to executive branch officialdom. Pat brought her as the surprise guest to a reception for the staff one summer evening in 1973, and a colleague invited me to come with him to meet her. We introduced ourselves, and my colleague Bill Fillmore informed Mrs. Eisenhower that he was planning to marry that fall. "Do you have any advice for newlyweds?" he inquired. Mamie, who to that point had been quietly demure, looked tiny next to her interlocutor. Suddenly, standing on tiptoe and grasping the lapels of Bill's jacket, she looked him in the eye and admonished "You tell her she'll get a lot further with honey than she will with vinegar!" Pat, standing nearby, laughed heartily as we struggled to maintain our composure.

There were times when Pat had to conceal her own surprise. Seated next to Chou en Lai at dinner during the historic trip to China, Mrs. Nixon reached for a cigarette case that was wrapped in tissue decorated with panda bears. Pat fingered the wrapping and commented to the premier that she had "always loved them."

"I will give you some," he replied.
"Cigarettes?"
"Pandas."

That is how the National Zoo in Washington, D.C., became home to the Chinese pandas, one of the most popular tourist sites in the nation's capital.

Pat was asked to define at various times her "cause" as first lady. While she launched the "Right to Read" literacy program, championed the arts and Amer-

ican artists in particular, and drew attention to volunteerism nationwide, she often simply alluded to her affection for people. Others viewed this as a special gift
and her greatest talent—"her boundless compassion for humanity"—but she herself never saw it as anything other than being herself. On one or two occasions
she did refer to her "personal diplomacy." If it can be called a style, it was one
that began well before her husband became president and it remains a viable
model of rhetorical effectiveness for a "silent partner."

Too prudent to be drawn into gratuitous confrontation, she apparently perceived as a violation of decorum the spouse-as-spokesperson, which seemed to
her to disregard the fact of who was the candidate in an election. What enjoyment a president's family might find in the perquisites of a presidency was, she
believed, balanced by concomitant obligations and sacrifice. Mrs. Nixon probably understood better than most the rhetorical risk of a voice with two faces, the
danger of intended harmony being perceived instead as contradiction. As she
was inclined to support almost all of Richard Nixon's expressed views, allowing
any possible confusion that might undermine his efforts by something she might
say was considered counterproductive, politically and personally.

There was public support for her conduct. Throughout the more than five
years of the Nixon presidency, Pat routinely led national and international popular opinion polls (Truman 1995, 192). Her style as a first lady was perceived as
consistent with her four predecessors[6], and, importantly, with herself. By 1969,
when she entered the White House, Pat Nixon was hardly a stranger in the popular sense. She had been a familiar face to the general public for nearly two
decades, since the Hiss case had propelled her husband into the national spotlight. In the 1968 presidential race, supporters and opponents alike looked for
anything that might hint of a distinction between the "new" Nixon and the
"old" Nixon as a strategy to gain voter support. Patricia Nixon may have sur-
mised that 1968 was not the time for a departure from personal conduct she
viewed as having been appropriate; after all, no one had blamed her for her husband's defeats of 1960 and 1962 (or, for that matter, any of his personal and
political setbacks). She, therefore, adhered to an image with which the public
appeared both familiar and comfortable. The value of this can best be appreciated in its historical context. Images that pervaded print and electronic media in
the early 1970s, those of Vietnam War protesters or increasingly agitated demonstrators, presented a stark contrast to any coverage of Mrs. Nixon's daily routine.
The drama provided by one set of photographs easily overwhelmed and obscured
the predictable appearance of the other. One gathers an impression that she
would still have opted for a "safe rather than sorry" course of action.

Apart from consideration of day-to-day public opinion, Pat Nixon was no
doubt aware of longer-term shifts in social and cultural perspectives regarding institutions and values. They included the presidency, the notion of privacy, and
the roles and rights of women in public and corporate spheres.

Richard Neustadt's redefining of the power of the presidency as the power to
persuade had proven valid and to Lyndon Johnson's advantage. His War on

Poverty and civil rights legislation both owed their support to the persuasive force of that one individual. But it could also backfire. Vietnam had become Johnson's war; it then threatened to become Nixon's. A personalized presidency posed the risk that anyone close to the president might become an issue and a problem for which the chief executive could and would be held accountable. The woman whose cloth coat and cocker spaniel had dogged her since 1952 was sensitive to what may become news and grounds for criticism. Her solution appears to be based on the adage: be mindful of unintended consequences.

Privacy in the era of Franklin Delano Roosevelt bore no resemblance to the brand of the late 1960s. Respect for the personal lives of public figures, violated infrequently, and accepted by Americans of the World War II era, had evanesced by 1969. The ways in which personal and family concerns had become public fare during the Johnson administration, detailed reporting of the Johnson daughters' social experiences and the tragedies and misfortunes of Johnson family friends, no doubt alerted the Nixon family (inclined to be private anyway) to be even more cautious before making public statements. Even so, Pat Nixon must have known that any effort to protect privacy came at a price. Her rhetorical approach, if at one time fitting, was not as conducive to increasingly staccato press coverage of the day. She needed to address the possibility that the mediated audience might perceive her as keeping the public at arm's length or lacking candor. The risk of having her disciplined nature viewed as Callicles' "dead men and stones" did in fact, occur. An unflattering image of a stiff and dispassionate consort was occasionally used to characterize Mrs. Nixon from the 1950s until the end of her husband's presidency in 1974. But reports of Pat Nixon taking any public position in contrast to the administration were, as she desired, nonexistent.

It was on the issue of women's rights that Mrs. Nixon gave the only indication of being more liberal politically than her husband. While she had indicated (via family and friends) that she favored initiatives in the 1968 and 1972 Republican Convention platforms which endorsed the Equal Rights Amendment, and that she supported the nomination of a woman to the Supreme Court, she must have been keenly aware of three constraints. First, there was little national consensus on these issues and her position would not resolve that. Second, her expressed sentiments would not likely change feminist opposition to the Nixon agenda. And third, the expanded world audience to which her husband was so keenly attuned included vastly divergent sentiments regarding the treatment of women in general and the outspokenness of political spouses in particular.

These factors, in addition to her personal preferences already noted, presented a tantalizing challenge to someone of Mrs. Nixon's political awareness and experience. She began with a savvy understanding that effecting political persuasion is not confined to registered or even eligible voters. While taking into account the breadth of an expanded world audience, she may have assessed those with whom interaction was personally most fulfilling. Already, she had defined her role as first lady, as she had consistently throughout her husband's public life, from the perspective of her status as a wife and mother. If such exemplification was not enthusiastically received by members of the media or politicians, neither did it spawn detractors in and of itself. Those inclined to like Mrs. Nixon approved the example she set; those politically opposed to her, or more precisely, to her spouse, took exception to other things. Criticism focused mostly on her manner: "reserve" became "robotic." In the popular press the term, "Plastic Pat" typically signified an unflattering news item. But for her, a domestic countenance appears to have been a natural and rewarding representation, one that permitted, even encouraged reaching out to others. Genuinely comfortable with young and old alike, and imbued by her upbringing with the demeanor of a caregiver, Pat Nixon was what Margaret Truman called "a small *d* democrat in her bones, someone who always preferred to iron her own dresses, wash her own clothes, who instinctively sympathized with the poor and unlucky of this world" (Truman 1995, 190).

A final aspect should not be casually dismissed. The office of first lady has come to convey a measure of dignity and distance that inspires curiosity, even awe. In her presence, an ordinary citizen might expect the display of gracious hospitality or pleasantness, but not necessarily the easy warmth of a friend. If members of the public had, in addition, any preconceived notions of a reticent Mrs. Nixon, they encountered a paradox that forced choosing between the "plastic Pat" they had read about and the laughing first lady who was patting their shoulder or squeezing their hands. An expression or spirit of unconditional warmth and acceptance takes on an implausible and therefore special significance when it originates in one who is perceived by an audience to be shy and reserved. This unintended aid may have been the secret to whatever success Pat Nixon's "personal diplomacy" enjoyed. As the advantage of the so-called "stealth bomber" is its ability to fly low, undetected by radar, so the strength of "personal diplomacy" may have been that it was so obvious and came to be taken so much for granted, that reporters often missed its effects completely. Two incidents in particular come to mind.

From the time of her departure following her husband's assassination, Jacqueline Kennedy had not returned to the White House. The official portraits of President and Mrs. Kennedy, painted by artist Aaron Shikler, were finished in 1971. Mrs. Nixon extended a hand-delivered invitation to Mrs. Kennedy and her children, inviting them to view privately the official portraits and to spend an afternoon in their former home. Surmising accurately that Mrs. Kennedy would not wish the press to be informed, she promised the former first lady privacy and not a word to the media. When Mrs. Kennedy accepted the invitation Mrs. Nixon did not share the reply with her press secretary Helen Smith, so that in the event the press might suspect or learn of the visit, Helen would be able to—and indeed, did—respond honestly that she knew nothing of the get-together. The three Kennedys arrived without fanfare, viewed both paintings and commented appreciatively on the prominent locations selected for each. Mrs. Nixon, who admired her predecessor's extensive efforts at White House restoration, briefed her on the progress in recovering White House antiquity. Mrs. Kennedy expressed admiration for the work of curator Clement Conger and Mrs. Nixon that was continuing based on Mrs. Kennedy's initiative. The Nixon daughters showed Caroline and John Jr. the family quarters and the rooms that had been their own. All three Kennedys wrote afterwards, thanking the Nixon women effusively for their gracious hospitality and more important for making every effort to guarantee the privacy of their visit. Jacqueline Kennedy wrote: "The day I always dreaded turned out to be one of the most precious ones I have spent with my children" (Eisenhower 1986, 310). Only later, by mutual agreement, was news of the event made public. Personal diplomacy admits loyalty and trustworthiness to an unusual degree. Mrs. Nixon could have violated the wishes of her predecessor and choreographed a press and photo opportunity without equal. Instead, she incurred the wrath of the press corps for withholding information. Helen Thomas, dean of the White House press corps and a personal favorite of Pat's had suspected something, leaked her suspicions, and felt betrayed by the White House's reluctance to confirm. Pat Nixon chose the path that hurt others least and paid the price herself.

In May 1972, the first lady accompanied her husband to the Moscow Summit and there is evidence to suggest that events occurred as a consequence of Mrs. Nixon's personal diplomacy. According to *U.S. News and World Report*, "[Mrs. Nixon's] friendliness seemed to captivate the Russians" ("Pat in Moscow: A Busy Week," 19). *Newsweek* reported:

> Three months ago she charmed them in Peking with her unfailing cheerfulness and tact. And last week in Moscow, Pat Nixon turned in another virtuoso performance as a goodwill ambassador extraordinaire, handling the people-to-people aspects of the Moscow summit trip with aplomb. . . . As a former schoolteacher herself, Mrs. Nixon seemed happiest while visiting children's ballet classes and Soviet classrooms. ("Ladies Day in Moscow," 31)

Washington Post reporter Robert G. Kaiser cited unprecedented media coverage to the summit by the Soviet media:

> Thirteen minutes of the 15-minute main news program was devoted to the Nixons' visit. . . . Such elaborate coverage is extremely unusual here, and it contradicts predictions by Soviet journalists who said that no big fuss would be made over the visit. On the contrary the Nixons have been given the sort of attention that is reserved for extraordinary events. . . . The impact of all this on ordinary Russians cannot be described with certainty. But there is no doubt that they will get the message that this visit is regarded as an extremely important event. (1972, A12)

Of Mrs. Nixon's impact specifically Kaiser wrote:

> Pictures of a smiling Mrs. Nixon at a Moscow school and in the city's subway system put the First Lady in a sympathetic light for Soviet citizens. Her neatly-coiffed good looks are a far cry from the hook-nosed snarling Uncle Sam who often represents America in Soviet cartoons. (1972, A12)

In mid-1973 Soviet officials, in the spirit of détente, reversed an earlier decision with the surprise announcement that the children's cast of the Bolshoi Ballet, with whom Mrs. Nixon had visited the previous spring, would be permitted to accept the invitation to perform in the United States for the first time. The *New York Times* reported that Mrs. Nixon had invited the entire membership of the ballet, young and old, to a reception at the White House when the tour came to Washington.

Preparations for the August event focused on the children. Fruit punch and an array of sweets adorned the buffet in the State Dining Room. The Marine Band played and the White House seemed unusually festive. But the arrival of the ballerinas signaled a change in mood. Huddled together, the young members of the troupe appeared apprehensive and skeptical. One of the chaperones whispered to a member of Mrs. Nixon's staff that a newspaper's unfavorable review of the previous evening's performance had been shared with the girls.[7] They had taken it personally and doubted whether their American hosts really wanted to be friends after all.

A receiving line was quietly formed, and invitations to eat and tour the house were extended. But as the children shook hands with the first lady their manner was dutiful and their expressions wooden. The reception looked to be a disaster. As one child extended her hand to greet the first lady, the interpreter standing beside her remarked, "Today is Zuhra's birthday." Mrs. Nixon brightened. Grasping the child's hand with both of her own and smiling at the young ballerina, she asked the interpreter "How old?" Before the interpreter could put the question to Zuhra, Mrs. Nixon had released the child's hand and ventured a guess as to her age, using her fingers. Zuhra responded almost immediately, holding up all ten fingers, and then raising a hand again to show one finger alone. As everyone in attendance watched, Mrs. Nixon reflected the gestured "eleven" response and then, in an almost seamless movement enfolded Zuhra in her arms. Zuhra clung to the first lady. Personal diplomacy had found expression in a birthday embrace for a child 5,000 miles from home.

But that was only the beginning. Ballerinas who had proceeded through the line abruptly turned and ran back to Mrs. Nixon, intent on "equal time." Chaperones tried in vain to restore the orderly procession of little girls, but they held tight to Mrs. Nixon who, laughing, made no move to stop the children. The reception became a birthday party, no one wishing to leave. The personification of an American mother, the first lady in fact, accompanied by the symbolic potency of a universal gesture, otherwise known as a hug. Détente, from that vantage on an August afternoon, seemed destined to succeed.[8]

Legacy

As the subject of rhetorical analysis, the wife of the thirty-seventh president is easily overlooked. She never sought the limelight; occasions at the podium were rare. To deflect attention she engaged in brevity, but her responses were purposeful and according to members of the media assigned to cover her, successful in the way she was able to connect with her audience for more than three decades in the public spotlight. Once asked to identify her favorite cause, the one with which she would endow the prestige and influence of her position, Patricia Ryan Nixon replied simply: "People are my project" (Eisenhower 1986, 267). Dean of the White House Press Corps and UPI reporter, Helen Thomas declared: "She was the warmest First Lady I covered and the one who loved people most" (Thomas 1975, 165).

The record of accomplishment set by Mrs. Nixon as first lady (1969–1974) is impressive. It includes restoration of White House antiquity, providing inspiration for illuminating federal buildings and monuments of the nation's capital, becoming history's most traveled first lady as an official guest of eighty-three countries, and the first to enter a designated combat zone on foreign soil. She was repeatedly honored by service organizations for revitalizing a spirit of volunteerism nationwide. Between 1959 and 1979, she climbed fourteen times to the heights of the Gallup "Most Admired Women" survey (Watson 2000, 179). And when she died in June 1993, friends and columnists paid tribute to her qualities of character and communicative behavior. Suzanne Fields recalled her "person-to-person attentiveness, her personal touch" (Fields 1993, E1). Ellen Goodman attributed to her a "steadfast" quality and stoicism: "Pat Nixon formed our classic image of the political wife. She was the woman who campaigned once with three broken ribs and another time with a swollen ankle. And she never mentioned it" (Goodman 1993, 33). Chris Matthews eulogized: "Through it all, the great power of Pat Nixon was the simple nerve" (Matthews 1993, F3). But because Mrs. Nixon was by nature reluctant to make herself the subject of conversation, Goodman began her memorial column: "We never knew her. Not really" (Goodman, 1993, A-11).

Ellen Goodman's statement prompts a question: Was Mrs. Nixon's approach, which entailed the preservation of a measure of personal privacy, worth what it cost her image? Though additional factors are attributed to the perception of Mrs. Nixon as remote, biographers, including Eisenhower, Thomas, Caroli, and Anthony all acknowledge to some degree in their biographies the truth of Margaret Truman's assessment that "Pat Nixon is the First Lady nobody knew" (Truman 1995, 188). Gutin goes so far as to suggest that Pat Nixon shirked her responsibility as first lady: "Pat Nixon never impressed her image on the consciousness of Americans. The consummate traditional political wife, she was a nondescript cypher, a woman who preferred to be neutral rather than committed. She was a woman who understood the enormous potential of her position and yet generally rejected it" (Gutin 1989, 61)

This is a difficult assertion to substantiate when applied to specific situations. Guests at the White House, treated to Mrs. Nixon's low-key, personalized approach, did not leave feeling shortchanged. Media access to these events, with rare exceptions, was not limited. Interestingly, however, it was a style so characteristic and expected of Mrs. Nixon that it was taken for granted and not often considered newsworthy.[9] If the ability to "make news" is the primary gauge of one's speaking style, Gutin may have a point. But relying exclusively on such a measure may cause critics to miss the wisdom of a strategy that reaches beyond conventional structural boundaries of a political and rhetorical situation to become uncommonly effective.

As a study of ethos, this essay has focused on two of the three qualities ascribed by Aristotle: character and goodwill. The third component, knowledge or expertise, is every bit as critical. In Mrs. Nixon's case, experience had given her a heightened understanding of people from varied backgrounds and nationalities. In her role as first lady, she put her knowledge to use. Though Caroli suggests that Mrs. Nixon's emphasis on domestic matters was excessive, the fact that fifteen years later Barbara Bush extolled Pat Nixon's style as one to emulate suggests recognition of qualities both endearing and enduring (Weinraub 1989, A20). What is meaningful for this study is that her conduct was grounded in her field of expertise, reflected her probity, and demonstrated her benevolence. It "revealed her character" and enhanced her credibility both nationally and internationally. It was not uniformly understood or appreciated, although somewhere in Russia a former ballerina (and now her children) probably recalls, with a certain fondness, the lady who embraced her on her birthday.

Personal diplomacy was a sophisticated rhetorical strategy, but there is nothing about Mrs. Nixon's demeanor to indicate that it was calculated. She appears to have possessed a capacity, if not instinctive, then impeccably disciplined to respond to heartfelt need. It is fair to say that by adulthood this is who Pat Nixon was as a human being. She did acknowledge in at least one interview: "I'm a perfectionist. I won't do a thing without trying to do it well" (Meyers 1960, 24).

She never aspired to the role of first lady, or a life in politics. Within the framework of public service she sought—and found—those who needed her. The inherent motivation that Kenneth Burke locates in human action is at least implied in Meyers' account of a rare, unguarded moment:

> Recently a young friend asked about the rigors of public life. Pat's eyes suddenly filled with tears. "I've given up everything I ever loved," she blurted, and looked out the window until composure returned. Then she continued: "The people who lose out are the children. Any of the glamour or reward in it comes to the grownups. It's the children who really suffer." (Meyers 1960, 25)

Patricia Nixon adhered rigidly and dutifully to protocol, traditionally understood and personally endorsed. But there were key moments in her career, a few described in this essay, when compassion overruled her strict sense of duty. Her impulsive departure from the decorum of the moment may have been persuasive in part because she so assiduously maintained strict decorum so much of the time.

Attention to the significance of balance may be what a study of Mrs. Nixon's self-styled personal diplomacy most strongly suggests. Her penchant for privacy has been noted. In her rhetorical demeanor, it extended beyond a sense of personal decorum to set a tone of conduct that appears to have satisfied a public need. Pat Nixon's image provided an equilibrium and fortitude when compared with that of her spouse in the era they shared. Edwin Black has written of the former president: "Experienced and skillful as he was a rhetor, he was never quite able to sequester his private life in the way that other public figures routinely do, or at least did prior to Nixon's presidency" (Black 1999, 1). Pat was, however, enabled or compelled by the events of Nixon's turbulent career to master the skill. Black notes that Richard Nixon himself recalled in two separate autobiographies the devastating effect that exposing personal and family financial details as part of the Checkers Speech defense in the 1952 presidential campaign had on Pat. Black keenly observes:

> Hannah [Nixon's mother] and Pat embodied privacy for Nixon, but they were not alone in their sensitivity to the pain of his disclosure. Anyone with a reverence for the privacy of family matters and a commitment to the pieties of the public-private allocation may have regarded Nixon's financial divulgence as an act of voluntary mortification, a brave and painful conquest of inhibition in the service of a higher candor. For an audience imbued with the values of privacy, the Checkers speech was a trial by embarrassment through which Nixon triumphantly passed before their very eyes. (Black 1999, 12)

Pat Nixon appeared to complete her husband's triumph. Her embodiment of the value of privacy with which many Americans identified certainly contributed to the pathos of the Nixons' financial disclosure episode in 1952. Her stoic dignity became an undeviating stance in times of crisis. Emotion overcame her only once, at Nixon's concession in Los Angeles the morning following the 1960 presidential election. Print and broadcast journalists conspicuously included mention of her stoic demeanor in reporting events of Nixon's political career. It signaled such a distinct contrast to her warmth and effusiveness that it served as a cue. Viewers observed the same resolute expression of the Checkers Speech broadcast in the gaze she maintained during her husband's resignation as he bid his staff farewell on August 9, 1974. It had become a demeanor on which the public could rely; its persuasive value may have been derived from its consistent maintenance.[10]

This demeanor continued to reflect Pat Nixon even after she left the White House. It was a period marked by silence. Prior to the debilitating stroke in 1976, she neither wrote nor commissioned a personal memoir. Her daughter Julie published the most comprehensive biography, but key staff members whose admiration for her was profound appear to have followed Mrs. Nixon's lead and are thus far content to let events of her life speak for themselves. Yet events encompass and contain facts. David Zarefsky (1998, 20) reminds those who would "do" rhetorical history, "Facts cannot speak for themselves; they must be spoken for."[11] A fuller understanding and appreciation of Mrs. Nixon's persuasive capacities will depend on the willingness of those who knew her well to share their recollections. Insufficient source material for comprehensive appraisal hinders any opportunity to appreciate forgotten virtues.

Civic virtue is persuasive, so long as it is perceived as genuine. But even in that event, it may be taken for granted and go unnoticed. Its short-term effect is apt to be confined to the context in which it occurs. If one's behavior as part of a rhetorical strategy needs to attract a certain attention, it is an inappropriate demeanor. If perceived as feigned, any appearance of integrity will likely prove counterproductive.

In the long term, however, the exemplification of civic virtue still has the capacity to ennoble a culture and its people, provided the virtues themselves continue to be valued and recorded as such. "The eyes of the beholder" or the identification that may occur between critic and subject will influence who emerges as heroic according to timeless and timely criteria. Socrates' dignity still inspires, but so too does Quintilian for preserving Socrates as he does: "he preferred that what remained of his life should be lost rather than that portion of it which was past. . . . he committed himself to the judgment of posterity [by] conduct honorable to his character as a man" (Watson 1856, Bk. II, ch. 11, p. 1). The persuasive effect of conduct may likewise depend on "the judgment of posterity." More than we realize may hinge on Zarefsky's "fourth sense" or as someone close to Patricia Nixon once said: "who writes the history" (Hobgood 1974e).

Questions for Discussion

1. Chapter author Linda B. Hobgood asserts in her essay that Pat Nixon remains a mystery to the American public. She quotes journalist Ellen Goodman who writes, "We never knew her. Not really." Do you agree that Pat Nixon is still a mystery? Why might this be so?
2. What strengths and abilities did Pat Nixon bring to the Nixon political partnership?
3. Did First Lady Pat Nixon champion a cause? Chapter author Linda B. Hobgood suggests that Mrs. Nixon's cause may have been her "boundless compassion" as manifested in her "personal diplomacy." What does Hobgood mean? Do you agree that Pat Nixon's cause was "people?"
4. Pat Nixon was often depicted in the media as aloof, distant, as "Plastic Pat." Yet those who knew her well or had personal contact with her say she was a warm, compassionate, and fun-loving person. What factors may have contributed to this paradoxical image of Pat Nixon? If you were hired as an advisor during her term as first lady, what rhetorical strategies would you recommend to her to help her control the image the press projected of her?

Internet Resources

http://www.archives.gov/nixon/
The Richard M. Nixon Presidential Library contains material on Pat Nixon. The website contains Mrs. Nixon's papers and photographs of her. You can search for material online, and access some of it over the internet.

http://www.nixonfoundation.org/TheNixons/PatNixon.shtml
The Richard Nixon Library and Birthplace Online contains a biography of Pat Nixon, complete with photographs of important events in her life.

http://nixonfamily.freeservers.com/
The Nixon Family website is an excellent source of articles and photographs of the
Nixon family. You can follow links to discover material on all members of the Nixon
family. Also accessible are election results and press reports of Richard Nixon's major campaigns.

http://www.geocities.com/pat_nixon_rwf/index.htm
The website, "Pat Nixon Republican Women, Federated," sponsored by a Cali-
fornia women's group is interesting to visit because it shows that the values Pat
Nixon stood for are still being championed by women today.

Notes

Portions of this essay were presented as "Conduct Becoming: Pat Nixon and the Rhetoric
of Personal Diplomacy," at the Southern States Communication Association Convention, Lexington, Kentucky, April 7, 2001.

The author extends appreciation to Welford D. Taylor, Jerry Tarver, and Kathleen J.
Turner for their valued suggestions and superb editing. Julie Eisenhower, Jinny Bartlett,
and Joe Bartlett, who provided similar assistance, graciously shared their knowledge and
recollections of Pat Nixon as well. My deepest thanks.

1. From Plato's *Gorgias* (Bennett 1993, 98–99).

2. Even before the Nixons moved into the White House, security had required the
parking of buses, bumper to bumper, so as to surround the White House grounds to protect the first family from the more violent demonstrators.

3. The term "fungible narrative" was, to my knowledge, first provided by Craig Allen
Smith in his text *Political Communication* (1990, 94–95). It refers to the fact that what we
do not know "about human motives, problems, relationships, and their resolutions," we infer from entertainment, from dramas we've seen. In other words, what we have no way of
knowing about Pat Nixon, we "absorb" (hence, fungible), much as a sponge absorbs mois-
ture, from such sources as Oliver Stone's film *Nixon* or reruns of *Saturday Night Live*. Eventually, what we know to be true and what we have inferred from entertainment sources
become blurred—too blurred to make distinctions.

4. Professor Kathleen Turner, who served as panel respondent at the SSCA Conference in Lexington, Kentucky, April 2001, described her own reaction watching Pat Nixon
during the Checkers Speech. Members of the panel audience nodded a unanimous agreement as she was apparently voicing their own impressions of the actual or taped broadcast.

5. Epitaph on cemetery monument at Mrs. Nixon's grave.

6. Though Lady Bird Johnson delivered 164 speeches during her husband's presidency,
Betty Caroli writes: "Unlike Eleanor Roosevelt, Lady Bird did not thrive on the controversies inherent in politics, and she disapproved of First Ladies who involved themselves
in issues that might divide the country" (1987, 237, 241). That Johnson's position was
more the expected norm for first ladies by the public audience of her era is implied.

7. The review actually praised the children's ballet performance, but found the adults'
performance less than impressive (Lewis 1973, D3).

8. The reception was hardly noted by the media. The best account is Tom Shales
(1973, D1, D3).

9. On one occasion in particular during the summer of 1974 when this author was especially moved by Mrs. Nixon's gesture of kindness to a visitor, her press secretary Helen McCain Smith rejected apologies for display of emotion saying, "No, it's good to be reminded of Mrs. Nixon's rare qualities. We see them so frequently, we can become too accustomed to her unique way with people."

10. It failed her only once as has been noted, during Richard Nixon's November 9, 1960, concession speech at the Ambassador Hotel in Los Angeles, shortly after midnight following his presidential election defeat. She learned from the experience. On the final day of Nixon's presidency, his family was unaware until they arrived on the main floor of the White House, that there was to be media coverage of the staff farewell. Pat Nixon acknowledged almost no staff members who were assembled in the East Room of the White House. When her husband finished speaking, the family proceeded to the South Lawn for departure. Afterward, she placed a call to Helen Smith. In her determination to retain composure, she had failed to say good-bye.

11. Similar commentary by Richard Weaver is: "The supposition that facts will speak for themselves is of course another abdication of the intellect" (1948, 58).

References

Anthony, Carl Sferranza. 1991. *First Ladies: The Saga of Presidents' Wives and Their Power, 1961–1990*, Vol. 2. New York: Quill/William Morrow.

Bennett, William, ed. 1993. Plato on Self-Discipline: Selections from *Gorgias*. In *Book of Virtues*. New York: Simon & Schuster.

Black, Edwin. 1999. Richard Nixon and the Privacy of Public Discourse. *Rhetoric and Public Affairs*, 2:1, 1–29.

Burke, Kenneth. 1954. *Permanence and Change: An Anatomy of Purpose*. Los Altos, Calif.: Hermes Publications.

———. 1969. *A Grammar of Motives*. Berkeley, Calif.: University of California Press.

Caroli, Betty Boyd. 1987. *First Ladies*. New York: Oxford University Press.

Cowan, Ruth. 1953. Pat Nixon's Story Pales Movie Script Writers' Best Try. *Washington Post*, 18 January.

David, Lester. 1978. *The Lonely Lady of San Clemente*. New York: Crowell.

Eisenhower, Julie. 1986. *Pat Nixon: The Untold Story*. New York: Simon & Schuster.

———. 2001. Interview on CNN's *Larry King Live*. Broadcast 20 June.

Fields, Suzanne. 1993. First Ladies' New First. *Washington Times*, 28 June.

Goodman, Ellen. 1993. Pat Nixon Was the First Lady of Virtue, Loyalty, and Family. *Richmond-Times Dispatch*, 26 June.

Gould, Lewis L. 1996. *American First Ladies: Their Lives and Their Legacy*. New York: Garland.

Gutin, Myra G. 1989. *The President's Partner: The First Lady in the Twentieth Century*. New York: Greenwood.

Hobgood, Linda. 1974a. Interview with Susan Dolibois, June.

———. 1974b. Interviews with Susan Porter Rose, June and July.

———. 1974c. Interview with Gwen King, July.

———. 1974d. Interview with Helen Smith, July.

———. 1974e. Interview with Richard M. Nixon, 5 August.

———. 2000. Interview with Mrs. William Broomfield (Jane), 26 October

———. 2001. Telephone Interview with Virginia B. Bartlett, 11 July.

Kaiser, Robert G. 1972. Soviet Media Play Up Nixon Visit. *Washington Post*, 24 May, A12.

Ladies Day in Moscow. 1972. *Newsweek*, 5 June, 79.

Lewis, Jean Battery. 1973. Less Than Inspired. *Washington Post*. 4 August, D3.

Matthews, Chris. 1993. Dignity and Grace in a Cloth Coat. *Washington Times*, 25 June.

———. 1997. *Kennedy and Nixon: The Rivalry That Shaped Postwar America*. New York: Simon & Schuster.

McPherson, Myra. 1975. The Blooming of Betty Ford. *McCalls*, September.

Meyers, Burt. 1960. The Silent Partner. *Time*, 29 February, 24–26.

Pat in Moscow: A Busy Week. 1972. *U.S. News and World Report*, 5 June.

Safire, William. 1975. *Before the Fall*. New York: Doubleday.

Sattler, William M. 1947. Conceptions of Ethos in Ancient Rhetoric. *Speech Monographs*, 55–65.

Schamber, Jon F., and Russell W. Vinyard. 2000. Cicero Revisited: A Look Back on Citizenship for the Rhetorician. Paper presented at the National Communication Association, Seattle, Wash., 9 November.

Shales, Tom. 1973. Stealing the Show at the White House. *Washington Post*. 4 August, D1, D3.

Smith, Craig Allen. 1990. *Political Communication*. San Diego: Harcourt Brace Jovanovich.

Thomas, Helen. 1975. *Dateline: The White House*. New York: Macmillan.

Truman, Margaret. 1995. *First Ladies*. New York: Random House.

Watson, John Selby. 1856. *Quintilian's Institutes of Oratory: Or Education of an Orator*. London: Henry G. Bohn.

Watson, Robert P. 2000. *The Presidents' Wives: Reassessing the Office of First Lady*. Boulder, Colo.: Lynne Rienner.

Weaver, Richard. 1948. *Ideas Have Consequences*. Chicago: University of Chicago Press.

Weinraub, Bernard. 1989. A Down-to-Earth Tenant for an Exclusive Address. *New York Times*, 15 January, A1, A20.

Will, George. 1975. Calculations. *National Review*, 12 September, 984.

Zarefsky, David. 1998. Four Senses of Rhetorical History. In *Doing Rhetorical History*, ed. Kathleen J. Turner, 19–32. Tuscaloosa, Ala.: University of Alabama Press.

CHAPTER SIX

Betty Ford
A Certain Comfort
from a Candid First Lady

Nichola D. Gutgold and Linda B. Hobgood

Being ladylike does not require silence.

—Betty Ford

Her White House stay was short-lived, but the lessons of Betty Ford's experience remain vividly instructive. By accident of a national political crisis which catapulted her to the rank of first lady in 1974, Mrs. Ford's tenure lasted a brief two years until her husband, Gerald R. Ford lost his bid for reelection. During that time, she developed a relationship of candor with the press and public. She spoke her mind on social and moral issues that were at the forefront of public debate. The positions she took were not always popular with the majority of Americans, many of whom complained bitterly especially after her notorious interview on CBS's 60 Minutes. Indeed, Mrs. Ford's rhetorical responses between 1974 and 1976 show how difficult it can be for a well-meaning public figure who must learn—"onstage"—to fill the role into which she had been so abruptly cast.

Taking full advantage of the considerable visibility and influence of the office of first lady, Betty Ford became a voice for the causes she supported. But public backlash and her reply are reminders that taking part in a controversy, even inadvertently, exacts a price. The risks taken by Mrs. Ford illustrate possible consequences when endearing traits of a first lady's character "collide" with the enduring values of many of her fellow citizens. An unintended effect of Mrs. Ford's experience demonstrates that presidential campaigns do prepare candidates and their wives for interaction with a national audience that is eager to know them. Unfortunately, Mrs. Ford did not have this benefit.

Mrs. Ford's persuasive efforts as first lady grew in sophistication as she gained experience in that position; she continued to build upon what she had learned from being the wife of a politician and the other roles she had played. We begin with an account of Mrs. Ford's childhood, education, work experience, and marriage to show some of the qualities of character that she brought to the office of first lady. We trace her experiences as the wife of a senator and mother of four children to indicate how "ready" she was rhetorically to assume the position of first lady. Using articles in print media and personal interview accounts, we discuss the role expectations that many Americans held for a president's wife at the time when Mrs. Ford was called to serve. Finally, we show how all of these factors came into play when she spoke her mind candidly to the American public. We use excerpts from Mrs. Ford's speeches, but focus primarily on CBS's televised interview on 60 Minutes between Mrs. Ford and interviewer Morley Safer. Aired on Sunday, August 21, 1975, this interview prompted thousands of letters, most of them negative. The way Mrs. Ford chose to answer her critics speaks to her own strength of character and her capacity to "measure up" and become accustomed to the demands of her position. Her rhetorical choices reveal an uncommon consistency. By virtue of those choices she was able to regain the admiration of an impressive majority of Americans, whose support she maintained through difficult times following her years as first lady. Indeed, over time Betty Ford learned to put her candor to use for the public good.

Biography

One can almost hear the enthymeme:

> Betty Ford is so honest and forthright, so humble and friendly!
> Well, of course—look where she's from!

To fully appreciate the character of Elizabeth Bloomer Ford requires understanding what it means to be "Midwestern." People from the Midwest are thought to be "comfortable with who they are. They have a common decency." There is more to it than mere birthright, though by virtue of her place of birth, Chicago, and her childhood home of Grand Rapids, Michigan, Betty Ford certainly qualifies as Midwestern. And despite subtle differences between, say, Hoosiers and Minnesotans, the similarities outweigh the differences and symbolically unify those who belong to the America's geographical "middle." If there is a single identifying attribute among "Midwesterners," it seems to be candor, including an appreciation for those who are straightforward in manner and speech.

New York Times reporter Jane Howard recalls:

> When the President [Ford] promised "straight talk among friends" in his Inaugural Address, he was speaking at least as much for his wife, whose low-key candor quickly surpassed his own. She was full of surprises, this kindly matron from Michigan. (Howard 1974, 64)

Betty Ford scholars (Anthony, Caroli, Gould, Gutin, and Truman among others) all highlight her frankness, but to this most attach another trait, a genuine sense of concern for and about others. They tend to assign regional distinction to this virtue as well. Observes Howard:

> In many ways she is ordinary, well schooled in the midwestern arts of assuaging and consoling. Her thank you notes are prompt and heartfelt. Nice gestures come naturally. . . . "Betty Ford was nice to me," recalls the ex-wife of one controversial Senator, "when other people weren't." But she's not just nice. No. The merely nice bypass the truth when it makes them or anyone else edgy, and that's something Betty Ford doesn't do. She never has. (Howard 1974, 64)

At least two additional qualities are implied in the kindness attributed to Betty Ford: a matter-of-fact, bedrock honesty, and a sense of humility. One of her friends, Jane Broomfield, who is the wife of a colleague of Gerald Ford's, offers tribute to this blend of honesty and self-effacement: "People in the Midwest are just open. Well, at least in Michigan they are. . . . They [the Fords] are great 'truth-tellers.' But she [Betty] could feel terrible and you'd never know it. There was no small talk about herself—ever" (Hobgood, 2000b). Biographer and daughter of another president, Margaret Truman, compared the preferences of two first ladies: "what Betty Ford shared with Bess Truman was a midwestern dislike for any and all kinds of pretentiousness" (Truman 1995, 133).

Mrs. Ford was not the first first lady to be embraced by "the folks back home" who claimed to know her best. For example, Lady Bird Johnson has, for many years, symbolized to Texans and non-Texans alike many of the qualities for which that state is so proud. But it is striking that Mrs. Ford is repeatedly viewed as personifying those same four virtues of frankness, concern for others, honesty, and humility. And while it is allowed that those qualities seem particularly evident among those whose origins are Midwestern, they are used in regard to Betty Ford in an apparent effort to associate her with qualities that are quintessentially American, too. Historian Lewis Gould, who calls her "outspoken—but never strident," assigns her other highly valued aspects of the American character such as an independent spirit and a sense of humor (1996, 553). Carl Anthony uses the first lady's own typically American tendency to convey her forthright attitude: "When somebody asks you how you stand on an issue," explained Betty Ford of her policy of candor, "you're very foolish if you try to beat around the bush—you just meet yourself going around the bush the other way" (1991, 553).

Mrs. Ford's character is thus clearly and uniformly understood, both by those who have known her and those who have studied her. According to Gutin, "Betty Ford is more sharply defined in the minds of Americans than most First Ladies" (1989, 122). One of the reasons for her popularity was the generally held opinion that this particular lady of the White House was the same person in Washington political circles as the one who had grown up in Grand Rapids and who had raised a family in the suburbs of Alexandria, Virginia. But as Anthony notes, perhaps wryly, there were occasions when "the private person collided with the public persona" (1991, 225). The events she considered significant in her own life and the people Betty Ford most admired might help to explain such "collisions."

Evident in both of her memoirs, *The Times of My Life* (1978) and *A Glad Awakening* (1987), is Betty Ford's genuine fondness for people. But she reserves highest praise for a special few among them, such as her parents. Born in 1918, she was the only daughter of parents she describes as attractive, hardworking, and devoted to each other. Her father's sales career meant constant travel; Betty recalls with tenderness that her mother wrote him every night when he was away. Betty's mother was "rather formal" and protectively firm. She insisted her daughter wear hat and gloves when they went shopping and while Betty didn't object to the accessories, she tried to explain to her mother that other girls went without them. Mrs. Bloomer was adamant, and Betty comments almost as an afterthought that her mother might not always approve the more lenient approach Betty used with her own daughter. In her first memoir, *The Times of My Life*, Betty remembers her mother's resolve, this time in the midst of a rainstorm:

> I can still feel my mother's arms around me, holding me as she stood on the porch and we watched a storm come rolling in across the lake, waves swelling, thunder crashing, lightning slicing the sky, and my mother telling me how beautiful it was. I found out later she was scared to death, but she taught me not to be afraid; I was safe in those arms. (B. Ford 1978, 7)

Later, she tried to emulate that resolve with her own children.

As an adolescent, Betty Ford enjoyed school and loved dancing classes. "Dance was my happiness," she wrote, and she dreamed of a professional dancing career. Her father's sudden, accidental death when Betty was sixteen meant, "It was rougher for everybody after that. . . . he was gone and we'd loved him" (B. Ford 1978, 22). Betty's dream of training in New York to further her career seemed extravagant and to her mother too risky for Betty at the time. "It wouldn't have done me any good to fuss, and I wasn't the kind to run away; the bond between my mother and me was strong" (23). Betty was, however, permitted to spend summers at the Bennington School of Dance in Vermont. It was there that she met Martha Graham, arguably one of the strongest and most lasting influences on Mrs. Ford's life. She says:

> It's almost impossible to describe the impression made by Martha Graham on a girl who came to her straight out of high school. I worshipped her as a goddess. She was a tough disciplinarian. . . . But, as I've said before, I admired that kind of strictness. You can't be a dancer without it; not only your body, but also your mind must be disciplined. (B. Ford 1978, 24)

Betty went to New York to study with Martha Graham's troupe, and she also found work as a fashion model. But at her mother's urging she returned to Grand Rapids where she taught dance. She married a friend from childhood, but it did not last. After the divorce, Betty devoted herself to a career in retail fashion at a local department store. In 1947, she met a very disciplined young man, Gerald R. Ford, whom Betty called "the most eligible bachelor in Grand Rapids" (B. Ford

1978, 47). She clearly admired his determination. In October 1948, they were married and within a month her husband defeated an incumbent congressman in his first election bid to the U.S. House of Representatives.

Neither Ford imagined that the victory in 1948 was the beginning of twenty-eight years in the nation's capital. The beginning of their marriage and the start of Jerry Ford's congressional career coincided. Betty recalls that she eagerly became dedicated to both. She was convinced that her husband's political success was made more likely by her support and involvement, but this did not always translate into traveling together back to the district, or routinely accompanying him on endless rounds of political and diplomatic engagements. In Betty's case, this meant remaining behind, managing a household flawlessly, and performing the role of both mother and father in the absence of her husband.

During these years, the Ford family grew to include three sons and a daughter, each of whom maintained an increasingly active schedule. Betty coordinated these schedules, provided all necessary transportation, and accepted the many volunteer tasks that school and extracurricular involvements demand of parents (B. Ford 1978, 64–69, 92–95). In addition, she did what many congressional spouses do to augment the constituent service provided by the congressional offices. She mastered the layout and schedule of activities in Washington, D.C., and became a travel guide for visitors from the Michigan district and elsewhere (B. Ford, 1978, 63). Furthermore, as her husband's stature and rank on the minority side of the aisle grew, so did Betty's understanding of the potential reach and influence of legislators' wives who volunteer in Washington-area civic and philanthropic activities. As her husband rose to the position of House minority leader, Betty's volunteer activities increased, and she helped to raise funds by drawing media attention and public support to a vast array of worthy causes (B. Ford 1978, 121–22). She goaded the wives of fellow Republican senators and congressmen into participating as models in charity fashion shows. Her own account is illustrative of her outlook:

> Since Jerry had become an important Republican, I had taken it upon myself to shake up the Republican wives. I thought the Democratic wives were more effective. "If anybody asks you to do anything, say yes," I advised my peers. "Get off your duffs. It's always the Democratic wives who model in the fashion shows for Multiple Sclerosis or the Heart Fund." I coerced a lot of women who'd never done any modeling in their lives into chasing up and down runways for charity, and they got so they liked it. Nobody made me take on these jobs; I was convinced it was my duty. (B. Ford 1978, 121–22)

Betty's role as an active wife and mother sounds remarkably typical for a congressional wife of the '60s and early '70s. But the degree to which she succeeded is not. What is more typical in political situations such as hers is the gradual loss of attention to some aspect of life or another. The balance of family life and political involvement can be daunting; the noteworthy element in this phase of Betty Ford's career while her husband served in Congress is her singular talent in achieving that balance. She was both model political partner and dedicated mother, and she remained as popular with congressional wives and with old friends in Grand Rapids as with the neighbors on Crown View Drive in Alexandria, Virginia. She had proven that she was a dedicated political partner who had even discovered ways to fit that lifestyle to her own particular talents. In some ways she appears to have thrived on the challenge of the balancing act. Had it not been for the aggravation of a pinched nerve that eventually led her to seek help from a psychiatrist, she might have survived painlessly, even triumphantly, a most demanding time (B. Ford 1978, 174–78).

In part, because of her physical discomfort, Betty had exacted a promise from her husband to retire from Congress. Watching his dream of becoming Speaker of the House grow dim in the early '70s, Jerry Ford had agreed to run one last time in 1974, and then retire. As minority leader he was attending more than 250 engagements annually and time with his family had become too infrequent. But the resignation of Vice President Agnew in the fall 1973 altered abruptly the Fords' plans. Instead of looking to retire, Gerald Ford was named Agnew's successor by President Nixon. Ten months later, Nixon resigned the presidency and on August 9, 1974, Gerald R. Ford was sworn in as president of the United States and Betty Bloomer Ford became first lady.

In the aftermath of the Watergate crisis, Gerald Ford made every effort to distance himself from former president Nixon and all that had characterized his presidency. Early on, he issued statements to indicate the kind of administration he intended to set up. The hallmark of his presidency, he vowed, would be a spirit of honesty and openness. Betty concurred in this commitment and tried to do her part. Both Fords were determined to be truthful and to them this meant being candid, even spontaneous in their interactions with the press. While not an uncommon initial approach for some candidates and their wives, political campaigns have a way of tempering this communication objective.

According to Jules Witcover in *No Way to Pick a President* (1999), national campaigns are essential to the electoral process. They help citizens assess candidates' fitness for office, and they help candidates articulate what values and initiatives to pursue. Campaigns also groom the teams of people closest to the candidates—family, staff, and aides—all of whom benefit from their interaction with media and public. They gather insights into national audience values and can then adapt their positions accordingly. Gerald and Betty Ford, thrust as they were into office by unusual circumstances, had no opportunity to learn from such national campaigns.

Gerald Ford, however, was accustomed to campaigning for state office; indeed, his seniority in Congress had been earned by twelve successful campaigns for the Michigan House seat. His constant travel on behalf of Republican colleagues had made him a familiar face across the country as well. But when Betty Ford considered what a national constituency might expect from her as a first lady, her thoughts turned to Grand Rapids and Crown View Drive. She had no familiarity whatsoever with any constituency beyond the Michigan congressional district. Her Alexandria neighbors who knew her best liked her just as she was. Historian James T. Baker wrote: "Untrained to be a President's wife, she could be just the one to turn the First Lady into a human being at last" (Baker 1976, 864). And Anthony quoted Mrs. Ford as saying "I've spent too many years as me. . . . I can't suddenly turn into a princess" (Anthony 1991, 224).

Rhetorical Activities as First Lady

"What state dinner?"

Less than twenty-four hours after her husband's swearing-in Betty Ford received a call informing her that within the week she was scheduled to host a White House dinner for King Hussein and Queen Alia of Jordan. For events such as these, Betty's years as a Washington hostess came in handy. "I've been coming up through the ranks, so it isn't like being thrown into the front lines straight from Grand Rapids," she reminds readers in her 1978 memoir (162). By experience thus mobilized, the new first lady and her husband made known their intended modus operandi, a policy of availability and openness. President Ford, addressing a joint session of Congress on August 12, "[told] legislators he [did not] want a honeymoon with them. 'I want a good marriage. . . . My office door has always been open and that is how it is going to be at the White House'" (B. Ford 1978, 163).

In this spirit, members of the Ford family made themselves accessible to the media. Statements made by the Ford children, however, promptly placed the president in the position of accounting for their remarks and dissociating himself from some of their more extreme statements. Ford explained that his children had always been encouraged to speak their minds, though he did not always share their views.

Betty, too, was eager to meet with members of the press and did so in the East Room of the White House less than a month after her arrival. In what Gutin calls the first official press conference by a first lady in twenty-two years (Gutin 1989, 131), Mrs. Ford answered questions and echoed her husband's acknowledgment that as parents they made no attempt to regulate their children's comments. Relaxed and unrehearsed, Betty's maternal persona projected the means by which she sought to identify with the American press and public. Determined to convey accessibility, she announced those programs to which she would direct her attention and presented an agenda of her own. She spoke in favor of ratification of the Equal Rights Amendment and of increased participation by women in public office. On the issue of abortion she expressed support for the pro-choice position.

These were not official positions of the Ford administration. As the president had always emphasized, the first lady had a right to her own opinion and she felt free to offer it. Mrs. Ford herself writes:

> I tried to be honest; I tried not to dodge subjects. I felt the public had a right to know where I stood. Nobody had to feel the way I felt, I wasn't forcing my opinions on

anybody, but if someone asked me a question, I gave that person a straight answer. I've been told that I didn't play it safe enough, but my husband has always been totally supportive. He's never stepped on my toes; he's never turned around and complained, "Well, that was a dumb thing to say." (B. Ford 1978, 205–6)

In any case, it became clear almost from the beginning of Ford's term that the statements coming from the East and West Wings of the White House in this administration might be distinctly different messages.

In mid-September 1974, President Ford issued a pardon for his predecessor, Richard M. Nixon. The pardon overwhelmed all actions prior to and many that followed Ford's decision. Betty recalls, "Jerry's administration had begun with a flood of good will and good wishes from all kinds of people who liked his decency, his friendliness, his accessibility, his ability to laugh at himself" (B. Ford 1978, 180). This amicable atmosphere (note Betty's use of the same "Midwestern" adjectives!) might have continued indefinitely, but President Ford's pardon of his predecessor marked its end. Then another one of those dramatic, unpredictable circumstances intervened to affect public opinion of the first lady in a manner both sympathetic and compelling.

Just weeks after the pardon, a malignancy was discovered during a routine medical examination of Mrs. Ford, and she underwent almost immediately a radical mastectomy. Gratitude for the assured success of the operation merged in Betty Ford's reaction to the ordeal with a sudden awareness of the power she held as a first lady:

> I got a lot of credit for having gone public with my mastectomy, but if I hadn't been the wife of the President of the United States, the press would not have come racing after my story. . . . Even before I was able to get up, I lay in bed and watched television and saw on the news shows lines of women queued up to go in for breast examinations because of what had happened to me. Lying in the hospital, thinking of all those women going for cancer checkups because of me, I'd come to recognize more clearly the power of the woman in the White House. Not my power, but the power of the position, a power which could be used to help. (B. Ford 1978, 194)

It is hard to imagine anything that could have brought this realization into focus with greater clarity or impact.

Recognition of the power of the office coincided with an oversight by the president, which, although pale by comparison, heightened the Fords' sensitivity to image and protocol. In November 1974, not long after Betty's return to the White House following her surgery, President Ford departed for a scheduled visit to Japan. At a formal dinner, he was photographed with Emperor Hirohito. Ford's dress trousers, "left over from college," appeared too short, and he suffered a fair share of ridicule from the media. Betty commented: "Well, if you're going to assume the office, you have to assume the striped pants that go with it. The public expects a president to dress well; he can't just say to hell with protocol" (B. Ford, 197).

As Betty gained experience in the office of first lady, she increasingly understood the purposes protocol serves beyond mere conformity to expectations. She acknowledged this to the Carters who followed the Fords into the White House when she said:

> The news out of the Carter camp was that they were going to do away with proto-col, but I think they're gradually coming around to understanding there's a reason for the forms and the ceremonies, a certain comfort in being prepared. (Howard 1974, 68)

The irony of this statement, coming from a woman hailed for her spontaneity and her "impromptu valor" is striking. The context of her statement was in-tended as commentary on the comparative advantages of coming to the White House from a House or Senate seat as opposed to a gubernatorial position. Nev-ertheless, after two and a half years and a presidential race that had proved gru-eling for the Fords, this first lady who didn't stand on ceremony had acquired an appreciation for decorum. Admittedly, she was not a fan of protocol for its own sake, but she wisely recognized its advantages in enhancing incumbency and in sustaining a certain public ethos.

There were times when she intentionally flaunted traditional norms and was heralded for doing so. Congressional wives invited to lunch at the White House were seated by an egalitarian method, reaching for a number in a hat, rather than the routine hierarchical arrangement according to their husbands' level of sen-iority or leadership rank. On more than one occasion, she impishly clowned for reporters, and they demonstrated their appreciation by showering her with fa-vorable attention. If taking credit for her husband's appointment of a woman, Carla Hills, to his cabinet, or an insistence that her mentor Martha Graham be awarded one of the nation's highest honors for her contribution to the arts seemed effrontery on Betty's part to some, it was praised by others. And when Rabbi Sage suffered a heart attack just as he was about to make a presentation to Mrs. Ford at the 1976 Jewish National Fund Dinner, she spontaneously led the assembled guests in prayer, amazing many by her sensitivity and presence of mind in a crisis. Betty Ford abandoned her prepared script and stated impromptu:

> Can we all bow our heads for a moment for Rabbi Sage? He is going to the hospi-tal and needs our prayers. Would you rise and bow your heads. (Pause) I'll have to say it in my own words. Dear Father in Heaven, we ask thy blessing on this mag-nificent man, Rabbi Sage. We know you can take care of him. We know you can bring him back to us. We know you are our leader. You are our strength. You are what life is all about. Love and love of fellowman is what we all need and depend on. Please, dear God. Let's all join together in a silent prayer for Rabbi Sage. (Silent prayer approximately 1 minute) Thank you very much. I know it will mean a great deal to him, and I know it means a great deal to me. (Ford Library, 1976)

In the aftermath of her episode with breast cancer, Mrs. Ford was unanimously praised for being so open with the public about her surgery, prognosis, and treat-ment in the months following the operation. In a phone interview with Linda

Hobgood (2000b), Jane Broomfield emphasized the unprecedented nature of the publicity that surrounded Betty Ford's cancer surgery. Prior to her potentially life-threatening experience, publication of such personal information and private details would have been unthinkable. As with so many events in her life, Betty Ford was denied the luxury of time to consider how she would share the news of her malignancy. Having acknowledged that she had sought help from a psychiatrist and benefited from his assistance, she must have judged breast cancer to be at least as important. Moreover, the first lady's experience might help to allay fears about cancer in other victims. Her decision to allow such publicity is one of several examples of what Gould refers to as "the combination of personality and circumstance [that] made Betty Ford a valuable First Lady who could not have been more in touch with her times" (Gould 1996, 553). After speaking with Mrs. Ford in a telephone interview, Nichola Gutgold (1998) calls this a reflection of Betty's "impromptu valor."

Still, there were those "collisions" noted by Anthony among others. Less than a year after her bout with breast cancer, Betty Ford began receiving, instead of the thousands of encouraging greetings from well-wishers around the world, expressions of indignation and resentment from those whose support the president most needed. This unfriendly mail, and the less-than-kind editorials that appeared in late August and September 1975, seemed something other than signs of a woman "in touch with her times."

Eleven days following Gerald Ford's official announcement that he planned to run for president in the upcoming 1976 election, CBS-TV promised "an unusual interview with an unusual woman . . . completely frank as she discusses her attitudes toward her role" for its popular Sunday evening program 60 Minutes on August 21, 1975. Gerald Ford had just marked the first anniversary of his swearing-in as president. Morley Safer, in an exclusive interview with Mrs. Ford in the family quarters of the White House, selected a series of questions, some never before asked of a sitting first lady. According to Anthony:

> She expounded on past revelations, speaking of seeing a psychiatrist, and on the Supreme Court Roe v. Wade judgment. The First Lady said it was "the best thing in the world . . . a great, great decision. . . . She thought smoking marijuana had become as routine for youth as the "first beer" had been for her generation. The one answer of Mrs. Ford's that would spin the nation's TV antennae, however, was not a view she'd previously expressed. When asked about whether it was immoral for young people to live together before marriage, she retorted, "Well, they are, aren't they?" She thought it might even limit the high divorce rate. Then Safer followed up with "the question." "What if Susan Ford came to you and said, "Mother, I'm having an affair?" For a brief second, Betty was silent, then calmly replied, "Well, I wouldn't be surprised . . . she's a perfectly normal human being . . . if she wanted to continue . . . I would certainly counsel and advise her on the subject." (Anthony 1991, 248)

Betty Ford described what followed in a wry understatement: "My stock with the public did not go up. It went down, rapidly" (B. Ford 1978, 206). *Newsweek* reported that 60 *Minutes* received more mail following the Betty Ford interview than at any time in the history of the CBS program. According to journalists Peer, Whitmore, and Whitman, "by October, the mail totaled more than thirty-three thousand pieces, with letters opposing her opinion outnumbering those supporting it by two to one" (1975, 19). Gould called the reaction to the interview "astonishing" (1996, 548), and Anthony listed a variety of organizations and individuals who took issue with Mrs. Ford's comments: "the Los Angeles Police Department [and] a Texas minister [W. A. Criswell who] called it [a] 'gutter type mentality'" (1991, 250). Betty Ford became the first first lady since Frances Cleveland to be censured by the Women's Christian Temperance Union (Peer et al. 1975, 19). President Ford himself anticipated fallout: "Jerry remained his usual dear funny self," recalled his wife. "He told the press that when he first heard what I'd said he thought he'd lost ten million votes. 'Then when I read about it, I raised that to twenty million'" (B. Ford 1978, 208). Prominent individuals including evangelist Billy Graham and popular entertainer Bing Crosby took exception to Mrs. Ford's comments. The governor of Georgia, Jimmy Carter and his wife Rosalynn were asked the same question about their daughter and reported they would be shocked by the circumstances that would not have surprised Mrs. Ford.

While most who registered a negative response cited disagreement with specific positions taken in the interview, at least one magazine, *Newsweek*, reported the obvious: "Not all Americans share Betty Ford's views—especially those who believe a First Lady should exemplify moral rectitude in speech as well as behavior" (Peer, Whitmore, and Whitman 1975, 19). Another editorial writer objected to her comments as representing "a manifest abuse of her position as First Lady. They constituted a failure of taste that reflected a failure of understanding":

> the issue is therefore, one of propriety. As First Lady, Mrs. Ford enjoys a wide audience and some cultural power. This circumstance prescribes a sense of restraint. Mrs. Ford ought to know that it is not up to her to rewrite the Ten Commandments over nationwide TV. At the very least she ought to realize that many Americans entertain very different convictions on drug use and abortion. . . . What this suggests on this and previous occasions, is not so much a beguiling "candor" as the desire to exploit her position in order to establish a particular public personality. ("This Week" 1975, 922)

Weighing the prospects for incumbent Ford and his major challenger for the Republican nomination, Ronald Reagan, columnist George Will quipped: "If Reagan supporters had their way, Mrs. Ford would have a prime time television talk show" (Will 1975, 984).

In her own defense Betty Ford wrote: "Morley Safer caught me off balance" (B. Ford 1978, 207). She had expected to be asked questions about women's rights, especially about the ratification of the Equal Rights Amendment (ERA). In early 1975, thirty-four states had ratified the amendment, which was four short of the number needed for its passage. Several state legislatures were in the midst of considering the measure. Mrs. Ford was an active proponent of the ERA, lobbying actively for its passage in several states such as North Dakota, Illinois, Nevada, Missouri, North Carolina, Indiana, and Arizona. Members of her staff provided her with background and tips on key legislators, whom she contacted and asked for support. With phone calls, letters, and telegrams, she laid out the case for the ERA (Gutin and Tobin 1993, 628).

After the interview, according to Gutin, Mrs. Ford was terrified by the reaction to her remarks. While Betty had vowed that nothing would interfere with her defense of women's rights, several of the questions posed by Safer had less to do with women's rights and more to do with parental responsibility. Such issues went to the heart of public sentiment in 1975; these were among the key values around which emerging candidates for the presidency were developing positions on which to run for office. If Betty was terrified, it was due to the growing certainty that her remarks might be a political liability for her husband (Gutin 1989, 132).

It was clear to all who knew her that Betty Ford was, above all else, a supportive spouse. That her answers to Safer's questions might have negatively affected President Ford's standing in public opinion surveys was anathema to her intentions. Anthony has observed that many Americans did not actually watch the Sunday night program, but instead heard or read sensationalized interpretations of it the next day (1991, 250). Stories about her comments far exceeded the dramatic impact of her own statements, removed as they were from their context. Betty had not experienced firsthand the epidemic influence of a news story in which she was the main figure; no sooner had she been buoyed by praise for her courage in facing cancer than she was cast into disfavor for frankness unbecoming to her stature.

In a personal interview with Linda Hobgood (2000a), Joe Bartlett, senior Republican staff officer of the House of Representatives who worked closely with Gerald Ford as minority leader, recalls Betty as "gracious always, to an incredible degree. . . . If she had an agenda it certainly was not obvious and it was not something that she brought into your presence. When you saw her you didn't see her as someone advocating a program. What you saw was a supportive wife." Her candor on 60 Minutes was more a rhetorical slip easily attributed to Betty Ford's limited experience in such media settings and to her impulsive frankness, suddenly more a liability than an asset. The incident was hardly a premeditated declaration of values she chose to present. It represents a classic example of "gotcha" in televised interview technique extending to the wife of a sitting president.

If it is true that being an asset to her husband mattered most to Betty Ford and if she further believed that the causes she supported would fare best by returning her husband to the White House, the interview itself merits a second look. An "old friend" of the Fords told Jane Howard of the New York Times: "Jerry's always turned to Betty for the sensitive point of view. . . . He's often said she was the smart one when it came to politics because she sees the forest instead of the trees" (Howard 1974, 66). Agreeing to chat with Morley Safer was wholly consistent with Mrs. Ford's policy of openness with the media. However, the timing of the taping on August 10, immediately following a demanding trip to Eastern

Europe with her husband was poorly planned by her staff. Press accounts of the European summit included speculation as to Mrs. Ford's health and were based on obvious signs of exhaustion in Belgrade, Warsaw, and Bucharest. In addition, she admitted that the sheets of papers Safer held were filled with questions that "terrified" her, and she claimed that the fact that "they were taping" made her feel forced to answer the questions posed. Her reply to Safer's leading, even am-phibolous question about people living together outside marriage—"Well, they are, aren't they?"—was actually very savvy, and shrewdly noncommittal. It es-tablished a rhetorical stance and cued her interviewer that she did not intend to use the interview to stand in judgment of others. Safer shifted, realizing he was eliciting the most "newsworthy" material from questions about her personal ex-perience—the same realm in which she was notoriously loath to dwell. If she was uncomfortable with "small talk about herself," she was not about to speak for the actions of her adolescent and grown children. She defended their capacity for making wise choices and went on record as saying she would be there for them in the event of unwise choices. She allowed youth a certain immaturity.

There is reason to believe that Betty Ford was eager to identify with, rather than alienate, as many Americans as possible. In her support of women's rights, for example, she presented herself as a traditional wife and homemaker who also had a career outside the home and understood the challenges of women in the workplace. She saw herself as an ideal spokesperson because she could be a bridge between women's traditional values and those values favored by advocates of the Equal Rights Amendment or proponents of the pro-choice decision rendered by the Supreme Court in *Roe v. Wade*. It is arguable that no two issues sparked more controversy among women in the latter half of the twentieth century, and they both reached an inflammatory tenor during the Ford administration. Whether she wished to be or not, Betty Ford found herself near the center of power when women in America were becoming more politically divided than ever, at least in a public way. This may be why, beyond matters of decorum that change over time, public figures—especially in a democracy, and particularly unelected lead-ers in a democracy, that is, first ladies—are well advised to maintain a certain distance. But this distance is contingent, of course, upon a first lady's desire to contribute to her husband's political success. There was no question as to Betty's devotion to Gerald Ford's success as president, but in trying to relate to and unite such disparate constituencies she instead drew attention to their differences. There is something paradoxical in Betty Ford's approach: those who admired her traditional life found fault with the liberal views she expressed, while those who favored her liberal views may have had little in common with her traditional lifestyle. When Mrs. Ford was first lady she was truly located at an unusual cul-tural crossroad of values.

Had any other woman leader of her day made remarks similar to Betty Ford's it would not have made news. Betty Ford had probably expressed many, if not all of these opinions before. That as first lady she expressed these thoughts and did so in public where young and old alike could see and read her comments sparked the charges of impropriety and irresponsibility. First ladies, Baker observed, are eminently imitable (Baker 1976, 863).

Anthony contends: "to present political motivation . . . one must at least attempt to understand human motivation" (Anthony 1991, 18). In 1975, 60 *Minutes* sought an interview with Betty Ford because she was the first lady and, not incidentally, the wife of a newly declared presidential candidate. But this woman, so comfortable with her own identity, knew better than most that "First Lady" was a title she just happened to hold. How long she would be a first lady was, she understood, beyond her control. As Mrs. Ford put it in a conversation with Jane Howard: "I don't feel that because I'm First Lady I'm any different from what I was before. It can happen to anyone. After all, it has happened to anyone" (Howard 1974, 87). The fact that she was not subdued by the position may have angered and irritated many. But beyond the causes she espoused and the husband she clearly admired and adored was an incorrigible "Midwestern" honesty. There was also that sense of common decency; Betty may well have known friends or neighbors who had struggled as parents with the very issues Safer raised in his interview. She had no intention of permitting anything she might say to hint of condemnation. Friendship meant a great deal to Betty Ford, and on those rare occasions when being first lady and being a friend appeared to necessitate a choice, Betty Ford invariably chose the latter.

The public came to see and value that. By the end of 1975, national polls showed the first lady's popularity was rising. From a dismal approval rating of 50 percent, she had soared in less than three months to 75 percent. *Newsweek* called her "Woman of the Year." The manner in which she and her staff were able to bring about this change in public perception clearly shows their growth in rhetorical acumen. One of the ways Betty Ford changed negative perceptions was to answer every adversarial letter she received in the aftermath of the 60 *Minutes* program. Significantly, her carefully worded reply was intentionally shared with the press. An excerpt, in which she defended her actions as reflective of any "mother next door" who is coping with the challenges of raising children in changing times, read:

> We (Betty and Jerry Ford) have come to this sharing of outlook through communication, not coercion. I want my children to know that their concerns—their doubts and difficulties—whatever they may be, can be discussed with the two people in this world who care the most—their mother and father. (Truman 1995, 140)

Legacy

Gerald Ford came tantalizingly close to winning the presidential election of 1976. Results were not known until well into the night, and Ford, having lost his voice in the final hectic days of the campaign was unable to speak above a whisper. Betty, who had exhausted herself throughout the long campaign, was by family consensus elected to read Ford's concession speech the following morning in the White House pressroom. The departing president and first lady retired to Rancho Mirage, California.

Failure to appreciate what Mrs. Ford described as being "an ordinary woman who was called onstage at an extraordinary time," dims regard for the remarkable stamina and resiliency imbued in the character of this nation's forty-second first lady. Any one of the major crises of these years—the suddenness of taking office, cancer and chemotherapy, the pardon of Richard Nixon, the hostility of the Equal Rights Amendment debate, the unanticipated political schisms that erupted over *Roe v. Wade*, and the *60 Minutes* interview and backlash—might easily have defeated someone with less fortitude. That her daughter Susan could say, following a White House state dinner that she looked across the room and saw "the same old Mother" is undoubtedly the compliment Betty Ford would most cherish.

Betty Ford is one of a handful of first ladies whose lives after leaving the White House has been enriched. But before her life became better, it first became bleak. Mrs. Ford acknowledged, in 1978, her addiction to alcohol and prescription medication. Her treatment, like so many things in her life, was public knowledge and led to greater national awareness of this life-endangering disease. The Betty Ford Clinic serves a worldwide clientele in the struggle to overcome substance dependencies. For her part in drawing attention to these challenges without drawing attention to herself, Betty Ford has, like her mother in the midst of a raging storm, sought to calm fears and lend a certain comfort. What Betty considered so "ordinary" about herself—her outspoken candidness—turned out to be an "extraordinary" part of her legacy to the institution of first lady.

Questions for Discussion

1. When Richard M. Nixon resigned as president in 1974, he was replaced by Gerald R. Ford. Do you think Betty Ford was ready at that time to assume the rhetorical demands of the position of first lady? Why or why not?
2. Betty Ford's relationship with the press and public was described as one of "candor" by chapter authors Gutgold and Hobgood. What do they mean by this? How did Mrs. Ford develop this kind of relationship with the press?
3. Describe the infamous *60 Minutes* interview between Betty Ford and Morley Safer. What questions did Safer ask Mrs. Ford, and what were her answers? How did the public react? How did Betty Ford use rhetoric to communicate with the American public after the interview?
4. As a first lady, Betty Ford suffered from breast cancer and drug and alcohol addiction. What rhetorical strategies did she use to turn these afflictions into gifts for the American public?

Internet Resources

http://www.ford.utexas.edu/
The Gerald R. Ford Presidential Library and Museum contains the first lady papers of Mrs. Ford. On this website, you can access her biography, photographs, documents, and selected speeches. You can also find a great deal of material

about issues that were pressing during the Ford administration such as Watergate and the Vietnam War.

http://www.bettyfordcenter.org/
Visit the Betty Ford Center website to learn about Mrs. Ford's problem with drug and alcohol addiction. Her problem was not unique. The website provides information about these addictions and suggestions for recovery.

http://www.komenswmichigan.org/bfordletter.htm
Betty Ford sent a letter to the Susan G. Komen Breast Cancer Foundation congratulating them on their twentieth anniversary. You can read the letter on this website, and use it as a springboard for discovering how much Mrs. Ford did to raise awareness in the American public about the need for early detection and self-examination.

Notes

The authors wish to thank the administration of the Gerald R. Ford Museum and Library who supported this research with a travel grant to visit the collection in Grand Rapids and Ann Arbor, Michigan. Sincere thanks also to Mrs. Betty Ford for granting a phone interview and to her staff for providing follow-up materials.

Chronology of Major Speeches

March 22, 1975	Gridiron Dinner, Washington, D.C.
October 10, 1975	International Women's Year Conference, Cleveland, Ohio
November 7, 1975	American Cancer Society Dinner, New York City
March 26, 1976	American Cancer Society's Courage Award, White House
April 8, 1976	Ladies' Home Journal Woman of the Year Award, New York City
June 22, 1976	Jewish National Fund Dinner, New York City
October 14, 1976	Martha Graham Medal of Freedom
November 1, 1976	Paul Harris Rotary Fellow Award and Rally, Harrisburg, PA
November 3, 1976	Concession Speech for Gerald R. Ford
December 1, 1976	American Cancer Society Communicator of Hope Award, New York City
December 19, 1976	University of Michigan Commencement, Ann Arbor, Michigan

References

Anderson, Karrin Vasby. 1998. Complicating Political Identity: A Rhetorical Biography of First Lady Hillary Rodham Clinton. Unpublished Ph.D. diss., Indiana University.
Anthony, Carl Sferrazza. 1991. First Ladies: The Saga of the Presidents' Wives and Their Power, 1961–1990, Vol. 2. New York: William Morrow & Company.

Baker, James T. 1976. The Former Miss Betty Bloomer of Grand Rapids. *The Christian Century* 13 October, 863–65.

Betty Ford Gaffe. 1975. *National Review*, 29 August, 920–22.

Caroli, Betty Boyd. 1987. *First Ladies*. New York: Oxford University Press.

Contest of the Queens. 1976. *Time*, 30 August, 31.

First Ladies of the United States of America. www.whitehouse.gov/wh/welcome.html, accessed 27 October, 2000.

Ford, Betty, with Chris Chase. 1978. *The Times of My Life*. New York: Harper and Row.

———. 1987. *Betty: A Glad Awakening*. New York: Doubleday and Company.

Ford, Gerald. 1979. *A Time to Heal*. New York: Harper and Row.

Gerald R. Ford Library. www.fordutexas.edu/, accessed 10 March, 1999.

Gould, Lewis L., ed. 1996. *American First Ladies*. New York: Garland.

Gutgold, Nichola. 1998. Phone Interview with Betty Ford, 16 September.

Gutin, Myra G. 1989. *The President's Partner: The First Lady in the Twentieth Century*. New York: Greenwood.

Gutin, Myra, and Leesa Tobin. 1993. You've Come a Long Way, Mr. President: Betty Ford as First Lady. In *Gerald Ford and the Politics of Post-Watergate America*, ed. Bernard J. Firestone, 625–32. New York: Greenwood.

Hobgood, Linda B. 2000a. Personal Interview with Joe Bartlett, 13 October.

———. 2000b. Phone Interview with Jane Broomfield, 26 October.

Howard, Jane. 1974. Forward Day by Day. *New York Times Magazine*, 8 December, 36, 64–72, 86–94.

McPherson, Myra. 1975. The Blooming of Betty Ford. *McCall's*, 101, 93ff.

Mrs. Ford Speaks Her Mind. 1975. *Christianity Today*, 29 August, 28.

National First Ladies Library. www.firstladies.org.

Peer, Elizabeth, Jane Whitmore, and Lisa Whitman. 1975. Woman of the Year. *Newsweek*, 29 December, 19–23.

Salmans, Sandra, Jane Whitmore, and Thomas M. De Frank. 1975. The Strain on Betty. *Newsweek*, 18 August, 21–24.

60 Minutes. 1975. Interview with Morley Safer. CBS, 10 August.

There's No Gilded Cage for Betty. 1975. *Time*, 1 December, 22.

Thimmesch, Nick. 1976. Ten-Four, First Mama. *Saturday Evening Post*, September, 62–65, 82–83, 120.

This Week. 1975. *National Review*, 27.33, 917–25.

Thomas, Helen. 1999. *Front Row at the White House: My Life and Times*. New York: Scribner.

Tobin, Leesa. 1990. Betty Ford as First lady: A Woman for Women. *Presidential Studies Quarterly*, 20:4, 761–67.

Truman, Margaret. 1995. *First Ladies*. New York: Random House.

Weidenfeld, Sheila Rabb. 1978. *First Lady's Lady*. New York: G. P. Putnam.

Will, George. 1975. Calculations. *National Review*, 12 September, 984.

Witcover, Jules. 1999. *No Way to Pick a President*. New York: Farrar, Straus, and Giroux.

CHAPTER SEVEN

Rosalynn Carter
Crafting a Presidential
Partnership Rhetorically

Diane M. Blair and Shawn J. Parry-Giles

There is no end to what I can do in the White House.

—Rosalynn Carter

More so than any first lady before her, Rosalynn Carter entered the White House keenly aware of the rhetorical opportunities for significant influence afforded a twentieth-century first lady. She reflected in her autobiography, "Before going to the White House, I knew that some First Ladies had had special areas of interest and, because of their influence, had been able to accomplish worthy goals" (1984, 270). In his book on first ladies, Carl Sferrazza Anthony concurred, "she had no doubts about her capabilities, no fears that she couldn't accomplish everything she wanted to" (1991, 278). First Lady Rosalynn Carter began her tenure in Washington, D.C., with an ambitious agenda for herself. Two months into her husband's administration, she proclaimed, "There's no end to what I can do in the White House" (Stroud 1977, 19). The Carters came to Washington with high hopes and expectations for making a difference, but by the end of their four-year term, the Carter presidency was facing a number of political crises from not only the Republicans but also from within their own party as well. Despite their best efforts, the Carters would be forced to leave the White House before they could follow through on many of their goals for improving the nation.

Although the Carters experienced many disappointments as the nation's first couple, historians generally judge Rosalynn Carter's first ladyship as more successful than that of her husband's administration (Caroli 1987, 271). She was a political advisor, an international ambassador, a tireless campaigner for her husband and other Democratic candidates, and an advocate in her own right for a number of social causes. She regularly attended cabinet meetings and met with the president for weekly "working lunches." She served as her husband's politi-

140

cal surrogate on a trip to Latin America, and she played a supporting role during the historical Middle East Peace Summit at Camp David. Rosalynn Carter also became a central spokesperson during her husband's political campaigns. While her husband tended to his languishing presidency, Rosalynn appeared in towns and cities across the United States telling voters why her husband was the kind of leader the country needed. Even the news media depicted her as the "spearhead" of the 1980 campaign (Avery 1979, 39). Rosalynn Carter's rhetorical activities and public discourse, thus, were a central component of the Carter presidency. In almost every way, Rosalynn's rhetorical activities—her image as a political advisor, her role as a political surrogate, and her own activist agenda—contributed to the creation of one of the closest working partnerships the White House has ever seen.

Biography

Several significant factors from Rosalynn Carter's biography help explain her broad rhetorical performance as first lady. These factors include: her religious upbringing and sense of moral obligation to help others, her view of herself as her husband's partner and equal, and her personal commitment to progressive social reform.

Eleanor Rosalynn Smith was born the oldest of four children in Plains, Georgia, on August 18, 1927. The town of Plains was small, only one square mile with a population of 600. According to Rosalynn, "We had no movie theater, no library, no recreation center, in Plains. Occasionally someone would open a restaurant, but it would never last long. The social life of the community revolved around the churches" (Carter 1984, 10).

Like many southern towns at that time, religion played a central role in the lives of its residents. Rosalynn was also raised in a devoutly religious family. Her grandmother was Lutheran, her grandfather was Baptist, and her parents were Methodist. Rosalynn attended all three churches and explained, "God was a real presence in my life." The vision of God that Rosalynn grew up with cultivated a sense of doing right by others, if not out of love, then out of fear of displeasing God. She wrote, "We were taught to love Him and felt very much the necessity and desire to live the kind of life He would have us live, to love one another and be kind to and help those who needed help, and to be good. But we were also taught to fear God, and though I loved Him I was afraid of displeasing Him all my young life" (Carter 1984, 10).

The Carter family, like many other families, saw hard times during the 1920s and 1930s. Her father lost his savings when the Plains bank failed in 1926. The family grew their own food and her mother made most of the family's clothes. Even so, Rosalynn claimed she and her siblings were unaware of any hardship. She remembered, "Our family didn't have much money, but neither did anyone else, so as far as we knew, we were well off" (Carter 1984, 12).

The Carter family suffered even further at the loss of its patriarch. When Rosalynn was thirteen, her father died of leukemia. Her father's death was a traumatic loss for her. According to Rosalynn, "My childhood really ended at that moment" (Carter 1984, 17). Her mother began to depend on Rosalynn to help with the younger children and to run the household. Rosalynn reflected, "She put me on my best behavior because I was the one she depended on to make all the right decisions" (Carter 1984, 19). This sense of personal responsibility and moral obligation also stemmed from her desire to honor her father's memory. She wrote, "Whenever I was faced with a decision or even a temptation, I would think about whether Daddy would like it or not" (Carter 1984, 19). As a teenager Rosalynn stayed away from alcohol and cigarettes and graduated valedictorian of her high school class. She had dreams of seeing the world beyond Plains, but she was forced, for lack of funds and family obligations, to attend Georgia Southwestern, a local junior college close to home.

When Rosalynn was seventeen, she fell in love with her best friend's brother. Ruth Carter kept a picture of her older brother, Jimmy, pinned to her bedroom wall. Jimmy Carter was three years older than Rosalynn and a midshipman at the U.S. Naval Academy. While on leave in the summer of 1945, Jimmy and Rosalynn went on a double date with Ruth and her boyfriend. He asked her to marry him the following Christmas leave. At first she refused, believing she was too young to marry, but a few months later she accepted. The couple was married on July 7, 1946.

The Carters' marriage was grounded in a sense of equality and interdependence. It was a partnership that would grow and expand as their lives developed and changed. In a 1976 campaign interview, Jimmy Carter characterized Rosalynn as "fully equal to me in every way in our relationship, in making business decisions, and she makes most of the decisions about family affairs" (Richardson 1998, 54). At the same time, he conceded that early in the marriage he was by far the more dominant person, and he suggested that "it was a struggle for her to achieve this degree of independence and equality in our personal relationship" (Richardson 1998, 54).

Indeed, Rosalynn Carter began her married life as a fairly traditional navy wife and mother of three young boys: John William (Jack), born 1947; James Earl Carter III (Chip), born in 1950; and Donnel Jeffrey (Jeff), born in 1952. Navy life, however, required that Rosalynn learn to manage a household on her own since Jimmy was absent at sea four to seven days a week. She came to love the independent life that she had achieved. Although military life took the family to such places as Virginia, Pennsylvania, Connecticut, Massachusetts, Hawaii, and New York, Jimmy Carter decided to leave the navy upon his father's death. It was at this time that the Carters moved back home to Plains so that Jimmy could take over his father's peanut business. The decision devastated Rosalynn. She remembers it being the most serious argument of their marriage, "Never had we been at such cross-purposes, I thought the best part of my life had ended" (Carter 1984, 36). Although Rosalynn resisted the move, she soon found herself taking on new responsibilities within the family business. She took on still more responsibilities as her husband's business partner when he began his political career.

Jimmy Carter started his political career on the local school board and then quickly moved to the state senate. Rosalynn's early involvement in her husband's political career was limited to mailing out campaign literature and posing for family photographs. In 1966, he ran for governor and lost the election, but he was determined to make another run for the governorship in 1970. During the second governor campaign, Rosalynn, now the mother of three sons and a three-year-old daughter (Amy was born 1967), wrote letters, kept files, and clipped news articles for Jimmy's campaign. Significantly, Rosalynn forced herself to overcome her fear of public speaking, which was so severe it caused her to become physically ill on occasion. She recalled, "The idea of standing up in front of people absolutely terrified me, even though I had had no difficulty speaking before my class in high school and actually enjoyed one-on-one political conversations at luncheons or receptions—even interviews with reporters" (Carter 1984, 69). She persisted, and before the end of the campaign she was making brief speeches frequently. The Carters were successful, and Rosalynn became first lady of Georgia in 1971.

The transition from Plains to Atlanta was a difficult challenge and a significant growing period for Rosalynn. She believed the move to the White House was much easier compared to this initial move. She wrote in her memoir, "Overnight, it seemed, we had become 'public' persons living in a fishbowl at the mercy of the press and sometimes the public" (1984, 91). She also reported that she used her husband's governorship years to gain confidence in her social and administrative abilities (Caroli 1987). During these years in Atlanta, Rosalynn developed an appreciation for what government could do to improve people's lives. She was determined to be a modern and socially involved first lady, "I didn't want to spend all my time taking care of that big house" (Carter 1984, 77). While first lady of Georgia, Rosalynn cultivated Special Olympics programs throughout the state. Inspired by Lady Bird Johnson, she started the Georgia Highway Wildflower Program. Rosalynn also met Betty Ford during the governorship years; she remembered, "I was anxious to meet her, for I had heard that Mrs. Ford and I had many things in common" (Carter 1984, 99). Another concern of Rosalynn's was the state's prison system, its inadequacies and inequalities. She worked with the Women's Prison Committee for the Commission of the Status of Women to improve prison housing conditions, and she helped create a Work Release Center. By the end of their stay in the governor's mansion, Rosalynn was an accomplished speaker and advocate, and she put those skills to work on behalf of her husband and his political agenda during his run for the presidency.

During the 1976 campaign, Rosalynn campaigned actively for her husband. Her days began at dawn and included between six or eight speeches, up to eighteen interviews, and three or four press conferences (Angelo 1976). The Carters believed that they could "cover more ground" if they campaigned separately (Caroli 1987, 265). Rosalynn was accompanied only by her good friend and her son's mother-in-law, Edna Langford, when she campaigned for the first time across the state line into Florida (Carter 1984, 112). Her strategy was to meet as many people and to get as much press coverage as possible "by knocking on the doors of radio and television stations and newspaper offices and saying, 'I'm Mrs. Jimmy Carter and I thought you might want to interview me'" (Carter 1984, 113). During the campaign, Rosalynn developed her own itinerary and wrote her own speeches. Careful lists were kept of the contacts made during the trip, and Rosalynn returned home with four campaign hints: "stop at the courthouse, look for large radio antennas, stay in people's homes, and muster the courage to intrude" (Smith 1996, 564). The Carters' diligence paid off, and they moved into the White House in 1977.

Rhetorical Activities as First Lady

Rosalynn Carter entered the White House with the expectation that she would be an active first lady. She told an interviewer for *U.S. News and World Report,* "I learned while Jimmy was Governor that I could help with anything. It didn't matter what it was. It was a position of influence, as the White House would be. You see the needs and you can do something about them" (Avery 1976, 27). Jimmy Carter described his wife as "an almost equal extension of me," and Rosalynn's first ladyship was in many ways an extension of her husband's presidency (Angelo 1977, 12). As first lady, Rosalynn Carter attended cabinet meetings, met with the president for weekly "working lunches," traveled nationally and internationally as a political surrogate, and was recognized as one of her husband's most influential advisors. By 1979, *Time* identified her as the "second most powerful person in the United States" (Sidey 1979, 22).

Mrs. Carter established early on that she had a number of significant goals that she wanted to accomplish as first lady. At the beginning of her husband's term as president, she explained to a reporter during a *Time* magazine interview: "I felt there would be all kinds of opportunities for me if Jimmy became President. And the more I saw all the problems, I thought, if somebody does something, it's got to be us" (Angelo 1977, 12). Her commitment to progressive social reform led to her active involvement in a number of projects and causes, including serving as the honorary chair for the President's Commission on Mental Health, advocating on behalf of the elderly, promoting community volunteer projects, and lobbying for the passage of the Equal Rights Amendment.

Rosalynn Carter was "an extremely active communicator who took maximum advantage of the national podium afforded her" (Gutin 1989, 150). Even though she was a newcomer to Washington, as first lady she compiled "a remarkable list of accomplishments in just four years" (Caroli 1987, 262). Her rhetorical activities, which included political advising, independent advocacy, and campaign surrogate, expanded the role of the first lady in significant ways and cultivated one of the closest political partnerships between a first lady and a president.

Political Advisor

The Carters moved to Washington as an established political team, and they continued to cultivate this image throughout Jimmy's presidency. As first lady,

Rosalynn Carter attended cabinet meetings, met regularly with the president to discuss substantive issues, accompanied her husband to the Camp David Middle East Peace Summit, edited her husband's speeches, and advised him on political appointments. She became known as the president's closest advisor (Ayres Jr. 1979). The news media seized on her potential influence early in the presidency. The *New York Times Magazine* anticipated: "Just as Mrs. [Eleanor] Roosevelt was called 'the Assistant President,' Rosalynn Carter could also have an impact on the making of national policy, advising on her husband's programs as well as advocating her own" (Stroud 1977, 19). While her attendance at cabinet meetings was already well established, *The New Republic* renewed attention to this unprecedented role for a first lady when it reported that in the absence of the vice president, Rosalynn Carter, entering a meeting late, quietly slipped into his chair (Osborne 1978). By 1979, *Time* declared, "The second most powerful person in the United States is Rosalynn Carter" (Sidey 1979, 22), and *Newsweek* referred to her as a "one-woman Kitchen Cabinet" (Mrs. President 1979, 22).

The Carters responded to this media image strategically. For example, when Jimmy wanted to promote his image as a "liberated" husband, he frequently emphasized Rosalynn's role as a "very equal partner" and a "perfect extension of myself" (Ayres Jr. 1979, 39). The Carters also argued that while Jimmy was occupied with the responsibilities of the office, Rosalynn's speaking engagements and travels helped keep him in touch with citizens' concerns. For example, he told Barbara Walters in an interview,

> When I am confined to Washington because of pressing duties and she [Rosalynn] goes out within the United States, she has a much easier relationship with people and can bring back to me an accurate assessment of what the hopes and dreams and fears and concerns of the American people are than I could get from any other possible source. She is a full partner in that respect. ("Interview" 1978)

He told the *New York Time Magazine* that "she helps form my positions because she has a sensitive way of understanding what other people feel. Also, she is able to get a much more frank and unbiased expression of criticism from people than I can" (Stroud 1977, 60, 63). Similarly, Rosalynn Carter would reiterate this important role for herself as first lady, "I can get closer to the people than he can, and then I can go back and talk to him about their hopes and dreams" ("Selling True Grit" 1979, 13). She also emphasized this image of a first lady's closer connection to the American people to justify her role in the speech-writing process, "If I can't understand something, then the American public is certainly not going to understand it either" ("I've Never Won" 1978, 13).

Suggesting that Rosalynn was the president's link to the people situated her advisory role squarely in the realm of benevolent helpmate and reinforced traditional gender expectations for the first couple. She could relate the fears and concerns of the public back to her husband who was concerned with the day-to-day business of running the government. This reasoning would also impact Jimmy's decision to have Rosalynn accompany him to the Middle East Peace

Talks. Jimmy wanted the wives of the leaders present to help maintain a "more congenial" atmosphere (Carter 1984, 239). While at Camp David, Rosalynn attended the meetings whenever she could, and took copious notes (over 200 pages typed). She also worked closely with Jimmy and Jody Powell (the president's press secretary) on a special international "call to prayer" for the success of the Camp David meetings. The wording of the prayer was delicate, she reflected, because it needed to appeal to and be approved by members of the Christian, Jewish, and Muslim faiths (Carter 1984, 245). Her role at the Camp David meetings and her support of the president was recognized formally when she was invited to join the procession, which included Prime Minister Begin, President Sadat, and the president of the United States, before a special joint session of Congress to announce the historic peace treaty.

In addition to supporting her husband's presidency, Rosalynn employed her image as her husband's closest advisor to boost her own credibility as first lady. When an American reporter asked what made her think she was fit to discuss serious matters with heads of state during her diplomatic tour of Latin America, Rosalynn replied, "I think I am the person closest to the President of the United States, and if I can help him understand the countries of the world, then that's what I intend to do" ("The President's" 1977, 17). Similarly, Rosalynn was not above promoting her personal influence on Jimmy when it came to improving opportunities for women. For instance, she told a group of women professionals,

> I want to assure you that I use my influence at home on behalf of women whenever I can. Now Jimmy and I try not to talk business after hours, but I have been known to, well, mention that he needs—more women on the White House staff—more women in departmental jobs—and a list of distinguished women just in case he finds himself looking for a woman Supreme Court Justice! (Carter 1979i)

President Carter's aides and White House staff also attested publicly to Rosalynn's influence. For instance, presidential aide, Tim Kraft told *Time*, "Jimmy places the greatest stock in her judgments of people. Her word is gospel" ("I've Never Won" 1978). Another unidentified occupant of the West Wing told the magazine, "If you want Jimmy to do something, you'd better get Rosalynn on your side first" ("I've Never Won" 1978, 13). Carter pollster, Patrick Caddell told *The New Republic*, "I think her political perceptions and judgments are very good. She's extremely shrewd, her instincts on people are generally good and during the campaign I found her to be a tremendous help, particularly in problems that needed to be brought to Jimmy's attention" (Osborne 1978, 14). At the same time, other White House staffers tried to temper speculation about her influence. For example, Jody Powell argued, "Her political judgment is very good. She senses repercussions, impact, the way things come across, very well." That said, he qualified, "We respect her judgment, but we don't always agree with her" ("I've Never Won" 1978, 13).

At times Rosalynn also seemed to downplay her influence as a political advisor—possibly as a strategic response to concerns raised about her proper role.

As Rosalynn's activities increased, grumblings of "Who elected her?" and the continuing issue of a first lady's "unappointed, unimpeachable status" created some concern that her prominence might be harmful to the Carter image (Troy 2000, 255–56). She told the interviewer for U.S. News and World Report, "I think Jimmy does respect my opinions about things that I'm interested in and know about, but I can't advise him on [Ugandan President] Idi Amin and things I don't know anything about." In this interview she emphasized instead her expertise on issues traditionally associated with women and family, "mental health issues, health programs, children, day-care centers, and things like that" ("Change Comes" 1977, 31). Similarly, in an article for Time, she insisted, "I don't consider myself a chief advisor, and I don't advise him on things I don't know anything about" ("I've Never Won" 1978, 13).

There were, however, times when her public discourse belied just how much influence she actually had on her husband's political decisions. For example, Rosalynn played a central role in Jimmy's cancellation of a highly anticipated policy address on the energy crisis. Rosalynn read the speech and told Jimmy that it said nothing new, and "nobody wants to hear it." The president then scheduled a series of Camp David sessions with leaders from "every segment of American life" to devise a new approach to energy policy, resulting in his major policy address, subsequently dubbed the "malaise speech," and a major shake-up of the cabinet and White House staff (Carter 1984, 302; Avery 1979). When questioned about the cabinet shake-up, Rosalynn confused her pronouns creating speculation about just who was making the decisions in the Oval Office. U.S. News and World Report wrote that in response to a question about the extent of her influence on the Camp David meetings, she responded, "I don't know that I had any. I sat in on the meetings, I listened with him, and then we—and then he made the decisions" (Avery 1979, 40). Similarly, Newsweek reported that when badgered with questions about the cabinet changes, she replied, "I just . . . uh . . . we . . . I . . . uh, Jimmy thought, and I agreed with him, that it was better to do it fast" (Mrs. President 1979, 22). Such bumblings may have reflected Rosalynn's effort to downplay her influence at the same time she sought to present a united front with her husband. Rosalynn rarely, if ever, disagreed with her husband in public. She told the press, "We [she and Jimmy] are very close together philosophically." And she suggested that when they do disagree, it is usually "when I don't understand something or when he doesn't understand how I feel" (Avery 1977, 41). Whatever their private debates, the Carters always supported each other's efforts in the public limelight. Rosalynn's support of her husband is also reflected in her own advocacy agenda.

Social Reform Advocate

Rosalynn Carter knew she could create a social and political agenda for herself as the wife of a twentieth-century political leader. When her husband became governor of Georgia, Rosalynn reflected that "A First Lady can pick and choose her projects and do almost anything she wants because her name is a drawing card, she is influential, and although legislators may not always support her, she can always get their attention, as well as the attention of other powerful people" (Carter 1984, 95). Rosalynn Carter understood the power of public discourse. She told an audience of women journalists and advertisers, "I think we are fortunate to be in the communications business—and I would like to include myself in your field today. We can choose our message. We can affect attitudes. We have influence" (Carter 1979i).[1] The problem, according to Rosalynn, was "which causes to be involved in, what to do, and how much to do" (Carter 1984, 95). As first lady, she pursued an advocacy agenda that extended above and beyond a single "pet" project. She advocated on behalf of a number of social reform projects, including mental health reform, issues of the elderly, volunteerism, expanding opportunities and rights for women (including ratification of the Equal Rights Amendment).[2]

While her pursuit of a number of worthy goals was admirable, her inability to concentrate or limit her advocacy was a source of criticism. Her activities were so numerous and her agenda so broad that some journalists believed it diluted her influence and "fuzzied" her public image (Holt 1978). Unlike Lady Bird Johnson who was known for her beautification project, Patricia Nixon who focused on volunteerism, and Betty Ford who was known for her candor in coping with breast cancer and speaking out on behalf of the ERA, Rosalynn was often criticized by the media for having no clear image or agenda (Quinn 1978). Rosalynn addressed her problems with the media directly in her public discourse. In a speech on April 26, 1979, before an audience of women communicators, she expressed her frustration with the media's lack of attention and criticism of her agenda, "I have been told that the problems of the mentally ill, the elderly, the handicapped and the poor are not 'sexy' issues for a First Lady. The media are not very interested. And I cannot tell you how much I dislike these negative attitudes" (Carter 1979i).

What is clear about Rosalynn's own advocacy is how well it complemented her husband's political agenda. Myra Gutin describes Rosalynn Carter's first ladyship and her husband's presidency as a "symbiotic relationship" (1989, 156). Indeed, in many ways their rhetorical activities and philosophies were so closely linked that it was hard to know where one's role performance stopped and the other began. In almost every way, her rhetorical advocacy on behalf of social reform allied strategically with her husband's presidency. She was fully aware that her interests might be relegated to the secondary status of first lady "pet projects," so she blended her agenda with her husband's. This rhetorical coordination can be seen in the social issues she addressed, the political philosophy she espoused, and the strategic linking of her activist agenda to her husband's political policies and accomplishments. Such a rhetorical coordination served both her own activist agenda and her husband's presidency.

The cause for which Rosalynn Carter's first ladyship is most closely allied is mental health. She first became aware of the issues surrounding mental illness during Jimmy's campaign for the governorship. In her autobiography, Rosalynn tells the story of meeting one woman in particular who revealed the difficulties of caring for a loved one with a mental illness. When Rosalynn met with Jimmy later that same day, she slipped into the receiving line to shake his hand and probed, "I want to know what you are going to do about mental health when you are governor." Jimmy immediately replied, "We're going to have the best mental health system in the country and I'm going to put you in charge of it" (Carter 1984, 73). Although Rosalynn was not placed in charge of the Governor's Commission to Improve Services to the Mentally and Emotionally Handicapped that was established during the Carter governorship, she was later named honorary chair of President Carter's Commission on Mental Health. Because of federal nepotism laws, Rosalynn could not be appointed the formal chairperson of the commission, and so had to settle for the "honorary" title.

Rosalynn was excited at the prospect of promoting a substantive issue, and she set out to promote the commission during her very first press conference following the inauguration. The media, however, showed little interest in Rosalynn's new project. Few of the major newspapers featured the commission; instead, they focused on Rosalynn's decision to serve only wine at White House functions (Carter 1984, 173). In spite of the lack of news media interest, Rosalynn persevered. The commission held public hearings, issued position papers, and eventually made 117 recommendations, including 8 "major" ones which resulted in the Mental Health Systems Act of 1980 (Troy 2000, 251). Rosalynn used her rhetorical first ladyship to lobby heavily for the act's passage. She spoke "everywhere I had a chance" to promote the legislation and raise awareness. She even testified before Congress, becoming the first first lady to do so since Eleanor Roosevelt. She explained her purpose, "I wanted to take mental illness and emotional disorders out of the closet, to let people know it is all right to admit having a problem without fear of being called crazy" (Carter 1984, 271). In September 1980, the Mental Health Systems Act became "the first major reform of federal, publicly funded mental health programs since the Community Mental Health Centers Act of 1963" (Carter 1984, 279). Unfortunately, Rosalynn's hard won effort on behalf of mental health would barely get off the ground, before Ronald Reagan's subsequent administration would cut the bulk of the funding for the project. Rosalynn described the fate of the project as a "bitter loss" (Carter 1984, 279).

Rosalynn's interest in "the problems of the elderly" and the "graying of America" came out of her work on the Mental Health Commission (Carter 1984, 281). Among her rhetorical activities on behalf of the elderly, she coordinated a roundtable discussion on aging and lobbied on behalf of several acts of legislation. After meeting regularly with Nelson Cruikshank, the counselor to the president on aging, Rosalynn decided to invite representatives from elderly advocacy groups to a roundtable discussion. Participants at this meeting "put together a brochure with fifteen recommendations of things people could do in their communities to help the elderly" (Carter 1984, 282). This brochure was then distributed to state agencies and local organizations, and Rosalynn often followed up with a visit to those organizations that implemented programs. Rosalynn spoke out on behalf of a variety of legislation intended to protect the rights of and ensure services for older Americans. Among her legislative efforts, Rosalynn lobbied for the Age Discrimination Act, which eliminated any mandatory retirement age in the federal government and raised the age limit from 65 to 70 in the private sector. She also lobbied on behalf of the Older Americans Act, which authorized substantial increases in appropriations for various social services for the elderly. In addition, she publicly supported Social Security reform and the Rural Clinics Act, which expanded medical services to underserved rural areas. She also lent her first lady ethos and public speaking skills to the American Nurses Association's education program for geriatric patients resulting in a training film (narrated by the first lady) entitled, *The Rosalynn Carter Nurse Training Program.*

Rosalynn's interest in mental health and the elderly are both examples of the blending of her own first lady projects with her husband's domestic policies. In her speeches, she frequently remarked on her own efforts in relation to health reform as an introduction to her larger purpose, which was to highlight and praise her husband's policies and accomplishments as president in such areas. For instance, in a prepared speech draft to be presented before a rally on Capitol Hill regarding hospital cost containment, she recounted the accomplishments of her husband's presidency in the first person plural,

> We have won some important fights in the past two and half years and we will win this one too. We won the fight to save the Social Security System. We won the fight for increased housing and other services for the elderly. We won the fight to free older Americans from the tyranny of forced retirement at 65. The battle for hospital cost containment is in many ways the toughest of all. And it is a battle we cannot afford to lose. (Carter 1979e)

Rosalynn's work with improving health services for the elderly also fueled her interest in promoting community volunteer efforts. In speech after speech, she encouraged her audiences to support local initiatives to create more caring communities and to solve their community's problems. Her focus on volunteerism and local community problem-solving also worked hand in hand with her husband's political philosophy of fiscal responsibility. In a preliminary draft of a speech for the Iowa Jefferson-Jackson Day Dinner, Rosalynn explained her plans to stump across the nation, "I want to have a chance to really talk to people about things that we need to do in our country and how we can do them—not how we can get government to do them, but how we can get together and do what needs doing where we are in our own communities" (Carter 1978a). Similarly, in a draft of a speech to be presented at the opening of a new Work Activity Center in Bartow County, Georgia, Rosalynn planned to tell her audience, "I hope we are growing through the mind-set that said, 'Let the government do it,' whatever it happens to be. Local initiative is critical" (Carter 1979j).

Rosalynn Carter's greatest disappointment in terms of her advocacy efforts as first lady was the struggle and failure of the Equal Rights Amendment. She suggested that she did "just about anything [she] could think of for the cause" (Carter 1984, 286). She gave numerous speeches, made phone calls to legislators in various states, wrote letters, attended fund-raisers, and held multiple events and meetings at the White House. She even agreed to be auctioned off at a dance to raise money for the effort. In the fall 1977, she appeared with former first ladies Lady Bird Johnson and Betty Ford at a Houston conference celebrating International Women's Year. Rosalynn fretted that the ERA had a serious image problem. Her rhetorical strategy was to try to draw media attention away from "those supporters who have appeared to be demanding and strident man-haters—mostly urban professional women" (Carter 1984, 287). Instead, she felt the public needed to see that "nice" women, "relatively traditional" women, like herself, supported the amendment, too (Carter 1984, 287, 289). In a speech before the New York Women in Communications she argued, "it is especially important to explain that women like me support the ERA. I am a relatively traditional person. I enjoy my roles as wife, mother, partner, and businesswoman. I care how I look—and what I think. I am not threatened by ERA. I feel freed by it" (Carter 1979i).

President Carter benefited politically from Rosalynn's advocacy on behalf of the ERA. Gil Troy argues that Jimmy understood the Democrats' political strategy of deepening the "gender gap" with the Republicans (2000, 251). In fact, Jimmy wasn't above promoting his own politically "liberated" image at his wife's expense. While Jimmy was governor, the ERA came up for a vote before the Georgia state legislature. To a crowd of anti-ERA protesters, Jimmy proclaimed, "I respect your right to oppose the ERA, but my mind is made up . . . I am for it—but my wife is against it!" Rosalynn was mortified and claimed she "[couldn't] believe he seriously thought I opposed it." When she confronted him about the incident, Jimmy "just grinned" in response to her indignation (Carter 1984, 101). In spite of this early misunderstanding between the Carters, Rosalynn frequently used her interest and support of the ERA to talk about her husband's accomplishments on behalf of extending opportunities to women. In a draft of a speech to be delivered via telephone to the American Baptist Churches Biennial Meeting, held on the campus of Southern Illinois University on June 7, 1979, Rosalynn and her speechwriters made this link explicit,

> All of you know my concern for women in America . . . I am proud and grateful for the progress we have made for women in the last 2 1/2 years. Jimmy is helping to give women a great new chance. Only five women have ever been appointed as Cabinet Secretaries in the history of our country—two in his administration. Only four women have been appointed as Under Secretary in the history of our country—two in his administration. (Carter 1979a)

The speech manuscript goes on to list the number of prestigious positions now held by women under the Carter administration. Rosalynn was to conclude this section of the address with one final praise for her husband's commitment to women, "In addition there are scores of women in many other strategic positions in the Administration and the government made possible by Jimmy's concern to give women their rightful place in American society" (Carter 1979a).

Perhaps more so than any other first lady, Rosalynn Carter's first lady activism and activities were intimately connected to her husband's presidential image and agenda. This complementary nature of their political agendas and philosophies, along with her established reputation as a close political advisor, enabled First Lady Carter to perform her most significant rhetorical role in the Carter administration—that of a rhetorical and political surrogate for the president.

Surrogate and Advocate for the President

In addition to advocating on behalf of mental health reform, the elderly, volunteerism, and opportunities for women, one of Rosalynn Carter's most important first lady projects was advocating on behalf of her husband's languishing presidency. She served as an extension of her husband, and one of the defining characteristics of Rosalynn Carter's first ladyship was the surrogate function she performed for her husband. One of the best and earliest examples was Rosalynn's diplomatic trip through Latin America. Her rhetorical activities became so central to the Carter presidency that when political necessity confined Jimmy Carter to Washington, Rosalynn Carter became a campaign surrogate for the 1978 midterm elections and the 1980 presidential campaign.

President Carter characterized First Lady Carter as a representative of the nation and his own personal surrogate. He told Barbara Walters and a national audience during a 1978 interview, "we had a special need to strengthen our ties, for instance with Latin America. And Rosalynn went on a full diplomatic mission representing me personally and also representing the nation" ("Interview" 1978). Her surrogate role began with the first lady's tour of Latin America as Jimmy's personal ambassador. According to Rosalynn Carter's autobiography, a few months after her husband's inauguration, "Jimmy came home one night and asked if I would go on a special mission for him." The new president explained that he was busy "setting in motion a host of domestic and foreign policy initiatives," and so he needed someone to take on the much needed task of promoting stronger relationships with our neighbors to the south (1984, 185).

The purpose of Rosalynn's trip was to explain the Carter administration's policies on human rights, nuclear weapons, and arms sales to neighboring nations. She also intended to listen to the concerns of the individual countries and take their messages back to the president. Her journey took her over 12,000 miles to seven different countries. The first lady visited Jamaica, Costa Rica, Ecuador, Peru, Brazil, Columbia, and Venezuela. She was the first high-ranking U.S. representative to visit Ecuador in twenty years. Her schedule was heavier than the president on his official visits because she assumed the duties of an ambassador plus her duties as first lady. Besides meeting with the leaders of each country, Rosalynn also had "receptions to attend, informal lunches with wives, side trips to show my interest in health and education projects, and the inevitable formal banquet held by the government" (Carter 1984, 200). Her dual role of surrogate president and hostess provided a glimpse into what role a woman U.S. president might someday play (Anthony 1991, 274).

Rosalynn's performance as a surrogate generated a lot of news media coverage and was not without controversy. An editor for *The Nation* remarked, "The wives of our Presidents have played all sorts of roles (mostly ceremonial), but never one quite like this" ("The Carters" 1977, 740). Even though Rosalynn sat through twenty-six hours of briefings by scholars and federal officials, some members of Congress and the media were critical of this new role for the wife of a president. According to *U.S. News and World Report*, the president's decision to send his wife "aroused suspicions among Latin Americans that the President does not take their countries seriously" ("Rosalynn's Turn" 1977, 36). Meg Greenfield, a writer for *Newsweek*, was critical of what she perceived to be Rosalynn's only qualifications for the world of policy making—her relationship to President Carter (1977). In response to some of the news media criticism, White House staff emphasized publicly that her role was not to negotiate or create policy with these leaders; rather, her role was mostly an informational gathering and exchange on behalf of her husband's administration (Goldman 1977).

Post-trip evaluations were also mixed. A national poll gave her a 74 percent approval rating for her role as "ambassador," and 72 percent considered her "a better source of diplomatic information for the president than the State Department" (Anthony 1991, 274). A writer for *Time* suggested that "she achieved her goal of convincing top leaders that President Carter wants to improve long-neglected relations with Latin Nations" ("Rosalynn Takes a Message" 1977, 26). Others were less enthusiastic. According to a *Washington Post* exposé, one former White House staffer claimed that Rosalynn's trip was ineffectual because South American leaders "treated 'her exactly as they would any wife of an American President: politely and nothing more'" (Quinn 1978, K3). Still others expressed concern not over her effectiveness as a surrogate but over whether or not such a responsibility was even proper for a first lady. In an opinion editorial for *Newsweek*, Meg Greenfield argued that Rosalynn's trip to Latin America in her husband's stead raised a fundamental question about the role of a president's wife. She told readers, "What we have here, in other words, is not an 'uppity woman' issue, but rather a question of the proper role in government of unelected kin of elected officials" (1977, 100).

Rosalynn's reflection on the controversy was that she had always been Jimmy's partner, and so it was only natural for him to turn to her "to take on a challenge that was special and personal to him" (Carter, 1984, 188). She continued in this role as Jimmy's personal ambassador and surrogate throughout his presidency. Drafts of her speeches frequently begin with a comment similar to this one expressed in her remarks at Harlem Church, "Jimmy wanted very much to be here. He sends his love, and wanted me to express his deep regret that he could not come" (Carter 1979d). In the draft of her testimonial for Governor Averell Harriman, she began, "Jimmy sends his greetings to you. And of course I am pleased that he sent me to be his special representative to honor America's most distinguished 'special envoy' Governor Harriman" (1979b). Her surrogate role was such a prevalent part of the Carter partnership, that First Lady Carter was granted the privilege of being the first woman to speak at the Gridiron Dinner for the president, and she began once again (this time for humorous effect) by addressing her role in her husband's absence:

> Jimmy really wanted to be here tonight with his friends in the press. Only matters of the highest and most urgent national importance could have kept him away. He just had to go to a town meeting in Elk City, Oklahoma. Actually, Jimmy was invited to the Gridiron by your former President Al Cromley of the Daily Oklahoman and Jimmy thought tonight's dinner was being held in Al's home state. Jimmy just called me from Elk City before I came over here, and he was pretty upset. He said he was the only person in Frankie's Diner who's dressed in white tie and tails. (Carter 1979g)

One of her biggest coups as Jimmy's surrogate came when she was given the privilege of officially greeting Pope John Paul II for his U.S. visit in 1979, an honor Vice President Mondale desired ("Playing" 1979).

Rosalynn Carter's surrogate role soon extended into the realm of political campaigning on behalf of the Democratic Party during the 1978 midterm elections and Jimmy Carter's 1980 reelection bid. In September 1978, she logged a cross-country campaign schedule speaking in support of Democratic candidates. According to Myra Gutin, the first lady was considered a superb campaigner and an effective fund-raiser. Gutin claimed she was "considered a Democratic heavyweight" (1989, 153). Newsweek reported that constituents claimed that of the two, "she's the most acceptable Carter to have at this time" ("Rosalynn on Road" 1978, 33). With her husband's presidency never quite finding its stride, Rosalynn's central goal for her public discourse seemed to be boosting her husband's image. She was, however, politically astute enough to offer the Democratic candidates "some distance from the ailing administration by calling each Democrat 'his own man' who would stand up to the President if necessary" (Troy 2000, 262).

Drafts of Rosalynn's "stump speech" suggest that she reminded her audience of the problems the nation was facing *before* Jimmy was president—highlighting the theme that her husband's administration "inherited a mess, but we are getting it under control" (Carter 1978b). She then reviewed the actions Jimmy took as president to resolve the problems, and she highlighted his accomplishments. For instance, on the issue of unemployment she pointed out that "there are more than six million more Americans on the job today than there were on Election Day 1976. That's the fastest increase in our nation's history" (Carter 1978b). After thoroughly covering domestic policies (the Farm Bill, Social Security reform, the Civil Service Reform Bill, plans to curb fraud and abuse of welfare and Medicaid programs), the speech draft reveals that Rosalynn turned her attention to foreign policy issues. She covered such topics as the Panama Canal treaties, efforts to control nuclear proliferation, human rights policy, and efforts for international peace. As a mother, she emphasized that she was particularly proud "that no American has died in battle anywhere in the world during Jimmy's presidency" (1978b). Her attention to both domestic policies and foreign affairs suggests that as first lady, Rosalynn Carter did not feel confined to a particular topic. Such a broad approach to her public discourse enabled her to expand her role as political surrogate beyond that of traditional topics of expertise for first ladies. It also enabled her to take on an even larger surrogate role for her husband, who by the end of his first term in office found himself facing numerous political crises—at home and abroad.

First Lady Carter's championing of her husband's presidency increased to a new level of responsibility during the 1980 election campaign. Her role as the president's surrogate would play a central role in the administration's campaign strategy. Rosalynn had encouraged Jimmy to hire public relations specialist Gerald Rafshoon to help with the president's image. Rafshoon recognized the value of the first lady for the president's campaign—"she could boast of his accomplishments in a way that Jimmy could not" (Anthony 1991, 303). Rosalynn Carter was designated the central traveling spokesperson for her husband's second presidential bid. *U.S. News and World Report* called her the "Spearhead of [the] Carter Campaign" (Avery 1979, 39). According to historian Gil Troy, "the Carters followed the Nixons' and Fords' reelection tradition of politicizing the First Lady and insulating the President" (2000, 268). President Carter was also constrained in his ability to campaign because of the Iran hostage crisis he was facing toward the end of his first term. In early November 1979, Iranian terrorists stormed the American embassy in Tehran taking sixty Americans hostage. The Iranians were demanding the return of the ailing shah who had come to the United States for cancer treatment.

As early as the late summer of 1979, Rosalynn began stumping to raise funds for her husband's reelection campaign. She made nine stops on a four-day tour that took her to Illinois, Arkansas, Texas, and California. She raised approximately $400,000 for Jimmy's "campaign war chest" ("The First Lady" 1979, 9). By October 1980, Rosalynn had appeared in 166 cities and raised $2.5 million. Reporters and political insiders praised her campaign abilities. According to Liz Carpenter, former press secretary to Lady Bird Johnson, "she's the salesman [sic]—a better salesman than he is" (Avery 1979, 39). A Dallas political consultant remarked, "You can't help but like the woman. She's attractive, charming, intelligent and totally committed to Jimmy. People eat up that sort of thing" ("Selling True Grit" 1979, 13). Even Republicans admired her efforts. Said Senator Roger Jepsen of Iowa, "she's the best campaigner Carter has. She represents him well" (Avery 1979, 39).

Not everyone, though, was impressed with Rosalynn's surrogate role. While her messages were generally well received, she did receive some criticism. During her speech before the National Urban League in Chicago, audience members were offended that she repeated the refrain, "he [or] she happens to be black" every time she referenced a person of color in relation to President Carter's appointments. The patronizing tone "drew outright hoots" from the audience, and Vernon Jordan be-gan his keynote speech by stating, "I'm president of the National Urban League and I happen to be black" ("Selling True Grit" 1979, 12; "Mrs. President" 1979, 23). Notes in the speechwriters' subject files suggest that Rosalynn's speech writing team frequently tried to adapt the first lady's speeches in order to highlight the Carters' appreciation for diversity and their understanding of the contributions and needs of ethnic and racial minorities. Various drafts of speech introductions are marked with titles like: "Language on Asian-Americans," "Language for Greek-Americans," and "Language for Irish-Americans" (Carter 1980).

Rosalynn's role as Jimmy's surrogate also created some tension with leaders of the women's movement. Gloria Steinem complained, "She never appears to say anything separate from him. More than any other president's wife I have seen there is no independent thought or phrasing separate from his" (Quinn 1978, K3). Rosalynn's own press secretary, Mary Hoyt, said that the first lady is best un-derstood as an "extension of the President" (Quinn 1978, K3). Journalist Sally Quinn argued that Rosalynn's performance had not lived up to the 1976 Carter campaign promise of a "much more influential role" for the first lady (1978). Ac-cording to Troy, "Quinn and her colleagues disapproved of Mrs. Carter's loyalty, selflessness and humanity. They missed Betty Ford" (2000, 261).

Rosalynn's public discourse reflected two primary goals: responding to her husband's critics and convincing the American public that they needed to re-elect Jimmy Carter for four more years so that he could finish what he started. The rhetorical themes of her discourse included: making concrete the accom-plishments of her husband's administration, testifying to his moral character and principled ideals, and explaining his vision for the future.

Rosalynn Carter responded aggressively to her husband's critics. She chastised them for being naysayers and for thinking him naïve. In her campaign speeches, she asserted, "They accuse him of thinking that any problem can be solved if you just look long enough and hard enough. And they were right. Jimmy Carter did think that. He does think that. He believes with all his heart that this country can solve its problems" (Carter 1978b). She told *U.S. News and World Report* that depictions of her husband as vacillating and weak stemmed from the news media tendency to try to intercept information and report what is assumed or speculated to be the president's position before he actually makes a decision. She defended Jimmy as a thoughtful, deliberate decision-maker who based his posi-tions on his informed convictions. She asserted, "He studies things, and when he makes a decision, it's *his* [her emphasis] decision." She also argued that Jimmy would not be swayed by his critics in his decision-making process, "You cannot make your decisions based on criticisms. You have to do what you think is right" ("Rosalynn Carter" 1979, 49).

Rosalynn believed that in spite of the various crises and obstacles her hus-band's administration faced toward the end of his first term, "we were having some successes" (Carter 1984, 304). She saw that her job on the campaign trail was to highlight her husband's accomplishments. This goal manifested itself in her discourse as a kind of chronological recounting of Jimmy Carter's accomplishments in office. The draft of her remarks before the Florida Democratic Convention is representative of her political stump speeches for the reelection campaign. Rosalynn began the speech by attending to the hostage crisis in Iran. Her discussion of the crisis reflected her broader goal of highlighting her husband's diligent and patient response to all the crises faced by the nation during his presidency by enumerating the specific steps the president took "to protect our interests and ensure justice" (Carter 1979h).

After the Iran crisis update, she turned her attention to enumerating her husband's accomplishments as president. Her speech covered Jimmy's accomplishments in terms of reducing unemployment, establishing an energy program that lessens the nation's dependence on foreign oil, addressing inflation, cutting the federal budget deficit (a deficit created by Republicans, she notes), increasing federal aid to education by 60 percent and establishing the Department of Education, saving Social Security from bankruptcy, reforming welfare but also making room in the federal budget for necessary programs for the elderly and the poor, and standing up for minority rights. After fully exploring his successes on the domestic front, she turned her attention to foreign policy issues featuring Jimmy's pursuit of world peace through a strong military, the Middle East Peace negotiations, the Panama Canal treaties, the Salt II treaties, and the administration's formal stand against apartheid in South Africa.

Her recounting of Jimmy's political accomplishments and goals were supplemented with depictions of her husband's character. Most of Rosalynn's campaign speeches, both during the midterm elections and the presidential campaign, created a strategic depiction of Jimmy Carter as a hard worker who was both bold in his initiatives and patient in implementing them. For instance, in a stump speech draft, she concluded her speech by stating, "When he [Jimmy] was inaugurated he offered not a new dream, but fresh faith in the old dreams that have made our nation unique among nations, and uniquely blessed. He has pursued that faith—with boldness, and with patience and the day-to-day persistence necessary to make dreams work" (Carter 1978b). She also depicted him as honest and principled—willing to meet difficult challenges regardless of political risk or gain. In her address to the Florida Democratic Convention, she asserted, "For three years he has not ducked or hidden. He has fought the hard battles. He has taken the heat" (Carter 1979h). In her public discourse she contextualized his lack of popularity in terms of his honesty, perhaps indirectly reminding her audiences of previous administrations who were not honest in their dealings with the American public. In a draft of the first lady's remarks to the Florida Democratic Convention, she argued that truth in politics was not always popular and often hard to come by: "Some people did not like what he [Jimmy] had to say. But people heard something that had long been lacking from our nation's leadership—the truth" (Carter 1979h). According to Rosalynn, her husband was willing to face and speak the brutal truth about the state of the nation and the work and sacrifice needed to solve the country's problems. In another draft of a stump speech, Rosalynn stated, "Jimmy has made the tough choices. He has faced our problems head on, rather than letting us bury our heads in the sand. He is always trying to make us see how much we still have left to do—so we tend to forget how much Jimmy has already done" (Carter 1979f). Throughout her speeches, she assured her audience that even though his decisions were not always popular, Jimmy's heart was always in the right place: "Jimmy loves our country. He is working night and day to do what is right for ourselves, our future, and our children. He wants a prosperous America, he wants a secure America, he wants an America at peace" (Carter 1979f).

Finally, Rosalynn's campaign discourse focused on explaining Jimmy's vision for the nation's future. However, her attempt to reassure the voters that the nation was on the right track was sometimes compromised by her rhetoric of self-restraint, sacrifice, and no easy solutions. For instance, even though she attempted to convince her audience that her husband had already accomplished so much, she also sought to remind her audience that "there are no magic cures" (Carter 1978a). She also compared the nation's current state with that of the Great Depression, "During the Depression, our deep problems led many to question whether even democracy could survive. . . . These are similar times." And yet, like the depression era, Rosalynn encouraged her audience, "With the work already begun, if we continue rebuilding our solid base, the 1980's can mean a stronger, more prosperous America. We can put behind us the talk of retreat and limited expectations" (Carter 1979c). In spite of the various domestic and international crises facing the Carter administration and the nation, Rosalynn's public discourse sought to restore her audience's faith in the White House. She told her audiences, "We know that today's problems are not permanent. They are difficult problems. But they are not insoluble. And America has lost none of the underlying strengths needed to solve them" (Carter 1979c).

Legacy

What distinguished Rosalynn Carter's performance of the first lady role from her predecessors was her keen understanding and public admission of how much influence she wielded. She clearly expanded the political power and rhetorical possibilities for the first ladyship, and her rhetorical activities contributed to one of the closest working, publicly acknowledged, presidential partnerships. As Carl Sferrazza Anthony has suggested, "unquestionably, Mrs. Carter had a degree of political power not seen since Eleanor Roosevelt," and as a couple, the Carters also "seemed almost replicas of fellow southerners James and Sarah Polk of the 1840s—pious, hardworking, and political" (1991, 275).

The Carter presidential partnership demonstrated the central, rhetorical role the wife of a president could play in an administration. Rosalynn's role as the president's closest advisor "added a new page to the evolutionary history" of first ladies. Other first ladies had been active advisors to their husbands, but no previous presidential couple was as open in acknowledging the influence of her advice (Smith 1996,

568). Both Carters acknowledged that Rosalynn was the more political of the pair. Although, they almost always put forth a unified front in public, she frequently disagreed with him privately, especially on the timing of announcements for his major decisions. According to Anthony, "Rosalynn was acutely aware that the problems Carter had to address were unpopular and controversial, and she feared the outcome of approaching them head on" (1991, 277). She argued that unpopular decisions should be made in the second term; the primary goal was to win reelection.

With Rosalynn's performance the office of the first lady also became a base for strong lobbying efforts and advocacy on behalf of substantive issues ranging from mental health reform, to age discrimination, to the ERA, to the Panama Canal, and the Salt II treaty. In addition to her numerous speeches, press conferences, and interviews supporting a variety of issues, Rosalynn was only the second first lady to testify before a congressional committee, Eleanor Roosevelt being the first.

Finally, Rosalynn's first lady performance demonstrated the rhetorical and political possibilities for a first lady as presidential surrogate. She took on the unprecedented role of representing the United States on substantive policy discussions with foreign leaders. Her trip to Latin America and her role as the president's representative marked a significant rhetorical development in the role. Previous first ladies, like Eleanor Roosevelt, traveled abroad as the president's representative, but their mission was not to explain American foreign policy to heads of state (Smith 1996, 570). Rosalynn's rhetorical performance was not limited to the "eyes and ears" role of the first lady; rather, she was charged with communicating persuasively the significant foreign policy themes of the Carter administration. In addition to her ambassadorship, her first ladyship also demonstrated the primary rhetorical role the wife of a president could play in election campaigns. Not only did Rosalynn stump for other Democratic candidates at midterm elections, during the 1980 reelection campaign she became the more "visible 'candidate' substituting for the president in the primaries" (Anthony 1991, 308).

Unfortunately, their bid for reelection was unsuccessful. Both Carters had big plans for the nation, but their term in the White House was short-lived. In spite of the miraculous accomplishment of a Middle East Peace Summit at Camp David, the Carter administration was plagued with problems including: the energy crisis; the struggling economy; the Russian invasion of Afghanistan, which forced President Carter to impose a grain embargo and cancel the U.S. participation in the 1980 Olympics; BillyGate; and last but not least, the Iranian hostage situation. In her autobiography, Rosalynn reflected that in spite of the obstacles for reelection, "I was so sure we could beat Ronald Reagan in the general election. I couldn't believe the people would fall for his rhetoric or support the platform laid out at the Republican Convention" (1984, 334). When it became clear that the Carters would not be remaining in the White House for a second term, Rosalynn admitted she was angry and resentful. She wrote:

> I was bitter at what I had seen on television for weeks that I thought was so unfair to Jimmy; bitter about the hostage situation dominating the news for the last

few days before the election as the media "celebrated" the anniversary of the hostage capture; bitter at the opposition for deliberately misleading the American people; bitter that they blamed Jimmy for the hostage crisis when they should have praised him for his sound judgment and patience. . . . Yes, I was bitter. (1984, 342)

Neither Carters allowed their presidential defeat to become a personal defeat. Instead, both maintained their sense of civic responsibility and social activism as they returned home to Plains, Georgia.

Both Carters remain actively involved in those causes and concerns that punctuated their time in the White House. Rosalynn Carter, for example, continues to serve as a public advocate for mental health. As a full partner in the Carter Center, she created and chairs the center's Mental Health Task Force, and every year she hosts the Rosalynn Carter Symposium on Mental Health Policy. She also works closely with a number of national community volunteer efforts including: Last Acts: Care and Caring at the End of Life (a national coalition of individuals and organizations advocating for more compassionate care for the terminally ill), Habitat for Humanity (a volunteer network that builds homes for the needy), Project Interconnections (a nonprofit organization that provides housing for homeless people who are mentally ill), and the Friendship Force (a citizens intercultural exchange program). In addition to her advocacy, Rosalynn Carter has published four books since her stay in the White House: *First Lady from Plains*, her autobiography; *Everything to Gain: Making the Most of the Rest of Your Life*, a book coauthored with her husband about life after the White House; *Helping Yourself Help Others: A Book for Caregivers*; and *Helping Someone with Mental Illness: A Compassionate Guide for Family, Friends, and Caregivers* (coauthored with Susan K. Golant). She continues to travel and speak throughout the world. Most recently she accompanied her husband on a historic visit to Cuba to meet with Fidel Castro.

Questions for Discussion

1. What are the factors from Rosalynn Carter's upbringing and life experiences that contributed to her rhetorical performance as first lady?
2. What were Carter's primary rhetorical activities as first lady, and did these activities expand the role in significant ways?
3. Rosalynn Carter devoted time and energy to a number of social reform projects. What were the causes she championed? Do you agree with her critics that her inability to concentrate on a single cause diluted her influence?
4. What were Carter's two primary rhetorical goals as a surrogate and advocate for her husband's presidency?
5. What do you believe is Carter's most important and enduring legacy as first lady?

Internet Resources

http://www.jimmycarterlibrary.org/
Located in Atlanta, Georgia, the Jimmy Carter Library and Museum houses the presidential and pre-presidential papers of Jimmy Carter as well as the papers of First Lady Rosalynn Carter.

http://www.cartercenter.org/aboutus/aboutus.asp?submenu=aboutus
The Atlanta-based Carter Center was founded in 1982 by President and Mrs. Carter. It is partnered with Emory University and is committed to promoting human rights and alleviating unnecessary human suffering throughout the world. The site includes a biography of Mrs. Carter.

http://rci.gsw.edu/home.htm
Formed by Mrs. Carter in 1987, the Rosalynn Carter Institute for Human Development is located at Georgia Southwestern State University (Mrs. Carter's alma mater) in Americus, Georgia. The Center promotes mental health research, education, and well-being of individuals, families, and caregivers.

http://www.ecbt.org/
Every Child By Two: The Carter/Bumpers Campaign for Early Immunization hosts this website. Rosalynn Carter and former First Lady of Arkansas Betty Bumpers have worked over the past three decades to enhance immunization efforts in order to reduce infant mortality. Both women are credited with the passage of laws mandating vaccination as a requirement for school-aged children.

Notes

The authors are particularly indebted to the archivists at the Jimmy Carter Presidential Library for their guidance in our search for Rosalynn Carter's public discourse.

1. Speech texts and interview transcripts were obtained from the Jimmy Carter Presidential Library, Atlanta, Georgia. Materials cited come from the Speechwriters Chronological File, the Speechwriters Subject File, Presidential Speechwriters File—Achsah Nesmith, and the Staff Office Files. Most of the speech texts cited are written working drafts and not necessarily the texts delivered. When multiple drafts were present, the last draft was cited. The citations in the bibliography include the dates of the drafts from which we quoted in our text. They may not reflect the date of the actual speech given. Even though the texts may not be "as delivered," they do evidence the themes Rosalynn Carter articulated in her public discourse. The Carter archival materials are just now becoming open to the public, and at the time of this essay, written drafts of her speeches were all that were available.

2. Many of Rosalynn Carter's speeches were drafted by Mary Hoyt, her press secretary, but she was also assisted by various members of her staff. According to Myra Gutin, sometimes entire speeches were drafted for the first lady and she merely made a few changes; however, most often the resulting speeches were a combination of Carter's ideas and

phrasing and the contributions of her speechwriters (1989, 155); see also Sally Quinn's article in *The Washington Post* (1978). The drafts of speeches in the files at the Jimmy Carter Presidential Library indicate that speech draft suggestions also came from White House speechwriters Bob Rackleff, Rick Hertzberg, and Achsah Nesmith.

References

Angelo, Bonnie. 1976. She's Running for First Lady. *Time*, 11 October, 27.

——. 1977. Rosalynn: So Many Goals. *Time*, 10 January, 11–12.

Anthony, Carl Sferrazza. 1991. *First Ladies*, Vol. 2. New York: William Morrow and Company.

Avery, Patricia. 1976. We've Worked Hard—I've Done All I Could Do. *U.S. News and World Report*, 18 October, 24–25.

——. 1977. Some Surprises as First Lady. *U.S. News and World Report*, 14 November, 40–41.

——. 1979. Rosalynn—Spearhead of Carter Campaign. *U.S. News and World Report*, 5 November, 39–40.

Ayers, B. Drummond, Jr. 1979. The Importance of Being Rosalynn. *New York Times Magazine*, 3 June, 39–50, 56.

Caroli, Betty Boyd. 1987. *First Ladies*. New York: Oxford University Press.

Carter, Jimmy, and Rosalynn Carter. 1995. *Everything to Gain: Making the Most of the Rest of Your Life*. Fayetteville, Ark.: University of Arkansas.

Carter, Rosalynn. 1978a. Iowa Jefferson-Jackson Day Dinner, 22 August. Speechwriters Subject File. Atlanta, Ga.: Jimmy Carter Presidential Library.

——. 1978b. Suggested Stump Speech, 4 October. Speechwriters File—A. Nesmith. Atlanta, Ga.: Jimmy Carter Presidential Library.

——. 1979a. American Baptist Churches Biennial Meeting, 1 June. Speechwriters Subject File. Atlanta, Ga.: Jimmy Carter Presidential Library.

——. 1979b. Averell Harriman Testimonial, 21 June. Speechwriters Subject File. Atlanta, Ga.: Jimmy Carter Presidential Library.

——. 1979c. First Lady's Campaign Remarks, 3 December. Speechwriters Subject File. Atlanta, Ga.: Jimmy Carter Presidential Library.

——. 1979d. First Lady's Remarks at Harlem Church, 4 December. Speechwriters Chronological File. Atlanta, Ga.: Jimmy Carter Presidential Library.

——. 1979e. Hospital Cost Containment Rally, 22 October. Speechwriters Subject File. Atlanta, Ga.: Jimmy Carter Presidential Library.

——. 1979f. Political Speech. Speechwriters Subject File. Atlanta, Ga.: Jimmy Carter Presidential Library.

——. 1979g. Remarks of the First Lady at the Gridiron Dinner, 24 March. Speechwriters Subject File. Atlanta, Ga.: Jimmy Carter Presidential Library.

——. 1979h. Remarks to Florida Democratic Convention, 16 November. Speechwriters Chronological File. Atlanta, Ga.: Jimmy Carter Presidential Library.

——. 1979i. Women and America—Rosalynn Carter Challenges Communicators, 26 April. Staff Office File—Sarah Weddington. Atlanta, Ga.: Jimmy Carter Presidential Library.

——. 1979j. Work Activity Center, 4 June. Speechwriters Subject File. Atlanta, Ga.: Jimmy Carter Presidential Library.

———. 1980. Material for Ethnic Audiences, 19 February. Speechwriters Subject File. Atlanta, Ga.: Jimmy Carter Presidential Library.

———. 1984. *First Lady from Plains*. Boston: Houghton Mifflin Company.

Carter, Rosalynn, and Susan K. Golant. 1996. *Helping Yourself Help Others: A Book for Caregivers*. New York: Random House.

———. 1999. *Helping Someone with Mental Illness: A Compassionate Guide for Family, Friends, and Caregivers*. New York: Random House.

The Carters. 1977. *The Nation*, 18 June, 740.

Change Comes to White House. 1977. *U.S. News and World Report*, 21 March, 31–33.

First Lady Becomes First Defender. 1979. *U.S. News and World Report*, 6 August, 9.

Goldman, Peter. 1977. Out on Her Own. *Newsweek*, 13 June, 15–18.

Greenfield, Meg. 1977. Mrs. President. *Newsweek*, 20 June, 100.

Gutin, Myra G. 1989. *The President's Partner: The First Lady in the Twentieth Century*. West Port, Conn.: Greenwood.

Holt, Don. 1978. Advocate-in-Chief. *Newsweek*, 4 September, 18.

Interview with the President and First Lady. 1978. 14 December. Speechwriters' Chronological File. Atlanta, Ga.: Jimmy Carter Presidential Library.

I've Never Won an Argument with Her. 1978. *Time*, 31 July, 12–13.

Mrs. President. 1979. *Newsweek*, 6 August, 22–25.

Osborne, John. 1978. White House Watch—Rosalynn. *The New Republic*, 19 August, 8–14.

Playing the Rosalynn Card. 1979. *National Review*, 12 October, 1274–75.

President's Closest Emissary. 1977. *Time*, 13 June, 17–19.

Quinn, Sally. 1978. Have You Heard What They're Not Saying about Rosalynn? *The Washington Post*, 25 June, K1–5.

Richardson, Don, ed. 1998. *Conversations with Carter*. Boulder, Colo.: Lynne Rienner Publishers.

Rosalynn Carter Takes on the President's Critics. 1979. *U.S. News and World Report*, 9 April, 49–50.

Rosalynn on the Road. 1978. *Newsweek*, 18 September, 33.

Rosalynn Takes a Message Home. 1977. *Time*, 20 June, 26.

Rosalynn's Turn at Diplomacy "Family Style." 1977. *U.S. News and World Report*, 6 June, 36.

Selling True Grit—and by God She's Good at It. 1979. *Time*, 6 August, 12–13.

Sidey, Hugh. 1979. Second Most Powerful Person. *Time*, 7 May, 22.

Smith, Kathy B. 1996. (Eleanor) Rosalynn (Smith) Carter. In *American First Ladies: Their Lives and Their Legacy*, edited by Lewis L. Gould, 557–82. New York: Garland.

Stroud, Kandy. 1977. Rosalynn's Agenda in the White House. *New York Times Magazine*, 20 March, 19–20, 58, 60, 63.

Troy, Gil. 2000. *Mr. & Mrs. President: From the Trumans to the Clintons*. Lawrence, Kans.: University Press of Kansas.

CHAPTER EIGHT

Nancy Reagan
Leading Lady, Supporting Actress, or Bit Player

Janette Kenner Muir and Mary Mooney

I must say acting was good training for the political life, which lay ahead for us.

—Nancy Reagan

Few first ladies can top the devotion that Nancy Reagan has shown over the years to her husband, Ronald Reagan, the fortieth president of the United States. Framed as one of the "great love stories of American politics," their love continues, even as he spirals deeper into Alzheimer's disease. Once a busy socialite with a late-blooming humanitarian bent, Nancy now spends her days caring for "Ronnie," and she continues to work both "on stage" and "behind the scenes" to ensure his place in history.

For many people, Nancy Reagan was and continues to be an enigmatic first lady. As a young woman, she said that her main goal in life was to be married and have a happy family; yet she seems to be disconnected from her two children, Patti and Ron. Even though she knew her actions as first lady were under continual press scrutiny and criticism for "her meddlesomeness," she remained a resolute participant in meetings with the president and his general decision-making. Many in the White House disliked her, and she was often referred to as "the Dragon Lady," yet her social elite friends recognized and appreciated her loyalty to her husband and their circle.

Much has been written about Nancy Reagan, and this chapter offers another perspective—a rhetorical perspective—in the continuing conversation about this former first lady. After providing a brief account of Nancy Reagan's life, from her early years through her role as a political partner in the campaigns of the up-and-coming Ronald Reagan, we consider her initial perceptions of the role of first lady. Unfortunately for her, these role expectations were far different from what she actually encountered, leading her to rethink her actions and words in more pragmatic terms. We discuss the rhetorical strategies she devised to overcome how she had been typecast by the press—as a socialite who was more interested in fashion than with the condition of America's poor and as a political spouse who meddled too much in presidential affairs. We look at Nancy Reagan's personal transformation as she projected a sense of humor at the 1982 Washington Press "Gridiron Dinner" and then became a passionate advocate of drug abuse prevention. Finally, we examine her current role as caretaker and surrogate as she attempts to provide meaning and structure in the former president's daily life, when he is only barely able to recognize her. Leading lady, supporting actress, or bit player? In truth, Nancy Reagan was all three.

Biography

Nancy Reagan's birth date and birth name have both been sources of dispute. A reproduction of her birth certificate, in *Nancy Reagan: The Unauthorized Biography* by Kitty Kelley, states that she was born Anne Francis Robbins on July 6, 1921, in New York City (1991, 1). However, many competing historical sources list her birth as two years later. Confusion about the difference is said to stem from her Hollywood days when it was common practice for studios never to list any female actress's age as more than twenty-five. Named for her two grandmothers, Anne Francis Robbins was always called Nancy for unknown reasons. Further confusion over her name was produced by her mother's name changes, first after divorcing Nancy's biological father and second after remarrying Nancy's adoptive father. It would seem the woman known as Nancy Reagan changed identity several times during the early part of her life.

Nancy's mother, Edith Robbins, was a stage actress who was known for her colorful vocabulary and spirit. Divorced soon after Nancy was born, she took her daughter on the road. Nancy was known as a "backstage baby"—traveling to every town where her mother performed. They parted after two years when the constant travel became too much for the young child. Nancy went to live in Bethesda, Maryland, with her maternal aunt's family. Living there with cousins and pseudoparents was a stable time, but a painful one as well. She saw her mother only occasionally when Edith visited Bethesda, or when Nancy traveled to New York.

Mother and daughter were reunited after six years, in 1929, when Edith married prominent neurosurgeon Loyal Davis and settled in Chicago. Nancy then became Nancy Davis by her own decision when she was fourteen years old. She discussed the adoption process with a judge, who was also a neighbor and friend of the family, then sought support from her biological father who agreed to the adoption.

As Nancy Davis, she was under the influence both of a mother with whom she had not shared a home for a number of years and a new father. These relationships were positive and both parents made strong impressions on Nancy. In her own words: "I learned a lot about how to be a wife, and about many other things from my mother. . . . She had a profound influence on the woman I turned out to be, as did her second husband . . . whom I have always considered my true father" (Reagan with Novak 1989, 66). Nancy's adult years illustrate vividly this influence. Although she eagerly adopted her mother's passion for the stage, she also developed character traits like her father who was "serious, dignified, and principled" (66).

Many stage actors who were friends of her mother also influenced her and helped shape the roles Nancy Reagan would play in life:

> Whenever Mother's old friends from the theater passed through town, they would stay with us. When I came home from school in the afternoon, it wasn't unusual to find Mary Martin in the living room, or Spencer Tracy reading the newspaper, or the breathtaking Lillian Gish curled up on the sofa, talking with Mother. Spencer Tracy stayed with us so often that he became practically a member of the family. (78)

These people greatly affected Nancy Reagan. Though she did not go immediately to Hollywood, they would soon become her friends and colleagues.

Nancy attended Smith College, double-majoring in drama and English. Her inclination toward drama was obvious, but she also shared her father's interest in English. As a doctor and teacher, Loyal Davis was a studied intellectual who wrote a book during Nancy's high school years and sent her silly word limericks while she was away at college. After graduating from Smith, she pursued a film career as Nancy Davis, often getting auditions, though rarely a part, through friends of her mother.

She lived in New York for a short time, then moved to Hollywood and landed a contract with MGM. When she first signed with the studio, she was asked to complete a questionnaire for the publicity department; one question asked her ambition. Answering with words that were telling of the woman she grew to be, Nancy wrote: "to have a successful marriage" (1989, 122). She made eleven movies in her career, including *The Next Voice You Hear*, 1950; *Donovan's Brain*, 1953; and *Hellcats of the Navy*, 1957, with Ronald Reagan. Her film career led to her next role as Mrs. Ronald Reagan.

The Nancy Davis/Ronald Reagan courtship was a love story filled with both modern-day circumstance and old-fashioned tradition. Although it was set in glamorous Hollywood, it was challengingly modern in that Reagan was recently divorced with two children. This was certainly rare in 1950. Ironically, foreshadowing their future in politics, the impetus for Nancy and Ronald's meeting came when her name was printed on a list of communist sympathizers. Ronald Reagan was president of the Screen Actors Guild at the time, and MGM studios suggested he contact her to clear her name.

It was a near miss in meeting, however, because there were several actresses named Nancy Davis in Hollywood, and Ronald was not inclined to pursue the issue. When Nancy stressed her continued worry, Ronald finally met her for dinner—just for reassurance. Nancy stated in her autobiography, *My Turn*, that upon opening the door for their dinner date, her first thought was, "This is *wonderful*. He looks as good in person as he does on the screen!" This event set the real-life stage for their undying attraction to one another (Reagan with Novak 1989, 94). As her memoirs described:

> Ronnie doesn't wait until he's going away on a trip to be affectionate; sometimes he kisses me when he's only leaving the room. He says 'I love you' frequently, and so do I. We are physically affectionate with each other, both in public and in private, and we're always holding hands. A reporter once told me that he and his colleagues were sometimes embarrassed to look at us, especially when I was meeting Ronnie's plane after a trip, because instead of a peck on the cheek, we would really kiss. (Reagan with Novak 1989, 121)

Their early time together was a happy process of discovering many uncanny commonalities, as they attended the Hollywood hot spots and appeared regularly in the press. One of the many qualities they had in common was that neither of them particularly enjoyed life in the "fast lane"; and thereafter they chose to spend quiet evenings together. Nancy made it no secret that she was anxious to marry Ronald, though he was less eager. Nevertheless, in spite of the fact that he was very recently divorced with two children from first wife, Jane Wyman, they were married in 1952. Following the traditional standards of the time, Nancy gave up her career to raise a family and support her husband's political ambitions ("Nancy Reagan Profile," 1). She moved quickly into the role of mother, having their first child seven months after their marriage. Nancy had two children with Ronald Reagan, Patricia Ann and Ronald Prescott and was stepmother to his two children from his previous marriage, Maureen and Michael. Nancy has remained in contact with Maureen and Michael but has been estranged from Patti and Ron. (Both children have, in recent years, softened toward their mother.)

Nancy Reagan's life was significantly shaped by the career moves of her husband. Ronald's acting career diminished over the early years of their marriage as he gradually worked more as a radio announcer and political campaigner than as an actor. In 1964, he came to the nation's attention with his speech for 1964 Republican candidate Barry Goldwater. Reagan's "A Time for Choosing" opened the door to a life in state and national politics that they had never anticipated (Reagan 1998, 11). The Reagans began their preparation for a public political life in 1965, when he ran for governor of California. Nancy was an active participant in this process. Stuart Spencer, a political consultant for all the Reagan political campaigns, described Nancy as:

> A born politician. They were a team. . . . We never held a meeting in the house with Ron and discussed strategic matters—which we did a lot in 1966—that she wasn't present. Listening. And, as time went on, asking questions. . . . Her political skills were better, in terms of what was best for Ron, than even his own. His skills were in the communication aspect and the beliefs and ideology. She was the personnel director of the Reagan operation. . . . She made a lot of decisions about

people coming and people leaving. She was right 90 percent of the time. (quoted in Colacello 1998a, 135)

After the election, Nancy persuaded Ronald that the family should live in the suburbs rather than in the run-down governor's mansion. Citing the children's safety as a concern, the Reagans moved to an English-style country home in the suburbs, paying the rent themselves until a group of their friends bought the house and continued to rent it to them (Reagan with Novak 1989, 140).

At this time in Nancy Reagan's life, being a wife and a mother were the most time-consuming of her jobs, but her early work as first lady of California focused on building an appropriate governor's mansion. Later, her attention turned to humanitarian projects such as hospital visits to soldiers, POWS, the elderly, and children. Her activities were similar during Reagan's second gubernatorial term.

In 1976, Ronald Reagan began his first bid for the presidency. Nancy Reagan remembers the campaign most vividly when she writes: "That campaign was so exciting, so dramatic, and so emotional. . . . that in my mind it almost overshadows Ronnie's four victories" (Reagan with Novak 1989, 178). She goes on to describe the campaign experience:

> You move from town to town, and the days and nights become a blur as one place melts into another. . . . But there can be a wonderful spirit of camaraderie in a campaign; everyone is working together and traveling toward the same goal. It reminded me of being on location for a movie. You become an extended family. . . . your whole life becomes those people and the plane you're on. (Reagan with Novak 1989, 184)

There were times though when Nancy would have to say "Enough!" as schedulers would press for more appearances, "Even then I felt the staff was there to look after Ronald Reagan the candidate, but I was there to look after Ronald Reagan the man" (184). While the election turned out to be a disappointment when Reagan did not receive the Republican Party's nomination, he was able to use the enthusiasm and support received during the campaign to pave the way to a landslide victory in 1980.

Rhetorical Activities as First Lady

One might think that being first lady of California would have prepared Nancy Reagan well for her role as first lady in Washington, but in many ways it did not. As she writes in My Turn, "I found out the hard way that nothing—nothing—prepares you for being First Lady" (1989, 20). The lack of privacy, continual public scrutiny, and critical press coverage barraged Nancy Reagan. She writes:

> My clothes. My friends. My taste in decorating. My relationship with our children. The way I looked at my husband! My entire life was suddenly fair game for com-

ment by the press and the public alike. . . . Washington can be a tough town, and I didn't know how to handle it. (Reagan with Novak 1989, 21)

Everything she did early on in her husband's presidency seemed to receive criticism. As time went on, she began to change her actions and words to better suit the press and public. For example, in what was perhaps a rare effort early on (1981) to control what appeared in print about her, Nancy Reagan authored a column on prisoners of war, missing-in-action soldiers, and their families. Her knowledge of their conditions came from her visits to wounded Viet Nam vets, senior centers, hospitals, and schools. She continued to gain popular support by working for other causes such as finding foster grandparents for handicapped children, described in her book, *To Love a Child* (with Jane Wilkie). In an effort to help the public get to know her, she wrote *Nancy* (with Bill Libby), then continued to explain herself and her actions from her own perspective in *My Turn* (with William Novak), written after she left the White House.

Throughout all of the self-presentations that map her evolution as a first lady, Nancy Reagan saw herself, above all else, as a wife. In her own words:

I threw myself into the various First Lady roles—spokeswoman, hostess, manager, and friend. I thought all of them were important, but there was one part of the job that outranked them all. Above everything else, the First Lady is the President's wife. (Reagan with Novak 1989, 60)

It was in the role of "wife" that she defined herself most fully as first lady, and it is a role that might prove to be the most challenging as she carries out her wifely duties caring for her failing husband. Yet, to understand better the rhetorical dimensions of her tenure as first lady, we need to examine how she played the roles of political partner, hostess, public relations specialist, and advocate.

Political Partner

Nancy Reagan has often stated that her life began when she met "Ronnie," as she is fond of calling the former president. Indeed, as she described their romance, his reticence to commit, their brief wedding, and the birth of their daughter Patty, it is clear that the most important role in Nancy Reagan's life was being the wife of Ronald Reagan. She was a partner in both his personal life and the political life they came to share. In addition, this partnership made her fiercely protective of him. In a 1987 speech about the role of the first lady, she noted:

In spite of everything I've learned these past six years, there's one thing on which I'm inflexible. The First Lady is first of all a wife. After all, that's the reason she's there. A President has advisers to counsel him on foreign affairs, on defense, on the economy, on politics, on any number of matters. But no one among all those experts is there to look after him as an individual with human needs, as a flesh and blood person who must deal with the pressures of holding the most powerful position on

Earth. . . . I think it's an important, legitimate role for a First Lady to look after a President's health and well-being. And if that interferes with affairs of state, then so be it. (Reagan 1987, 10–11)

Nancy Reagan's devotion to her husband was based upon the way she defined her role as first lady and this definition generated much press and public commentary, thus creating for her a significant rhetorical exigence. She wanted to be there for him—all of the time—in every aspect of his life. To some, this seemed intrusive, and Nancy had to answer charges that she was running the White House. Although she claimed she never tried to influence policy directly, she did have a strong influence with people close to Reagan, such as James Baker and Michael Deaver. She was responsible for hiring personnel, and both Baker and Deaver understood that they had to be accountable to her. Richard Burt, former assistant secretary of state under George Shultz, commented, "I'd go so far as to say that Nancy Reagan was the most powerful First Lady of the last 35 or 40 years. And she went about it in the right way, the appropriate way—entirely behind the scenes" (quoted in Colacello 1998b, 115). Muffie Brandon, the White House social secretary from 1981 to 1984, noted that even though Nancy Reagan did not want to appear to be in charge, she was much more influential than she cared to have known. According to Brandon, "I once asked her, 'Don't you ever think about your place in history?' She looked at me and she said, 'Oh, no. It's Ronnie. And Ronnie's place in history'" (quoted in Colacello 1998b, 115).

Much has been written about the level of influence Nancy Reagan had on her husband behind the scenes. Some of the president's advisors were particularly critical of her actions, saying that she tended to interfere with the president's schedule and wanted to be too much involved. After the 1981 assassination attempt on Reagan's life, Nancy acknowledged that her attention to her husband increased because no one else was focused on his personal needs.

The assassination attempt played a crucial role in Nancy's attitudes about her husband's work. She began to consult astrologer Joan Quigley because she was terrified that something might happen to him again. To Nancy, "Joan's recommendations had nothing to do with policy or politics—ever. Her advice was confined to timing—to Ronnie's schedule, and to what days were good or bad, especially with regard to his out-of-town trips" (Reagan with Novak 1989, 48). Advisors closest to Nancy and Ronald Reagan were respectful of her concerns and tried to accommodate her. Many times this meant that she went along with her husband on trips. She always believed that if she had been there on March 30, 1981, the day the president was shot, she might somehow have prevented it.

Throughout Ronald Reagan's two terms in office, Nancy Reagan was an active, engaged member of his circle, and there were times when her opinion was the only one that mattered. Her influence on her husband was credited with elevating the role of first lady to the level of "Associate Presidency" (Caroli 1996, 39). When Ronald Reagan was convalescing in 1985 the press reported that there were three people in control: the president, his chief of staff, and the first lady (77).

They were definitely a team. Nancy Reagan not only read newspapers and watched television news reports, but she also used an elaborate telephone network to make things happen. Despite her involvement from the outset, there were some who were surprised that she would have opinions and refuse to be silenced. She noted in a speech to the Associate Press Publishers:

> I'm a woman who loves her husband, and I make no apologies for looking out for his personal and political welfare. We have a genuine, sharing marriage. I go to his aid. He comes to mine. I have opinions. He has opinions. We don't always agree. But neither marriage nor politics denies a spouse the right to hold an opinion or the right to express it. And if you have anything less, it's not marriage, it's servitude. (Reagan 1987, 14–15)

In discussing the ways that women are silenced in their roles as first ladies, Nancy relates her first stage role where she played a character who was kidnapped and kept in an attic. She describes her small part in the second act, drawing the analogy to the treatment of first ladies: "I ran down the stairs, said my one line; whereupon they captured me and took me back to the attic. . . . there are those who think First Ladies should be kept in attics, only to say our lines, pour our tea and then be put away again" (15–16). Here she describes a tension in the public's expectations of first ladies. On one level, they are expected to be neutral standard bearers for their husbands while remaining silent about their own views on policy issues. On another level, however, first ladies are expected to take risks and determine their own places in history. Media constructed images of Nancy Reagan as a conspicuous consumer of material goods and fashions as well as a blind supporter of her husband were difficult for her to overcome. Feminist Betty Friedan criticized Nancy as "an anachronism . . . denying the reality of American women today . . . what they'd like to see a First Lady represent" (Caroli 1996, 334), while other objectors charged her with having little that she stood for on her own.

Even though she was often ridiculed, the important role she played in Ronald Reagan's political world could not be ignored, and many of her husband's advisors agreed on her value to him politically. For example, Michael Deaver said she deserved as much credit for Reagan's success as did he. Both Deaver and James Baker have commented that they often used Nancy as a sounding board and asked for her advice and help regarding the president. Even historians, who have rated Nancy Reagan low as a first lady, have admitted how valuable she was to her husband, and she is still credited with being the one person most skilled at protecting his image (Caroli 1996, 274).

At a state dinner, Canadian prime minister Brian Mulroney, who had developed a friendship with the Reagans, asked Nancy, "What do you think is the most important thing you do?" She remarked: "I protect Ronnie from himself. . . .

He trusts everybody, and he doesn't see when he's being blindsided, or when people are acting out of motives that are less than noble. And he never acts upon it once he does. I do" (quoted by Mulroney in Colacello 1998b, 173). In response to criticism about her influence on the president, she noted, "No First Lady need make apologies for looking out for her husband's personal welfare. . . . The First Lady is, first of all, a wife" (McAllister 1988, A1). Nancy Reagan's view of being a good wife involved being concerned about the issues her husband addressed. She commented, "A First Lady should discuss policies with the President. . . . When they go up to their living quarters at night, is she supposed to talk about dresses and hairdressers? Any man who married a woman that vapid shouldn't be President anyway" (A1). Two issues that reflected the extent of Nancy Reagan's influence were the replacement of Donald Regan and the United States–Soviet détente. Both of these areas were highlighted during Reagan's second term.

Donald Regan Dismissal

During Ronald Reagan's second term in office, Nancy took on a broader supporting role, which resulted in increased influence on the president to the extent that some of the president's advisors were afraid of her. Presidential assistant Helene Von Damm noted with surprise Ronald Reagan's unfailing support of Nancy. Above all, Nancy was his protector. She protected his human needs as well as his political image, and, with the president's advancing age and illnesses, she tried to shield him from negative influences. The Iran/Contra Affair was a devastating blow to the president's credibility and suggested that those who surrounded him were not keeping him informed. Nancy's involvement in the dismissal of Donald Regan, Ronald Reagan's chief of staff, was questionable and added to the perception of influence she had over the president. In his 1988 book, *For the Record*, Donald Regan writes that Nancy vetoed dates for the president's trips and news conferences after consultations with her astrologer, kept the president convalescing too long after surgeries, and described her generally as the "dragon lady." Helene Von Damm, who worked for twenty years as Ronald Reagan's secretary and finally as his director of presidential personnel, described Nancy Reagan's role as manipulative rather than supportive in the firing of Regan:

> Though she always claimed that her sole motivation was making her husband look good, I was very distressed by the open fashion in which she attempted to manipulate him over Don Regan's dismissal. Far from making him look good, her practically open interference made him look pathetic and weak. (Von Damm 1989, 229)

Of course, Nancy Reagan's viewpoint on the firing of Donald Regan was quite different. She saw her role, once again, as one of supporting her husband. In *My Turn* she provided excerpts from her daily journal that speak of her anguish and concern over Regan's lack of popularity with the staff and his way of handling the president. Although she knew people believed that she was influencing Regan's removal, she admitted that while she wanted him to leave, it was, ultimately, the president's decision to make. Leaks to the press implied that she was in control, and an article by William Safire underscored the Von Damm position that the first lady had "staged a coup":

> [A]t the time he most needs to appear strong, President Reagan is being weakened and made to appear wimpish and helpless by the political interference of his wife . . . the power-hungry First Lady . . . an incipient Edith Wilson, unelected and unaccountable, presuming to control the actions and appointments of the Executive Branch. (Safire 1987, A17)

In her memoirs, Nancy Reagan described this article as the most vicious and unbelievable article ever written about her. Other reporters came to her aide and took exception to his view—specifically the lead editorials in the *New York Times* and a column by Judy Mann, who was usually critical of Nancy Reagan's actions. Mann countered Safire's remark and was quoted in *My Turn*:

> First Lady Nancy Reagan managed to do what nobody else was able to do–namely, rid the administration of someone who was literally crippling the Presidency. White House Chief of Staff Donald Regan hung on in an unprecedented display of supreme arrogance, placing his own self-interest above that of President Reagan and, certainly, above the welfare of the country. Calls, pleas, messages through the media, and personal visits from Republican leaders could not move the President to replace him. . . . The Republicans and conservative power brokers ought to be sending her bouquets of long-stemmed red roses. Instead, she's being depicted as a power-hungry dragon lady. . . . The President didn't look like a wimp. He had a wife who understood what had to be done and was willing to do the dirty work. That makes him a pretty lucky man. (Reagan with Novak 1989, 348)

According to Nancy, most people wanted Regan to leave, but no one was willing to convince the President that he needed to dismiss him. She spoke to her husband about it, not to the press. Rather than denying her power behind the scenes, she claimed to have merely facilitated an action that others were too afraid to take.

American/Soviet Détente

In a *Vanity Fair* interview, Nancy Reagan discussed her influence on Ronald Reagan in building the relationship between the United States and the Soviet Union. Referring to it as "the whole Russian thing," she said, "I couldn't have influenced this if he didn't really come to believe it. I just felt, here were these two superpowers sitting here, and it was silly not to get together" (Colacella 1998b, 171). Ronald Reagan's position on the Soviet Union was clear from the beginning of his presidency. Massive military buildup, the MX long-range missile system, the Evil Empire Speech, and the Strategic Defense Initiative (Star Wars) all revealed Reagan's skeptical position on the possibility of developing a relationship with the USSR.

In 1989, Nancy Reagan referred again to this influence and how it was perceived by the media, "You can't imagine how surprised I was to read I was calling the shots on the nuclear arms race" (Reagan 1989b). Yet, she did influence the way her husband handled the Soviet Union. In fact, many people credit Nancy Reagan's behind-the-scenes advice as central to the détente that developed between Gorbachev and Ronald Reagan. Though it was a series of talks and a complicated process, the first lady was involved at all times in the details.

Nancy has spoken of her relationship with Raisa Gorbachev, a degreed historian, and the perceived competition that developed between the two. Because of the constant media attention, the two women were very self-conscious about meeting and interacting. In Nancy Reagan's memoirs she noted, "Every nuance of my encounters with Raisa Gorbachev was scrutinized. Every meeting between us was treated like a test of wills. Every time we appeared together, we were seen as contestants in some international pageant" (Reagan with Novak 1989, 336). In the end, however, they developed a relatively warm relationship. Said Mrs. Gorbachev at a luncheon during a visit to New York and the United Nations: "I will miss you and your husband. . . . As for the two of us, it was destiny that put us at the place we were, next to our husbands, to help bring about the relationship that our two countries now have" (379).

It seemed impossible that the end of the Reagan era would see the collapse of the Berlin Wall, the breakup of the Soviet Union, and the end of the Cold War. While this occurred over a very long and tedious series of talks, Nancy Reagan was with her husband as his life and political partner throughout the process, pushing from behind the scenes for peace.

Hostess

Just as relentless as the attention paid to the social interactions of Nancy Reagan and Raisa Gorbachev was the daily scrutiny of social affairs the first lady hosted or attended. Meeting high expectations and playing the tireless, hospitable, prepared, and gracious hostess was another important role Mrs. Reagan performed well for her husband and country. The White House itself illustrates this point.

When the Reagans moved into the White House, the building had not been renovated for a number of years. The private living quarters needed painting, the floors needed work, there were cracks in the walls, and there was general disarray. While Nancy Reagan approached the renovations as necessary for reclaiming "some of the stature and dignity of the building" and for meeting the hostess duties of the first lady, she did not expect that it would provoke great anger and controversy. Nancy began a campaign to raise $200,000 for the White House renovations. The greatest contributors to this fund were her friends from California, known as "the Kitchen Cabinet" and criticized by the press as "an exclusive, wealthy club" (Reagan with Novak 1989, 22). While those in the White House were pleased with the changes, others outside were more critical. Reports of the renovations were contrasted with rising unemployment and homelessness. Some critics opined that the renovations had been paid for with public monies.

Others thought it inappropriate for the Reagans' personal friends to contribute to the White House renovations (24–25). The press heavily criticized Nancy Reagan for excessive spending and lavish decorations (Caroli 1996, 100). The image of Nancy that emerged was that of a rich woman who needed to acquire expensive things. In reality, however, she was continuing the work of First Ladies Jacqueline Kennedy and Patricia Nixon, who also made renovating the White House a priority. Similarly, Rosalyn Carter made efforts to acquire fine American paintings for the White House collection (Reagan with Novak 1989, 224).

Nancy's successors were also grateful because her renovations made their work easier. New wall and floor coverings, refinished doors, upgraded wiring, and renovated bathrooms were passed on to First Ladies Barbara Bush and Hillary Clinton, so that these women had only minor refurbishing to do. Barbara Bush wrote of her gratitude: "Nancy Reagan got lots of criticism for redecorating the White House when we all should have been on our hands and knees thanking her. . . . As her successor, I was eternally grateful to her for that" (Bush 1994, 165).

From the first lady's perspective, refurbishing the White House was an attempt to bring a sense of dignity and royalty back into it. This effort contrasted directly with the Carter years when the White House was filled with children, grandchildren, and animals. From the socialite following to the lavishly expensive inaugurals, the Reagans appeared to some to be trying to elevate the presidency to a level consistent with its need to entertain foreign heads of state and royalty. Yet in redecorating, Nancy was providing an environment in which she could fulfill the social hostess aspect of her role as first lady as she defined it.

The replacement of the White House china was an example of the perceived opulence surrounding the Reagans' time in the White House. Although the funds to purchase it came from private donations and the china was clearly needed (sets had to be mixed and matched for large dinners), critics argued that donors gained tax advantages and would want special treatment from the White House. For the press, the china served as a symbol for Nancy Reagan's ongoing extravagance during a time of recession.

The manner in which the Reagans dressed directly added to these perceptions, and Nancy Reagan was well known, and criticized, for borrowing expensive dresses from popular designers. To her critics, Nancy commented:

> And I wonder: What would have happened if I *had* stopped borrowing dresses and had started wearing only the clothes that I could actually afford to buy? Before long, instead of calling me extravagant, the press would have started referring to me as "dowdy" and "frumpy." And the newspapers would soon have been keeping track of how many times they have seen me in the same outfit. I don't think I could have won this one. (Reagan with Novak 1989, 32)

Although the media have always focused on the way first ladies dress and look, the attention paid to Nancy Reagan's clothing was extreme, dominating much of the coverage of her. The criticism women writers lavished on her may have been due to the campaign of 1980 and the first year of the presidency in

1981. "With few exceptions," she wrote, "they described me as a woman who was interested only in rich friends and fancy clothes, a supercilious and shallow socialite, a lady who loved shopping and going out to lunch. In other words, an airhead" (Reagan with Novak 1989, 35). In some ways, the press descriptions were true. Nancy had (and continues to have) a circle of very rich, supportive friends. When she campaigned with her husband and after his election to the White House, she did wear designer clothes and was rarely seen in the same outfit twice. She definitely traveled in social circles, but she questioned the criticism that was continually directed toward her. In talking about the press coverage at this time, she noted the various names and jokes that were told about her:

> And the *Chicago Tribune* surely deserved a prize for squeezing the greatest number of negative references into a single sentence when it described me as "Queen Nancy the Extravagant, an aloof former debutante and movie star whose main concerns are fashion, decorating and lunching with rich girlfriends, whose idea of hard times is tablecloths that shrink, whose doe-eyed devotion to her husband leads to hard-eyed terrorizing of her aides." I was called more names than I can remember. Queen Nancy. The Iron Butterfly. The Belle of Rodeo Drive. Fancy Nancy. The Cutout Doll. On the *Tonight* show, Johnny Carson quipped that my favorite junk food was caviar. (Reagan with Novak 1989, 36)

Even today, a tension exists in the different ways that first ladies are talked about in the media. Rarely are they discussed without reference to the clothes they wear and the designers who have influenced them. During the 2000 presidential campaign, great emphasis was placed on the clothing and fashion styles of Laura Bush and Tipper Gore. This focus is supported by the Smithsonian Museum of American History's First Lady Exhibit, which focused originally on the inaugural gowns worn by first ladies. Today, the exhibit focuses on the first ladies' political role and public image, although inaugural gowns are still included as a significant part of the exhibit (Mayo and Meringolo 1994).

Public Relations Specialist

In retrospect, Nancy Reagan realized that she was probably responsible for perpetuating many of the press's attitudes by retreating from rather than directly addressing their charges. Many critics viewed her lack of reaction as snobbishness rather than as self-protection. Nevertheless, the image the press projected of Nancy Reagan was supported by her actions during the first year of her husband's presidency.

As we have already suggested, her public image created a significant rhetorical exigence that Nancy Reagan needed to address. To do so, she began to pay more attention to public relations. Her goal was to recover her reputation and shift the negative perceptions that also surrounded her husband's administration.

The contrast between the poor and unemployed Americans and the perception of a wealthy, extravagant White House created great tension for the Reagans. By the end of 1981, Nancy Reagan had the highest *disapproval* rating of any first lady in modern times. The president's economic recovery plan was not working, and from mid-1981 to late 1982 the country underwent the worst economic recession since the Great Depression. Unemployment and homelessness were on the rise. Polls showed that 52 percent of Americans felt Reagan favored the rich (Colacello 1998b, 170). In her memoirs, Mrs. Reagan wrote:

> During Ronnie's first term, I was portrayed as caring only about shopping, beautiful clothes, and going to lunch with my fancy Hollywood friends. During his second term I was described as a power-hungry political manipulator, a vindictive dragon lady who controlled the actions and appointments of the executive branch. . . . Part of the problem is that while the President's job is clearly defined, nobody really knows exactly what the First Lady is supposed to do. The Constitution doesn't mention the President's wife, and she has no official duties. As a result, each incoming First Lady has to define the job for herself. (Reagan with Novak 1989, 57)

Acting in the role of public relations specialist, Nancy Reagan attempted to overcome these perceptions and develop her own rhetorical persona. Her appearance at the annual Press Gridiron Dinner did just that.

The Gridiron Dinner is considered by Washington insiders to be one of the most important annual events in Washington, D.C., for journalists and politicians. The program is usually the same—members of the press perform skits that poke fun at Democrats and Republicans, followed by speakers from each party and a toast to the president. In 1982, Nancy Reagan found out that someone had planned to do a song about her. Sheila Tate, Nancy's assistant, came up with the idea that she should sing an attack on the press. Nancy refused to do that saying, "If I'm going to do this at all, I think I should make fun of myself" (Reagan with Novak 1989, 39).

The white-tie crowd was definitely surprised when Nancy showed up in a mismatched costume, with yellow rain boots, a boa, and a red straw hat with feathers. She sang "Second Hand Clothes," a parody of Fanny Brice's "Second Hand Rose." The lyrics were:

> I'm wearing second-hand clothes
> Second-hand clothes
> They're quite the style
> In the spring fashion shows
> Even my new trench coat with fur collar
> Ronnie bought for ten cents on the dollar.
>
> Second-hand gowns
> And old hand-me-downs
> The china is the only thing that's new.
> Even though they tell me that I'm no longer Queen,
> Did Ronnie have to buy me that new sewing machine?
> Second-hand clothes, second-hand clothes

I sure hope Ed Meese sews.
(Reagan with Novak 1989, 41)

As part of the finale, Nancy Reagan smashed a replica of the White House china to pieces. The crowd cheered and cried, "Encore! Encore!" (Caroli 1996, 170). This song, along with her willingness to sing it and make fun of herself, showed the press corps that she was not as humorless and distant as she had been portrayed. Clearly, this rhetorical act directly overcame the exigence characterized by Nancy Reagan's perceived aloofness and royal image. "From that night on," she wrote, "my image began to change in Washington. . . . It is not often in life that one is lucky enough to enjoy a second beginning, but during one five-minute period in the spring of 1982, I was able to make a fresh start" (Reagan with Novak 1989, 38, 41). In her memoirs, she included a quote from the *Washington Post* that described the journalists' reactions to her act, saying, "The sophisticated audience of journalists, politicians and their friends responded to her performance as though she had undergone a major change. A number of those image-makers left the ballroom saying that Nancy Reagan's song-and-dance number had transformed her image" (Reagan with Novak 1989, 42).

In reflecting on this event and the initial impressions she had to overcome when first in the White House, Nancy Reagan discussed her time as first lady in a speech for the Southern California Conference on Women in September 1989. She talked about the highs and lows of those years and the bad publicity she had received over replacing china, remodeling rooms, and wearing designer dresses. Media scrutiny both "hurt and frustrated her." "There was a time when I never wanted to hear the word china again." She explained again that the china and dresses were donated, costing taxpayers nothing (1989b). The turning point for attitudes, however, appeared to be her performance at the Gridiron Dinner. She proved that she could be a good sport, leading some members of the press to soften their stance toward her.

Further determined to help her husband's administration and still wanting to address her own low popularity ratings, Nancy Reagan turned her attention to the fight against drug abuse. She realized she would be the "object of attention no matter what" and wanted to do something positive (Reagan with Novak 1989, 57). Initially her advisors were not pleased with the topic because it seemed too negative and depressing. However, as she noted at an Associated Press publishers' luncheon, a first lady should do whatever she wants because she will "never again be in this unique position to make such a contribution" (Reagan 1987, 17). Nancy Reagan had always had an interest in the drug issue, and if the issue worked with the American public, it could be important for her image. The effort to remake Nancy's image was acknowledged by several advisors who worked directly with her. During an hour-long television program on Nancy Reagan in 1985, presidential aides talked about "working out a plan" and developing a "public relations campaign" to increase Nancy Reagan's appeal to the American public.[1]

Advocate

Nancy Reagan's most public role was as an advocate against drug abuse. To spotlight the "Don't Do Drugs" program Nancy Reagan traveled nearly 250,000 miles throughout the United States and several other countries. She appeared on talk shows such as *Good Morning America*, taped public service announcements, appeared on the situation comedy *Diff'rent Strokes*, wrote guest articles, and visited prevention programs and rehabilitation centers across the country. She also narrated two PBS specials—*The Chemical People* and its follow-up program, *Chemical People II*—which encouraged community members to organize against drug abuse.

The press covered Nancy Reagan's initial efforts, but soon grew weary of the repetitiveness of her message. However, subsequent approval ratings showed that the issue was popular with the American public. Within just a few months of the beginning of the campaign, she had gained twenty points in public approval polls and had a staff of several dozen because the project had grown far beyond what one person and a few volunteers could do (Caroli 1995, 60).

In April 1985, Nancy Reagan expanded her drug-awareness campaign to the international level, inviting first ladies from around the world to attend conferences in Washington, D.C. She went to the Vatican to speak with Pope John Paul II about drug abuse. She continued her crusade by appearing in June 1986 at the World Affairs Council in Los Angeles. The speech, "The Battle against Drugs," was published in *Vital Speeches of the Day* and laid out her basic platform and appeals for involvement in the campaign. She began by acknowledging the privilege of speaking to such an audience:

> I can't tell you how honored I feel to be speaking before the World Affairs Council. I know of great leaders and intellects who have appeared in the place where I am standing today–and it's a little overwhelming. I certainly don't put myself on their plane, but I believe what I want to discuss with you is just as important as anything previous speakers have discussed. (Reagan 1986, 645)

Nancy told the story of how she became aware of the drug issue in the sixties when she was first lady of California. At that time, she received calls from distressed friends whose children were getting caught up in drugs, and she later integrated some of these stories into her speeches.

> [A]ll the statistics, all the clinical studies, all the expert briefings in the world can't match the reality of one deeply suffering young person. When people learned I was interested in drug abuse, I began getting letters that would simply pierce your heart, letters of pain and loneliness and confusion—thousands of them. (Reagan 1986, 646)

She continued to describe the results of her five years of speaking around the country and the world to raise awareness about the dangers of drug abuse. "We now have 9,000 parent groups that are . . . closing down head shops, becoming involved in school drug programs, and forming support groups for one another" (Reagan with Wilkie 1989, 646). Youth peer groups and "Just Say No" clubs were forming to counter the increased pressure to try drugs. Internationally, she commented that the number of concerned first ladies was on the rise. Nancy's primary appeal in this speech was to everyone's moral responsibility to take a personal stand against drugs. The appeal to moral obligation was interspersed throughout the rest of her speech and put drug use and the denial of abuse onto a moral high plain that gave no room for middle ground. She strongly declared:

> Those who believe that people who use drugs aren't hurting anyone but themselves are wrong. Drugs hurt society. The money spent on drugs goes into the hands of one of the most ruthless, despicable lots ever to breathe—the drug producers. They are often murderers. They are sometimes terrorists. They are always criminals. They represent man at his most debased. They are the people who are financing the death and destruction of our young people. And by doing nothing when you know of drug use, you're conspiring with them as they line their pockets with even more blood money. (Reagan 1986, 647)

In October 1988, Nancy Reagan became the first American first lady to address a United Nations General Assembly. At this gathering she did not lay blame on other countries that import illegal drugs, but admonished the United States for its lack of responsibility in dealing with its drug users. She noted:

> It is often easier to make strong speeches about foreign drug lords or drug smugglers . . . than to arrest a pair of Wall Street investment bankers buying cocaine on their lunch break. . . . It is far easier for the United States to focus on coca fields grown by 300,000 campesinos in Peru than to shut down the dealer who can be found on the street corners of our cities. (Reagan 1988c, 1)

The focus on what the United States should be doing to prevent drug abuse was at the heart of all of Nancy Reagan's speeches. She was most interested in keeping young people off drugs, creating drug-free zones in school yards, and preventing drug abuse from starting. Too much attention, she also argued, was placed on the suppliers. Drug abuse must be stopped by directly decreasing the demand for drugs, and keeping children away from drugs from the beginning would have a definite impact on that demand. As she developed her platform, Nancy Reagan wove in poignant stories from parents and teenagers about their struggles to quit using drugs.

In a speech for the 43rd Session of the United Nations, she appealed to the audience that "as mothers we are concerned, as First Ladies we are committed, and as citizens of the world we pledge to do all that is possible to stop this scourge" (Reagan 1988c, 1). In a description of the various speeches she has given over the years, Nancy claimed, "I have found that there is a powerful, unified international resistance to illegal drugs that is developing. This is a different type of international conspiracy, a conspiracy of compassion" (2). She argued for education and commitment. Countries must become responsible:

> My chief concern is for the children—the children of America and of the world—that they will say "no" to drugs, that they will choose life, and learn to live in the world that God made, not in the nightmare world of drugs. The children need our help; and as you carry out your important responsibilities, what better guide can there be than what is best for our children will also be best for our nations. (2)

Nancy Reagan was successful with this cause in many ways. First, parents' groups, student peer groups, and local support groups sprang up all around the country. Second, more first ladies from other nations signed up for the program as the issue progressed over the years when Ronald Reagan was in office. Finally, her image was enhanced because her advocacy work was successful as a public relations effort. This was evidenced by a 1985 NBC report showing that she ranked second only to Jackie Kennedy Onassis among recent first ladies (Caroli 1995, 335).

Legacy

Despite the ups and downs of her relationship with the press and public, Nancy Reagan's legacy as a first lady must include the positive contributions she made to improve social conditions. Although she had received awards of different kinds before she entered the White House, as first lady she received public service awards for her work against drug abuse and numerous humanitarian awards from the American Camping Association, the National Council on Alcoholism, the United Cerebral Palsy Association, and the International Center for the Disabled (Who's Who, 2).

After leaving the White House, she also contributed to the public good by establishing the Nancy Reagan Foundation to continue her work with drug abuse. In 1994, the foundation joined forces with the BEST Foundation For A Drug-Free Tomorrow and developed the Nancy Reagan Afterschool Program, a drug-prevention and life-skills program for youth.

In her speech to the Southern California Conference on Women, Nancy Reagan called her campaign a "five-year battle to convince America that drugs are indeed a national problem" (Wride and Eng 1989, 3). She continued that battle in a testimony before Congress on March 9, 1995, when she noted that the antidrug crusade she had championed "appears to be fizzling because of a lack of leadership and overemphasis on treatment rather than prevention" (Hook 1995, A4). She commented:

> I am not here to criticize or place blame, but after the great strides that were made just a few years back, I'm worried that this action is forgetting how endangered our children are by drugs. . . . Why is it we no longer hear the drumbeat of condemnation against drugs coming from our leaders and our culture? Is it any

wonder drug use has started to climb again, and dramatically so? (quoted in Hedges 1995, A1)

Mrs. Reagan's appearance was part of a larger celebration of conservatism on Capitol Hill. Her appearance at this hearing, along with that of former drug czar William Bennett was important in reminding the public of her agenda. Bennett and his former aide, John Walters, commented that President Clinton "is virtually invisible on this issue" and, if trends continue, 1996 would mark "the greatest increase in drug use in American history" (*On Capitol Hill* 1995). This increase in drug abuse was attributed to Clinton's appeal to youth, his famous "I didn't inhale" line, and his general "liberal" attitude ("Nancy's Back" 1995, A4).

Today, the most important aspect of Nancy Reagan's life is her devotion to her husband—placing his life and needs ahead of her own, working to secure his place in history. Feminists have criticized her for "excessive devotion," but others view her focus on marriage as a result of childhood insecurities within her family. Her main goal in life when she moved to Hollywood was to "have a happy marriage" (Leamer 1981, 64), and Ronald Reagan became the object of this goal, leading her into her future roles as helpmate, political partner, social hostess, public relations specialist, and antidrug advocate.

As Ronald Reagan's health wanes, his mind fading under the ravages of Alzheimer's disease, Nancy Reagan still carries his torch, reminding the world of his role in securing democracy and freedom for many in the twentieth century. Now called "the world's most popular caregiver" and "the Grand Dame of the Conservative Movement," it is clear that Nancy Reagan has come into her own. Her presence at the 1996 Republican National Convention provided a personal, poignant moment, reminding people of the Reagan era and legacy. She said:

> Just four years ago Ronnie stood before you and spoke for what he said might be his last speech at a Republican Convention. Sadly, his words were too prophetic. When we learned of his illness. . . . he made the decision to write the American people and the people responded as they always do. I can't tell you what your cards and letters have meant to both of us. The love and affection from thousands of Americans have been and continue to be a strengthening force for Ronnie and me each and every day. . . . As you all know, I am not the speechmaker in the family, so let me close with Ronnie's words, not mine. In that last speech four years ago, he said, "Whatever else history may say about me when I'm gone, I hope it will report that I appealed to your best hopes not your worst fears, to your confidence rather than your doubts, and may all of you as Americans never forget your heroic origins. Never fail to seek Divine Guidance, and never, never lose your God-given optimism. (Reagan 1996b, 1)

Even in that moment of acknowledgment, she used her husband's words to remind Americans of his legacy. Nancy Reagan has become, for many, the pulse of the Reagan era—the person most able to keep his memory alive.

It is not an easy role for the former first lady. Friends describe her as tired and lonely, unable to spend much time away from the man who now barely recognizes her. She attempts to carry on a normal life with Ronnie—arranging golf games and seeing that he spends time at his office and, on occasion, greets tourists at his presidential library. It is a different world for them, one filled with silence and isolation. Once the most powerful man in the world, the Great Communicator who implored Gorbachev to "tear down that Wall," Reagan is now fading into the darkness of disease. Despite the circumstances, the storybook romance lives on, as Nancy Reagan declares that her love for Ronnie grows deeper as they struggle to find meaning and purpose in their lives together. In a speech for the National Alzheimer Association in New York, October 1996, she compares her trials and tribulations to those of Job, explaining that

> Job stops asking and simply commits himself to go on living. It's his wife who shares her incredible understanding of faith and love. . . . I found that too. I found that even though the person I love and have loved for 44 years is slipping away my love for him grows. As he changes, if I stop asking why, and simply love, I do grow. (Reagan 1996c, 2)

Nancy Reagan represented her husband at the dedication of the Ronald Reagan Building and Trade Center, the largest U.S. structure except for the Pentagon (Reagan 1996a). She also represented him at the dedication of the George Bush Presidential Library and in the 2000 presidential campaign. And so it appears that Nancy Reagan is not quite ready for the final curtain call. There is still much to be done and her husband to care for. The elegant parties, the meetings with world leaders, the cheering crowds at political rallies are all sweet memories of the Reagan era. The dreams they relive in old videos and film clips help the former president to remember the past.

After all the pomp and circumstance and the endless photographers and media scrutiny, the first lady is, as she reminds us, a wife. She has played many roles within that spotlight, leading up to and during her tenure as first lady. She has successfully secured Ronald's place in history, and, inevitably, her own as well. She is a model of participation for the roles of political partner, hostess, public relations specialist, and advocate. But, it is as a wife that Nancy Reagan finds her most challenging and rewarding role. Leading lady, supporting actress, or bit player? Actually, Nancy Reagan was all three.

Questions for Discussion

1. Nancy Reagan met her future husband, Ronald Reagan, during her acting career. Did her career as an actress prepare her for being a first lady? In what ways was she unprepared?

2. When Mrs. Reagan moved into the White House, she faced criticism for her extravagant decisions to change the china collection, to redecorate, and to adorn herself with designer clothes. What rhetorical strategies did she use to persuade the press and public that she was more than a "fashion statement?"

3. One of the turning points in the Reagan administration was the assassination attempt on the president. How did Nancy Reagan cope with this near tragedy? Was the public responsive to her actions?

4. Nancy Reagan's "Just Say No" antidrug campaign received mixed reactions from the press and public. Do you think this cause was a good choice for a first lady in office in the 1980s? What rhetorical strategies did she use to convince young people to "say no" to drugs? Do you think the same strategies would be effective in today's society?

5. Given her husband's steadily declining health, Nancy Reagan made her husband's legacy her responsibility. What do you think his legacy might be? Did she leave a legacy of her own?

Internet Resources

http://www.reagan.utexas.edu/
You can find biographies of the Reagans as well as photos and audiovisual material on this official website of the Ronald Reagan Presidential Library and Museum. Nancy Reagan's papers as first lady are archived here and finding aids are online.

http://www.reaganfoundation.org/
The Reagan Foundation website provides information about forums, lectures, and conferences held today. You can access material on Nancy Reagan such as her biography, films, and information on her "Just Say No" campaign.

http://abcnews.go.com/sections/Primetime/US/nancy_reagan_040205-1.html
http://abcnews.go.com/sections/primetime/2020/PRIMETIME_010628_nancyreagan_feature.html
These two websites provide a unique glimpse into Nancy Reagan's post–White House years as Ronald Reagan's caretaker. They are especially helpful in understanding how she is constructing a legacy for her husband and herself.

Notes

A sincere thanks to Cate Sewell and others at the Ronald Reagan Library in Simi Valley, California, who generously assisted in the attainment of Mrs. Reagan's speeches. We also wish to acknowledge C. Claire Smith and Eve DeAngelo for their careful proofreading and editing.

1. NBC Documentary on Nancy Reagan, 1985. This documentary featured presidential aide Michael Deaver and White House pollster Richard Wirthlin outlining plans to make Nancy Reagan more appealing to the American public. By the summer of 1985, NBC reported that the plan had worked because an NBC poll showed Nancy Reagan as ranking second only to Jackie Kennedy Onassis among recent presidential wives.

Selected Chronology of Major Speeches

August 15, 1986   The Battle against Drugs
May 4, 1987   Remarks for Associated Press Publishers' Luncheon
June 9, 1988   Remarks for the World Gas Conference
August 15, 1988   Remarks to the Republican National Convention
October 25, 1988   Address to the United Nations
June 3, 1989   White House Memoirs: A First Lady's Perspective
September 5, 1989   Address to Southern California Conference on Women
August 12, 1996   Remarks to the Republican National Convention

References

American Presidency: First Lady—Nancy Reagan. www.gi.grolier.com/presidents/aae/ first/40pw.html, accessed 26 May 1999.

Benedetto, Richard. 1998. Reagans Allow Peek at Their Home Life. *USA Today*, 8 June, A7.

Bush, Barbara. 1994. *Barbara Bush: A Memoir*. New York: Charles Scribner's Sons.

Caroli, Betty Boyd. 1995. *First Ladies*, expanded edition. New York: Oxford University Press.

———. 1996. *America's First Ladies*. Pleasantville, New York: Reader's Digest Association, Inc.

Colacello, Bob. 1998a. Ronnie and Nancy. *Vanity Fair*, July, 76–88, 134–42.

———. 1998b. Ronnie and Nancy: The White House Years and Beyond. *Vanity Fair*, July, 110–22, 169–76.

Creative Quotations from Nancy Reagan. www.bemorecreative.co//.htm, accessed 26 May 1999.

Hannaford, Peter. 1983. *The Reagans: A Political Portrait*. New York: Coward-Mccam.

Hedges, Michael. 1995. Clinton Faces Criticism for Setback on Drug War. *Washington Times*, 10 March, A1.

Hook, Janet. 1995. Drug Crusade Waning. Nancy Reagan Says. *Los Angeles Times*, 10 March, A 4.

Kelley, Kitty. 1991. *Nancy Reagan: The Unauthorized Biography*. New York: Simon and Schuster.

Leamer, Lawrence. 1981. *Make Believe: The Story of Nancy and Ronald Reagan*. New York: Harper & Row.

McAllister, Bill. 1988. First Lady Defends Her White House Role. *Washington Post*, 10 June, A1.

Mayo, Edith, and Denise D. Meringolo. 1994. *First Ladies: Political Role and Public Image*. Washington, D.C.: Smithsonian Institution.

Nancy Reagan Documentary. 1985. NBC.

Nancy Reagan Profile. www.who2.com/nancyreagan.html, accessed 26 May 1999.

Nancy's Back. 1995. *USA Today*, 10 March, A5.

On Capitol Hill. 1995. Newsletter. Securities Industries Association. April.

Radcliffe, Donnie. 1988. Nancy Reagan's Hard Line: At UN Talking Tough on Drugs. *Washington Post*, 26 October, D1.

Reagan, Nancy. 1986. The Battle against Drugs. *Vital Speeches of the Day*, LII: 21, 15 August, 645–47.

———. 1987. Remarks for Associated Press Publishers' Luncheon. 4 May. Simi Valley, Calif.: Ronald Reagan Presidential Library and Museum.

———. 1988a. Remarks for the World Gas Conference. 9 June. Simi Valley, Calif.: Ronald Reagan Presidential Library and Museum.

———. 1988b. Remarks to the Republican National Convention. 15 August. Simi Valley, Calif.: Ronald Reagan Presidential Library and Museum.

———. 1988c. Address to the United Nations. 25 October. Simi Valley, Calif.: Ronald Reagan Presidential Library and Museum.

———. 1989a. White House Memoirs: A First Lady's Perspective. 3 June. Simi Valley, Calif.: Ronald Reagan Presidential Library and Museum.

———. 1989b. Address to Southern California Conference on Women. 5 September. Simi Valley, Calif.: Ronald Reagan Presidential Library and Museum.

———. 1996a. Remarks at the Dedication of the Ronald Reagan Building and International Trade Center. 5 May. Simi Valley, Calif.: Ronald Reagan Presidential Library and Museum.

———. 1996b. Remarks to the Republican National Convention. 12 August. Simi Valley, Calif.: Ronald Reagan Presidential Library and Museum.

———. 1996c. Remarks at the Gala Event for the National Alzheimers Association. 31 October. CNN Morning News. Transcript #96103112V28.

———. 1997. Remarks at the George Bush Presidential Library Dedication. 6 November, Simi Valley, Calif.: Ronald Reagan Presidential Library and Museum.

———. 1998. Forward. In *A Shining City: The Legacy of Ronald Reagan*, ed. D. Erik Felton. New York: Simon and Schuster.

Reagan, Nancy, with Bill Libby. 1980. *Nancy*. New York: Berkeley Books.

Reagan, Nancy, with William Novak. 1989. *My Turn: The Memoirs of Nancy Reagan*. New York: Dell Publishing.

Reagan, Nancy, and Jane Wilkie. 1989. *To Love a Child*.

Regan, Donald. 1988. *For the Record: From Wall Street to Washington*. New York: Harcourt Brace Jovanovich.

Safire, William. 1987. First Lady Stages a Coup. *New York Times*, 2 March, A17.

Von Damm, Helene. 1989. *At Reagan's Side: Twenty Years in the Political Mainstream*. New York: Doubleday.

Who's Who. Academic Universe. web.lexis-nexis.com/universe/, accessed 2 June 1999.

Wride, Nancy, and Lily Eng. 1989. Nancy Reagan Opens Women's Conference: Talk Focuses on Anti-drug Drive. *Los Angeles Times*, 6 September, 3.

CHAPTER NINE

Barbara Bush
Her Rhetorical
Development and Appeal

Molly Meijer Wertheimer

You have two choices in life: You can like what you do, or you can dislike it. I have chosen to like it.

A more literate America would benefit every single thing I worry about: crime, unemployment, pollution, teen-age pregnancy, school dropouts, women who are trapped into welfare and therefore poverty, etc.

—Barbara Bush

Two weeks before George Bush was elected president in 1988, he predicted that Americans would fall in love with Barbara Bush (Radcliffe 1989, 3). That prediction came true. In the first three months of her taking residence in the White House, she received 35,000 letters (Kilian 1992, 162); by the end of her first year as first lady, she averaged 3,000 letters a week (Anthony 1991, 422) During her next three years as first lady (1991 through 1993), she was ranked number one in Gallup's annual "Most Admired Women" poll, and she continued to rank in the top five throughout the 1990s (Gallup 1999). Today, she remains popular with Americans in her new identity as first mother—the only woman to be both wife and mother of a president in her lifetime.[1]

What is it about Mrs. Bush's enactment of her public roles that continues to interest so many of us? Is it her "naturalness"—that she seems comfortable with herself? Is it her "honesty"—that she calls it like she sees it? Is it her feisty wit— that she uses humor to disarm her opposition? Is it her maternal persona—that she projects concern for family, friends, and community? Is it her commitment to service—that she works hard to promote family literacy and volunteerism? Is it her endurance—that she continues to campaign even as she grows advanced in years? Those of us who study her rhetorical activities would say that it is all of those projected qualities because she makes such skillful rhetorical use of them.

Barbara Bush was not always a consummate rhetorician. When she first moved to Washington, D.C., in late 1966, the wife of a newly elected member of the House of Representatives, she stayed out of public view. Yet as George Bush's career advanced, she could no longer avoid publicity. Although she had always been "talkative and opinionated in private," she had to learn to speak in public. She had to find the right balance between being candidly "outspoken," but not seeming too "impudent" or "caustic" (Radcliffe 1989, 50, 53). In short, she had to develop skills as a rhetorician. According to first lady scholar Lewis L. Gould, Mrs. Bush learned to manage "the media and her own image with a great deal of deftness" (1996, xviii). By the time of her husband's inauguration, Kati Marton contends, Mrs. Bush was "so skilled . . . at manipulating her image that she gave almost everybody something to like about her (2001, 275). "Media smart" is how biographer Donnie Radcliffe describes her (1989, 50). Mrs. Bush also developed her public speaking skills to the point where she was selected to speak at the Republican National Conventions in 1988 and 1992. Her popularity and political value was so great that she was even asked to campaign by herself during off-election years. One question this essay raises is: How did she become so accomplished?

Barbara Bush developed her public speaking skills through years of experience. At first she used a slide show that she narrated; this device allowed her to extemporize as her staff member advanced the slides. After that, she learned to speak without using the slides by constructing basic speeches and then amplifying her points with stories that she collected and honed. She used her talent as a storyteller—including timing and mimicry—to enliven her presentations. She also perfected her use of humor—using self-deprecating humor to diffuse those who would provoke her with nasty questions or try to entrap her to reveal *her* position on thorny political issues. She also became a master at manipulating the news media for her own purposes. She learned to project a wholesome image of motherhood—of maternal service to others; her "matronliness," says Marton, "was . . . carefully packaged" (2001, 275).

This essay traces some of the "methods" Barbara Bush used to develop her presentational skills as well as commenting on her interpersonal communication skills—her "social style"—developed from long years of participating in social activities both to promote her husband's agenda as well as her own. Her *A Memoir* provides illuminating detail to support her claim that critically important diplomacy happens when political leaders meet informally in social situations (Bush 1994, 87–88). By the time she entered the White House she had been the wife of a man who was a member of the House of Representatives, ambassador to the UN, head of the National Republican Party, liaison to China, head of the CIA, and vice president. During her eight years as second lady Mrs. Bush—known as a "traditionalist"—did not "sit home and eat bonbons" (Bush 1994, 166). According to her own tally:

In the 2923 days of the vice presidential years: 1629 days were spent out of Washington traveling, including visiting all fifty states and sixty-five different foreign countries, many of them more than once . . . George and I traveled an estimated 1.3 million miles, which is 54 times around the world . . . when I was in town, I hosted 1,192 events at the Vice President's House and attended 1,232 other events in Washington. (Bush 1994, 167)

Her activity as first lady was every bit as busy. Although these tallies reveal the many opportunities she had to develop and practice her rhetorical skills, they do not reveal how well she performed. A second purpose of my essay is to review her performance and comment critically on the rhetorical legacy she has left the office of first lady, even today as she breaks new ground as "First Mother" of George W. Bush and "First Mother-In-Law" to Laura Welch Bush.

Biography

Barbara Pierce was born in New York City on June 8, 1925, to parents Marvin and Pauline Pierce.[2] The Pierces lived in Rye, New York, a quiet town of eight thousand people just two train stops away from Greenwich, Connecticut, home of her future husband George Herbert Walker Bush. Although an affluent suburb, Barbara's family lived modestly, but well; even during the depression, the children "never wanted for anything." Barbara remembers especially the wonderful food served at her house and mealtimes shared with members of her family. Afterwards, the Pierces would often spend the evenings together "with everyone enjoying a favorite book or magazine."

Barbara's father worked his way through Miami University of Ohio, waiting tables and tending furnaces after his wealthy Pennsylvania family lost their fortune in the 1880s. Described by Barbara as "really bright" and athletic, Marvin Pierce graduated Phi Beta Kappa, receiving nine letters from playing on athletic teams. He met Barbara's mother, Pauline, a "striking beauty" who was studying to be a teacher, and they fell in love. Her family was from Marysville, Ohio; her father was an attorney who served on the Ohio Supreme Court in the 1920s. When Barbara was born, Marvin worked for the McCall Corporation, becoming its president in 1946. Her mother was the disciplinarian of the family and an accomplished gardener who "knew how to keep an exquisite home." She filled her home with antique furniture and china, purchasing it from vendors from all over the country and paying for it on the installment plan. Her hobbies kept her quite busy.

Barbara related to her father and mother differently. She was especially close to her father who often took her side in family squabbles; in A Memoir she writes: "some of my happiest times were walking with daddy to the station in the morning," then she would take her own bus to school (5). Her mother was often preoccupied with her younger brother who was in and out of the hospital for years. As an adult, Barbara understood better what her mother was going through, but as a young girl she missed the attention. She learned lessons from both of her parents that she would use when she raised her own children; from her father she learned to teach by example, to give her children a good education, and lots of love. From her mother she learned to appreciate what she had instead of what she didn't have: "She was a lucky women," writes Barbara, "who had a husband who worshiped the ground she walked on, four loving children, and a world of friends. Her ship had come in—she just didn't know it" (Bush 1994, 9).

Outside of school, Barbara played with her friends, cutting out paper dolls from McCall pattern books, riding their bikes, and reading literature and poetry together. They acted out some of the stories they read as plays. Barbara developed a biting sense of humor and an irreverence that became a permanent part of her personality. She could mimic people well, sometimes using the ability to put people down. Years later, she admitted that she shouldn't have behaved this way and she forbid her own children to make fun of others. As an adult, her humor became self-deprecating—she made fun of herself.

Kati Marton attributes the development of Barbara's sharp wit to her size and weight: "As the large-boned daughter of a coolly critical mother and the younger sibling of a thin and graceful older sister, she survived by irreverence . . . [and] a cutting wit" (2001, 281). Whether true or not, twelve-year-old Barbara weighed 148 pounds and was five feet eight inches tall. She remembers her mother telling her thin older sister, Margaret, to eat up, but warning Barbara not to eat any more at meals. An athletic and solidly built young girl, Barbara reminisces in A Memoir about the dance classes she and her friends took on Fridays. Probably because she was tall and there were more girls than boys, Barbara often volunteered to take the role of the boy; that way she could avoid being the last girl asked to dance.

Barbara attended public school until she was in sixth grade, then enrolled in Rye Country Day School, a private school, through the ninth grade. For tenth, eleventh, and twelfth grades she went to Ashley Hall in Charleston, South Carolina, an exclusive preparatory school with limited enrollment (150 students) that offered a classical curriculum. At Ashley Hall, she made good grades and always followed the rules; she enjoyed swimming and acting in plays. About public speaking she wrote: "I was so shy at the time and never could have gotten up and given a speech." One of her classmates remembers her as "just the prettiest thing and very outgoing and athletic" (Kilian 1992, 31); by the time she was a teenager, Barbara had grown more slender.

During Christmas vacation in 1941, sixteen-year-old Barbara Pierce met seventeen-year-old George Bush at a dance at the Round Hill Country Club in Greenwich, Connecticut. She describes her reaction to biographer Pam Kilian: "He was the handsomest-looking man you ever laid your eyes on," and "I could hardly breath when he was in the room" (1992, 34). George was smitten with her, too, for he later wrote his mother, "I have never felt toward another girl as I do toward her" (quoted in Marton 2001, 278). During that vacation, they met at another dance and went on a date. They wrote to each other from school, and during spring break, they went to a movie. At the end of George's senior year, he took Barbara to the prom.

George joined the navy in June 1942, becoming the youngest pilot to earn his navy wings (he was eighteen). Barbara wrote to him during her senior year and when she was a freshman at Smith College. She was preoccupied with George's safety since he was on active duty in the Pacific. In the fall 1944, she received a letter from a pilot in George's squadron saying that his plane had been shot down. She spent three anxious days waiting until she heard that he had been rescued. They were married on January 6, 1945; Barbara was nineteen, George was twenty. In commenting about their young age, she writes: "In wartime, the rules change. You don't wait until tomorrow to do anything" (Bush 1994, 22).

During the first eight months of married life, Barbara joined George as his schedule allowed. In three of the twenty-nine moves she would make during their forty-four years of married life, Barbara set up housekeeping in Michigan, Maine, and Virginia Beach; their accommodations were modest—dark rented rooms, a one-room efficiency, a basement apartment—showing the personal financial situation of this young couple from privilege. Barbara learned to cook, clean, and do laundry, she "wandered the streets" when she was bored and read good books. In Virginia Beach, the Bushes relaxed on the beach, and she chased George's golf balls as he and a friend learned to play. She was very much in love. After the bombs were dropped on Hiroshima and Nagasaki, August 1945, George was released from the navy, the recipient of two air medals and a Distinguished Flying Cross. They headed for New Haven, Connecticut, so George could attend Yale (Bush 1994, 24–26).

The Bushes lived in three different places during the two and a half years they were at Yale—some of them involved living arrangements that were quite communal, sharing kitchens and bathrooms. Barbara was not interested in finishing her education, though she could have done so. Instead, she played bridge, went to the movies, worked part-time in a co-op, kept score for George's baseball team, and had her first child, George Walker Bush, "Georgie," known today as "George W." George graduated from Yale after two and a half years, and then he accepted a position with Dresser Industries to work at one of their holding companies, Ideco Oil. He drove to Odessa, Texas, in a red Studebaker his father had given him as a graduation present, sending for Barbara and Georgie after finding a place to stay.

The Bushes lived in Odessa, while George learned the oil business; then, in 1949, they moved to California, living in four different places as George changed positions within Dresser Industries. Barbara became pregnant, and she visited a clinic for prenatal care, the kind of clinic where you see anyone who is on duty. She did not meet the doctor who delivered her daughter Pauline Pierce Bush, "Robin," until the night she was born on December 20, 1949. This experience later helped Mrs. Bush empathize with other women in similar situations. In 1950, the Bushes moved back to West Texas; they lived in a motel, a small house, and then a slightly bigger house. George's career advanced, and at age twenty-six, he formed his own oil company, Zapata Oil, with a neighbor. In 1953, Barbara gave birth to John Ellis Bush, "Jeb."

Also in 1953, Robin was diagnosed with leukemia and died several months later. This was a heartbreaking episode for the Bushes; Barbara was inconsolable. She was in her late twenties and her hair began to turn white. George helped her through this difficult time, as did son Georgie, who was only seven years old. In *A Memoir*, Barbara describes how Georgie cheered her up and helped the family overcome their sadness by using humor. In 1955, Barbara had another child, Neil Mallon Bush, and less than two years later, Marvin Pierce Bush was born; Barbara gave birth to her last child, a daughter, Dorothy Walker Bush, "Doro," in 1959, the same year the Bushes moved to Houston.

For the next ten years, as George continued to build his business, Barbara did "what every mother in America does: taxiing children to the doctor, the dentist, birthday parties, baseball games, tennis matches, and so on" (Bush 1994, 55). She discovered that her son Neil was dyslexic, and spent considerable time learning about the disorder and helping her son learn to read. She set the tone for the family and was the disciplinarian. George W. said she was like a "drill sergeant," while Jeb said she was the family's "chief operating officer" (Kilian 1992, 57, 66–67). She was highly organized, coordinating all of the children's activities and family moves. These were the kinds of experiences she brought with her when George entered politics.

In 1962, George ran for chairman of the Republican Party of Harris County, Texas. Barbara described this first race as a mean political battle. George campaigned in all 210 precincts of Harris County, and Barbara went with him. Although she did no public speaking at this time, she sat on stage and listened to her husband's speeches. In *A Memoir* she writes: "The evenings could be long and tedious. That's when I took up needlepoint," which turned out to be an effective conversation starter with other stitchers at the rallies (Bush 1994, 57). She attended mixers before and after her husband's speeches where she proved a valuable asset because she had an outgoing personality and a good memory for names, faces, and conversations. She also helped her husband "read character," judging who would and would not serve him well. Over the years, George would learn "to rely on her judgment of people." According to Lud Ashley, one of George's close friends, "it is hard to imagine George going as far as he did without Barbara" (quoted in Marton 2001, 281). George won the election, and then turned his attention to a run for the U.S. Senate.

During the 1963 Senate primaries, John F. Kennedy was shot and Texan Lyndon B. Johnson became president. According to Mrs. Bush, "with Johnson at the top of the Democratic ticket, we did not have a chance." Her use of the pronoun "we" here shows that she considered herself very much in the race with her husband as his political partner. That same tone of "politics as a shared ambition" carries through *A Memoir*, each of the Bushes contributing his or her share as dictated by traditional gender roles. Barbara went door-to-door with members of her husband's staff, wearing a name tag that simply read "Barbara." She felt that she could secure more truthful reactions from voters if she remained incognito (Bush 1994, 60; Kilian 1992, 85; Parmet 1997, 109). George lost that election, but he ran three years later for the U.S. House of Representatives and won.

The Bushes spent the next four years very busy in Washington, D.C. (1967–1971). George was appointed to serve on the prestigious Ways and Means Committee, and their social life escalated. Barbara was George's social partner, attending receptions, dinners, and luncheons both with and without him. Early in January, they attended two days of briefings for new Republican members of Congress and their spouses. During the second day session for wives, she learned about protocol as well as tips about dressing. She felt the information was outdated because the speaker talked about calling cards and long white gloves. She "tried everything once," she said, including briefings at the State Department, Republican meetings, Congressional wives meetings, luncheons, and dinners. She joined the International Club II, perhaps because George's mother had been a founding member (Bush 1994, 67–68). Lady Bird Johnson and Betty Ford had also been members of this group. There were plenty of opportunities for "networking" among these political wives, and Barbara "tried hard never to miss one of those meetings."

Barbara also became an active member of the 90th Club, consisting of the wives of members of the 90th Congress. The women met to study issues; eventually, eleven women became close friends. One of these women, Janet Steiger, introduced Barbara to slide shows. Mrs. Steiger used a slide show of the sights of Washington when she was invited to address constituents; she shared the idea with other wives who were often issued similar invitations. According to Mrs. Steiger, Barbara improved the slide show, she "perfected it to the extent that she had a series of shows, one on the gardens of Washington, another on the buildings, and so on. 'I ended up borrowing her slides. They were so much better'" (quoted in Radcliffe 1989, 151).

At first Barbara was fearful of making presentations. She was invited to talk at a garden club in her home district, for example, and she couldn't say no. But she was scared to death. She told her friend Shirley Pettis Robertson that there was no way she could give the speech. According to Shirley, she put much time into those speeches. Often Shirley would see her lights on late at night as she worked on them (Radcliffe 1989, 157). Marion Chambers, another friend, told a story about finding Barbara on her doorstep one day. Barbara had come to Marion's to rehearse a speech: "She stood in front of the fireplace and we both started laughing because we could hear her knees knocking . . . that was the last time I ever heard them knock" (quoted in Radcliffe 1989, 158). With practice, Barbara developed the slide show into an effective campaign tool.

George made many friends as well, and the Bushes often entertained, inviting friends and neighbors for informal lunches on Sundays, much as they had done when they lived in Texas. Apparently, Barbara kept index cards of all the friends they had made throughout the years, and according to Marton, by the mid-1970s she had between four and five thousand cards (2001, 283). In addition to socializing, Barbara's life "settled into a nice routine" that included carpooling, housekeeping, meetings, losing weight, and coloring her hair (Bush 1994, 71). George was busy most of the time and frequently traveled back and forth to Texas. Barbara remained in charge of the children, taking them all over Washington to see the sights: "every single weekend," she said, "I dragged those poor young people around Washington, taking hundreds of pictures." Later, she used those pictures in her slide shows. "It certainly was an easy way to give a speech," she wrote. "The slides were almost a protective shield, something you could hide behind" (68). During George's second term, Barbara wrote a monthly newspaper column called the "Washington Scene" that was published in Houston newspapers.

In 1968, George was reelected to the House of Representatives, and in 1970, Republican leaders, including Richard M. Nixon, urged him to run again for the Senate. George lost that election, and the Bushes were faced with the question of what to do next. He asked Nixon for a recently vacated position as ambassador to the United Nations. Many were surprised when Nixon said "Yes," because George Bush had no real experience with foreign affairs. But the Bushes had important social skills: "He [George] and Barbara would get to know all the right people, attend all the right receptions, and give all the right parties. . . . Most of all, they, as a team, would do what they did best, and that required no foreign policy skills—make friends." After a round of trips to Europe to orient the Bushes, they moved to New York. "All the evidence suggests," writes George Bush biographer Herbert S. Parmet, "the Bushes succeeded brilliantly" (1997, 150).

"George loved to entertain and came up with extraordinary and fun ideas," wrote Barbara in A Memoir (1994, 85). They also went to "several receptions every evening, many dinners, and quite a few lunches." These social functions were heaven for Barbara: "I loved all of that. In fact, I was born to the job: I love people and I adore eating" (Bush 1994, 87). But they were also work. Barbara stressed the diplomatic importance of such socializing: "At the ambassadors' level, much of the real work of the United Nations was conducted at these social functions. Especially if there was a problem between two countries, the only communications the ambassadors had was 'after hours.' Your guest list was often composed of people who wanted to meet but couldn't on an official level" (87–88). When asked if she was ever given any guidelines or told what to do at such functions she said: "Certainly I was given advice on protocol, and occasionally what to wear . . . , but, for the most part, I just depended on the manners my mother taught me" (86). To overcome the language barrier, she said: "a touch, many smiles, much interest, and lots of honest affection were a universal language" (88).

In 1972, both of the Bushes campaigned for Nixon's reelection; Barbara traveled with other cabinet wives and by herself. After his reelection, Nixon recalled George from the United Nations position and appointed him head of the Republican National Committee, a position Barbara did not want him to accept. News about the Watergate break-in and cover-up was coming out, and Bush's job was "to coordinate efforts at damage control" (Gutin 1996, 61; Kilian 1992, 96). George was kept very busy, traveling around the country, holding the Republican Party together. Barbara kept busy, too, working as a volunteer in a nursing home and for the party, and hosting weekly cookouts for twelve to twenty-five people after church on Sundays. Her family presented her with C. Fred, a cocker spaniel, on her forty-eighth birthday; he eventually became a traveling companion and "coauthor." When Nixon resigned, George asked the new president, Gerald R. Ford, to appoint him the official diplomat to China—the title was "Chief of the U.S. Liaison Office to the People's Republic of China."

The Bushes moved to China, taking only C. Fred, who attracted considerable attention everywhere they went and so functioned as a conversation starter. The Bushes studied the culture and language, and entertained many different groups and individuals from China, other countries, and the United States. For the most part, the Bushes stayed in their quarters in Beijing, but they were also allowed to visit Red China, Hong Kong, and Canton. Ready with her camera, Barbara snapped shots of interesting sights (Kilian 1992, 97–98), gathering material to use as slides later to raise money for charities and to help her husband campaign for president. In Beijing, Barbara toured the Forbidden City, the Great Wall of China, the Ming Tombs, and she peddled her bike around the city often with C. Fred attached by his leash to her handlebars. The Bushes also entertained a constant flow of guests from the United States, including Henry Kissinger and President Ford as well as family members and friends. According to Mrs. Bush, "everyone wanted to come to China. It was all so new and exciting." But the only way an American could travel there was "if invited by the ambassador to stay in his residence" (Bush 1994, 118). After two years and considerable hostessing, President Ford recalled the Bushes and appointed George head of the CIA.

Morale in the CIA was at an all-time low in early 1976, because a tell-all book by Philip Agee, *Inside the Company: CIA Diary*, had blown some of the agents' covers: one was murdered. The Bushes set off on a morale boosting trip, staying with CIA employees in many countries. This trip must have been a learning experience for both of the Bushes, but George's position required much confidentiality, and Barbara found herself closed out of this part of his life. "I was very depressed, lonely and unhappy," she wrote in *A Memoir*. She was fifty-one at the time and probably going through menopause. The women's movement was in full force, and she began to feel that "her life had been wasted," especially since she may have viewed the CIA job as the end of George's political career. Kati Marton also suggests that Barbara may have been fed up with Jennifer Fitzgerald, George's "executive assistant" ("office-wife"), who had accompanied them to China and made the move with George into "the covert operations of the CIA" (2001, 288–89). Nonetheless, Barbara turned her attention to her public speaking engagements and traveled around the country showing her slides of China "to civic groups, schools, and churches . . . at fund raisers for different charities . . . and at political gatherings." According to Barbara, "China was still a 'hot' item. I tried to have a fast-moving program with *no* pictures of George, me, the children, or C. Fred. I wanted to be completely non-partisan so civic groups would feel comfortable inviting me to speak" (1994, 135). How different this would be from the slide shows she would put together when she campaigned for George for president. When Jimmy Carter defeated Gerald Ford later that year (1976), the Bushes began house hunting for a place in Houston.

In May 1979, George announced that he was a candidate for the presidency; Barbara brought organizational skills developed from years of child rearing and home management to his campaign (Kilian 1992, 102), and she continued to hone her abilities to speak on issues, deal with media, and refine her image.

During 1979 and 1980, "Barbara Bush was on the road almost every day for two years, campaigning for her husband—first for president, then for vice-president. Most of this time, especially in 1979, she traveled with just one aide," Becky Brady (now Beach) who was new to politics herself (Kilian 1992 103, 105). As the wife of a little-known candidate, Barbara did not attract much attention. She and Becky would fly into a city where a local Republican would act as their guide. They would attend five or six one-hour engagements a day. Her typical audience was a handful of Republican women who would meet in someone's living room for tea and coffee (Kilian 1992, 104). Barbara would present her slide show of China, now modified for partisan purposes. At first, she was not very comfortable and used the slides to "get in the swing of making speeches" (Kilian 1992, 104). Her aide Becky said: "She wasn't accustomed to speaking. But she was fabulous. She put the audience at ease. It was new to her and she didn't realize how well she was doing, but they loved it" (quoted in Kilian 1992, 106). Barbara would narrate the slides using her storytelling ability and Becky would advance them; sometimes Barbara extemporized at length, and Becky would hurry Barbara along by advancing a slide (Kilian 1992, 110). She stuck with the China slide show for about a year, "then decided she could speak on her own without it" (Kilian 1992, 111). She worked out "a basic speech with George Bush as the focus, talking about her family life, his accomplishments, and his goals" (Kilian 1992, 106). She and Becky took the speech to every state except Alaska, and all ninety-nine counties in Iowa (Kilian 1992, 109). Although George Bush was not nominated the Republican presidential candidate in 1980, Ronald Reagan invited him to run as his vice president. Suddenly, Barbara Bush was thrown into the national spotlight and would begin campaigning for the Reagan/Bush ticket.

During the primaries, Barbara had grown familiar with her speech material—highlighting George's personal qualities and his stance on issues. She was not familiar, however, with Reagan's views, so she talked about the problems of the Carter administration. Stressing the negative was not what she liked to do, but initially she had little else to say. She was also not very knowledgeable about literacy, a cause she had chosen to advocate since everything she worried about, she said in A Memoir, "would be better if more people could read, write, and comprehend" (145).

Invariably, she was put into situations where she was asked to speak about subjects she had not yet mastered. This raises the question of how well Barbara did as an impromptu speaker. She related an incident in *A Memoir* to explain how she tried to make the best of unexpected situations. During a campaign stop at Cardinal Stritch College in Milwaukee, for example, she was greeted by Sister Camille who said: "We are so excited about your visit. I have collected literacy experts from all around Milwaukee, some forty-five of the most informed people, and they are waiting to hear you. We are just thrilled." Sister Camille introduced Barbara to an audience of experts by saying, "Well, here she is. We can't wait to hear what you have to say." Although Mrs. Bush was unprepared, luckily, she said, "it suddenly came to me what to do." She made a few introductory remarks, and then asked her audience a question: "If you were married to the President and had the opportunity to really make a dent in the field of illiteracy, what one thing would you do? How would you go about it? We'll start on the right and go around the room" (145–46). She said that their two hours ran out before she was halfway around the room. Her audience was happy and she learned about literacy from experts. She also invented through desperation a strategy she could use on other occasions.

She tells about other kinds of impromptu speaking situations and how she handled them in *A Memoir*. Over the years, reporters had asked her questions spontaneously and often she was not given the opportunity to present well-considered answers. Probably the most difficult questions included those designed to catch her taking a stance on thorny issues that was different from her husband's, Ronald Reagan's, or the Republican Party platform. For example, she was often asked about abortion. Donnie Radcliffe claimed the only time she ever heard Barbara sound incoherent was when someone asked her about abortion: "In March 1989, when asked by reporters if she thought the Supreme Court should overturn Roe v. Wade," Mrs. Bush replied, "Now listen . . . you can try this every way you know—I am not going to discuss that. But that really—first of all, I don't think it is very presidential. I don't think it's—it's not—I don't think it's—I'm not going to talk about it. I'm not—because, see, if I start talking about one issue, then I'll have to move into another, and another, and another" (quoted in Radcliffe 1989, 187). She was also asked questions about gun control, the ERA, and personal questions such as: "Did she regret dropping out of Smith College? Did she miss having her own career?" (Kilian 1992, 116) At first her answers were "defensive, snippy," but in time she became good humored and sophisticated.

For example, during the 1980 primary in New Hampshire, she was asked by the *Today Show* to put an open microphone on her belt during an entire day of campaigning. The day included a half-hour interview with Jane Pauley who asked her on camera: "Mrs. Bush, people say your husband is a man of the eighties and you are a woman of the forties. What do you say to that?" (Bush 1994, 148). Mrs. Bush described her reaction in *A Memoir*: "Why didn't she just slap me in the face? She was darn lucky I didn't burst into tears and say that was the worst question I had ever heard. I was speechless and heartsick. I finally answered, 'Oh, you mean people think I look forty? Neat!' I went on to say, 'If you mean that I love my God, my country, and my husband so be it. Why, then I am a woman of the forties'" (149).

In addition to Jane Pauley's interview, Barbara was forced to think about the public impact of her physical appearance by other events. Early in the campaign, she was invited to participate in a press conference at the Waldorf in New York with the wives of the other candidates, including Nancy Reagan and Elizabeth Dole. In *A Memoir*, she compares the conference to a cattle show; the wives were not allowed to speak, they just posed for pictures. "I had the best candidate," she wrote, "but in a beauty contest or best-dressed competition, I didn't have a chance." Mrs. Bush wished she could speak about her husband's qualities, so confident had she become in her ability to address an audience. Kati Marton speculates that as a person, Mrs. Bush "didn't want the burden of beauty. . . . [because] she lacked the narcissism required for its maintenance" (2001, 281). Instead, she relied on her wit to develop what would "become her signature style as first lady." She evolved a self-deprecating humor that allowed her "to turn every potential negative into a positive: her age, her weight, her wrinkles, even her privileged lifestyle" (Marton 2001, 275).

The eight years that Mrs. Bush served as second lady were busy: "I believe the busiest of my life" (Bush 1994, 166). Of course, she moved yet another time into the vice president's house, which "needed a lot of work." She helped plan the renovations and raised private funds to pay for them. She also organized renovations of a house the Bushes had purchased in 1980, in Kennebunkport, at Walker's Point. There the Bushes entertained many U.S. and foreign leaders, as well as members of their large family and friends. She also worked on her image by buying new designer outfits and by meeting designers who would make clothes for her, especially Arnold Scaasi (Bush 1994, 160). In Washington, she set up a staff headed by Susan Porter Rose. She also campaigned for Reagan/Bush during the presidential campaign in 1984, and for Bush/Quayle in 1988.

The Bushes' foreign and domestic travel as well as their entertaining performed important social/political functions. Some of the places they visited outside of the United States included a trip to Ghana in honor of the twenty-fifth anniversary of the Peace Corp. They attended the inauguration of President Marcos of the Philippines, the funerals of Anwar Sadat and Brezhnev. In *A Memoir*, Mrs. Bush explained the usefulness of attending these affairs. About funerals, she said, "George met with many current or future heads of state at the funerals he attended, enabling him to forge personal relationships that were important to President Reagan—and later, President Bush." At all of these functions, Mrs. Bush met new people and deepened her friendships with those she had known before. She continued to learn about the problems and challenges facing other world leaders. The same might be said for her travels in the United States and the entertaining she did both at the vice president's house and at Walker's Point. In fact it was a conversation at a dinner with Nelson and Sandy Doubleday that helped her publish her first book.

As second lady, Barbara promoted the cause of literacy both in direct and indirect ways. *C. Fred's Story*, the book she wrote "with" her cocker spaniel to raise money for literacy, was published in April 1984. The project came about when George told Nelson not to kick C. Fred because the dog was writing a book. This prompted Nelson to inquire about the project and to set up Barbara with an editor to help her. Presented like a slide show, the book shows photographs of C. Fred with George and Barbara in many of the places they lived or visited. The text relates humorous "conversations" the dog had with Barbara, and these episodes perform rhetorical functions: they present the Bushes as "cozy" down-to-earth people who have forged warm personal relationships with many international leaders. Surprisingly, the book raised about $100,000—all donated to the Literacy Volunteers of America and the Laubach Literacy Action (Bush 1994, 188). Mrs. Bush held several book signing events in public libraries, and she went on a media tour to promote the book. She appeared on the *Today Show* and was interviewed again by Jane Pauley. In *A Memoir*, she gave a clear indication of how much she had learned about being interviewed:

> She [Jane Pauley] raced on the set, and as she was putting on her mike, she said something like, "Let's make this fun and not talk about literacy." Not talk about literacy? No way. That was what I was there for. Her first question was, "Mrs. Bush, why would a dog write a book?" Knowing that this might be my only chance, my answer was that he was worried about illiteracy in our country, and then I got in as many facts as possible before I let her get another word in edgewise. (1984, 189)

Mrs. Bush promoted literacy in indirect ways as well. For example, in *A Memoir* she described one of the media savvy methods she used: "It struck me that I worked so hard all year long for literacy and got little or no press coverage, and then I would do something frivolous like going up in a cherry picker [to put the star on top of the national Christmas tree] and my picture is seen around the world. So one year I took Rita and Rex Saurus, two puppets who encourage children to read" (1994, 175). Now the media coverage would be put to good use.

Mrs. Bush's work with literacy groups continued throughout George's second term as vice president, as she worked with Harold McGraw to marshal the support of American businesses and corporations (Bush 1994, 215). She also worked with many of the states' literacy councils and with PLUS (Project Literacy U.S.), a public/private partnership between PBS and ABC. She summarized the work she did during her eight years as second lady as follows: "I participated in 537 literacy related events and another 435 events related to volunteerism." Newspaper coverage of these events, together with articles on literacy that were published in popular magazines, helped raise public awareness of illiteracy and of how this problem could be solved (Bush 1994, 218).

Mrs. Bush continued to use the media for her own purposes, but she was not always successful. Or was she? A highly publicized remark of hers raises the question of whether her "slip ups" with the press were strategic, or whether she could save a mistake by the kind of spin she would later put on what she said. On a plane trip to New York, Barbara was in the press section talking to two reporters about the presidential debate the night before when Fritz Mondale had asked

President Reagan about his rich, elite running mate. Barbara made a remark to reporters about Mondale's running mate, Geraldine Ferraro, in what she thought was an off-the-record conversation: "That rich . . . well, it rhymes with rich . . . could buy George Bush any day." Of course, her comment made immediate radio and TV news. When interviewed by the press after the story broke, Mrs. Bush added her own spin on the story by telling reporters she had already apologized to Mrs. Ferraro for calling her a "witch" (Bush 1994, 195–96). About this "slip up," Kati Marton contends: "even her [Mrs. Bush's] slip-ups seemed calculated. Though she apologized profusely to Ferraro, she had made her point. It was an old Nixon trick: putting negative remarks into circulation by apologizing or denying them" (2001, 292).

No sooner was George Bush inaugurated as vice president in 1985, then the Bushes began to think about his run for president in 1988. "For the first couple of years," according to Barbara, "the campaign consisted of getting out and meeting as many people as possible and attending receptions and dinners. By 1987, it was in full swing." George W., the Bushes' oldest son, moved his family to Washington to help with the campaign.

During the Democratic National Convention in July 1988, Ann Richards, then governor of Texas attacked George Bush in her speech in a way that made Barbara feel sick to her stomach (Bush 1994, 225). Once Dan Quayle was announced as her husband's vice presidential running mate, the liberal press "trashed" Quayle; among other things, he was alleged to have had an affair with Paula Parkinson (Greene 2000, 36). Probably, most hurtful for Barbara was that the same accusation was made about George, who was alleged to have had an affair with his executive assistant, Jennifer Fitzgerald (Grimes 1990, 163–74; Bush 1994, 240) What made matters worse was the concurrent criticism of what was called the Bushes' "affection gap"—that they "were not lovey-dovey enough in public." Although their handlers told them to be more affectionate, neither of them took that seriously. At the Republican National Convention, both joked with exaggerated affection at a luncheon given in Barbara's honor, George calling Barbara "sweetie-pie," and Barbara asking the audience "to see if he looks at me as adoringly . . . as I looked at him" (Bush 1994, 227).

Probably one of the most important campaign speeches Barbara made was at the Republican National Convention in 1988. Even though she had been campaigning for years, she still felt nervous when she gave a highly formal presentation. She rehearsed the speech by standing at the podium at the convention center, "because she wanted to get a feel for the speech and the room" and "to combat the nervous sensation that hit her when she thought of addressing the thousands of delegates who would fill the empty room" (Kilian 1992, 143).

During the speech, Mrs. Bush said: "You've probably heard to the point you're sick of hearing it of all the important, big deal jobs George has held." Acknowledging "the tremendous energy and commitment" those jobs demanded, she told the audience that she respected her husband the most because of his performance as a husband and father: "But do you know what I respect about George. . . . In spite of those important, time-consuming jobs, our family has always felt an enormous part of his life." She continued to detail examples of his concern as a spouse, especially when they lost their four-year-old daughter to leukemia, and as a father, for example, when George told a reporter that his proudest accomplishment was that "the kids still come home." She concluded by reminding the delegates, "You should be proud. You have nominated for the presidency a man who is as strong and caring as America herself" (quoted in Inman 1988).

During the last month of campaigning, Mrs. Bush seems never to have stayed in one place longer than a few hours. She used her slides to show George as "a leader and happy family man." "There were also slides of George with world leaders, George at the Berlin Wall, and George at the Wailing Wall. Sometimes there was a videotape of George describing Barbara's life, with an emphasis on the humorous" (Kilian 1992, 137). According to biographer Donnie Radcliffe, Barbara increasingly used humor well. She made "self-deprecating humor an art. Joking about her white hair and her ample silhouette was a deliberate attempt to be funny, get a laugh, warm up a crowd." She thought that jokes about herself were better than jokes about others (1989, 9–10). Eventually, she had a "whole gag bag filled with stories about herself that she could draw from for any occasion. One anecdote poked fun at the allegations about George's affair: "'George Bush sleeps with two girls,' she deadpanned, pausing for effect, 'Millie [her springer spaniel] and me'" (quoted in Kilian 1992, 137–38). Kilian emphasized especially Barbara's use of timing. She became a favorite with campaign audiences.

Throughout the campaign season, there were still those who wanted to redo her, such as the woman who took a picture that had appeared in *Life* magazine, altering the haircut, earrings, necklace, clothes, and makeup (Bush 1994, 243). She told Roger Ailes, George's media advisor, "I'll do anything you want, but I won't dye my hair, change my wardrobe, or lose weight" (quoted in Radcliffe 1989, 4). She talked about the advantages of her drip-dry style: "I wash my hair every day of my life and probably washed all of the color out. But I can exercise, play tennis, I don't ever have to say to George, 'I'm sorry, I can't do that, I just got my hair done.' You have to set priorities in life and that's just not one I have. What you see is what you get." (quoted in Radcliffe 1989, 7) When George Bush was elected president, she carried this line of thinking—packaged with self-deprecating humor—into the White House.

Rhetorical Activities as First Lady

Mrs. Bush had been an incredibly active second lady and she continued this level of activity when she became first lady, leading one of her staff members to conclude that she was probably "one of the busiest first ladies ever" (Gutin 1996, 620). Together with her husband and by herself, she entertained many heads of state and their spouses in the White House, at Camp David, and at Walker's Point; they also visited many heads of state in their own countries, often staying in their homes or with Americans who worked for the U.S. government abroad.

One cannot read *A Memoir* without gaining an appreciation of the political importance of such interpersonal relationships, developed over many years by the Bushes' diplomacy of friendship. They also entertained other friends, family, staff, politicians, and members of the press. Early in George Bush's administration, they held a number of dinners and parties for members of Congress to begin the healing process after a tough campaign; they also held other receptions, luncheons, and parties for the press (252–53) Reports of Mrs. Bush's activities in the press were mostly positive, and she quickly rose in popularity with the American public. She promoted her husband's agenda as well as her own through statements to members of the press, interviews, and through hundreds of formal and informal speeches.

If anyone had asked Mrs. Bush during the 1988 campaign to project her post-election popularity, she probably could not have imagined how well she would be received by the American public. The campaign for president had been "hurtful," she said. Less understated, John Robert Greene, author of *The Presidency of George Bush*, referred to the campaign as "jugular politics" (2000, 27–43); Ann Grimes called it "grueling" (1990, 283). Yet Mrs. Bush's political skin had thickened; "she had become media smart," adept at using the press to manipulate her image (Radcliffe 1989, 50). She quickly discovered that, as first lady, she "attracted media attention wherever she went" and "almost everything she or her family did, no matter how insignificant, was of interest to the public" (Radcliffe 1989, 37). In the first one hundred days, she "scooted around the country to some forty solo publicity events . . . in an effort to capitalize on media attention that inevitably would fade" (Grimes 1990, 267). She preferred to draw attention to good causes and constructive people—to points of light—and not to herself.

Both press and public were eager to compare the incoming Bushes to the outgoing Reagans. With her white hair and full figure, Barbara was an easy contrast to the petite, immaculately coifed Nancy. Headlines forecasted their differences: "Bye Bye Glamour" and "Goodbye, First Fashion Plate—Hello First Grandmother" (Brown 1988, 42). At a tribute given to her at the Kennedy Center, Barbara humorously suggested to an audience of nearly six thousand people that she and Nancy had vastly different values: "Giving her 'Bush Blue' Arnold Scaasi jacket a tug and striking a model's pose," she said: "Speaking of glamour . . . I want you all to look at me. Please notice the hair, the make-up, designer dress. Look at me good this week, because it is the only week" (quoted in Radcliffe 1989, 15). These comments defined her style and early set the tone of the administration. Her words and actions carried the subtext "I am not Nancy Reagan" (Gould, quoted in Grimes, 267). Journalists at the *New Republic* called her, "Mrs. Not Nancy Reagan," and Kati Marton claims that the way she distanced herself from Nancy at the inaugural was brilliant: "She presented herself as the unNancy: plain spoken, authentic, and unthreatening" (2001, 274–75).

Another way in which Barbara Bush contrasted herself with Mrs. Reagan was in how she spoke about the White House. She intended to fill the White House with visits from her children and grandchildren, and she did not plan to redecorate. Instead, she talked about the beauty of the White House *as she found it*, about how much she enjoyed *what was already there*. During an interview, she told journalist Charlotte Saikowski of the *Christian Science Monitor* that the White House is "so much more beautiful than I thought." She said, "The food is the most beautiful food you have ever laid your eyes on. Today, I had lunch off of (Woodrow) Wilson's plates, sometimes I have lunch off of Lincoln's plates" (1989, 14).[3] Her comments marked a glaring contrast with Nancy Reagan, whose slim figure indicated that she did not share Barbara's relish of the White House food and whose efforts to procure a new set of China implied her dissatisfaction with what was there.[4] Although Mrs. Bush projected complete satisfaction with her new home, as a matter of fact, she did redecorate three or four rooms, but she never received any negative press. For example, she converted a "beauty salon" to an office/birthing room for her springer spaniel, Millie, as well as making other changes. According to Grimes, she "kept saying she didn't need to change a thing" and quietly made the changes. "That is a masterful political way to handle the situation" (1990, 279).

Barbara Bush also made it clear that she would not become involved in her husband's work except to promote his agenda and that she would not comment on controversial political issues. The press and public had chided Nancy Reagan for meddling in presidential affairs; Mrs. Bush was determined to avoid making the same mistake. She frequently said: "I don't mess with George's office and he doesn't mess with my house" (quoted in Grimes 1990, 325). Of course, no one doubted her private influence on her husband; in fact, "reports of her private influence circulated throughout the Bush tenure; she was christened by some observers as 'the Silver Fox'" (Greene 2000, 148). According to Grimes, she was viewed in Washington as a "key behind-the-scenes operator" (1990, 293) and Kati Marton, quoting Roger Ailes, George Bush's media advisor, said, "She would not express her opinions in public . . . but she was a strong and respected voice inside" (2001, 297).

An early incident reinforced her resolve to refrain from making controversial statements in public, basically to do "what she . . . dubbed 'muzzling' herself" (Grimes 1990, 296). Two weeks after the inauguration, she was asked a question about gun control and told reporters that she was afraid of guns and would not own them. She also said that the AK-47 was and should be illegal. These remarks caused quite a stir since George Bush did not favor a ban on the AK-47. Thereafter, her press secretary announced that she would not be commenting about any controversial issues. Instead, she would only talk about ideas that interested her, such as women, work, and literacy (Kilian 1992, 159–60; Grimes 1990, 298).

Mrs. Bush found an ingenious way to garner press attention on her terms. She used a strategy that may best be described as "deflection." Millie, her springer spaniel, "married" Tug III during the week of the inauguration, and this marriage along with the subsequent "honeymoon," pregnancy, delivery, and White House brood claimed media attention throughout the first hundred days of the Bush presidency. Acknowledging the rhetorical power of the paw, Chuck Conconi, staff writer for *The Washington Post*, called Millie and her pups a "major public relations asset" (1989, E3). John Hughs of *The Christian Science Monitor* contrasted Millie's treatment with Lucky's, the Reagan's dog "who was banished to California because he could not contain himself in the White House" (1989, 18). Kilian put the point well when she said that Millie "filled the anecdote quota during the early weeks of the administration. Her puppies got a stupendous amount of attention; at one point, more than one hundred photographers were on the White House grounds taking pictures" (1992, 160).

Millie not only helped Mrs. Bush with her public relations activities, she also helped with hostessing and diplomacy. As C. Fred had done before, Millie was present during many White House activities and accompanied Barbara to Camp David and Walker's Point. There are many episodes reported in *A Memoir* suggesting how Millie's presence tended to cut through protocol, allowing the Bushes and their guests to interact in more informal ways. According to Grimes: "A dog running around the White House chomping on a tennis ball . . . functions well as an icebreaker and helps cut through protocol pretty quickly" (1990, 283). Millie also helped Barbara raise money for one of her major causes—literacy.

Mrs. Bush understood the power of her position as first lady. Citing Lady Bird Johnson's notion of the first lady's office as a bully pulpit, she assembled a staff and told them her priorities. She retained Susan Porter Rose as her chief of staff and Laurie Firestone as her social secretary; she hired Anna Perez as her press secretary and rehired Julie Cooke as her director of projects (1994, 253).[5] She told her staff: "each day we should do something to help others" (272). Julie Cooke scheduled many events that "either highlighted a need, helped encourage volunteerism, or focused on literacy." To begin with, she wanted to promote George Bush's "thousand points of light," by celebrating all of the volunteers in the country (Radcliffe 1989, 33). But as we have seen, literacy was her chief focus. In *A Memoir*, she explained why: "a more literate America would benefit every single thing I worry about: crime, unemployment, pollution, teen-age pregnancy, school dropouts, women who are trapped into welfare and therefore poverty, etc." (274–75). The Barbara Bush Foundation for Family Literacy became official in March 1989 (Bush 1994, 251).

As first lady, Mrs. Bush promoted literacy all over the United States and internationally. She attended an important meeting in fall 1989 at the University of Virginia. Meeting with governors' wives, Mrs. Bush asked them what they were doing in their states to help the cause (Bush 1994, 309–11). In *A Memoir* she also referred to a literacy meeting held in the White House on February 21, 1991, at which she raised $3 million (398–99). She read to children on the radio during a program called "Mrs. Bush's Storytime." Later, these readings were released on audiocassettes (360). She appeared on the *Oprah Winfrey Show* to discuss literacy, and she authored a *Reader's Digest* article, "Parenting's Best-Kept Secret: Reading to Your Children," that had great exposure (Gutin 1996, 619). Mrs. Bush also opened an international conference on literacy in Ottawa in October 1990 (Bush 1994, 368). And when she visited other countries, she often included trips to local schools to read stories to children. Altogether, she participated in several hundred literacy events. According to Gutin, "she would ask her sponsors what they wanted her to tell the press who would write stories about the event and whether they needed contributions or volunteers" (Gutin 1996, 620). Her presence gave great media exposure to groups whose mission and activities she helped publicize.

Perhaps her most unusual fund-raising project for literacy was *Millie's Book* (1990), a volume she "wrote" with her springer spaniel much like its predecessor, *C. Fred's Story* (1984). *Millie's Book* was released amidst a media blitz that included appearances on the *Today Show, Good Morning America*, and the *CBS Morning Show*. Mrs. Bush also appeared on the cover of *Good Housekeeping* (August 1990). The publicity worked, and the book's reception was greater than anyone had imagined; it was even ranked number one on the *New York Times* "Best Seller List" and remained on national bestseller lists for many months (Kilian 1992, 23). Over 400,000 copies were sold, raising more than $1 million for literacy. It was translated into Japanese and German and released in paperback. By the summer of 1990, Millie needed her own volunteer to handle her correspondence (Bush 1994, 352). Earlier, when the puppies were born, Millie's mail had also been extensive.

Mrs. Bush, herself, received a great deal of mail: her yearly average was about 100,000 pieces (Bush 1994, 279). She had a staff to help her respond to these letters, many of which were positive and some of which were about "silly things" like George's dislike of broccoli—a theme she later developed as she campaigned for him for reelection. About 100 letters a day were invitations for her to speak. Especially busy was graduation time—her office would be swamped with more invitations than she could accept. Members of Barbara's staff read the letters and attached notes to them, and then she would look them over. She said: "We tried very hard to select those that would represent a cross-section of schools and regions" (335). Once she had selected the schools, Barbara and her staff worked together to write a general speech that represented what she wanted to say as well as allowing room for adaptation to local conditions.

In *A Memoir*, Mrs. Bush described the inventional process she and her staff used:

> My staff and I had been working on *the* [graduation] speech off and on all spring. We asked Ed McNally from George's speech writing department to help. So he joined our brainstorming sessions, which included Susan Porter Rose, Julie Cooke, Anna Perez, Susan Green, Jean Becker and Sondra Haley. We sat around and talked about the things I wanted to say, and tried to choose the theme for this year. They reminded me that I always say, "You have two choices in life. You can like it or not. I chose to like it.". . . We talked about my dad and the things he told me. . . . I suggested that we end with the marvelous story from one of Robert Fulghum's books about "where do the mermaids fit into a world of wizards, giants, and dwarfs" . . . Somehow, out of all these ramblings, a speech began to take shape. (337)

This was the core of all the graduation speeches Barbara would give that season, even at Wellesley.

While planning the generic graduation speech, Mrs. Bush and her staff became aware of a controversy brewing at Wellesley College, where she was scheduled to present a graduation speech. She was not the students' first choice as a speaker; Alice Walker was, but Walker was not available. Although a majority of the 600 graduating seniors wanted Barbara Bush to speak, 150 signed a petition in protest and presented it to university president Dr. Nan Keohane. The petition read: "To honor Barbara Bush as a commencement speaker is to honor a woman who has gained recognition through the achievements of her husband, which contradicts what we have been taught over the past four years" (quoted in *Chicago Tribune* 1990, 2). The press reported the controversy in articles and editorials, and it also became a subject discussed widely on television news and talk shows. According to Mrs. Bush in *A Memoir*: "That darn Wellesley flap" took on "a life of its own." Homemakers across the United States were offended, and Mrs. Bush received many encouraging letters. She also received a letter from Chris Bicknell, who had been selected to be the student speaker at Wellesley's graduation. She thanked Mrs. Bush for being so understanding of the students' position and for expressing that understanding to the press (338–39). Mrs. Bush had told a small group of reporters over lunch in the White House family quarters: "I thought they were very reasonable. . . . They're 21 years old and they're looking at life from that perspective. . . . I hope they won't opt not to have families, and I hope they won't opt not to be great parents" (quoted in Robinson 1990, 1).

The controversy was boiling when Mrs. Bush and her staff met a second time to refine the graduation speech. "I told my staff," Barbara said, "that I did not want to make a special speech catering to Wellesley. I also did not want to complain, explain, or apologize in any way. By the end of the meeting, we had settled three things I wanted the students to consider: You have to get involved in something larger than yourself; Remember to get joy out of life; Cherish human relationships." She read the speech to her husband, who suggested that she add: "Read to your child." And she added, "Hug your child." She said, "We cut and pasted and were ready to start the graduation trail" (Bush 1994, 377).

Mrs. Bush presented the same basic speech at many locations, including the University of Pennsylvania, St. Louis University, and Wellesley College. She added local color to the speeches, but altered the speech a bit more for the special interests of students at Southeast Community College in Cumberland, Kentucky, the heart of coal-mining country. Most of these students were the first in their families to go to college and they were, to Mrs. Bush, "truly a group of courageous students" (Bush 1994, 337), quite a contrast to the more privileged students at Wellesley.

What seems not well known about the Wellesley speech situation is that Mrs. Bush almost turned down the invitation. The date conflicted with a visit from the Gorbachevs, an event regarded as critically important to U.S./USSR relations. Instead of declining the invitation, Mrs. Bush asked Dr. Keohane if Raisa

Gorbachev could also speak to the seniors. This would be a treat for all because it would be Mrs. Gorbachev's first speech in the United States. Moreover, Raisa was a first lady, but she also had an independent career of her own. Once the flap started, bringing Mrs. Gorbachev perhaps signaled to the students that Mrs. Bush was sensitive to their concerns, even if she didn't agree with them.

On the plane ride to Boston, Mrs. Bush took out her speech and went over it "just one more time" (Bush 1994, 340). Despite the protests, the petitions, and the press coverage, she said, "I had just quit worrying about the whole thing once the speech was written because I felt good about what I wanted to say to them" (341). When she arrived at Wellesley, she discovered that a number of students had circulated a second petition and the results were released right before she spoke. The petition praised the choice of Mrs. Bush as the commencement speaker and commended unknown women who had devoted their lives to serving others. The petition also urged Mrs. Bush to support legislation on day care, welfare, and wage equity between men and women (Gutin 1996, 622).

The Wellesley speech is an excellent example of Mrs. Bush's wit and self-deprecating humor with which she was able to win over her audience. During the speech, Mrs. Bush told the group that family is important in life: "As important as your obligations as a doctor, a lawyer or a business leader may be, your human connection with spouses, with children, with friends, are the most important investment you will ever make." She told them: "At the end of your life, you will never regret not having passed one more test, not winning one more verdict or not closing one more deal. You will regret the time not spent with a husband, child, a friend or a parent." Moreover, she told her audience that she knew she was not their first choice as a speaker: "Now I know your first choice today was Alice Walker . . . known for 'The Color Purple.' Instead you got me, known for the color of my hair." She told the audience that she expected great achievements from them and ended by saying: "Who knows somewhere out in this audience may even be someone who will one day follow in my footsteps and preside over the White House as the President's spouse. And I wish him well" (Bush 1990b; 1994, appendix C).

Mrs. Bush's speech was well received by her audience. According to coverage in the *New York Times* (June 2, 1990), audience members interrupted her speech several times with applause and laughter. A headline in the *Washington Post* announced: "Barbara Bush: Wowing Wellesley" (Radcliffe 1990, C1) and their television critic, Tom Shales, called it "a rock 'em–sock 'em smash hit" (Shales 1990, C1). NBC's Tom Brokaw said it was "one of the best commencement speeches I ever heard" and *Boston Globe* staff writer John Robinson reported: "the rave reviews on the nation's front pages and television shows confirmed her victory" (1990, 1). Not only did the press praise the speech, they also commented on the two first ladies' "symbolic summit": "The picture of the two women forging a friendship over live television symbolized the growing potential of women as leaders in the global quest for international cooperation. . . . Some Washington observers are beginning to call the current US-Soviet summit 'Barbara's summit,' a tribute to her contribution to the tone and atmosphere of the event" (Robinson 1990, 1).

Mrs. Bush gave another important speech while she was first lady—at the Republican National Convention in 1992, when George Bush was running for reelection against Bill Clinton. At the time, public opinion polls showed that she had a high approval rating with the American people, while her husband trailed Clinton. Republican Party leaders counted on her to boost her husband's ratings by driving home their message on family values. Even though this prime-time speech was probably the most important one of her career, or at least the one most widely seen and heard with an estimated audience of 26.5 million people (Kubasik 1992, 35), she described it beforehand as a "trifle," "a Mickey Mouse thing," "nothing at all." But this was the 1992 convention and all eyes were on the four women who were "running" with their husbands: Barbara Bush and Marilyn Quayle versus Hillary Clinton and Tipper Gore. Many members of the press drew a sharp contrast between Barbara Bush, a "career" wife and mother and Hillary Clinton, a "radical feminist" (Couture 1992, B5).

Despite her calling the speech a trifle, she and her staff worked very hard on it. I have examined at least five drafts of the speech and many pieces of correspondence related to it in the "First Lady Office, Press Files" at the George Bush Presidential Library and Museum. A letter addressed to George Bush, written by California citizen Jay Wilson, was among the documents. This letter asked President Bush what he meant by "family values" and explained that he lived with several other unrelated people whom he considered his "family." Sent from the president's staff to the first lady's staff, this letter seemed to crystallize the primary exigencies for Mrs. Bush's speech—define "family values" broadly, show how "family values" connects to American values, and illustrate how the Bush family "lives" what they talk about (also see "1992 Events Files, GOP Convention," OA/ ID 07474).

Mrs. Bush and her staff wrote several drafts of the speech, giving great care to the tone and content. They were particularly concerned about what they meant by "family values." Taking great pains not to give the impression that they were only talking about traditional families, they used a series of examples to emphasize the many different kinds of "families" found in the United States today— traditional families, single-parent families headed by men or women, and extended families of grandparents, foster parents, adoptive parents, divorced parents, aunts and uncles, brothers and sisters, even neighbors and communities. They wanted to emphasize the importance of the family through "tough" times and especially the role of the family in passing down the values that are central to the American character.

During the speech (Bush 1992b), Mrs. Bush stated that regardless of the kind of "family" a child comes from, each must learn values such as "integrity, strength, responsibility, courage, sharing, love of God, and pride in being an American." She told the audience that her husband—"the strongest, the most decent, the most caring, the wisest man"—was determined to preserve a nation of strong families and strong communities. She also recognized the many roles that women are free to choose or are forced to play by circumstances. She presented herself as accepting, without regret, the choices she had made in her own life as well as accepting, with respect, the choices of her daughter and daughter-in-law, both of whom worked and had children. She said: "You may be exhausted from working a job, or two jobs, and taking care of your children, or you may have to put your career on hold. . . . Either way, you may wonder, as I did every now and then, am I doing the right thing? Yes, you are." Mrs. Bush introduced her eldest grandson, sixteen-year-old George P. Bush, Jeb's son, whose remarks were part of her presentation. Echoing points she made in her speech, he added: "In a Presidential campaign, it's hard for people to get a sense of what makes the candidates tick. The family is what makes my grandfather tick." He ended his speech with: "Viva Bush" (Bush 1994, appendix D). They were joined on stage by Mrs. Bush's five children, their spouses, and her twelve grandchildren. Making a surprise appearance, President Bush also joined the group.

Mrs. Bush seemed to be saying visually through this assemblage of twenty-four people: "the rest of you may talk about family values, but George Bush and I live them!" *New York Times* journalist Elizabeth Kolbert made this point when she said: "the show of Bush family solidarity . . . presented a triumphantly simple visual . . . the phrase 'family values' seemed to have a clear meaning" (1992, A12). Even Molly Ivans, who described herself as a "salty Democrat," told *USA Today*: "I liked (her) speech. Her political timing is impeccable. I can't help it. I loved it. I even like the tough slightly bitchy side of her" (quoted in Kelly 1992, D4). Kati Marton also highlighted the usefulness of Mrs. Bush to her husband when she wrote: Mrs. Bush "was . . . the source of one of Bush's strongest assets: his image as the patriarch of a large and appealing brood" (2001, 276). First lady scholar Myra Gutin wrote approvingly that this "speech was another triumph for Barbara Bush" (1996, 623).

Mrs. Bush frequently gave other kinds of campaign speeches. Of course, she campaigned actively for her husband during the 1992 presidential race, but she also campaigned for other Republicans during the midterm elections of 1990, including "thirty-three candidates in twenty states and twenty-nine cities" (Bush 1994, 370). She made most of these trips without her husband, as she would continue to do during the 1992 presidential election, when she and George "rarely traveled together" (487). She went on two types of campaign trips, some were big rallies and others were "smaller fund raising lunches or dinners." Mrs. Bush and one of her staff members, Anna Perez, worked on two speeches—"one to be given at the rallies . . . and a second warm and cozy talk for the smaller groups." Like the graduation speech, their approach was to draft a generic or "core" speech and then adapt it to the particularities of the situation. The bulk of this core speech was a list of George Bush's accomplishments as president, with room left mostly at the beginning and end to insert comments about local candidates, campaign organizers, and conditions. Interspersed throughout the speech were bits of humor—about herself and her family—that had become her trademark.[6]

Especially after the Republican National Convention, Mrs. Bush's campaigning increased dramatically. In A Memoir she logged visits to "eleven cities in seven states . . . including eight fund-raisers; five school, library, or literacy events; two cultural centers; three rallies, and one fair" (Bush 1994, 489). The last week of the campaign was especially busy, she "literally criss-crossed the country . . . did unending radio, TV, and print interviews," went to mall after mall, and appeared on the Larry King Live Show (475). None of this hard work was rewarded because George Bush lost the election to Bill Clinton, and the Bushes had to make plans to leave the White House.

Legacy

First lady scholar Myra Gutin reports that members of Mrs. Bush's staff said "she was probably one of the busiest first ladies ever" (1996, 620). She performed many traditional roles such as hostess, surrogate, and political partner. In addition, she promoted her husband's agenda as well as her own in indirect nonverbal ways as well as by giving literally several hundred informal and formal speeches. A document among Mrs. Bush's papers in the George Bush Presidential Library and Museum lists 455 speeches that Mrs. Bush gave between 1989 and 1992 (OA/ID 08383). The way she performed these activities modified the "institution" of first lady. I will summarize the lessons she has left us as her legacy.

As we have seen, First Lady Barbara Bush was active as a hostess—in the White House, at Camp David, and Walker's Point. She entertained with her husband and alone, both formally and informally with various kinds and numbers of guests. In reading her A Memoir as well as the two books she wrote with her dogs, C. Fred's Story and Millie's Book, it is quite clear that many of the Bushes' political goals were furthered through their interpersonal diplomacy of friendship.

Mrs. Bush also acted as George Bush's surrogate on many occasions, two important occasions that have not been discussed are her visits with Desert Storm personnel and their families[7] and the toast she gave impromptu when her husband became sick during dinner on a trip to Japan.[8] As we have seen, Mrs. Bush was quite the campaigner and she enabled her husband to get his message to many more people by taking that message to them herself. As Lee Atwater told The Washington Post: "she's by far the most sought-after surrogate we've got" (quoted in Grimes 1990, 174).

Mrs. Bush was also very much her husband's political partner, helping him get "into office and keep him happy while . . . there" "Publicly," according to Ann Grimes, she carried "out her purely decorative, symbolic role, but behind the scenes, as her children and friends say, she . . . [was] a full partner in the family business of politics" (1990, 324–25). Grimes continues: "few in Washington . . . doubt [her] enormous influence with the president, despite her pro forma disclaimers" (325). Yet, her influence was like "Bess Truman['s], . . . who entered into almost every decision Harry Truman ever made" (326). Kati Marton makes a similar point when she writes: "Barbara did not think it in the Bushes' interest for the public to know how influential she was. . . . She had an upstairs/downstairs attitude about voicing her views—not in front of the staff and not in front of the reporters" (2001, 297). In the end, the kind and extent of her influence, especially how much she has had on her husband's policies, remain open and may never be answered fully. Unfortunately, as Betty Boyd Caroli explains, "much of the influence went undocumented and unquantified because it occurred off the record" (1995, 287).

Many people looked to Mrs. Bush as a liberal voice in an otherwise conservative administration. Moderate Republicans were also reassured by her presence, as Marton points out: "through subtle pauses, inflections, [and] body language, she gave [them] . . . a feeling that she was with them, that they had an ally in the Bush White House" (2001, 277). Her private influence on policy may have been to make some issues more visible to her husband such as funding for Aids research, and to move other issues on her husband's agenda upward in priority such as with the AK-47 legislation. Her influence was most obvious when George Bush signed the National Literacy Act of 1991 into law. As a symbol of how much Barbara Bush had done to bring literacy to the attention of the American public and legislature, President Bush gave her the pen he used to sign the bill, and it is now in the George Bush Presidential Library and Museum. For her part, she credits many people with passage of the legislation, but her words show how proud she was of the achievement: the act was "the first piece of legislation—and to date, the only one—ever enacted specifically for literacy, with the goal of ensuring that every American adult acquires basic literacy skills. . . . But even more than that, the act seeks to strengthen our nation by giving us more productive workers and informed citizens" (1994, 425).

Mrs. Bush also left another kind of legacy with regard to literacy. During her eight years as second lady and her four years as first lady, she promoted literacy in many different ways. One week after becoming first lady, she began the Barbara Bush Foundation for Literacy and worked to raise money so that the foundation could fund needy programs across the country. Her books alone raised more than $1 million, and she continues to promote literacy even after she has left the White House. Her daughter-in-law and former librarian, First Lady Laura Bush, has continued and extended the project to highlight the value of reading to children. When Laura Bush established her own foundation—the Laura Bush Foundation for America's Libraries—Barbara Bush pledged $50,000 and joined her daughter-in-law on June 4, 2002, to listen to papers presented at a White House Conference on School Libraries.

In regard to public image, Mrs. Bush popularized a natural look that reflected the reality of a life spent enjoying good food, sunshine, exercise, and activity. Her look said that she was concerned with her appearance, as she had to be given her position, but she was not *overly* concerned with it. Her white hair and sun-wrinkled skin became trademarks, along with her triple strand of fake pearls. She legitimized the role of matriarch or grandmother, celebrating motherhood right down to her two dogs and Millie's litter. The cover of *Life* magazine (May 1989), coinciding with Mother's Day, captured this persona well: we see a smiling Barbara shown with a smiling Millie who is nestled with her brood of very photogenic puppies. She stressed motherhood as well when she framed her literacy campaign as an effort to teach mothers to read to their children and when she appeared on stage with her children and grandchildren during the Republican National Convention.

In regard to press relations, we learn from Mrs. Bush's experience and her advice. In *A Memoir* she writes: "One of the lessons someone in public life must learn is: THE PRESS HAS THE LAST WORD" (emphasis hers, 442). This statement is especially significant coming from a woman who has been called "our most unflappable First Lady" (Truman 1995, 317). As we have seen, she had to learn to face interviewers' questions both on camera and off. Beginning with an initial tendency to be sarcastic and teasing, she learned to moderate her words, to direct the conversation to areas that furthered *her* purposes, and to poke fun at only herself. She also learned that nothing might be off the record, that the purpose of the interview could be changed, that the interaction during the interview could be misinterpreted. Yet given all of the constraints in dealing with journalists, they also presented vitally important opportunities to promote the cause of literacy. In the end, Mrs. Bush wrote that there were probably many more decent reporters than nasty ones (498–99).

In regard to public speaking, Mrs. Bush's example teaches that everyone can improve as a public speaker through capitalizing on individual personality traits, shaping them artistically for public performance. Mrs. Bush began her career as a speaker by using slides to deflect attention away from herself—this helped with her nervousness. Using slides also helped with speech organization, for once the slides were arranged in trays, the topics and their sequence were easy to remember by virtue of visual clues. Narrating stories about the images projected made excellent use of her storytelling skills, sense of humor, ability as a mimic, and her comedic timing. As she grew comfortable in front of audiences, her presentations became more "oratorical," only in that she stopped using the accompanying images and concentrated more on set speeches. But even here we learn that she and her staff worked out different basic speeches or "speech templates" for kinds of occasions (genres)—graduation speeches, campaign speeches—and they adapted those general speeches by adding "local color." She instructed her staff to keep her speeches short and funny, and she developed her self-deprecating humor to an art. Myra Gutin, first lady scholar and communication professor, has judged Mrs. Bush's public speech very highly. So have two of George Bush's staff members. Pete Teeley, a former press secretary, who has said, "She is a good speaker . . . she's very composed in terms of what she wants to say. She has real presence" (quoted in Kilian 1992, 111). Victor Gold, a senior campaign aid and coauthor of George Bush's autobiography, has said: "In some ways, she was better before an audience than George. 'When she talks to an audience, there is straight projection. The audience feels this is a real person. She is able to assert strength, ideas, and feelings of personal warmth without trying . . . Barbara is a direct link with her audience'" (quoted in Radcliffe 1989, 158).

After leaving the White House, the Bushes relocated to Houston and traveled extensively visiting family and friends in the United States and abroad. Mrs. Bush retained her interest in the Barbara Bush Foundation for Family Literacy, still claiming that making people more literate will solve many social problems. She also became a member at large of AmeriCares and joined the boards of many other institutions (1994, 521–22). She has attempted to keep up with her correspondence. That is one reason why she published A *Memoir*. She made an interesting comment at the end of that book about the lack of funding for first ladies after they leave the White House. Although she didn't think former first ladies should receive funding, she said she wondered "how I was going to answer my mail and cope with public appearance requests." She wrote A *Memoir* to help finance this work (506).

Perhaps her most active role since leaving the White House has been campaigning for her son George W. during his presidential race. Early in Campaign 2000, she was called in for damage control when George W. ran into a flap for his alleged use of cocaine as a young man. Karen Brown interviewed Mrs. Bush in New Hampshire on WMUR, and a portion of that interview was carried nationally on CNN and ABC's *Good Morning America*. Mrs. Bush was still so well liked and respected that it seemed if she said the drug issue was too old to be relevant, then others would agree with her. She also became very active during fall 2000, as she participated in a "W is for Women" campaign swing with Laura Bush and others. Now that W is president, she has achieved something no other first lady has achieved: been first the wife, then the mother of two U.S. presidents in her lifetime. With a family as large as hers and as interested in political service, she may yet achieve other distinctions such as becoming the first women to be a grandmother of a U.S. president, if George P., dubbed the "Ricky Martin of the Republican Party" during the 2000 Republican National Convention, or one of her other progeny chooses that kind of life (Crowley 2000, A18).

Mrs. Bush was presented with many honors when she was first lady, including at least nineteen honorary degrees at many colleges and universities.[9] A rose was named in her honor and presented to her when she visited France (Kilian 1992, 205). Part of her legacy is the lesson she learned from her mother: to appreciate what we have and not long for what we cannot have. About her own life she says: "Imagine knowing heads of every country, on a fairly personal basis in many cases. . . . Or imagine traveling to all those foreign countries. I feel like I have had the best, the most exciting, thrilling life anyone could ever have" (quoted in Kilian 1992, 207). Not even mentioning the heartbreak of losing Robin or the agony of defeat to "draft-dodging, pot smoking" Bill Clinton, Mrs. Bush's rhetorical sense remains strong. All must agree that her achievements have far exceeded what anyone could have expected from a career homemaker and college dropout.

Questions for Discussion

1. When George Bush began his political career, Barbara Bush was a home-maker. She was frightened to stand up before an audience to give a public speech. What strategies did she use to overcome her stage fright?
2. What cause did Barbara Bush champion during her eight years as second lady and four years as first lady? Why did she choose to promote this cause? What rhetorical strategies did she use?
3. Barbara Bush helped her husband campaign for the presidency in 1980, 1988, and 1992. Describe the rhetorical strategies she used during those years. Did she employ different strategies as she gained experience?
4. In 1990, Barbara Bush was invited to present a commencement address at Wellesley College. Describe the students' reactions to her choice as a speaker. What did she say to win the students over?
5. Some scholars consider Barbara Bush to be a "traditional" first lady. Given her activity as a first lady, do you agree or disagree with this characterization? Why?

Internet Resources

http://bushlibrary.tamu.edu/index.php
The George Bush Presidential Library and Museum is a rich resource for material on Barbara Bush. You can access her biography as well as many photographs of her and her family. Thanks to a request filled through the Freedom of Information Act, all of Barbara Bush's speech materials have been processed and are available to students and researchers. Use the online finding guides to see the resources available.

http://www.barbarabushfoundation.com/
The Barbara Bush Foundation for Family Literacy's website describes its mission. Check it out to learn more about a cause very dear to the heart of former First Lady Barbara Bush.

Notes

I would like to acknowledge the generous help of Dr. Robert Holzweiss, archivist, and other staff members of the George Bush Presidential Library and Museum in College Station, Texas. They helped me find texts and audiotapes of Mrs. Bush's speeches as well as relevant files kept by members of her staff.

1. Abigail Adams was the only other woman to be both wife and mother of a president. Mrs. Adams died in 1818, and John Quincy Adams did not become president until 1925.

2. I have used material from Mrs. Bush's A Memoir to write this section, supplemented by material from two biographies: Pam Kilian's Barbara Bush: A Biography (1992) and Donnie Radcliffe's Simply Barbara Bush: A Portrait of America's Candid First Lady (1989). Unless otherwise indicated, the material is from A Memoir.

3. She spoke similarly of the White House in *A Memoir* when she said that even the most ordinary events, like lunch, could seem magical: "I ate off President Cleveland's white china with touches of navy blue and gilt." And she said, "The butlers loved trying to make me guess whose china I was using. Imagine being served a meal on dishes that Abraham Lincoln ate from!" (Bush 1994, 277).

4. Defending the purchase, Nancy Reagan explains in *My Turn* that she ordered the china because the White House didn't have enough pieces from any one set for a state dinner. She also explains that the American people did not pay for the china; rather it was a gift purchased by the Knapp Foundation (1989, 27–29).

5. Her final staff consisted of nineteen people: see appendix A in *A Memoir* for their names and positions.

6. There are two drafts of this core as well as an example of how the core was amplified with local material in Anna Perez's "Political Speech Research File" (OA/ID 08737) in the George Bush Presidential Library and Museum. The same file also contains a list of how Barbara should answer questions about George's accomplishments and about his position on various social issues, such as abortion, women's issues, and so on.

7. Mrs. Bush discusses the military bases she visited, both with and without her husband in *A Memoir*. She often met with the wives, mothers, and fathers of soldiers who were killed in action or missing in action; see 385–408.

8. Mrs. Bush was unprepared to present a toast at a dinner held by the prime minister of Japan. Because her husband got sick during the dinner and was rushed out on a stretcher, she was asked to give a toast in his place. She relied on her sense of humor to put a light touch on the otherwise embarrassing event; she simply said that her husband was a poor sport having earlier lost a game of tennis to the emperor of Japan and the crown prince: see *A Memoir*, 448–51.

9. A list of Mrs. Bush's honorary degrees may be found in Anna Perez's "Political Speech Research File" 2 of 3 in the George Bush Presidential Library and Museum.

References

Anthony, Carl Sferrazza. 1991. *First Ladies: The Saga of the Presidents' Wives and Their Power, 1961–1990.* New York: William Morrow & Co.

Brown, Patricia Leigh. 1988. The First Lady-Elect: What She Is and Isn't. *New York Times*, late city final ed., 11 December, 42.

Bush, Barbara. 1984. *C. Fred's Story: A Dog's Life.* Garden City, N.Y.: Doubleday & Co.

———. 1990a. *Millie's Book: As Dictated to Barbara Bush.* New York: William Morrow & Co.

———. 1990b. Choices and Changes: Your Success as a Family. *Vital Speeches of the Day*, 1 July.

———. 1992a. Events Files, GOP Convention OA/ID 07474. College Station, Tex.: George Bush Presidential Library and Museum.

———. 1992b. Family Values: The Country's Future Is in Your Hands. *Vital Speeches of the Day*, 1 September.

———. 1994. *Barbara Bush: A Memoir.* New York: Charles Scribner's Sons.

Butterfield, Fox. 1990. Family First, Mrs. Bush Tells Friend and Foe at Wellesley. *New York Times*, late ed., 2 June, A1.

Caroli, Betty Boyd. 1995. *First Ladies*, expanded ed. New York: Oxford University Press.

Chicago Tribune. 1990. First Lady Represents U.S. on Trip, 8 May.

Conconi, Chuck. 1989. Personalities. *Washington Post*, 4 April, E3.

Couture, Dan. 1992. Convention '92. *Houston Chronicle*, star ed., 20 August, B5.

Crowley, Brian. 2000. He's Hot, He's Hispanic—and He's a Bush; Campaign Finds Nephew an Asset. *Atlanta Journal and Constitution*, home ed., 3 August, A18.

Gallup Organization. 1999. Most Admired Men and Women: 1948–1998. www.gallup.com/poll/specialreports/pollsummaries/polls_this_century_index.asp, accessed, 13 December.

Gould, Lewis. 1996. The First Lady as Symbol and Institution. In *American First Ladies*, ed. Lewis L. Gould, xiii–xx. New York: Garland.

Greene, John Robert. 2000. *The Presidency of George Bush*. Lawrence, Kans.: University of Kansas Press.

Grimes, Ann. 1990. *Running Mates: The Making of a First Lady*. New York: William Morrow & Co.

Gullan, Harold I. 2001. *Faith of Our Mothers: The Stories of Presidential Mothers from Mary Washington to Barbara Bush*. Grand Rapids, Mich.: William B. Edermans Publishing Co.

Gutin, Myra. 1996. Barbara Bush. In *American First Ladies*, ed. Lewis L. Gould, 608-29. New York: Garland.

Hughes, John. 1989. The Bush White House. *Christian Science Monitor*, 20 January, 18.

Inman, William. 1988. Barbara Bush Praises Her Husband. *United Press International*, 18 August.

Kelly, Katy. 1992. Ivans Has Her Say about GOP's Big Guns. *USA Today*, 21 August, D4.

Kilian, Pamela. 1992. *Barbara Bush: A Biography*. New York: St. Martin's Press.

Kolbert, Elizabeth. 1992. The Media and the Message: Campaign Watch; On TV, a Victory in Family Numbers. *New York Times*, late ed., 21 August, A12.

Kubasik, Ben. 1992. No Barbara Bounce on Nielsen Scale. *Newsday*, 21 August, 35.

Marton, Kati. 2001. *Hidden Power: Presidential Marriages That Shaped Our Recent History*. New York: Random House.

Parmet, Herbert. 1997. *George Bush: The Life of a Lone Star Yankee*. New York: Scribner.

Radcliffe, Donnie. 1989. *Simply Barbara Bush: A Portrait of America's Candid First Lady*. New York: Warner Books.

———. 1990. Barbara Bush, Wowing Wellesley; With Raisa Gorbachev on Hand, the Speech Carries the Day. *Washington Post*, final ed., 1 June, C1.

Reagan, Nancy, with William Novak. 1989. *My Turn: The Memoirs of Nancy Reagan*. New York: Random House.

Robinson, John. 1990. Mrs. Bush Replies to College Flap. *Boston Globe*, city ed., 3 May, 1.

Saikowski, Charlotte. 1989. At Home in the White House. *Christian Science Monitor*, 16 February, 14.

Shales, Tom. 1990. The First Lady, at the Head of the Class. *Washington Post*, final ed., 2 June, C1.

Truman, Margaret. 1995. *First Ladies*. New York: Fawcett Columbine.

Watson, Robert P. 2000. *The Presidents' Wives: Reassessing the Office of First Lady*. Boulder, Colo.: Lynne Rienner Publications.

CHAPTER TEN

Hillary Rodham Clinton
Using Her Vital Voice

Anne F. Mattina

I'm often asked if what I am doing in Washington creates a new role model for first ladies. And I always say I don't want to create any new stereotype. I want to free women to live according to their own needs and desires. I do not want to create a new category that anyone after me must somehow fit into. I want all women to be given the respect they deserve for the choices they may make.

—Hillary Rodham Clinton

Long before she met her husband, Hillary Rodham had established herself as a public speaker. From the small venue of the Wellesley College commencement in 1969, to the international stage of the United Nations World Conference on Women in 1995, Beijing, China, she has contributed no small amount to public discourse. With her election as senator from the state of New York, we can expect her to continue to use the spoken word to achieve her political and humanitarian goals. While political pundits and media sages have debated her "place" as a first lady, and her image has undergone numerous revisions in the press, Rodham Clinton's message has remained unchanged. She has committed much of her life, her intellect, and her considerable rhetorical skill to empowering women and improving the lives of children.

Rodham Clinton's public image remains a contested site among scholars, the press, and the American public. Admired and loathed with equal passion, the last first lady of the twentieth century is not easy to capture within the confines of a book chapter. She came of age during a period of massive social upheaval, when traditional roles, especially for women, were challenged and boundaries expanded. Her life reflects the experience of many other middle-class white women given access to higher education in the latter half of the twentieth century. Taking their cues from the second wave of American feminism, this first cohort of professional women blazed trails into all areas of public life, all the while struggling to maintain familiar roles of wife and mother. While not all such women chose to embrace multiple (often divergent) roles, many, including the young Hillary Rodham, did.

Though she may share similar experiences with other women from the postwar generation, she is unique in significant ways. Obviously, very few women have had the opportunity to inhabit the White House in so visible a manner. No other first lady since Eleanor Roosevelt seized upon the potential power of that nonelected office with quite the same vigor as Rodham Clinton. And no other predecessor has run for a seat in the U.S. Senate (or any other elected office for that matter), while occupying that role. As her husband left the presidency after a tenure marked by both great joy and sorrow, Rodham Clinton began a new phase in her already remarkable life as a U.S. senator from New York.

In what follows, a biography of Hillary Rodham Clinton is presented, which examines early influences on the future first lady. Significantly, she was influenced by her Methodist upbringing and a strong identification with her mother's experiences as a child of divorce. Next, her rhetorical activities during her White House years will be documented, focusing especially on the Vital Voices initiative. Then follows a discussion of several recurrent themes in Rodham Clinton's rhetoric, namely, her passion for promoting women's and children's rights both at home and abroad.

Biography

"I don't believe there's ever been a full portrayal of Hillary Clinton as a person, a full blown painted picture of her as a person," asserted her press secretary, Lisa Caputo, during a televised discussion on the night Senate candidate Rodham Clinton was to address the Democratic National Convention. "She's a transitional figure in history covered by not a consistent press corps, so there is not a context of her, so what you're seeing are all these different snapshots" (*Lehrer Report* 2000). The hackneyed analogy that Rodham Clinton is a "Rorshach test" for the multitude of perspectives on American womanhood is, nonetheless, accurate. Responses to this first lady in the media and other public venues are largely based on the individual's comfort level with women who push the boundaries of social norms.

Who exactly is Hillary Rodham Clinton? She is a highly educated, professionally competent person who is unfailingly devoted to her marriage and child. She is deeply religious and conservative in ways that few people have noticed. She truly believes in the power of government, and she is very much the product of her time.

Hillary Rodham was born in 1947, in Chicago, to Hugh and Dorothy Rodham. The oldest of three, she described her childhood as "a family that looked like it was straight out of the 1950s television sitcom Father Knows Best" (Rodham Clinton 1996b, 21). Her father, a Republican, owned a small business and her mother did not work outside of the family home.

Hugh Rodham was a significant influence on his daughter's life. His expectations were high and Hillary worked hard for his approval. An oft-repeated anecdote was his response to her straight-A junior high report card. He said, "Well,

Hillary, that must be an easy school you go to." His daughter would later write of this experience, "By raising the bar, he encouraged me to study even harder, and in fact, comments like that spurred me on" (1996b, 22). Hugh Rodham required his children to read the newspaper and to participate in dinner conversations about current events (Kennedy, 2000a).

Hillary's mother also had an equally profound influence on her life and her future choices. Dorothy (Howell) Rodham's childhood had been a difficult one at best. Born to young parents who had little in the way of resources, Dorothy and her sister were bereft after their mother and father divorced. The two small girls were sent by train from Chicago to California to live with their paternal grandmother, a "severe and arbitrary disciplinarian," according to Hillary (1996b, 34). They traveled alone; Dorothy, aged eight, was charged with the responsibility of taking care of her sister, aged three. By age fourteen, Dorothy was employed as a live-in domestic at a neighbor's home. In 1937, she moved back to Chicago and married Hugh Rodham in 1942. Her childhood experiences shaped much of her adult worldview, as well as that of her daughter. The roots of Hillary's passion for children may be found in her mother's unhappy past. Indeed, her mother's story is one that Hillary recounts in almost all detailed discussions of her own life.

Raised a Methodist, Rodham Clinton also notes the centrality of church life in her upbringing. "My brothers and I went faithfully to Sunday school," she recalled, "and were usually back at church at least one more time during the week for youth group meetings, athletic competitions, potluck suppers, or play rehearsals" (1996b, 26–27). According to biographer Lewis L. Gould, young Hillary was active in her church youth group and was influenced by her pastor, a man "interested in theology as it applied to the problems of society." In 1962, the church youth group attended a speech by Reverend Martin Luther King Jr., calling for an end to racial injustice. Afterwards, Hillary met the civil rights advocate, an event that left a deep impression (1996, 632).

Her religious upbringing is a fundamental part of her personality and is essential to understanding her rhetoric. "Hillary Rodham Clinton is as pious as she is political," asserts reporter Kenneth Woodward. "Methodism, for her, is not just a church but an extended family of faith that defines her horizons" (1994, 23). Her public advocacy is best understood through the lens of her faith, a subject to be explored further in this chapter.

During her high school days, Hillary Rodham was a student leader and a member of the National Honor Society. She worked on the school paper, was on the debate team, and was a novice public speaker as well. In her sophomore year, she enrolled in a public speaking class, populated largely by the football team. Years later, the first lady recalled how the players had sat in front making catcalls, trying to "rattle her." "After that, Washington was nothing," she joked (Kennedy 2000a). During her junior year, she ran for Student Council president, an event that shocked many in her suburban world, as no other female student had attempted such a feat. Though she lost to the captain of the football team, she expressed satisfaction with the way her campaign had been run and with her speeches (Kennedy 2000a).

Hillary was active in politics at a very young age. Adopting the political lean-ings of her conservative father, she was a "Goldwater Girl," supporting the Re-publican candidate in the 1964 presidential campaign.

She was voted "most likely to succeed" by her classmates and ranked in the top of her class. After graduating, Rodham headed east to Wellesley College, where her political views began to change. Though she served as an intern for the House Republican Conference in 1968, she, like so many others of her generation, be-gan to question the status quo. She joined protests of the Viet Nam War and wrote her senior thesis on the community-action programs of Lyndon Johnson's Great Society. Hillary was not, however, a campus radical. She went to the 1968 Democratic National Convention in Chicago, not to protest, but to observe. "She did not want to destroy the status quo," Carl S. Anthony asserts, "she wanted to wake it up and have it take responsibility. She wasn't anti-establishment, she was reestablishment" (1999, 111). Hillary worked within the system, a choice she would make throughout her life.

Hillary was both intellectual and popular at Wellesley. She was elected presi-dent of her class in her junior year and represented her school on the nationally televised program College Bowl. Her classmates also chose her to be their gradu-ation speaker in 1969. Though she had prepared a text with input from her class-mates, Rodham instead delivered an impromptu rejoinder to the keynote speaker of the day, Senator Edward Brooke of Massachusetts. Questioning the relevance of Brooke's speech, she seized the opportunity to challenge his remarks and offer an alternative to her classmates. Harkening to themes that would emerge during her tenure as first lady, she asserted, "The challenge now is to practice politics as the art of making what appears impossible, possible" (quoted in Gould 1996, 633). Not only did her speech capture the attention of her audience, it also landed her in *Life* magazine, earning her national exposure at the age of twenty-two. "It was an auspicious end to her rewarding undergraduate experience at Wellesley" (Gould 1996, 633). Hillary's acceptance at a top law school was all but assured.

She applied to several, including Harvard. While visiting that campus, how-ever, Hillary met a professor who explained that the law school did not need any more female students (*Current Biography Illustrated*). Undeterred, she enrolled at Yale. Before beginning her law classes, Hillary took a job in a fish-canning plant in Alaska. She was fired for questioning the manager about the quality of the fish (Anthony 1999, 113).

While at Yale, she served on the editorial board of the *Review of Law and So-cial Action*. She also worked with the staff of the Yale–New Haven Hospital to help draft guidelines for the treatment of abused children. While working on this project, the future first lady met another person who would play a large role in her life professionally and personally. Marian Wright Edelman, a Yale alumna and the first African American woman to pass the bar in Mississippi, spoke at Yale in the spring of 1970 about her work with the poor and children's rights.

Inspired by the civil rights activist, Rodham joined Edelman's staff of the Wash-ington Research Project as a summer intern. The work was unpaid, so Rodham secured a grant from the Law Student Civil Rights Research Council and spent her time interviewing families of migrant laborers. Upon completing her work, she reported her findings to a Senate subcommittee (*Current Biography Illustrated*). Rodham's relationship with Edleman continued long past that first summer, providing her with future job and advocacy opportunities throughout her adult life.

Her interest in family law, combined with her work in a legal aid clinic and her experiences at the New Haven hospital, culminated in a book chapter on the relationship between children and the judicial system. Included in *Beyond the Best Interests of the Child*, Hillary's chapter challenged received wisdom regarding adoption, a subject she would continue to work on throughout her adult life.

It was also at Yale where she met Bill Clinton, a classmate. Their courtship began in the law library and soon Hillary and Bill were teaming up for mock trial debates. In the summer 1972, they traveled to Texas to work as organizers for Senator George McGovern's presidential campaign. Hillary registered Hispanic voters in San Antonio, while Bill managed the local campaign. Returning to Yale for her last year of law school, she provided legal research for the Carnegie Council on Children, specializing in the rights of children to education and medical care (*Current Biography Illustrated*).

After graduating in 1973, the future president returned to his home state to teach at the University of Arkansas law school and to prepare a run for Congress. Hillary added an extra year to her curriculum, studying child development at the Yale Child Study Center. Upon completing this program, she joined the staff of Edelman's Children's Defense Fund in Cambridge, Massachusetts.

In 1974, she went to Washington, D.C., taking a position with the House Judiciary Committee investigating what was to become known as the Watergate scandal. She impressed supervisors and peers with her energy, objectivity, and knowledge of legal procedures. The position ended with the resignation of President Richard Nixon, whereupon Rodham was "deluged with offers of high-paying jobs at prestigious law firms on the East Coast" as well as an offer to return to her position at the Children's Defense Fund (*Current Biography Illustrated*). Instead, shocking friends and colleagues alike, Hillary traveled to Arkansas to help with Bill Clinton's (unsuccessful) congressional campaign.

By this point in her life, Hillary Rodham had met Martin Luther King Jr. and worked for Marian Wright Edleman. She had earned a Yale law degree and campaigned for George McGovern. She had testified before Congress and played a role in the final chapter of the Nixon presidency. She had appeared in *Life* magazine and on network television. She was twenty-seven years old.

Bill and Hillary married in October 1975, in a small ceremony in Little Rock, Arkansas. Hillary continued to use her birth name, Rodham. The future first lady joined the faculty at the University of Arkansas law school, teaching criminal law.

In 1976, Bill Clinton was elected to the office of attorney general of Arkansas, and then was elected governor two years later. Clinton lost his second term race for that office, and according to Gould, "one source of voter resentment" was Hillary (1996, 636). Evidently, some voters did not agree with her decision to keep her birth name. "In Arkansas, at that time, there was very little appreciation for pushy, uppity women," explained former state senator Jerry Brookout ("The Clintons" 1999). "I've not wanted to upset anybody," Hillary said at the time. "I really thought I was doing it for the right reason. So, I'm thinking of perhaps changing my name to Martha Washington, or something, I don't know," she joked with an audience at the time ("The Clintons" 1999). As her husband prepared for a political comeback, she added his surname to hers. Clinton was successful in regaining the governor's seat in 1982 and held the position until winning the presidency ten years later.

Chelsea Victoria Clinton, their only child, was born in 1980. "Chelsea's birth transformed our lives," wrote Rodham Clinton, "bringing us the greatest gift of joy—and humility—any parent could hope for" (1996b, 9). The Clintons settled in to what would prove to be an active political and professional life. As the governor's wife, Rodham Clinton not only practiced law, she chaired the state's Education Standards Committee and founded the Arkansas Advocates for Children and Families. She launched a preparedness and literacy training program for parents, the Arkansas Home Instruction for Preschool Youth, and served on the board of Arkansas Children's Hospital.

As chair of the education committee, she traveled around the state, holding hearings and getting a sense of the breadth and depth of the issues, again a precursor of things to come. She developed tough policies designed to improve the system, and though they were unpopular, they worked. She was invited to testify before a joint Arkansas Senate–House Education Committee about her plans, and, according to one state senator, she "mesmerized" and "hypnotized" her audience with her command of the issues. Her concluding remarks were met with silence until one wag broke the "spell" by announcing, "Well, boys, it looks like we elected the wrong Clinton." ("The Clintons" 1999) Many observers have noted that it was the success of education reform that catapulted then governor Clinton to center stage at the 1988 Democratic National Convention, where he introduced the nominee, Michael Dukakis. His lengthy prime-time speech made headlines and earned him an invitation to Johnny Carson's *The Tonight Show*, where he charmed the national audience with self-deprecating humor.

Rodham Clinton was named Arkansas Woman of the Year in 1983, and Arkansas Mother of the Year in 1985. She was also named one of the Top 100 Lawyers in America by *American Lawyer* magazine ("Hillary for Senate") While being both very visible and active in Arkansas, she nonetheless maintained that being Chelsea's mother was the most important role she played in her life. Both supporters and detractors alike frequently note her devotion to her daughter and to her husband and marriage, even though the latter two have caused consternation among those same groups of people (Schindehette 1999, 78–88).

Much has been speculated and written about the Clinton marriage, but Hillary herself has been consistent in her support of her spouse. In early 1992, just as the presidential primary season was getting under way, candidate Bill Clinton was faced with the humiliating spectacle of an alleged mistress's "tell-all" confession in a tabloid newspaper, detailing a twelve-year relationship. Going on the offense, the Clintons agreed to an interview on 60 *Minutes* with reporter Steve Kroft. "Hillary was really the one in charge," asserts Kroft, "she just really knew what she wanted to do" in the interview ("The Clintons" 1999).

With their political future on the line, the Clintons faced a difficult situation. And while the candidate may have hedged in his responses to direct questions regarding his fidelity, Hillary demonstrated no such hesitation. "I'm not sittin' (sic) here like some little woman standing by my man like Tammy Wynette," she declared. "I'm sittin' here because I love him, and I respect him and I honor what he's been through, and what we've been through together. And if that's not enough for people, then heck, don't vote for him" ("The Clintons" 1999). The door was closed on the subject, at least for a while. All agreed Hillary's unwavering support saved the candidacy of Bill Clinton.

There was a backlash, however, against what people perceived as Hillary's rebuke of traditional women evinced by her offhand country music analogy. The months remaining in the campaign were far from smooth. During the primaries, both she and her husband introduced themselves to the American public as a partnership—"buy one, get one free," was how the marriage was billed early in the campaign. This strategy was not ill advised given their success in Arkansas.

However, they did meet with resistance on the national level, most pointedly in reaction to another quote, taken out of context, which made it appear (again) that Rodham Clinton was belittling traditional female roles. While being pressed by reporters to defend herself and her husband against charges levied by an opponent that she had benefited financially from Clinton's political station in Arkansas, Rodham Clinton responded,

> This is the sort of thing that happens to the sort of women who have their own careers and their own lives. And I think it's a shame but I guess it's something that we're going to have to live with. Those of us who have tried to make a career, tried to have an independent life and make a difference and certainly like myself who has children but other issues, uh you know I've done the best I can to lead my life but I suppose it'll be subject to attack but it's not true and I don't know what else to say except that it's sad to me. (quoted in Jamieson 1995a 27)

Her impromptu response and "fragmented syntax suggests that she is groping for an answer," concludes Kathleen Hall Jamieson (1995a, 26). Next, Rodham Clinton was asked if there wasn't a way to avoid the appearance of conflict, and she replied,

> I wish that were true. You know I suppose I could have stayed home and baked cookies and had teas but what I decided to do was fulfill my profession which I entered before my husband was in public life. And I've tried very, very hard to be as careful as possible and that's all I can tell you. (quoted in Jamieson 1995a, 27)

The uproar over her remarks was swift and intense. The tempest subsided a bit, but the furor over the possibility of a feminist first lady, one who had her own career, did not disappear. Rhetorical critic Karlyn Kohrs Campbell tells us that Rodham Clinton holds the "dubious distinction of being the first presidential candidate's wife to be the focus of a major opposition strategy" (1993, 7). Indeed, her tenure as first lady was marked by extremes in terms of press coverage and popularity. Ultimately, she negotiated the difficult terrain on her own terms, becoming the first presidential spouse to win an elective office as a New York senator, simultaneously fulfilling her duties of first lady.

Rhetorical Activities as First Lady

From the moment she entered the White House, Hillary Rodham Clinton made the role of first lady her own. Observed writer Kati Marton, "She sprung out at the beginning with this incredible force that she has. . . . A woman who is that overt about her own intelligence and that level of self-confidence . . . we were not used to that" ("The Clintons" 1999). What we were used to was some degree of public activism by a first lady. In fact, many twentieth-century presidential spouses have used their positions to advocate for various causes. Rodham Clinton's experience was unique, however, as an observer stated, "most modern First Ladies wielded influence behind the scenes" (Thomas and Rosenberg 1999, 28). This was not the way Hillary Clinton would operate.

Early in his first term, President Clinton appointed his wife chair of his task force on National Health Care reform. Much as she had done when appointed to the Arkansas Education Reform Committee, Rodham Clinton began to travel the country holding hearings and speaking directly to all involved constituencies. One of her first official meetings was with a congressional subcommittee, testifying and answering questions for over two hours under the glare of the national press. She was undaunted and impressed everyone with her knowledge and poise. Coverage in the national press was favorable, and her overall approval ratings rose accordingly (Jamieson 1995a, 47; Anderson 1999, 604).

The Clinton administration was not prepared for what came next. Though she enjoyed a brief "honeymoon" with the press regarding this unprecedented foray into policy, her methods and motivations were soon savaged by the media and callers to radio talk shows nationally. The powerful insurance and medical lobbies responded to her efforts with a series of well-crafted television commercials designed to undermine confidence in her plan. Small business owners, one group particularly anxious over proposed changes, also marshaled forces. These combined efforts were very successful, and the backlash was intense. During a speech in Seattle, the first lady was met by an angry group of protestors chanting, "Socialized medicine makes me sick!" and brandishing signs with messages such as, "Nyet Comrad Hillary." The Clinton administration retreated from the fray, health care reform was no longer a viable option for the young administration.

Conventional wisdom holds that Rodham Clinton then receded from public activism, but even the most cursory research proves that false, as *Newsweek* reports,

After the collapse of her campaign to remake the nation's health care system she was thought to have retreated into the more traditional role of First Lady, visiting hospitals and worrying about her hairdo. In truth, her hairstyles have changed more than her agenda. She is, and always has been a missionary. Her all consuming task is to do good as she sees it, especially for children. (Brant and Thomas 1996, 20)

Anthony recalls her pledge to continued activism given in a speech at a symposium on the role of first ladies in 1994,

A hushed audience had gathered expecting to hear Hillary ooze contrition . . . but when a poised and confident Hillary began to speak, it was obvious that the first lady had no intention of offering the expected mea culpas. She would continue to be active in public life, she declared. If she did otherwise . . . "my husband and friends would probably have me committed. I, for better or worse, have spoken out on public issues for 25 years." Some kind of first lady amnesia would not have been very credible. (1999, 110)

Rodham Clinton never did back down, choosing instead to use the role of presidential spouse as a "bully pulpit," although much of what she accomplished was outside of the media spotlight. Her response to the whole health-care experience was to change tactics. Hillary was following a pattern set early on in her life, not to accept defeat, but rather to step back, devise a plan, and try again.

During an interview soon after the health care fiasco, Rodham Clinton attempted to put her actions into perspective. Speaking of the president she said,

We have been partners for so long, we are just connected to each other in so many ways that our partnership in some respects is even stronger than it ever has been . . . although it is different, there are certain expectations that go along with the role I'm in, which I take very seriously. ("The Clintons" 1999)

During the ensuing years in the White House, Rodham Clinton went beyond traditional hostess duties, playing a significant role in many legislative and policy decisions, but she did not deliberately seek out the spotlight. Indeed, in early 1999 when many reporters and columnists were speculating whether or not she would run for the Senate, Jonathan Alter writing in *Newsweek* opined, "The real problem for Hillary is her record. She doesn't have one. With health care a failure, she has nothing to show for her years as First Lady" (1999, 32). Though many public observers during the Senate campaign echoed his words, that assessment is woefully inaccurate.

Rhetorical Roles
The roles a first lady plays are multiple: "chooser of visitors, provider of hospitality, emissary to and contact with worthy enterprises, setter of tone, selector of projects and so forth." Such are "real functions, they are also important. They are representative, political, diplomatic" (Greenfield 2000, 58). Though she came to the White House with her own career, Rodham Clinton fulfilled all of these roles

expected of a first lady. In addition to being appointed chair of the President's Task Force on Health Care Reform, she also served as chair of the President's Committee on the Arts and Humanities and spearheaded the Save America's Treasures Campaign.

Rodham Clinton also worked closely with the Departments of Education, Interior, and Housing and Urban Development, forging partnerships within and outside of the government to facilitate change. Along with Attorney General Janet Reno, she helped to form the Department of Justice's Violence against Women office (Anthony 1999, 138).

With Secretary of State Madeleine Albright, Rodham Clinton formed the Vital Voices Global Democracy Initiative, the goal of which was to make women's issues a foreign policy objective. The initiative sought to provide women with access to resources such as business microloans and other paths to empowerment.

While first lady, Rodham Clinton proved a tireless advocate for a myriad of causes, most of them focused on women and children. She kept a daunting public speaking schedule—she visited fifty-one countries sometimes delivering two or more speeches a day—and also authored, "Talking it Over," a syndicated weekly newspaper column for several years. Another pivotal role she played during her husband's administration was that of "chief defender," specializing in damage control in events such as those surrounding his impeachment.

What is noteworthy about all of this activity is that so little of it earned media attention. What did interest the mainstream media had almost nothing to do with policy. For example, soon after a speech she gave in 1998 on international violations of children's rights, an acerbic column appeared in the *New York Times* by Maureen Dowd. No mention of the speech was included in the piece; rather, the columnist centered on the fact that Rodham Clinton had attended a movie premiere with the actress Gwyneth Paltrow. "There was a time when there were large and real accomplishments that she wished to achieve. Historians will long wonder how Mrs. Clinton came in as Eleanor and left as Madonna," Dowd concluded (quoted in Anthony 1999, 113). Such criticism was commonplace throughout Rodham Clinton's tenure, but was very short-sighted.

Rhetorical Messages

Of particular interest to this chapter are the speeches and public activities of Hillary Rodham Clinton. Her official website as first lady archived a total of 284 speech texts, listed under broad subject areas: 45 percent centered on "Advancing Democracy," with fifty-nine of those texts on topics of "Human Rights" and "Women as Citizens." Other texts focused on the needs of families and children, particularly in the areas of health care and education reform. An examination of these texts clearly reveals Clinton's deep commitment to empowering women and bringing children's issues into the realm of public policy. Indeed, her political agenda is coherent and it is one she has maintained throughout her public life.

A typical speech by Rodham Clinton begins with immediate recognition of the audience and the context of the event. She consistently prefaces her remarks by recognizing (by name) others on the dais and in the immediate audience. Throughout a speech, she employs examples of particular women as evidence to support her thesis. Quite frequently, her speeches pay homage to notable women of the past, making their names and deeds accessible to modern audiences.

She is a trained public speaker, comfortable enough on the platform to include impromptu remarks. Ann Douglas notes that Rodham Clinton made "ardent fans" of the White House photographers on her Save America's Treasures Campaign because of her ability to "surprise them" by "veering off from her prepared text . . . adding new thoughts and words, responding to the particular audience she was addressing" (1998, 233). However adept she is at identifying with particular audiences, her message remains consistently authentic as she skillfully combines narrative, empirical data, and her own personal vision in each of her speeches. Karlyn Kohrs Campbell observes that her rhetorical style is characteristically masculine,

> Hillary Rodham Clinton's style of public advocacy typically omits all of the discursive markers by which women publicly enact their femininity. Her tone is usually impersonal . . . her ideas unfold deductively . . . all kinds of evidence is used . . . She is impassioned but very rarely emotional. (1998, 6)

Concluding her description of Rodham Clinton's style, Campbell asserts that Mrs. Clinton, "plays the roles for which she has been professionally trained, the roles of lawyer, advocate and expert" (1998, 6).

However, Rodham Clinton's rhetoric is not exclusively "masculine." One device she employs frequently is narrative, a technique considered "feminine" by analysts. "Traditionally, women are a family's storytellers," explains Kathleen Hall Jamieson, "In both primitive and advanced cultures, women are the repositories of parable-like dramatic vignettes, concise stories that transmit the common wisdom from woman to woman and generation to generation" (1995b, 808). Rodham Clinton explains why she thinks narratives are effective in public advocacy in a speech given on March 4, 1999, to the United Nations,

> I appreciated the Secretary General sharing some stories from his own experience. Because sometimes stories make the point much better, don't they than all the statistics and all of the talking that we can engage in at great forums. One single story can pierce through and make it clear that we are all in the same story, we all face the same challenges. (1999a)

Emphasizing the role of narrative in bridging generations, she adds: "What lessons will we bring from this 20th century into the 21st? How will we honor the past?"

A significant, but often overlooked, influence on Rodham Clinton's rhetoric is her religious faith. "Her faith is critical: Mrs. Clinton sees herself as a serious Christian," assert reporters Eleanor Clift and Howard Fineman (1996, 36.) She brings the gospel of women's empowerment and democracy wherever she goes. It is my contention that this rhetorical persona is linked to her Methodism, a denomination that embraces the credo, "Be doers of the word and not hearers only."

Rodham Clinton has been quoted as saying she derives much inspiration for her daily life from the Book of James in the New Testament (Martin 1994, 1095). James "is a known figure and possesses a standing enabling him to speak with authority" (*New American Bible* 1970, 341). The first Book of James asks, "My brothers, (sic) what good is it to profess faith without practicing it?" James asserts "without works faith is idle . . . faith without works is as dead as a body without breath" (343–44). James' admonition resonates throughout Rodham Clinton's life and rhetoric.

The basic argument Rodham Clinton makes repeatedly is, "If women are to advance, democracy must advance as well," and she uses the power of her position to spread this thesis internationally ("United Nations Speech," 1999a). No matter where the stage or what the circumstance, she urges this and other notions upon her listeners, especially the need for women to have a voice. For example, on September 5, in Beijing China, she said, "If there is one message that echoes forth from this conference, it is that human rights are women's rights and women's rights are human rights. Let us not forget that among those rights are the right to speak freely and the right to be heard" (1995).

She acknowledges the essential connection between voice and empowerment in a speech given on October 16, in Argentina,

> I would like to talk about voices, powerful voices, the voices of women in this country and my country, throughout our hemisphere and our world, and what we can do to make all of our voices heard. To have our voices heard about our shared commitment to advancing the cause of women's rights, advancing the cause of democracy, and making clear that the two are inseparable. (1997)

This theme of voice resonates throughout many of her speeches. She explains why "voice" is imperative in women's lives, when she says at Seneca Falls on July 16, "we must tell and retell, learn and relearn, these women's stories, and we must make it our personal mission, in our everyday lives, to pass these stories on to our daughters and sons" (1998b). Only those who have a voice can share their experience and pass their wisdom to their children. And only those with a voice can advocate for the well-being of others.

Rodham Clinton demonstrates her enactment of James as she pursues her agenda around the world. At the United Nations on March 4, 1999, she says, "We have learned the lessons about what importance we must place on the role of women, we know that we must continue to speak out on our own." She also offers herself as a witness to the testimony of women worldwide, "In Romania and Russia, I've heard the voices of women struggling to recreate a civil society where they had only known authoritarian rule and there had been no tradition of democracy. They are attempting to be sure that their voices are heard and their contributions recognized" (1999a). Thus, "freedom and equality for all," often repeated by Rodham Clinton, "depend first on whether or not a citizen truly has a voice" (1997).

If a particular group is silenced through custom, culture, or oppression, she offers herself as their voice to the rest of the world. She also offers other women

leaders for emulation. In a July 16, 1998, speech commemorating the 150th anniversary of the first American woman's rights convention, Rodham Clinton
presents suffragist Elizabeth Cady Stanton as a role model whose experiences can
teach modern audiences:

> Stanton was inspired, along with the others who met to rewrite our Declaration of
> Independence, and they boldly asserted, "We hold these truths to be self-evident
> that all men and women are created equal." "All men and all women." It was the
> shout heard around the world, and if we listen, we can still hear its echoes today.
> We can hear it in the voices of women demanding their (full) civil and political
> rights anywhere in the world. I've heard such voices and their echoes from women
> around the world, from Belfast to Bosnia to Beijing, as they work to change the
> conditions for women and girls and improve their lives and the lives of their fami-
> lies. We can even hear those echoes today in Seneca Falls. (1998b)

In the same speech, Rodham Clinton invites her listeners to join the struggle for
women's rights, and she does so artfully by using a narrative to tell the story of a
glove maker, Charlotte Woodward, a young woman who attended the first convention. She begins by asking her listeners to imagine what it must have been like
on the road that warm summer day so long ago; how unsure Charlotte was about
the personal consequences of attending the meeting, but nonetheless still determined to go. Showing considerable rhetorical skills, Hillary uses the road as a
powerful metaphor and invites her audience to join her on the journey of American women's rights. Thus, her speech positions her listeners to appreciate what
their forebears have accomplished and to commit to continue this vital work.

The Seneca Falls address concludes by linking the right of American women
to vote to their responsibility to participate in the democratic process. Mrs. Clinton asserts that through a long struggle, women have gained access and can make
a difference through the agency of the vote. This theme resonates throughout
many of her speeches.

The predictable universal routine of women's lives is also a source from which
she draws inspiration and identifies with her audiences. In Northern Ireland on
September 2, 1998, for example, Rodham Clinton observes,

> Wives. Mothers. Daughters. Sisters. Few were household names. But, having seen
> their lives and communities torn apart by violence, women came together as
> women have always done—around kitchen tables, at the market, in gatherings like
> this. It was women whose whispers of "enough" became a torrent of voices that
> could no longer be ignored. If we listen carefully, their voices still echo through this
> room and lift ours up today. (1998a)

And in her August 27, 1996, speech in Chicago at the Democratic National
Convention, she confides to her audience of millions,

> I wish we could be sitting around a kitchen table, just us, talking about our hopes
> and fears about our children's futures. For Bill and me, family has been the center

of our lives, but we also know that our family, like your family, is part of a larger community that can help or hurt our best efforts to raise our child. (1996a)

Thus, she provides a powerful form of identification with her listeners. Though they may not share her status (or her visibility), they can relate to the images of their everyday existence as invoked by Rodham Clinton.

However, she acknowledges the risks women take when they speak out. "If we listen," she tells her audience in Northern Ireland, "we can hear the voices of women who withstood jeers and threats, prejudice and violence to make themselves heard in a political world once reserved primarily for men" (1998a). Rodham Clinton has experienced firsthand the vitriol reserved for women who speak out.

She exhorts her listeners in Seneca Falls to "help us imagine a future that keeps faith with the sentiments expressed here in 1848," and to "be on the right side of history, no matter the risk or cost" (1998b). This is a powerful testament to her own experience as a rhetor.

Referring to the women of Seneca Falls in her speech given on March 3, 1999, in New York City, Rodham Clinton advises her audience,

They [early women's rights advocates] understood something that we also have to understand, and that is that those who advocate for progress and change will often pay a price, but if we persevere, if we see that kind of commitment through, the changes that can happen, will benefit . . . our daughters and our granddaughters. (1999b)

She is personally aware of the cost of speaking out, as she has suffered a good deal of abuse for her activism. As Karlyn Kohrs Campbell notes after describing some particularly egregious examples of this, "no prior presidential spouse has occasioned the kinds of attacks that have been directed at Hillary Rodham Clinton" (1998, 2). But again, no prior presidential spouse has challenged the status quo in the quite same way as Rodham Clinton. Undeterred, she states emphatically, "If I'm going to be criticized for doing what I believe in, I might as well just keep doing what I believe in" ("Working Women Interview").

We gain additional insight into her personal conviction from the Seneca Falls Speech, in which she speaks of Harriet Tubman's accomplishments, risking her own life countless times to bring others to freedom,

[Tubman's] rule for all of her Underground Railroad missions was to keep going, once you started—no matter how scared you got, no matter how dangerous it became—you were not allowed to turn back. That's a pretty good rule for life. It describes the women who gathered in Wesleyan Chapel in 1848, but it could serve as our motto for today. We, too, cannot turn back. We, too, must keep going in our commitment to the dignity of every individual—to women's rights as human rights. We are on that road of the pioneers to Seneca Falls, they started down it 150 years ago. But now, we too must keep going. (1998b)

Such willingness to take on the responsibility and the inherent risks in doing so are hallmarks of Rodham Clinton's rhetoric. She reminds her audience in Uruguay on October 2, 1998,

Today, more than at any other time in history, women have the opportunity and the responsibility not only to raise our own voices but to empower others to raise theirs as well . . . But think of the thousands and thousands and thousands of women throughout the Americas for whom no one speaks. Who believe they are not worth anything. . . . What will we do to raise our vital voices for them? (1998c)

In the aftermath of the terrorist attacks of September 11, 2001, Senator Clinton reflects on her personal experience with this "unreasoning hatred that is focused on an individual you don't know, a cause that you despise." Referring specifically to the Seattle health-care reform speech, she says, "One of the most difficult experiences that I personally had in the White House was during the health care debate, being the object of extraordinary rage. I remember being in Seattle . . . [where] radio talk show hosts had urged their listeners to come out and yell and scream and carry on and prevent people from hearing me speak" (quoted in Lemann 2001, 41). Arrests were made and weapons were found among the audience. Video footage shows Rodham Clinton facing the threats head-on, not retreating from the podium, and instead vigorously defending her plan. As a speaker and advocate, her resolve is unwavering, from the football players in the high school speech class to the hecklers in Seattle to shouldering the humiliating spectacle of her husband's infidelity, she continues her fight.

Legacy

Examination of her rhetorical record leads to the conclusion that Hillary Rodham Clinton envisioned the role of first lady as a powerful one, indeed. She imbued it with her missionary zeal to spread the gospel of democracy and women's rights, and has never backed away from the challenge of her advocacy.

During her Senate campaign, a reporter compared her role to that of a senior presidential adviser and asked whether she went "beyond the job" of first lady, "Mrs. Clinton laughed out loud and said, 'I'm not going to have it any more. And the next first lady doesn't have to do it.'"

Rodham Clinton's adult life has been a blending of the personal and political. Though many question her loyalty to Bill Clinton in light of the evidence of his infidelity, I would offer this. As first lady of the United Sates of America, Hillary Rodham Clinton was afforded an opportunity few women have ever had: an international stage from which to espouse her personal and political views. Though the American media seemed all consumed by her hairstyle, her "failure" at health care reform, and her husband's infidelity, Rodham Clinton kept to her message and shared it at every opportunity she was given. She has said,

As I travel around the world, I am very grateful for the opportunity that I have to meet with women and to listen to them. Their dreams, their aspirations, their hopes, their concerns. And these are the women . . . who we must do all that we can to ensure that their voices are heard, heard in city halls and board rooms, and trade union offices and political parties, in academia, in families. (1998c)

Empowered by her position, education, deep religious conviction, and feminism, hers was a "bully pulpit" which served to launch her into the next phase of her life, that of United States senator.

Rodham Clinton exemplified the feminist credo "the personal is political." As she said in her address to the 1996 Democratic National Convention, "For Bill and me, family has been the center of our lives, but we also know that our family, like your family, is part of a larger community that can help or hurt our best efforts to raise our child" (1996a). Much of her rhetoric as first lady resonated with this duality.

Postscript

In November of 2000, Hillary Rodham Clinton was elected to the U.S. Senate from New York. Not only was she the sole first lady to serve in an elected office, she was also the first woman to win a state-wide election in New York. Her first months in office were spent learning the ropes, largely out of the media spotlight. This situation changed as the terrorist attacks of September 11, 2001, catapulted New York and its new senator into the national and international spotlights. After gaining her footing, Senator Clinton emerged as a passionate spokesperson and advocate for her state. She has earned high praise from both sides of the aisle for her dedication to her job, her knowledge of the issues, and her political savvy. In 2003, her White House memoir *Living History* was an immediate best seller and her public book signings drew record crowds across the country. Senator Clinton continues to use her vital voice for issues important to children and families. Though she has resisted calls to run for the presidency thus far, it would not be surprising if she achieves this other "first" for a first lady.

Questions for Discussion

1. What were the two most significant influences in Hillary Clinton's childhood that led to many of her later choices as a public figure?
2. How did Hillary Clinton understand her role as first lady? What experiences in her life led to that understanding? How did her role as first lady evolve through her husband's two terms?
3. What experience(s) as first lady prepared her to hold a seat in the U.S. Senate?
4. After reading this chapter, have you changed your view of Hillary Clinton as a first lady? Do you see her as more traditional, more moderate, or more radical? Why?

Internet Resources

http://clinton2.nara.gov/WH/EOP/First_Lady/html/HILLARY_Home.html
This website is a valuable resource for anyone who wants to do research on Hillary Clinton. It provides access to the speeches she gave as first lady and de-

scriptions of the issues she advocated. You can also access her biography and look at photos of her.

http://clinton.senate.gov/
Hillary's Senate website provides information about issues before the Senate, about constituent services, and it has an email address you can use to send her a message.

http://www.congressmerge.com/onlinedb/cgi-bin/newmemberbio.cgi?member=NYJR&site=congressmerge
To find out what Senate committees Hillary Clinton is on, how she votes, and more, go to this website.

References

Alter, Johnathan. 1999. Paging Mrs. Roosevelt. *Newsweek*, 1 March, 32.

Anderson, Karrin Vasby. 1999. "Rhymes with Rich": "Bitch" as a Tool of Containment in Contemporary American Politics. *Rhetoric & Public Affairs*, 2, 599–623.

Anthony, Carl Sferrazza. 1999. Hillary's Hidden Power. *George*, November, 108–40.

Brant, Martha, and Evan Thomas. 1996. First Fighter. *Newsweek*, 15 January, 20–24.

Campbell, Karlyn Kohrs. 1993. Shadowboxing with Stereotypes: The Press, the Public and the Candidates' Wives. Research Paper R-9, in *The Joan Shorenstein Barone Center for the Press, Politics and Public Policy*. Cambridge, Mass.: Harvard University Press.

———. 1996. The Rhetorical Presidency: A Two-Person Career. In *Beyond the Rhetorical Presidency*, ed. Martin J. Medhurst, 178–95. College Station, Tex.: Texas A & M University Press.

———. 1998. The Discursive Performance of Femininity: Hating Hillary, *Rhetoric & Public Affairs*, 1:1, 1–19.

Clift, Eleanor, and Howard Fineman. 1996. How Hillary Keeps Going, *Newsweek*, 8 July, 36.

Clinton, Hillary Rodham. 1995. Address to the United Nations Fourth World Conference on Women. Speech given at Beijing, China, 5 September. www.whitehouse.gov/wh/eop/first_lady/html/generalspeeches, accessed 17 January, 2000.

———. 1996a. Address to the Democratic National Convention in Chicago, 27 August. www.dncc96.org/day2/speeches/, accessed 6 January 2000.

———. 1996b. *It Takes a Village: And Other Lessons Children Teach Us*. New York: Simon & Schuster.

———. 1997. Remarks by the First Lady at the United Nations. Speech given in New York City, 16 October. www.whitehouse.gov/wh/eop/first_lady/html/generalspeeches, accessed 28 January 1998.

———. 1998a. First Lady Hillary Rodham Clinton Remarks at Vital Voices Conference. Speech given in Belfast, Northern Ireland, 2 September. www.whitehouse.gov/wh/eop/first_lady/html/generalspeeches, accessed 14 September 1998.

———. 1998b. Remarks by the First Lady Hillary Rodham Clinton 150th Anniversary of the First Woman's Rights Convention. Speech given in Seneca Falls, N.Y., 16 July. www.whitehouse.gov/wh/eop/first_lady/html/generalspeeches, accessed 30 October 1999.

———. 1998c. Vital Voices of the Americas: Women in Democracy. Speech given in Montevideo, Uruguay, 2 September. www.whitehouse.gov/wh/eop/first_lady/html/generalspeeches, accessed 26 April 1999.

———. 1999a. United Nation's International Women's Day Speech on Women's Rights. Speech given in New York City, 4 March. www.whitehouse.gov/wh/eop/first_lady/html/generalspeeches, accessed 14 March 1999.

———. 1999b. Women's Leadership Forum, Speech on Women and Politics. Speech given in New York City, 3 March. www.whitehouse.gov/wh/eop/first_lady/html/generalspeeches; accessed 15 April 1999.

———. 2000. Remarks at the Democratic National Convention, Los Angeles, Calif. www.dncc96.org/day2/speeches/, accessed 6 January.

The Clintons: A Marriage of Power. 1999. Television Documentary. The Learning Channel, air date 15 February.

Current Biography Illustrated. n.d. Hillary Rodham Clinton www.hwwilson.com/databases/cbhillary.htm, accessed 13 September 2001.

Douglas, Ann. 1998. The Extraordinary Hillary Clinton. Vogue, December, 231–39.

Gould, Lewis L. 1996. American First Ladies: Their Lives and Legacy. New York: Garland.

Greenfield, Meg. 2000. First Ladyhood. In Speaking of Hillary: A Reader's Guide to the Most Controversial Woman in America, ed. Susan K. Flinn, 57–58. Oregon: White Cloud Press.

Hillary for U.S. Senate. n.d. www.hillary2000.org, accessed 27 February 2001.

Jamieson, Kathleen Hall. 1995a. Beyond the Double Bind: Women and Leadership. New York: Oxford University Press.

———. 1995b. Eloquence in an Electronic Age. In Rhetoric: Concepts, Definitions, Boundaries, ed. William A. Covino and David A. Jolliffe, 801–11. Needham Heights, Mass.: Allyn & Bacon.

Kennedy, Helen. 2000a. The Girl Who Became Candidate Hillary. New York Daily News, 6 February. www.nydailynews.com, accessed 13 September 2001.

———. 2000b. 60s Turmoil Turns Scholar Into Rebel. New York Daily News, 7 February. www.nydailynews.com, accessed 13 September 2001.

Lehrer Report. 2000. PBS, air date, 14 August.

Lemann, Nicholas. 2001. The Hillary Perspective. New Yorker, 8 October, 41.

Martin, Marty E. 1994. Methodist in Deed. The Christian Century, 16 November 1095.

New American Bible. 1970. Encino: Benzinger Publishing.

Osborne, Claire G., ed. 1997. The Unique Voice of Hillary Rodham Clinton. New York: Avon.

Schindehette, Susan. 1999. The Ties That Bind. People, 15 February, 78–88.

Thomas, Evan, and Debra Rosenberg. 1999. Hillary's Day in the Sun. Newsweek. 1 March, 25–31.

Woodward, Kenneth. 1994. Soulful Matters. Newsweek, 31 October, 23.

Working Women Interview. 1994. www.abcnews.com, accessed 17 June 1999.

Laura Bush
Using the "Magic of Words"
to Educate and Advocate

Molly Meijer Wertheimer

The power of a book lies in its power to turn a solitary act into a shared vision. . . . As long as we have books, we are not alone. . . . There is no magic like the magic of the written word.

I have a lifelong passion for introducing children to the magic of words.

—Laura Bush

In *A Charge to Keep*, George W. Bush made a prediction about his wife Laura's future popularity: "As America gets to know her," he wrote, "they will love her as I do" (1999, 93). According to an early *USA Today*/CNN/Gallup Poll conducted December 14–16, 2001, that prediction is coming true. Mrs. Bush topped the list of the "Most Admired Women" in the United States only a year after she had received too few mentions to be ranked (McQuillan 2001, A3; Jones and Carroll 2001, 52–55). By September 2003, Frank Newport, Gallup Poll Editor-in-Chief, could say during an interview on CNN: "when we tested her last job approval as a first lady, Laura Bush had one of the highest that we have in our Gallup Poll history" ("America's Voice" 2003).

If she seemed a reluctant first lady during her first one hundred days, consider her starting point. When Laura Lane Welch married George W. Bush, it was on condition that she would never have to become a public person—the kind who makes statements to the national press and gives speeches to a national audience. But she was marrying a man who, as journalist Frank Bruni of the *New York Times* put it, had "politics in his plasma": "Her vow of silence was doomed from the start" (2000a, A1). She gave her first political speech in Muleshoe, Texas, where she ran out of things to say and mumbled her conclusion. As her husband's political career advanced from governor of Texas to president of the United States, she could not avoid publicity. Slowly, by speaking to supportive audiences such as Republican women's groups, she gained experience and made great strides in skill and confidence as a rhetorician. If she continues to draw upon her love of literature and uses the "magic of words" to inspire her speaking, her messages will become increasingly memorable. She has made a start in that direction, for example, when she borrowed a poet's phrase to call music "the speech of angels" or when she called jazz "the language of America." Her former press secretary Noelia Rodriguez has aptly said: "You don't rule anything out when it comes to Laura Bush."

During spring 2001, Mrs. Bush was becoming known nationally as an advocate for education, especially early childhood cognitive development. She unveiled her "Ready to Read, Ready to Learn Initiative" and traveled around the country promoting various aspects of it. True to her husband's promise to be the "Education President," Mrs. Bush stayed closely on topic, though she branched out occasionally to speak about subjects such as American libraries and librarians, authors and readers, and more. Her advocacy gained momentum gradually and would have continued to do so had it not been for the events of September 11, which thrust her into full visibility onto the nation's stage in a matter of moments. Through her actions and words, she became the nation's consoler-in-chief, helping those who heard and saw her to focus their attention on acts of kindness among strangers. Increasingly, during fall 2001 through spring 2004, she became an international advocate for the rights of women and children to an education and to full participation in their societies. She promoted women's health, discussing both breast cancer and heart disease; and she promoted, from 2003 forward, Preserve America, an initiative designed to protect and cherish America's historical sites and communities.

Before her husband was inaugurated, journalists speculated about what kind of first lady Mrs. Bush would be. Some contrasted her sharply with activist Hillary Clinton, associating her instead with traditionalist Mamie Eisenhower known for her quip: "Ike runs the nation; I turn the lamb chops." Probably the lowest expectations of her came from Gil Troy, political scientist at McGill University, who predicted that she would "retraditionalize" the White House and have little to do with policy issues, except perhaps education, which he described as "constructive, yet benign, and suitably feminine" (Boswell 2000, B1). Sympathetic with his position was Betty Boyd Caroli who said Mrs. Bush's focus on education "is about as safe as it gets. Right up there with apple pie" (quoted in Gamerman 2001, A3). Others such as Carl S. Anthony and Lewis L. Gould stressed Mrs. Bush's complexity, warning that she should not be viewed as a one-dimensional woman (Barta 2000, A4). Because they did not know much about her, still others made her into a fashion target—her hair, dress, and shoes all became synecdoches by which to infer her character (e.g. Givhan 2000, C01).

At the time of this writing, Mrs. Bush has completed three years as a first lady. She has become popular with the American public and the media, appearing on television shows such as *Good Morning America*, *The Oprah Winfrey Show*, *The*

Jay Leno Show, *60 Minutes*, *20/20*, MTV, and the Disney Channel; her photographs have also been on the covers of *Good Housekeeping*, *Ladies' Home Journal*, *Reader's Digest*, *Parade Magazine*, and *Newsweek*. She has testified before the Senate Committee on Health, Education, Labor, and Pensions and the House Committee on Education and the Workforce. She has presented speeches all over the country on behalf of early childhood education, American libraries, women's health and other issues, and has had the distinction of being the first first lady to give an entire radio address to the nation on her own. She has made solo diplomatic trips abroad, calling the world's attention to abuses of human rights in Afghanistan and traveled to France on a fence-mending mission. If she stays on her current trajectory using her white glove pulpit to do good deeds, she will far exceed the low expectations some commentators have had of her.

Biography

In the small West Texas oil-boom town of Midland, Laura Lane Welch was born on November 4, 1946, the only child of Harold Bruce Welch and wife, Jenna Hawkins Welch.[1] Her father was a successful contractor and her mother kept her husband's books while remaining at home. Later in life, Laura would credit her parents with instilling in her a passion for learning, a desire to do her best, and a deep faith.

Laura's childhood was filled with the girlish pleasures that come from giggling at sleepovers with friends, Brownie and Girl Scout activities, playing the piano, singing in the church choir, and playing with her pets. Reading was what she liked to do most. From the time she was a baby, Laura's mother read to her, and when she was old enough, her mother took her to the local library. Years later, Mrs. Bush would praise her mother for giving her "a most precious gift—a lifelong passion for reading." Her favorite books as a child were Laura Ingalls Wilder's *Little House on the Prairie* books, which she saved and passed on to her own daughters.

Laura attended several schools when growing up: North Elementary and James Bowie Elementary Schools, San Jacinto Junior High School, and Robert E. Lee High School. She was popular, studious, and lived a carefree life with parents who made her feel secure and loved. Probably, her only low point during these years was a car accident. Her car went through a stop sign, collided with another car, killing the driver—her close friend Michael Douglas. Laura was traumatized, but slowly she learned to put the accident into perspective and learn from it—how precarious life is and how much a gift.

She attended Southern Methodist University, majoring in education. From the time she was seven years old, she wanted to be a teacher. She tells how she would line up her dolls and teach them lessons. While at SMU, she took courses in Child Growth and Development, Teaching Reading in the Elementary School, Children's Literature, the Child and the Elementary School, as well as other courses in subjects such as math, language arts, social studies, and so on

(Felix 2002, 40). She graduated in 1968 with a bachelor of science degree in education.

She began her career teaching third graders at the Longfellow Elementary School in Dallas, a position she kept for a year. Next, she taught second-graders at the John F. Kennedy Elementary School in Houston—a predominantly African American school. She said, "I particularly wanted to teach in a minority school. . . . I just learned about the dignity of every human and every child . . . how important every single child is, and how important each one of their lives are" (quoted in Felix 2002, 42). She held this position until 1972. Subsequently, she moved to Austin and enrolled in a Master of Library Science Degree Program at the University of Texas. She took courses in "Children's Literature, School Libraries, Literature for Adolescents, Library Materials, Cataloguing and Classification, and Library Administration" as well as studying "about the history of libraries and information systems in various civilizations . . . [and] understanding the role of books and libraries in today's society" (Felix 2002, 43–44). Laura completed her degree in 1973, and then accepted a position as children's librarian at the McCrane-Kashmere Gardens Library in Houston. Because her position did not involve working with children, she returned to Austin in 1974, to become a librarian at the mostly Hispanic Mollie Dawson Elementary School. She remained in that position until 1977. She felt comfortable with Spanish speaking students because she had studied that language in high school and had taken a Spanish language and cultures course in Monterrey, Mexico.

Although Laura Welch and George W. Bush attended the same junior high school in Midland, according to Barbara Bush, "they had not been aware of each other" (1994, 140–41). The two also lived in the same apartment complex—the Chateau Dijon—the two times Laura worked in Houston. Laura's official meeting with George W. was at a barbecue given by their mutual friends, Joey and Jan O'Neill. The first time they invited her over to meet him, she turned them down, saying she had little interest in politics. Eventually, she accepted the invitation.

At the time, George W. was already planning to run for a seat in the U.S. House of Representatives. He was ready to settle down, and their meeting was fateful for both of them. Laura thought George was "really cute" and a lot of fun. She told her mother: "The thing I like about him was that he made me laugh." George W. also liked her; he told his parents: "I found her to be a very thoughtful, smart, interested person—one of the great listeners. And since I am one of the great talkers, it was a great fit" (quoted in Minutaglio 1999, 184). He also wrote in his autobiography: "If it wasn't love at first sight, it happened shortly thereafter. . . . My wife is gorgeous, good-humored, quick to laugh, down-to-earth, and very smart. I recognized those attributes right away in roughly that order. . . . We both, very quickly, fell in love with one another" (G. W. Bush 1999, 79–80). They were married three months later, November 5, 1977, the first date Vice President George Bush had free and one day before Laura's thirty-first birthday. Laura left her position and moved to Midland after their short honeymoon in Mexico.

The Bushes continued to get to know each other as they campaigned all across West Texas. Although Laura had always considered herself a Democrat, she became a Republican through marriage. Before they were married, George had promised Laura that she would never have to give a political speech, especially without him being there. She was happy to help him in other ways—as a confidant, with emotional support, and so on—but she had no desire to step onto the political stage. Three months after they were married, however, George was scheduled to be in two places at one time. Laura had to act as his surrogate in Muleshoe, Texas. This was her first campaign speech, and she was not very comfortable. Although she felt confidant as a teacher in front of little children, campaigning for political office was a very different kind of speech situation. As she stood on the courthouse steps in front of a small audience, she began to utter the remarks she had prepared, but too soon she ran out of things to say, "her speech dwindling down to nothing" (Minutaglio 1999, 16–17). In an interview granted to television's Matt Lauer, she said, "I had a really great start to my speech, but I hadn't gotten far enough to have a very good ending. So I stood up and gave my few—what I thought were really pretty good—lines at the start and then I had to mumble and sit down" (quoted in Felix 2002, 77). She was embarrassed, but also angry with herself for not preparing better.

One night during that same campaign as they were driving home after George W. had delivered a campaign speech, he asked Laura whether she liked it or not. Her mother-in-law had warned her not to criticize his speeches, but Laura told him candidly that she did not think his speech was very good. He listened to her, became distracted, and then drove the car straight into the wall of their garage (G. W. Bush 1999, 83). Despite his less than perfect speech, George W. won the Republican primary in June 1978, but lost the general election to his Democratic opponent.

On November 25, 1981, Laura gave birth to twin daughters Barbara and Jenna, named after their two grandmothers. George W. was in the delivery room when they were born. Afterwards, he helped Laura take care of the children: "There was never any question that I would help take care of them," he said, "I was a modern dad" (G. W. Bush 1999, 86). For the next several years, Laura devoted herself to raising the children as her husband worked to build his energy company. They were both active members of the First United Methodist Church and were engaged in community service—Laura, the Junior League and George, the United Way. Their lives were settled—happy, peaceful.

In late 1986, Vice President George Herbert Walker Bush assembled the family at Camp David to announce his run for the U.S. presidency. To help with the campaign, George and Laura moved their family to Washington, D.C., and remained there for eighteen months. They were actively involved in campaign strategy; sometimes they traveled around the country with George Bush as he campaigned, other times they campaigned without him (Barbara Bush 1994, 242; George W. Bush 1999, 179). After he was inaugurated the forty-first president of the United States, George W. and Laura returned to Dallas, Texas. Both had learned a great deal from their experience in Campaign 1988, and from George Bush's presidency.

Together with other investors, George W. purchased the franchise for a baseball team, the Texas Rangers, and worked as a managing partner until 1994, when he ran for governor of Texas. While he managed the team, Laura volunteered for a number of causes; she served on the board of the Friends of Dallas Public Library and Executive Committee, she was a member of the Parent Teachers Association, and library liaison at her daughters' school, the Preston Hollow Elementary School. She was involved with charity balls and fund-raising activities in Dallas society. These experiences were not enough, however, to help her feel comfortable with the idea of living her life on the public stage. When her husband became interested in running for governor, she was not sure that she wanted to be "a career politician's wife." There were other reasons for her reluctance as well. George W.'s opponent would be incumbent Ann Richards, who was enormously popular in Texas, especially with women, African Americans, artists, writers, and musicians. Richards was thought to be unbeatable. She had also trashed Laura's father-in-law in a speech at the 1988 Democratic National Convention, saying that Bush senior was born "with a silver foot in his mouth." Laura was not sure her husband wanted the office for the right reasons. Was he running to achieve a kind of payback, as part of a family script, or to make Texas a better place to live? She was also afraid her husband might lose, and the Bush family had just suffered a heartbreaking defeat when Bill Clinton won the presidency in 1992 (Minutaglio 1999, 268–69).

When George W. began his campaign for governor, politically Laura was "an unproved asset." She was "still learning to tamp down the knots in her stomach when she was approached for a comment by the media or asked to speak to a civic group." When "she was pressed to give a talk, she was frequently worried about not having the speech in her hands" (Minutaglio 1999, 244). Her husband was sympathetic, and did "not push her to make speeches or public appearances." He said, "She wasn't really comfortable doing a lot of campaigning, which was fine with me" (George W. Bush 1999, 90) He treated her discomfort with humor, joking in his speeches that his wife's idea of a speech is "to put her fingers to her lips . . . [and] tell the children, 'Shhhhhhh!'" Unhappy with the comment, Laura felt it perpetuated a negative image of librarians. Laura did speak to Republican women's groups across the state, which were supportive and nonconfrontational. By the end of the race, she had traveled to 30 of Texas's 254 counties" (Minutaglio 1999, 301). On November 8, 1994, George W. Bush won the race for governor of Texas, and the Bushes moved to Austin, January 17, 1995.

First Lady of Texas

After her husband won the election, Mrs. Bush quickly realized that she could do something about the issues she cared about most such as early childhood education. Her husband said: "I don't think Laura ever anticipated her life would turn out this way. . . . Nor did she dream growing up, 'Gosh, if everything works out,

I just may be the first lady of Texas.' But when she got out there, [and] started giving speeches . . . she realized people listened to her" (quoted in Romano 2000, A01). She grew increasingly confident as a public speaker. She set up an office in the Texas governor's mansion, the first first lady ever to do so (Leonard 2000a, A1), and she used the office to make a difference in people's lives.

One of the first events Mrs. Bush planned was a literary celebration. She invited seven Texas writers to read from their works as part of her husband's inaugural festivities. She was nervous about speaking at the event; according to biographer Antonio Felix, she had anxiety dreams the night before (2002, 100). Some of the authors had neither supported her husband, nor voted for him. However, their inclusion early set a bipartisan tone to her husband's administration. One writer, Sarah Bird, told her audience how impressed she was to have been invited to read because she considered herself a "raging liberal." The fact that she was invited, she said, boded well for the administration (Felix 2002, 99). It also boded well for the kind of political partnership the Bushes would develop. During her time as first lady of Texas, Mrs. Bush promoted many bipartisan initiatives to support the visual and literary arts, education, and other issues such as breast cancer awareness.

Mrs. Bush's signature issue was early childhood education and literacy, as it would continue to be when she became first lady of the United States. This was consistent with her husband's agenda, especially during his reelection campaign of 1996, when he emphasized "reading and literacy, the things his mother and wife were associated with." Politically, these were important issues that would appeal to women and minority voters (Minutaglio 1999, 313). They were also issues to which Laura Bush, as a former teacher and librarian, felt strongly committed. In the two terms she served as first lady of Texas, she either supported or launched many programs aimed at improving education in Texas schools. She worked with legislators, social service personnel, and literacy experts on an "Early Childhood Development Initiative," which consisted of four components: a Family Literacy Initiative, Reach Out and Read, Texas Ready to Read, and *Take Time for Kids* (a parenting magazine).[2]

According to Bill Minutaglio, George W.'s biographer, Laura Bush's "crowning achievement" as first lady of Texas was the Texas Book Festival (1999, 313). In 1996, Mrs. Bush joined together with the Texas Library Association, the Austin Writers League, and the Texas State Library and Archives Commission to inaugurate a celebration of writers and readers. The only one of its kind in the country, the Texas Book Festival was a combination of literary event and fund-raiser. Authors read from their works and signed books, while children listened to stories, made bookmarks, watched jugglers, and more. Money raised by the event was donated to the state's public libraries for the purchase of books. From 1996–2000, nearly 400 Texas libraries shared the nearly $1 million dollars raised. Not only did the libraries and the authors benefit, but the Bushes gained political capital because many of the authors celebrated "had once been unabashed supporters . . . and champion fundraisers for liberal causes and issues" (Minutaglio 1999, 313).

These are just some of the initiatives Mrs. Bush promoted in Texas and would continue to promote on a national scale when she became first lady of the United States. She was an active first lady of Texas, thought by some to be the best ever to serve in that role. As an advocate for literacy and breast cancer awareness, according to journalist Hillary Rose, Mrs. Bush was "perceived to be one of the most effective Governor's wives in the state's history" (2000, n.p.). On education, Frank Bruni of the *New York Times* credits her with helping to "write, lobby for, and secure passage of legislation . . . to teach preschool children in Texas to read" (2000a, A1). Mary Leonard of the *Boston Globe* writes that Laura Bush was the only first lady of Texas "to have achieved major policy success" (2000a, A1). Even Liz Carpenter, a Texas Democrat who worked for Lady Bird Johnson, comments that Mrs. Bush's projects and personality made her "beloved and appreciated" across the state (quoted in Leonard 2000a, A1). Her popularity in Texas, writes journalist Julie Bonin, was ubiquitous: "Tortilla vendors, wealthy businessmen, and even Democrats sing her praises" (2000, A18).

Campaign 2000

As an active first lady of Texas, Mrs. Bush gained considerable experience as a public speaker, and she was ready, if initially reluctant, to help her husband advance his political career. In 1998, George W. began to explore a run for the presidency; a year later, his campaign was in full swing. Once again, Mrs. Bush was hesitant about stepping into the spotlight—this time, the national spotlight of a presidential campaign. However, she had been a political apprentice for years, campaigning in state and national contests run by her husband and father-in-law. She had become part of the Bush "family business" of politics. Setting her reluctance aside, Mrs. Bush proved to be a valuable asset on the campaign trail.

Laura Bush spent about 100 days on the Campaign 2000 trail, traveling solo about 75 percent of the time and with George W. about 25 percent of the time. During the primary season, she spoke mainly to Republican women's groups and read to children in elementary schools. By the fall, after her daughters had left for college, she was by her husband's side with a microphone in hand, introducing him to audiences and even taking her own questions after their speeches. Her early speeches emphasized the difference between George W.'s character and Bill Clinton's: "Governor Bush has represented Texas with dignity and honor. . . . I'd love to see him do the same thing for our nation in our highest office" (quoted in Felix 2002, 118). She made a glaring contrast to Hillary Clinton, exhibiting no political ambition of her own, although these two women are the only first ladies who have earned advanced degrees. Mrs. Bush also focused on education in her speeches, helping to persuade voters that education would be a Bush administration priority that would get results. She appealed to women and minority voters for whom these issues were key.

Laura Bush's official debut before a national audience was her speech at the Republican National Convention, July 31, 2000. This was not the first time she had spoken to a national audience or at a major convention. In 1996, she had addressed the GOP Convention in San Diego and earlier in 2000 (June), she had spoken before the Texas GOP Convention. This speech was especially significant, however, because it was the first major event of the convention, delivered prime time. Together with Colin Powell, who spoke immediately after her, Mrs. Bush was given the responsibility of "jump-starting" the four-day jubilee (Bruni 2000a, A1).

Newspaper articles appeared before her speech, introducing her to the public as a woman who gives her husband a steadiness, evenness, who reins him in. George W. acknowledged her positive affect on him when he said: "I feel like a better candidate when Laura is with me" (quoted in Simon 2001, 220). She also functions like a "radar detector," according to Mark McKinnon, George W.'s campaign media director. Mrs. Bush "could sense when the campaign was running off track . . . She can read him [her husband] better than anybody, so she has a good sense of when he is not being well-served or when his agenda is not being properly communicated" (quoted in Copp 2001, 17). Journalists also contrasted Mrs. Bush with Hillary Clinton, saying she is not personally ambitious, only reluctantly doing the best she can to help her husband. In an interview with Frank Bruni (2000a, A1) before her speech, she admitted to getting butterflies in her stomach just thinking about it.

Even before Mrs. Bush began to speak, she communicated her priorities to her national audience visually. Appearing on stage with her were rows of minority students from a Houston school, who were dressed in red and blue shirts and were sitting at school desks. Much as her mother-in-law, Barbara Bush, had sent a visual message about "family values" to the American public when she assembled the Bush clan on stage during her 1992 RNC speech, so Laura showed the audience where her and her husband's priorities would be—educating children.

Mrs. Bush began her speech by saying she was "a little overwhelmed" to help kick off the convention ("Education and Responsibility" 2000). She told the audience they had made an excellent choice in nominating her husband. She used humor to say that she and her husband were about to become empty nesters, and running for president seemed an extreme way to handle the situation. Laura turned her attention to her husband's record on education in Texas. To promote credibility and foster identification with teachers, she talked about her early love of teaching and her experience teaching second and third graders to read. She admitted that more needs to be done to help teachers with this difficult task. She cited a study to show that strides had been made to improve reading while George W. was governor of Texas. She pledged to continue this work on a national scale and to focus on children younger than school age. She pledged that George W. would make Head Start an early reading, early learning program. Before she ended her speech, she talked about her husband's character, comparing it to that of President Clinton's. Using a veiled attack, which was heartily received by her immediate audience, Mrs. Bush said that people often approach her husband saying: "I'm counting on you. I want my son or daughter to respect the President of the United States." She ended her speech by talking about the future, saying George W. Bush would make a great president!

After the speech, George W. said he realized "how at ease" his wife had become in her public role as he "watched her deliver flawless remarks before a national television audience" (1999, 92–93). Other commentators spoke positively about her performance: political communication specialist Rita Willock of Southern Methodist University, Laura Bush's alma mater, praised the speech saying, "it was very much in her own language. It was not a spun speech. . . . Laura's speaking effuses a sincerity that draws people to her" (quoted in Barta 2000, A4). According to *Baltimore Sun* journalists Ellen Gamerman and Gerard Shields (2000, A6), delegates interviewed at the convention said they were pleasantly surprised by her speech. They waved signs that read "Laura for First Lady," and they called her a "hidden asset" and the Republican Party's "secret weapon."

Like the wives of other politicians, Mrs. Bush played an important role in helping her husband win votes, and the pressure on her to do so increased during fall 2000. At the time of the Republican National Convention, Celinda Lake, a Democratic pollster who studies gender voting patterns, put George W. ahead of Al Gore with male voters, but in "a statistical dead heat" among female voters (Leonard 2000b, p A8). By the third week of September, Al Gore pulled ahead among female voters (Mitchell 2000, 16A), and by the middle of October, Gore's lead with women increased (Gore 46 percent to Bush's 39 percent). Polls also indicated that women made up the largest group of undecideds in the country (70 percent); they were not convinced that either candidate would represent their interests (Muir 2000, n.p.). Journalist John Lange underscored the important role Laura played during fall 2000 when he wrote, "wives on the platform can make the difference of several percentage points in an election" (2000, A8). Drafting her mother-in-law into service, as well as other well-known Republican women—Condoleezza Rice, Lynn Cheney, and in some venues, Cindy McCain—Laura Bush took to the road on a "W is for Women" campaign trip (Harnden 2000, 19). Their purpose was to convince women voters that George W. would represent women's interests well.

The races in Michigan, Pennsylvania, and Wisconsin, all rich in electoral votes, were very close. The Bush women campaigned in several venues in all three states. Barbara Bush, recovering from back surgery and still enormously popular, introduced her daughter-in-law to the audiences; Laura was the featured speaker. Both talked about what George W. was like as a son, husband, and father. They showed mutual affection and respect for each other, teasing each other playfully in front of their audiences. In many respects, Barbara Bush was passing the torch to her daughter-in-law. Laura had the last word at rallies and ran the press conferences. One of her more pointed comments to the media was when she was asked why her husband was trailing behind Al Gore with women voters. She answered the question by saying that her husband was doing well with women, but the important question was why Gore was not doing better with men (Bruni 2000b, A30).

The election between George W. Bush and Al Gore was the closest in American history. Voting day was November 7, 2001, but the outcome of the race was debated for days. The election turned on the vote in Florida, which was so close election officials called for a recount. However, the recount itself proved problematic for many reasons. Some people said the ballot was confusing, and they voted for the wrong person. Others said the polls closed too early. Lawyers for George W., Al Gore, and others debated all aspects of the case to no resolution, and then the Supreme Court made the final decision. During this time, Laura Bush said that the seven-week wait gave the Bushes time to put the election into perspective. Regardless of the outcome, she said, she knew they would be OK. On December 12, George W. Bush was announced the winner; on January 20, 2001, he was sworn in as the forty-third president of the United States. Laura Bush became the first lady.

Rhetorical Activities as First Lady

When Laura Bush became first lady, she was well positioned to play the roles expected of her. Although she admired many former first ladies, especially fellow Texan Lady Bird Johnson, she looked to her mother-in-law as a role model: "I have learned a lot . . . from watching her," she said (quoted in Romano 2000, A01). As a first lady, Barbara Bush had served as her husband's surrogate, political partner, traveling companion, and hostess. Significantly, she had also served as an advocate for literacy, actively raising public awareness of the problem by her speeches and public appearances. Through the Barbara Bush Foundation for Family Literacy and from the proceeds of C. *Fred's Story* and *Millie's Book*, she raised several million dollars to support literacy programs. Her husband acknowledged her influence on legislation when he gave her the pen he had used to sign the National Literacy Act of 1991 into law (Barbara Bush 1994, 425). Using what she learned from her mother-in-law as well as from her own experience as first lady of Texas, Laura Bush was well aware of the opportunity she would have to effect change. To show that she would use a different approach than her immediate predecessor, Hillary Clinton, she moved the first lady's office back to the East Wing. She also hired a staff and was ready to serve as an active first lady on projects she knew and cared about. "I know about education," she said, "I know about things that I've worked on. . . . Most other issues I don't know that much about. And just to put in my two cents—I don't think it is really necessary" (quoted in Bruni 2000a, A1). With some degree of trepidation natural for a woman described as "private," she was determined to make a difference. In her first week as first lady, she acknowledged: "I have a forum. . . . I won't always have it. The time is now."

Getting Started

Even before her husband was inaugurated the forty-third president of the United States, Mrs. Bush helped to set a bipartisan tone for the new administration by focusing public attention on one of her abiding interests—American authors. The first event she planned was a tribute to literature called "Laura Bush Celebrates

American Authors." Using a painted library as a backdrop and standing in front of painted bookcases, Mrs. Bush told her audience: "Traditionally, inaugurations include a tribute to the first lady, but my tribute is to the thousands of people who have contributed to my life—our great American authors" (quoted in Jayson 2001, A6). She said she would use her time in the inaugural spotlight to highlight her belief that "reading is the most important skill that children learn in school." She cited books such as Thomas Paine's *Common Sense* and Harriet Beecher Stowe's *Uncle Tom's Cabin* that helped "create major changes in American Society." She mentioned other authors such as Herman Melville, Willa Cather, and Richard Wright, whom she said have helped "shape the American identity." She said, "The power of a book lies in its power to turn a solitary act into a shared vision. . . . As long as we have books, we are not alone. . . . There is no magic like the magic of the written word" (quoted in MacPherson 2001, A6). Helping children to share in that magic, one of her aids early announced, would be among the first lady's top priorities; her signature issue would be early childhood education, especially prereading skills. During the coming months, she would unveil her "Ready to Read, Ready to Learn Initiative" and travel around the United States promoting different components of it. She would also offer unmistakable support for many other priorities such as American libraries, literacy volunteers, and breast cancer and heart disease research, and so on.

The Ready to Read, Ready to Learn Initiative

Mrs. Bush announced the chief area of her advocacy, early childhood education, in a speech given on February 26, 2001, at Cesar Chavez Elementary School in Hyattsville, Maryland. She began her speech by saying that her interest in education is consistent with her husband's priorities as president:

> President Bush made education his number one priority. He wants to give American teachers and schools greater flexibility, freedom and support . . . so that every child is educated and no child is left behind. . . . From the crib to the classroom children need parents, teachers, and other adults to help them prepare for success in school and in life. Some of America's schools need extra help, and President Bush has a plan to help them succeed. He wants to help you chart your own course to success through local control, high standards, accountability, and research based reading programs. This is the President's plan. And this is the President's promise. I want to help him keep that promise. ("Ready to Read" 2001a)[3]

Mrs. Bush described the component parts of her "Ready to Read, Ready to Learn" Initiative, "I want to help recruit more teachers . . . spotlight early childhood programs . . . [and] give parents, teachers, and caregivers the right kinds of information about learning and development." She discussed each component, suggesting strategies on how to achieve those goals nationally.

Mrs. Bush pledged her help in recruiting new teachers. She highlighted successful recruitment programs such as the New Teacher Project (NTP), which recruits professionals to become teachers in low-income schools; Teach for America, which recruits college graduates to make two-year teaching commitments; and Troops to Teachers, which trains retired military personnel to teach in the classroom. As part of his education package, Mrs. Bush announced that her husband proposed to increase funding for this last program tenfold.

Mrs. Bush told her audience about successful early childhood development programs such as the LEAP curriculum (Language Enrichment Activities Program) used at a Dallas, Texas, Head Start Center. She also mentioned the Early Reading First Program, which studies the effectiveness of teaching Head Start children math and reading skills. She cited a successful Boston based program, Reach Out and Read, which gives young children and their parents valuable information on the need to read. Mrs. Bush supported this program when she was the first lady of Texas and said, during the speech, that she would like to work with leaders of the program to expand nationally.

Mrs. Bush told her audience that valuable research about early learning should be shared with parents and teachers. That research indicates how important early cognitive stimulation of the brain is as a prerequisite for later higher-level functioning. She said she would work with Dr. Paige, the new education secretary, to publicize material on their website: "How Will I Know a Good Early Reading Program When I See One?" Mrs. Bush ended her speech by reiterating her husband's ideas about accountability and not allowing children to be victimized by the "soft bigotry of low expectations."

During the spring and summer 2001, Mrs. Bush promoted different aspects of her Ready to Read, Ready to Learn Initiative. She promoted teacher recruitment in speeches given at "Teach for America" events in Los Angeles ("Occidental College" 2001d) and New York City ("Teach for America" 2001h). On both occasions, she told her audiences that she plans to help Teach for America "triple the number of program participants over the next four years." She also promoted teacher recruitment at two "Troops to Teachers" events at the San Diego Naval Base ("Troops to Teachers" 2001e) and at Fort Jackson, South Carolina, on National Teachers Day ("Troops to Teachers" 2001j). Mrs. Bush asked her audience to turn their "attention to the home front . . . to Uncle Sam's classrooms . . . where we need your service as teachers." She mentioned her husband's commitment to boost funding to the program.

In other speeches that Mrs. Bush made during spring 2001, she spotlighted successful schools, teachers, and programs. Accompanied by Vincente Fox, president of Mexico, Mrs. Bush spoke at an elementary school in California on March 22, to a largely Latino audience of 300 students, parents, and teachers ("Morningside Elementary School" 2001c). "I wish the rest of the country could see your school," she told her audience, "You care about what is going on in the classroom." Indeed, parents at this school promised to perform fifteen hours of volunteer work at the school and to read to their children twenty minutes a day; the gains the students made on standardized tests were impressive (Ritsch 2001, B1). True to her word, Mrs. Bush's appearance gave media attention to a successful educational program, one that could be a model for other schools.

Mrs. Bush spoke in Chicago at an event honoring teachers as mentors and role models. Using examples from her own life and from students' letters, she praised teachers who are influential in the lives of students ("Golden Apple Teacher Awards" 2001k). Mrs. Bush also spoke at two Reach Out and Read events, one in Chicago on May 14, and the other in Boston on June 1 ("Reach Out and Read" 2001l, 2001m). In both speeches, she praised members of her audience for showing children how valuable they are and how important reading is. She said that parents trust their pediatricians, so they take a "prescription" to read to their children seriously. She said she was proud to support the Reach Out and Read Program as it expands nationally, and in Boston, Mrs. Bush acknowledged Dr. Klass and Dr. Zuckerman, two founders of the successful program, who were in her audience.

Mrs. Bush spoke at a K–12 Education Symposium in Washington, D.C., on February 28, 2001 ("Hoover Institution" 2001b). During the summer, July 26 and 27, she cosponsored a White House Summit on Early Childhood Cognitive Development with U.S. Secretaries Rod Paige (Education) and Tommy G. Thompson (Health and Human Services). Held at Georgetown University, the rationale for the summit was to share information. Over 400 experts came from government, education, and community agencies to give presentations and to learn from others. Mrs. Bush spoke early in the summit, outlining its mission and setting its tone ("Summit on Early Childhood" 2001n). She told her audience that the summit features some of the "nation's foremost researchers, policy makers and experts" on "early childhood cognitive development and brain research" as well as those who run pediatric-based programs for language acquisition, and model preschool programs. She asked her audience to rise above partisan politics to help children learn before they reach age five.

Mrs. Bush also spoke about education at the Senate Spouses Luncheon on April 3, 2001, and at the Congressional Club on May 2, both in Washington, D.C. In both speeches, she gave members of her audience an assignment. To the senate wives (spouses) she said:

> Let me emphasize that President Bush and I firmly believe in the power of local control. You are the experts on what's best in your states. You know what your school children need; you know the programs that work; and you know what best can be done. But as a nation, we need results, and we need the evidence that shows whether our children are learning. I hope you will help us carry out a mission of better education in each of your states. ("Senate Spouses Luncheon" 2001f)

She made a similar assignment to the members of the Congressional Club, asking them to do what they can in their home districts to further the Bush's education goals ("Congressional Club" 2001i). In all of the speeches that she gave that spring, she functioned very much as her husband's political partner, helping his administration achieve their education goals.

Support for American Libraries and Librarians

Though not directly part of the Ready to Read, Ready to Learn Initiative, as a former librarian, Mrs. Bush actively promoted America's libraries. She spoke during National Library Week at the American Library Association's "@ Your Library" event. Held at the Northeast Neighborhood Library, this event kicked off a five-year initiative to promote the use of resources in today's libraries. Speaking to an audience of twenty-five children and seventy-five adults, Mrs. Bush said: "the most valuable item in my wallet . . . [is] my library card." She praised librarians: "Our nation runs on the fuel of information and imagination that libraries provide every day, and librarians are in charge of collecting, cataloguing, and distributing it to patrons. Librarians help educate and inform the public, . . . they strengthen our great democracy." Calling libraries "community treasure chests," she said, "a wealth of information [is] available to everyone, equally . . . and the key to that treasure chest is a library card." She encouraged all Americans to sign up for cards at their local libraries and to become library volunteers ("@ Your Library" 2001g).

To further support the nation's libraries, Mrs. Bush announced the creation of the Laura Bush Foundation for American Libraries. The mission of the foundation, issued in a press release from the Office of the First Lady, is to provide grants to libraries for books:

> As school budgets have become stretched, school districts have had to apply their resources to programs and services other than libraries. It is not uncommon for libraries to receive funds for computers and related technology instead of books. As a result, some libraries lack up to date books and reference materials. . . . One of the purposes of the Laura Bush Foundation is to help libraries find a balance between technology and contemporary books by providing needed funding for book purchases. ("Laura Bush Foundation" 2001o)

For Mrs. Bush, "The new Foundation provides yet another opportunity to share with American children the magical world of books and reading."

On September 7 and 8, 2001, Mrs. Bush cosponsored a National Book Festival with James H. Billington, librarian of Congress. Held in the Library of Congress and on the east lawn of the U.S. Capitol, the festival was a consciousness raiser, not a fund-raiser. In a speech given at the festival, Mrs. Bush called the Library of Congress an "American Treasure," home of "many of our countries great written treasures." She described the purpose of the festival in an interview: "This event gives us an opportunity to inspire parents and caregivers to read to their children as early as possible and to encourage reading as a lifelong activity" (quoted in Felix 2002, 141). First Librarian Billington stated the case somewhat differently when he said, "We must all try, in every way we can, to send the message that reading is critical to our lives and to the life of our nation."

Like the Texas Book Festival, the gala atmosphere drew press attention as well as crowds. Events scheduled included author readings and book signings, panel discussions, a copyright workshop, and tours of the Library of Congress. Interested guests attended demonstrations of the new technologies and learned to do high-tech research in the National Digital Library Learning Center. Teachers learned to use the library's online collection, called American Memory. Small children met book characters such as the Cat in the Hat and Peter Rabbit, and older children met professional basketball players who promoted a "Read to Achieve" program. Authors from other cultures and nations told stories; musicians ranged from a mariachi band to bluegrass. Unfortunately, national press coverage of this event was largely eclipsed by the terrorist attacks on the World Trade Center and the Pentagon.

September 11 and Its Aftermath

On September 11, Mrs. Bush was on her way to testify before a Senate committee when a Secret Service agent told her a plane had struck one of the World Trade Center Towers. Just before Mrs. Bush met Senator Ted Kennedy, agents told her a second plane had struck the South Tower. Immediately, she knew these were acts of terror. Mrs. Bush was taken to a secure location, but not before making a statement to the press: "Our hearts and prayers go out to the victims of terrorism, and our support goes to the rescue workers" (quoted in Fiore 2001, 1) Journalist Larry McQuillan of USA Today asked her: "What do you say to the children?" Mrs. Bush told reporters that parents should reassure their children. Answering that question became one of her chief priorities over the next several weeks. Through her words and actions, Mrs. Bush became what many commentators called the nation's consoler-in-chief. From the tragedy forward, according to first lady scholar Myra Gutin, "It will be much harder to take a step back to having a lower profile . . . . This is her emergence" (quoted in Fiore 2001, 5:1). Although Mrs. Bush had been an active first lady during her first eight months, she had received little national coverage prompting some to wonder what she had been doing; this situation changed overnight.

The day after the attack, Mrs. Bush wrote two letters to children—one for younger, another for older children ("Elementary School Letter" and "Middle and High School Students" 2001p), which she sent to states' top educational officials for distribution to the nation's 100,000 schools. She varied the letters slightly to adapt her message to the two different age groups. Both letters were consoling, telling children that sad things sometimes happen, but each and every one of them is important and loved. She told them they now have an opportunity to do good things for other people—to show how much others mean to them. Mrs. Bush also broadcast short messages to children on the Disney Channel, and she appeared on five networks to tell parents to turn off their television sets, to share meals with their children, to read and comfort their children. She appeared on the Oprah Winfey Show and relayed the same message to parents; she also talked with Leslie Stahl on 60 Minutes about helping children cope with the images shown and shown again on television and with the horrible realities of the attacks.

Children were not the only ones Mrs. Bush consoled. In the first two days after the attacks, Mrs. Bush visited survivors of the Pentagon attack at the Walter

Reed Army Medical Center and Washington Hospital. She thanked blood donors at the Eisenhower Executive Building, and helped her husband choose speakers for the National Prayer Day held on September 14. On September 17, she traveled to western Pennsylvania, Shankesville, to offer solace to the families and friends of the victims of United Airlines Flight 93. Speaking to an audience of approximately 250–300 people, she said, the "heartache and loss" they are experiencing is the kind that "none of us could have ever imagined" ("Memorial Service" 2001q). Members of her audience were overwhelmingly grateful. A week later, she made another public statement at the "Concert for America." She dedicated the concert to the victims of September 11, and to those who answered "grief and adversity with kindness and courage." She said that it was time for us to return to the good things in life, and borrowing a poet's phrase, she called music "the speech of angels" and said "it brings a special comfort to our nation" ("Kennedy Center" 2001r).

Before the end of September, Mrs. Bush traveled to New York City and met with different kinds of audiences—children, firefighters, and teachers. She visited P.S. 41, an elementary school that hosted children who had been evacuated from P.S. 234 during the attacks. She visited Battalion 9, a firehouse that had lost thirty-one men when the World Trade Center Towers collapsed. She left sunflowers tied with red, white, and blue ribbons, and left a message in their journal: "To the firefighters of Battalion 9, You showed the world that honor and bravery are alive in New York City. Thank you for being heroes. God Bless you, Laura Bush." Probably her most substantive speech was the one given at Madison Square Garden to 2000 volunteers from the "Learning Leaders," a nonprofit organization that trains volunteers to help in schools. This event had been scheduled before September 11, but she used the occasion to acknowledge members of the group as "cool-headed heroes who shepherded, sheltered, and saved" children by guiding them away from a school near the World Trade Center. She thanked teachers and school staffs for their dedication in comforting children, and called the volunteers who help them "one of the blessings that have been revealed in the aftermath ("Learning Leaders" 2001s).

During October, Mrs. Bush continued to make the aftermath of September 11 a key theme in her public appearances and speeches. In the beginning of the month, she addressed the anti-Muslim, anti-Arab feelings that were surfacing in the country by calling attention to the need for tolerance. At an event called "Close the Book on Hate," Mrs. Bush read *Amazing Grace* to two dozen children in a Washington Barnes and Noble bookstore; this is a story about an African American girl who overcomes her prejudice. She also helped address the problem of intolerance through lessons she planned as part of Teach for America Week. Her lessons developed themes related to the September 11 attacks such as understanding others, being compassionate, and embracing diversity. She combined these themes with lessons on geography, social studies, and phonics. At the end of the month, she met with recipients of Liberty Scholarships, given by the United Negro College Fund. The scholarships went to three students who had lost parents or guardians in the September 11 attacks. Mrs. Bush called the scholarships "a truly meaningful response to the tragic events of September 11" ("United Negro College Fund" 2001u). Finally, Mrs. Bush spoke at a Women's Day Awards Luncheon in New York City on October 30, 2001, to honor women who have made significant contributions in many fields. Even in this kind of speech, she connected their good deeds with the good deeds of others. So many people have acted generously, she said ("Women's Day Awards" 2001v).

When Mrs. Bush spoke at events that had little to do with September 11, she made some mention of the attacks. For example, at a three-state summit for early childhood development on October 3, she began her speech by talking about the aftermath, especially how much children need routines to feel safe ("Cognitive Development Summit" 2001t). Significantly, most of this speech detailed aspects of her Ready to Read, Ready to Learn Initiative: it was the first speech I read where, after mentioning the events of September 11, she allowed them to recede into the background.

Mrs. Bush continued to console the nation in speeches given during November. A difficult speech she gave early in the month was at a "Best Friends for Our Children" event on November 7 at the Bertie Backus Middle School in Washington, D.C. This school had lost children and teachers who were on the hijacked plane that struck the Pentagon. She presented each child in the school with a book and gave the school a collection of books for their library ("For Our Children" 2001w). Once again, she was encouraging.

Probably the most far-reaching speech she gave in November was at the National Press Club. On November 8, she spoke to nearly 200 journalists and public relations staff members for thirty minutes and accepted questions. She acknowledged the importance of Larry McQuillan's question asked on September 11: "What do you say to the children?" She said his question functioned as a "wake up call," and she quickly turned her attention to the nation's children. An underlying theme of all she said was Psalm 27: "Your face Lord do I seek . . . I believe that I shall see the goodness of the Lord in the land of the living." Throughout her speech, she cited examples of police, firefighters, teachers, and children who acted with great courage and compassion. She reminded her audience of the major role they play as journalists and publicists, and she gave them an assignment:

> You have a real opportunity to make sure that, as time passes, Americans are still informed about ways they can exercise their compassion. You have a real opportunity to highlight the needs in your communities so people know what they can specifically do to make life better where they live. ("National Press Club" 2001x)

After the speech, Mrs. Bush answered more questions than she had done in previous speeches. One journalist commented favorably on her performance, especially during the question-and-answer period when Mrs. Bush spoke without a text: "It shows when a public figure's life has been immersed in literature" (Himes 2001, A46).

Also, in November, Mrs. Bush broke with tradition to deliver, instead of her husband, a radio address in support of children and women of Afghanistan ("Radio Address" 2001y). This was the first time in U.S. history that a first lady presented an entire radio address by herself. Mrs. Bush condemned the terrorists, not only because of what they had done in our country, but also because of what they had done to their own people. She stated the point directly: "Good Morning. I am Laura Bush, and I am delivering this week's radio address to kick off a worldwide effort to focus on the brutality against women and children by the al-Qaida terrorist network and the regime it supports in Afghanistan, the Taliban." She talked about the brutal repression of women and children: "One out of every four children won't live past the age of five because health care is not available. Women have been denied access to doctors when they are sick. . . . Women cannot work outside the home or leave their homes by themselves. . . . the Taliban forbid education to women." She also encouraged Americans to continue to support the fight against terrorism.

After the speech, leaders of women's groups and women in Congress discussed the issues; Mrs. Bush met privately at the White House with women leaders from Afghanistan. She also received a great deal of media coverage probably because no one expected her to speak out so forcefully for the international rights of women and children. Melanne Verveer, one of Hillary Clinton's former staff members and head of Vital Voices, an international women's group, said about Mrs. Bush's speech: "For Mrs. Bush to be speaking out about women's rights is like Nixon going to China. . . . It's so counterintuitive and unexpected that it is having a very powerful impact and a positive value." Feminist Gloria Steinem also praised the speech: "I'm glad to hear from Mrs. Bush. Now we will find out who she is" (both quoted in Leonard 2001, A15).

During the month of December, the most significant message from Mrs. Bush to the American public was the inscription she chose for the White House Christmas card: "Thy face, Lord, do I seek: I believe that I shall see the goodness of the Lord in the land of the living" (Psalm 27: 8, 13). That was not the original Bible verse selected, but the alternative deemed more fitting after September 11. Interestingly, this is the same Bible verse the chaplain at Camp David used immediately following the terrorist attack, and it is the verse Mrs. Bush cited in her National Press Club speech. In fact, the theme runs through most of the messages she presented during fall 2001. She read the message to the American public when she showed the card to Barbara Walters during the televised tour of the White House Christmas decorations (Walters 2001). She talked about it as well on *Larry King Live*. During a discussion of how good could come from bad, Mrs. Bush said:

> The Christmas card was already well into the works by September 11. We had the artist do the artwork way last summer and it was actually at the printer. But I changed the verse to Psalm 27, the part that read, "I believe I shall see the goodness of the Lord in the land of the living." Because that's what I think happened. We saw a handful of people commit a horrible crime, but at the same time we saw

hundreds and thousands of people do good things. And that's what I really think happened on September 11. (King 2001)

Resuming Advocacy: Old and New Priorities

In the first six months of 2002, Mrs. Bush continued to attend events that focused primarily on the attacks of September 11 and their aftermath. She also resumed her advocacy of early childhood education and continued to work hard on the recruitment of teachers and librarians. Significantly, she also began to step out solo on the global stage to speak about the international rights of women and children—to an education and to participation in public life. This was especially evident in her support of the inclusion of women in the newly forming governments in Afghanistan and in Iraq after the fall of Saddam Hussein. She continued to celebrate American authors and literature, and after he husband issued a presidential directive, she began to promote America's historic places through the Preserve America initiative. Her advocacy of women's health expanded to include not only breast cancer but heart disease which claims more women's lives each year than any other single cause. Both directly and indirectly, she continued to enhance her husband's political capital especially with groups who traditionally vote for Democratic candidates such as teachers, women, African Americans, and environmentalists. From 2002 through 2004, she traversed the nation campaigning for Republican candidates. Laura Bush also raised considerable funds for her husband's bid for reelection in Campaign 2004.

Back to The Ready to Read, Ready to Learn Initiative

Like First Ladies Eleanor Roosevelt, Rosalynn Carter, and Hillary Clinton, Mrs. Bush was invited to testify before congressional committees on the need for early childhood education ("Senate Committee" 2002c). On January 24, 2002, she spoke as a mother and former teacher before the Senate Committee on Health, Education, Labor, and Pensions on the development of language in young children. She compared her own daughters' early experiences of letters, sounds, and language structures to those of the children she taught in the inner-city schools in Houston. Some of her students had not developed adequate prereading skills, and it was an uphill battle for them to learn to read. She recommended the inclusion of prereading activities in programs such as Head Start. Including mention of September 11 in her testimony, she said, "I have seen the faces of children who were directly affected by the attacks" and I am "doubly committed to using my voice to help give our youngest Americans a real chance to succeed in the classroom." Following her husband's lead, she called reading "the new civil right." Her testimony before the House Education and Workforce Committee on March 14, 2002, was similar, but here she stressed the need for strong teachers in our nation's schools ("House Committee" 2002h). Calling teachers "the heart and soul of our schools," she spoke of the need to recruit the brightest teachers and to train them with the best possible programs. Commenting on her Senate testimony, journalist Ann Gerhart of the *Washington Post* said that Mrs. Bush used her "signature style," a blend of "homey personal anecdotes with educational theory and current science" (2002a, C01).

Mrs. Bush engendered bipartisan support for her Ready to Read, Ready to Learn Initiative when she teamed up with Senators Hillary Clinton (D-NY) and Kay Bailey Hutchison (R-Texas) to spotlight the need for more teachers. On February 26, 2002, the trio attended a Transition to Teaching/New Teacher Project event at Powell Elementary School in Washington, D.C. She talked about the need to replace 2.2 million teachers who will retire in the next ten years ("Transition" 2002e). She encouraged the audience to consider teaching as an alternative occupation for midcareer professionals, saying "teaching is the greatest community service of all," while Mrs. Clinton said: "Uncle Sam wants you to teach." Both women supported an amendment Mrs. Clinton had introduced to an education bill, which would allow some professionals to begin teaching without completing the traditional training program (*Hillary Watch* 2002, 16).

As she had done during her first year as first lady, Mrs. Bush continued to help publicize successful educational programs and extraordinary teachers. One noteworthy example is the speech she gave at the Ebenezer Church in Atlanta to honor Doctor Martin Luther King ("Martin Luther King Jr. Day" 2002b). She praised the education he had received as a child and his life as an inspiring teacher of others. Putting him on par with Lincoln, she said, "American history is unimaginable without him." She also told her audience that she believed Doctor King would have applauded the passage of the No Child Left Behind Bill and the bipartisan support that made that possible.

The East and West Wings of the White House worked together to sponsor a conference on education, which Mrs. Bush hosted. Held on March 5, 2002, the White House Conference on Preparing Tomorrow's Teachers brought together 150 "university and business leaders, teacher education advocates, teachers' unions, public policy organizations, and foundations from across the country." The conference was part of Mrs. Bush's Ready to Read/to Learn Initiative, but it was also designed to address one of the provisions of the No Child Left Behind Bill, which commits federal resources to making sure that every child in America is taught by a qualified teacher. Mrs. Bush set the agenda for the conference very directly in a speech she gave at the beginning of the meeting ("Opening Remarks" 2002f): "We all know that the most important ingredient in a child's education is a good teacher. And we all know that teachers need training, tools, and our support to help children succeed in school." She talked about her experiences as a new teacher in the inner-city schools in Houston: "Many times I didn't know enough to make the right instructional decisions." To show that the problem was not with her, the school where she had taught, or the university where she had received her degree, she added, "I took pride in my educational training, but the job was much harder than I had imagined." By recognizing the difficulties of the task instead of finding fault with the teachers, Mrs. Bush inspired a spirit of cooperation among her audience. *Washington Post* journalist Ann Gerhart credits Mrs. Bush's approach with helping her husband's administration win the support of educators, labor unions, and key politicians such as Ted Kennedy: "Her steady public respect for teachers has helped forge the administration's ability to push for improved teacher training without excoriating educators" (2002a, C01).

During 2003 and 2004, Mrs. Bush continued to present many education related speeches. Her website lists at minimum ten speeches and press releases between January 2003 and April 2004. Her effectiveness as a recruiter of new teachers cannot be denied. Through the Troops to Teachers Initiative, the New Teacher Project, and Teach for America, she has helped recruit 15,500 new teachers. She has expended a great deal of effort as well on recruiting librarians.

Resuming Support for American Libraries

During the early months of 2002, Mrs. Bush continued to support American libraries and librarians. On January 9, she spoke at the Topeka and Shawnee County Library in Kansas, telling that group that the president included in his 2003 budget a fivefold increase in funding to help libraries recruit and train professionals ("Library Gala" 2002a). She cited statistics from the *Library Journal Magazine* and *Labor Review*, stating the high percentage of librarians and directors who will retire in the next decade. Especially targeted for recruitment are librarians who can help parents and teachers choose material to read to preschool children and who can speak in other languages. She also sponsored a White House Conference on American Libraries in June 2002, the purpose of which was to bring together leaders in library research and those who run successful programs. She welcomed all of the participants in an opening address on June 4, and then she and her mother-in-law, former first lady Barbara Bush, listened to the presentations given in the East Room of the White House. At the close of the conference, Laura announced that the Laura Bush Foundation for American Libraries had received pledges of $5 million dollars since its inception in 2001, $50,000 of which was pledged by Barbara Bush ("Closing Remarks" 2002o).

Perhaps the most interesting speech Laura Bush gave at a library was during September 2003, when she spoke at the First Ladies Library in Canton, Ohio, to help dedicate their new Education and Research Center. "As a former teacher and librarian and a first lady," she said, "the memorabilia and personal artifacts of our first ladies are priceless." Quoting Lady Bird Johnston who pointed out that the constitution remains silent on the role of the first lady, Mrs. Bush reminded her audience, "a podium is there if she cares to use it." She also praised the Library's collection of "books, information, and artifacts," because they allow the researcher to discover how "the role of the first lady has broadened and changed" since the days of Martha Washington. After citing some of the contributions first ladies have made to their husbands' administrations, she closed her speech by saying "Thanks to the First Ladies Library, the history of America's first ladies will continue to be told—one remarkable woman at a time" ("First Ladies Library" 2003).

Celebrating American Authors, Literature, and Historic Places

Mrs. Bush's fondness of history is consistent with her love of stories. As we have seen, she celebrated American authors and literature when she was the first lady of Texas through Texas Book Festivals and during the inaugural festivities in early 2001. As a first lady, she helped organize National Book Festivals and to date three have been held in Washington, D.C., through the combined efforts of Mrs. Bush, her staff, and the Library of Congress. She has celebrated American authors at White House symposiums on the Life and Works of Mark Twain, the Harlem Renaissance, and Women of the American West. Invited to the celebrations are scholars, writers, students, and authors, who spend a day together talking about significant issues raised by these distinctive American voices. It was during the planning stages of a symposium dedicated to "Poetry and the American Voice," scheduled for February 12, 2003, that Laura Bush probably made her only rhetorical blunder as a first lady. One of the poets invited to the symposium was passionately against the impending war in Iraq. Through a call he placed on the internet to other poets, Sam Hamill planned to take anti-war poetry to the White House to present to Mrs. Bush. Luckily, she discovered the plot in time to cancel the symposium; however, there was a great deal of bad press generated by the episode (Wertheimer 2003).

Less challenging have been the speeches Mrs. Bush has presented in support of Preserve America, an initiative created by President Bush as an executive order on March 3, 2003. The purpose of the initiative was to provide federal funding to maintain American historic places and communities. In a speech given at the National Association of Counties in March 2003, Mrs. Bush said that "many of our historic sites and monuments are deteriorating and need to be preserved." She provided many examples of work being done such as efforts to preserve a trail that Sacagawea used to lead Lewis and Clark on their expedition. She encouraged members of her audience to work with Preserve America to protect our heritage where they live.

Promoting Women's Rights and Health at Home and Abroad

After Mrs. Bush's second year as first lady, she began to address the issues of women's and children's rights and women's health at home and abroad. She continued to meet international leaders in her role as presidential spouse and hostess, and to entertain them at the White House and at her Crawford home. For example, the British prime minister and his wife stayed with the Bushes at their ranch many times, especially right before and during the war in Iraq. In early April 2002, comments appeared in the press about how Laura Bush and Mrs. Blair had little in common, even though both women had spoken out six months before on behalf of the women and children of Afghanistan. However, the two women shared an interest in promoting research for breast cancer since both knew victims. Laura's mother was a breast cancer survivor, and Mrs. Blair lost an aunt and best friend to the disease. During that visit, the two first ladies spoke at a Dallas Breast Cancer Fund-raiser, each in her own way. Days later, on April 9, Mrs. Bush functioned as her husband's surrogate when she led the U.S. delegation to the funeral of the Queen Mother of England ("Presidential Delegation" 2002k). There she made a brief statement on behalf of President Bush and the American people about "a truly remarkable woman" ("Queen Mother" 2002l).

Throughout spring 2002, both at home and abroad, Mrs. Bush continued to advocate for the education of women and children in Afghanistan. On January 29, she spoke at a USAID event with Hamid Karzai, at the time the interim chairman of the Afghan Authority. She spoke about U.S. involvement in an international coalition to rebuild that country, and noted especially "our support for the women and children." She reinforced U.S. commitment to make sure "the women of Afghanistan again have the freedom and the resources to pursue an education and a profession" ("USA Event" 2002d). She made a similar statement on March 8 to the UN Commission on the Status of Women in honor of International Women's Day. She talked about the educational supplies, including 40,000 backpacks recently sent to Afghanistan for children who would return to school later that month ("United Nations" 2002g). In commenting on this speech, *Washington Post* journalist Lynne Duke pointed out a change in the first lady's style of speaking: Mrs. Bush "sounded very much an advocate . . . speaking more forcefully and in greater detail than she did . . . last fall. And in so doing, the first lady, who before September 11 seemed guarded in her speechmaking, spoke today with uncommon flourish about human rights in general" (2002, C01).

Mrs. Bush also helped raise money for school uniforms and other materials by networking behind the scenes. Sima Simar, Afghan minister for women's affairs, requested 200 manual sewing machines, 450,000 yards of fabric, buttons, thread, shoes, and socks. She wanted Afghan women, widowed by the war, to have a means to support their families. Mrs. Bush phoned Elaine Chao, U.S. labor secretary, and secured a commitment for funds to pay these women to sew uniforms (Neuffer 2002, E1). Later that month on March 20, 2002, while introducing her husband in a speech given at the Samual W. Tucker Elementary School, she thanked American corporations for their gifts of material and money ("Back-to-School" 2002i). She also thanked the children of America for raising $4 million to help the children of Afghanistan, $2500 of which had been raised by the children in her audience, many of whom were Moslem (Wax 2002, B04).

During the first six months of 2002, Mrs. Bush's foreign travel evolved from simply accompanying her husband to Asia with little substantive diplomacy of her own to her solo trip to Europe where she presented speeches at large venues, including another radio address to the people of Afghanistan. During her trip to Asia in February, her schedule was separate from her husband's, but her activities remained low-key and ceremonial, visiting with the Girl Scouts in South Korea and reading *Curious George* to children in Japan. A month later, at the end of March, Mrs. Bush accompanied her husband on a four-day trip to Latin American. Her diplomatic role during this trip was more substantial. She presented a speech in Peru on March 23 entitled: "Early Education to Eradicate Poverty and Promote Social Integration." She told her audience about initiatives used in the United States to help children learn and then mentioned new initiatives that have been proposed to help educate children in all of the Americas. She talked about "Centers for Excellence in Teacher Training" that will operate in the Andes, Central America, and the Caribbean. The purpose of the centers is teacher training, she said, especially for setting up reading programs in schools. Significantly, she pledged U.S. support for Peru's National Network for Girls Education and the Rural Girl's Education Law, both of which promote the education of girls ("Eradicate Poverty" 2002j).

From May 13 through 22, 2002, Mrs. Bush traveled to France, Hungary, and the Czech Republic. The purpose of her first solo diplomatic trip was to promote "education, social issues, and economic assistance" to the people of Afghanistan, but she did more than that. Traveling with a staff of fifteen people, including, significantly, presidential spokesperson Karen Hughes, Mrs. Bush also drew the attention of the world to the crises in the Middle East and her husband's commitment to help broker peace between Israel and Palestine.

In Paris, Mrs. Bush drew public attention to the brutality of the Taliban when she visited fragments of Buddhist art that had escaped destruction. She also presented a twenty-five-minute speech, "Education: The Door of Hope" (2002m) on May 14, to an audience of 700 people at the Organization of Economic Cooperation and Development (OECD) Forum 2002. Here she praised education as "the most important gift we can give the world's children," saying that it is the gift "most likely to lead to future peace and prosperity." Echoing a point President Bush had made in his State of the Union Address (2002), she said, "All Mothers and Fathers the world over love their children and want the very best for them." She talked about suicide bombers and said that all children should be taught "to respect human life—their own life and the life of others." In a section of the speech that she had reworked on the plane to include mention of a recent suicide bombing that took the lives of seventeen Russian children, she quoted one Russian mother as saying: "The person who did this . . . could not have been born of a mother." After her speech, reporters asked her if she felt uncomfortable commenting upon events in the Middle East, and she answered, "not really." She said she could easily identify with parents who are afraid to let their children go to the grocery store or to a bowling alley. When asked if she could identify with the Palestinians, she replied, "Can I empathize with a mother who sends her child out to kill herself and others? No." Then she added more tactfully that both sides have to come to the negotiating table (quoted in Gerhart 2002c, C01).

In Budapest, Mrs. Bush met with officials to thank them for their help in fighting against terrorism. She spoke with prominent women, telling them to "lead the way toward making women full partners in this vibrant new society (quoted in McQuillan 2002, 5A). She also met with physicians and pharmacy executives to announce a grant to help them establish a woman's health initiative. Hungary has one of the highest rates of cancer in Europe; significantly, that night Mrs. Bush met with the U.S. ambassador to Hungary, Nancy Brinker, who founded the United States Susan G. Komen Breast Cancer Foundation, which sponsors the Race for the Cure (Gerhart 2002d, C01). Years earlier, Mrs. Brinker, a friend of the Bushes from Texas, had helped Mrs. Bush become active in charity and fund raising activities before she became the first lady of Texas (Minutaglio 1999, 237).

Mrs. Bush next traveled to Prague, capital of the Czech Republic. While there, she drew public attention to the crises in the Middle East when she visited a Nazi concentration camp outside of Prague and, within that city, six synagogues where Jewish women and children had been murdered over the centuries (Gerhart 2002e, C01). She also visited Radio Free Europe/Radio Liberty, which helped her, together with Radio Free Afghanistan and Voice of America, to send a message to the people of Afghanistan on May 21. She began this speech by acknowledging all of their suffering and pledging the commitment of the American people to help them. She spoke about the efforts the United States and other countries are making in the areas of agriculture, education, and health care. Most poignant were the messages she read from American children who raised money for the children of Afghanistan. She also addressed the women of that country, encouraging them not to stand on the sidelines as new leaders of their country are selected:

> I understand the lives of women in America and the lives of women in Afghanistan are very different, and I respect our differences and your decisions. Yet I want you to know that the isolation the Taliban regime forced on you is not normal—not by international standards, not by Islamic standards, and not by Afghanistan's own standards. Before the Taliban, women were elected representatives in Afghanistan's parliament. Women worked as teachers, doctors, and professionals. Women were educated and women were a vital part of Afghanistan's life. I hope you will be again because a society can only achieve its full potential when all of its members participate. ("Radio Address" 2002n)

Mrs. Bush concluded her speech by saying that she wished the people of Afghanistan would build their country the way the people of Hungary and the Czech Republic have done. She reiterated the same message later that day in a statement presented during a roundtable discussion at Radio Free Europe/Radio Liberty. Again, she mentioned how difficult it must be for the women of Afghanistan to leave their isolation after so many years of being forced to remain, uneducated, in their homes. They may need help, she said, to take their places as active participants in society. Mrs. Bush ended her solo trip when she joined her husband on May 22 to continue their diplomacy in other European countries. Her time by herself, however, helped those who read about her trip shed any lingering impression of her as "a quiet first lady."

In September 2003, Mrs. Bush returned to France on a fence-mending mission to help secure the support of President Jacques Chirac and other European leaders to shoulder the burdens of the war in Iraq. She was accompanied by

Karen Hughes, former communications officer for President Bush; Hughes has often been recalled for special projects since the time she resigned. One of the highlights of that trip included the photographs of Mrs. Bush who "grimaced," "smirked," "blushed" (all descriptions were used) when Jacques Chirac took her hand and kissed it gallantly. Flashes popped and video cameras rolled and the "French kiss" became a print and television media event. Another highlight of the trip, more important for our purposes, was the speech she gave in France acknowledging her husband's decision to recommit the United States to join the United Nations Educational, Scientific, and Cultural Organization (UNESCO) after 19 years of absence.

Laura Bush began the UNESCO speech by talking about the importance today in a world plagued by terror of principles that were set down 58 years ago in the wake of World War II—"To further universal respect for justice, for the rule of law, and for the human rights and fundamental freedoms which are affirmed for the peoples of the world, without distinction of race, sex, language, or religion." She focused on the value of education, claiming it to be "the birthright of every human being—all the world's sons and all the world's daughters." She divided the remainder of her speech into four key areas of education, beginning with universal literacy. The examples and statistics she used to develop this point were largely—and surprisingly—feminist. "Two-thirds of the nearly 900 million illiterate adults in the world are women," she said. And "for people throughout the world, and especially women and girls, education is power, the power to control their own lives." She turned to the difference education can make by considering women in Afghanistan, some of whom are now learning math and science in schools. She cited one young girl who wants to become a lawyer, "because . . . [she] want[s] to bring justice and freedom" to her country, especially for women." Laura's second point was that education must be quality education—meaning that what is taught should help show the students that there is more than hate and hopelessness in the world. To explain her third point, which was to institute post-conflict education, she used Iraq as an example: "One tragic legacy of Saddam Hussein's rule," she said, "is an overall adult illiteracy rate of 61 percent—and a staggering 77 percent—or three in four women in Iraq—cannot read." Her last point was that education or the ability to read can save lives, and she talked about teaching people how to avoid HIV and AIDS. She ended her speech by saying that "literacy and liberty" are natural allies, and she hoped that all parents, teachers, and leaders everywhere will "condemn the terrible tragedy of men, women and children killing themselves to kill others." She asked the civilized world to stand together against terror.

Education not only helps women to gain employment, take care of their children, and participate in their communities, it also helps them take care of themselves. Breast cancer awareness was an important subject for Laura Bush and she spoke about it both at home and abroad. During the middle of her term as first lady, she also began to address the problem of women and heart disease. President Bush had made several proclamations—one a year for four years (2001–2004)—declaring

February to be American Heart Health Month. The first proclamation followed a women's health symposium held in March 2001, where 70 physicians met to develop a national strategy to reduce the number of women dying from heart disease. Facts listed on Mrs. Bush's website are surprising and scary. Women between the ages of 40 and 60 begin to become susceptible to heart disease, and one out of three postmenopausal women die from the disease. Moving her husband's agenda forward, Mrs. Bush participated in a Healthy Heart Initiative which was designed to educate the American public about the causes of heart disease and how to prevent them by eating right and exercising. The Red Dress Project became a symbol through which women were encouraged to take care of themselves.

Probable Legacy

Mrs. Bush is the first first lady of the twenty-first century and as such she brings to the position a unique blend of conservative and liberal tendencies. Much as her predecessors who straddled the nineteenth and twentieth centuries, Mrs. Bush continues to balance the traditional demands of the role—wife, mother, hostess—with the modern demands for a first lady to be a political partner, a savvy public relations expert, and an independent advocate for those issues in which she takes special interest. Although commentators early predicted that Mrs. Bush might be more traditional than modern, given her activity as a first lady those who had the lowest expectations of her would have to admit that she is doing pretty well. During a *Today* show interview with Katie Couric, Laura Bush described herself as both traditional and modern: "I think I am both ways," she said (quoted in Gerhart 2004, 112). The final assessment of her tenure as first lady, undoubtedly, will have to include both her traditional and modern tendencies, especially how she strikes a balance between them.

Before Laura Lane Welch married George W. Bush at age thirty, she had earned a bachelor's degree in education, a master's degree in library science, and she had worked for ten years as an educator and librarian teaching inner-city minority students to read. She thought of herself as a Democrat, although she was not interested in politics. After her marriage, she gave up her career and focused on raising her children, helping her husband launch a political career, and serving her community as a volunteer. When her husband became governor of Texas, she drew on her full set of experiences as a teacher and mother to help her husband focus squarely on early childhood education and what could be done to improve it. Mrs. Bush also lobbied legislators, corporations, foundations, and individuals to raise funds to initiate research-based and tested educational programs.

As first lady of the United States, Mrs. Bush continues to function as her husband's political partner on education and other initiatives. Each brings to the partnership different kinds of experience and expertise, hers as an educator and librarian and his as a politician, though they seem to have learned a considerable amount from each other over the years. Together, they present a common desire to improve different aspects of education on a national scale. Both view education as the new civil right, and after September 11, both have begun to present education on the international stage as a human right and a precondition to world stability and peace. The war in Iraq, so troublesome for all, has taken some of the president's and first lady's attention away from domestic concerns, and after the "Poets against the War" fiasco in early 2003, Mrs. Bush stepped out of the national spotlight for a few weeks (Allen 2003, C1), making "few personal appearances" (Mason 2003, 1). She did, however, launch new initiatives—"heart healthy" and "Preserve America"—as well as continuing to discuss subjects such as reading and teacher training.

On the national stage, Mrs. Bush functions effectively as an advocate for her Ready to Read, Ready to Learn Initiative. She travels across the country using her celebrity as a first lady to spotlight national attention on different components of it. At the time of this writing, it is difficult to predict how much long-range good she will do, but her testimony before Senate and House bipartisan committees, the large number of teachers she has recruited, and the education summits she has planned—bringing together educators, legislators, researchers, unions, foundation administrators, and so on—doubtless will have some positive effect on education in this country. Mrs. Bush has also actively promoted related initiatives such as support for American libraries, recruiting librarians, celebrating books and their authors, and honoring volunteers who serve their communities by helping people learn to read. Though she speaks for other causes such as breast cancer and women's heart disease, the evolving pattern of her advocacy grows increasingly systematic the longer she serves as first lady, and this includes her advocacy for the education of women and children internationally. It is as though Mrs. Bush is bringing a librarian's sense of organization to the messy closet of miscellaneous educational initiatives and interests. Building on her mother-in-law's insights on literacy: "everything I worried about would be better if more people could read, write, and comprehend" (Barbara Bush 1994, 145), Laura is adding: to learn to read, children must have basic prereading experiences, which presuppose parents who can read to them and social programs to reinforce what is done (or not done) in the home. They must have free access to libraries where families can borrow materials and to knowledgeable librarians who can recommend age-appropriate material even to those who do not speak English.

Of course, Mrs. Bush has also acted as a traditional hostess. She has made sure the Bushes home in Crawford, Texas, Prairie Chapel, is a comfortable retreat for relaxing as well as for diplomacy. The Putins, Blairs, and others have been able to taste American hospitality and see American values in action in an informal situation—with a minimal of protocol. Mrs. Bush has also presented ceremonial speeches and followed in her mother-in-law's footsteps by providing a more liberal counterbalance to her husband's conservatism. She has helped him secure the support of those who typically vote Democratic such as teachers not by excoriating them but by focusing on issues of concern to them. She has also raised considerable funds for his reelection campaign.

Laura Bush continues to be a steadying influence on her husband, both before and after September 11, when she became more visible and helped to steady the nation during a time of tragedy. As the "Consoler-in-Chief," Mrs. Bush comforted children and told parents how to help their children through the crises. In the aftermath, she helped the country focus on the kindness exhibited by many as the nation dug through the rubble and prepared to build a stronger, more vigilant nation. Working with advisors such as Karen Hughes, Mrs. Bush became an advocate for the rights of women and children—in Afghanistan and in other countries as well. Commenting on Mrs. Bush's performance post–September 11, Carl Anthony has said, "Her performance has been stellar. . . . It is really in moments of crises . . . that you see the true character of a first lady" (quoted in Thomma 2001, A10).

At the time of this writing, Mrs. Bush has served as first lady for nearly three and a half years. It is not possible to say how many years she will continue to serve or how far she will take us in forging a role model for first ladies of the twenty-first century. Her greatest strength may be helping the Bush administration further its education initiatives. If *she* had to choose what her legacy would be, she would probably say: "I would like to be known as an advocate for children" (quoted in Romano 2000, A01). In April 2001, she told journalist Tara Copp of the *Chicago Sun-Times* that she hopes "we really have recruited more teachers. . . . I hope schools around the country are making sure their children can read. Those are the issues that are most important to me" (17).

Mrs. Bush has grown tremendously as a public speaker since her first appearance as surrogate for her husband in Muleshoe, Texas. Although it is too early to write a rhetorical biography of her, this chapter has presented evidence of her development as a public speaker from the early days as she campaigned by her husband's side for U.S. representative to her solo diplomatic trips as first lady. Marveling at her accomplishments, her husband told reporters before he was elected president, "If I'd have said, 'Honey, you'll be the kickoff speaker at the Republican Convention in the year 2000,' she would have said, 'You've totally lost your mind and I'm not marrying you'" (quoted in Bruni 2000a, A1). What would she have said if her husband had told her that in 2002 she would be speaking to an international audience of 700 on a solo diplomatic trip to Europe or addressing the people of Afghanistan via Radio Free Europe? Or in 2003 she would be visiting the French President Jacques Chirac on a fence-mending mission?

Questions for Discussion

1. What experiences did Laura Bush have as a young girl, college student, working woman, wife, and mother that helped her forge her role as first lady?
2. Describe Laura Bush's evolution as a public speaker.
3. What issues did Laura Bush promote when she became first lady? Were they consistent with her husband's initiatives and priorities?

4. Laura Bush has been called a traditionalist as a first lady by some commentators and a modernist by others. How would you describe her position? Why?

5. What do you think Laura Bush's legacy will be as a first lady?

Internet Resources

http://www.whitehouse.gov/firstlady/
At present, the best website to learn about Laura Bush is the White House website, especially the "First Lady" pages. There you will find information about Mrs. Bush's initiatives as well as texts of all the speeches she has given since becoming first lady. You will find photographs of her, a biographical sketch, and even some of her favorite recipes.

http://www.laurabushfoundation.org/
The Laura Bush Foundation for American Libraries also provides information about one the initiatives near and dear to the first lady's heart—supporting American readers by providing grants to libraries. You can read about Laura Bush and her passion for reading on this website.

Notes

1. I have relied on material from Felix (2002) and Stone (2001) as well as from Laura Bush's biography on the White House website to write the "biography" section. There were also many profiles of Mrs. Bush in newspapers published throughout 2000 and 2001, during Campaign 2000 and the inauguration. Material that occurs in several of the sources I have not provided citations for in the text.

2. In 1996, Laura Bush received almost $1 million from the Barbara Bush Foundation for Family Literacy to help finance her first lady's Family Literacy Initiative. She used the money to support at least fifty programs throughout Texas, including a literacy program for the deaf, programs with Head Start, and Even Start (G. W. Bush 1999, 91).

3. I have cited Mrs. Bush's speeches in the text by using an abbreviated title of each speech and the year in which it was delivered. I have made every attempt to cite the day the speech was given and the location in the text. At present, Mrs. Bush's speeches are on the White House website (www.whitehouse.gov/firstlady/news-speeches/). On this page, the reader can click on the date of the speech and the text will come up.

References

America's Voice: First Lady's Popularity. 2003. CNN Live at Daybreak. 30 September. http://www.cnn.com/TRANSCRIPTS/0309/30/lad.02.html, accessed 3 May 2004.

Barta, Carolyn. 2000. Laura Bush, an Updated Traditional First Lady. *Seattle Times*, 26 December, A4.

Bonin, Julie. 2000. Speech May Shed Light on Reticent Half of Texas' First Couple. *Atlantic Journal and Constitution*, home ed., 30 July, A18.

Boswell, Randi. 2000. First Lady Power to Take Dramatic Shift. *Ottawa Citizen*, 16 December, final ed., B1.

Bruni, Frank. 2000a. Quiet Strength: For Laura Bush, a Direction She Never Wished to Go In. *New York Times*, 31 July, final ed., A1.

———. 2000b. Barbara Bush Joins GOP Women on Stump to Try to Bridge Gender Gap. *New York Times*, final edition, 19 October, A30.

Bush, Barbara. 1994. *A Memoir*. New York: Charles Scribner's Sons.

Bush, George W. 1999. *A Charge to Keep*. New York: William Morrow and Co.

Bush, Laura. 2000, Aug. 15. Education and Responsibility. *Vital Speeches of the Day*, 66: 21, 650–51.

———. 2001a. Ready to Read, Ready to Learn. Speech delivered in Hyattsville, Md., 26 February. www.whitehouse.gov/firstlady/news-speeches/, accessed 15 October 2001.

———. 2001b. Remarks of Laura Bush to the Hoover Institution. Speech delivered in Washington, D.C., 28 February. www.whitehouse.gov/firstlady/news-speeches/, accessed 15 October 2001.

———. 2001c. Remarks of Laura Bush at Morningside Elementary School. Speech delivered in San Fernando, Calif., 22 March. www.whitehouse.gov/firstlady/news-speeches/, accessed 15 October 2001.

———. 2001d. Remarks of Laura Bush to Occidental College. Speech delivered in Los Angeles, 22 March. www.whitehouse.gov/firstlady/news-speeches/, accessed 15 October 2001.

———. 2001e. Remarks for Laura Bush at Troops to Teachers Event. Speech delivered in San Diego, 23 March. www.whitehouse.gov/firstlady/news-speeches/, accessed 15 October 2001.

———. 2001f. Remarks of Laura Bush at Senate Spouses Luncheon. Speech delivered in Washington, D.C., 3 April. www.whitehouse.gov/firstlady/news-speeches/, accessed 15 October 2001.

———. 2001g. Remarks for Laura Bush for National Library Week Celebration and American Library Associations @ Your Library Event. Speech delivered in Washington, D.C., 3 April. www.whitehouse.gov/firstlady/news-speeches/, accessed 15 October 2001.

———. 2001h. Remarks of Laura Bush at Teach for America Gala. Speech delivered in New York City, 1 May. www.whitehouse.gov/firstlady/news-speeches/, accessed 15 October 2001.

———. 2001i. Remarks of Laura Bush at the Congressional Club. Speech delivered in Washington, D.C., 2 May. www.whitehouse.gov/firstlady/news-speeches/, accessed 15 October 2001.

———. 2001j. Remarks for Laura Bush at Troops to Teachers Event. Speech delivered in Fort Jackson, S.C., 6 May. www.whitehouse.gov/firstlady/news-speeches/, accessed 15 October 2001.

———. 2001k. Remarks of Laura Bush at Golden Apple Teacher Awards. Speech delivered in Chicago, 14 May. www.whitehouse.gov/firstlady/news-speeches/, accessed 15 October 2001.

———. 2001l. Remarks of Laura Bush at Reach Out and Read Event. Speech delivered in Chicago, 14 May. www.whitehouse.gov/firstlady/news-speeches/, accessed 15 October 2001.

———. 2001m. Remarks of Laura Bush at Reach Out and Read Event. Speech delivered in Boston, Mass., 1 June. www.whitehouse.gov/firstlady/news-speeches/, accessed 15 October 2001.

———. 2001n. Remarks of Laura Bush at the White House Summit on Early Childhood Cognitive Development. Speech delivered in Washington, D.C., 26 July. www.whitehouse.gov/firstlady/news-speeches/, accessed 28 March 2002.

———. 2001o. Mrs. Bush Announces Creation of Laura Bush Foundation for America's Libraries. Office of the First Lady Press Release, 30 July. www.whitehouse.gov/firstlady/news-speeches/, accessed 15 October 2001.

———. 2001p. Elementary School Letter & Middle School Letter. 12 September. www.whitehouse.gov/firstlady/news-speeches/, accessed 15 October 2001.

———. 2001q. Remarks by Mrs. Bush at Memorial Services in Pennsylvania. Speech delivered in Shankesville, Pa., 17 September. www.whitehouse.gov/firstlady/news-speeches/, accessed 15 October 2001.

———. 2001r. Remarks by Mrs. Bush at Kennedy Center. Speech delivered in Washington, D.C., 24 September. www.whitehouse.gov/firstlady/news-speeches/, accessed 15 October 2001.

———. 2001s. Remarks by Mrs. Bush Learning Leaders. Speech delivered in New York City, 25 September. www.whitehouse.gov/firstlady/news-speeches/, accessed 15 October 2001.

———. 2001t. Remarks by Mrs. Laura Bush to Early Cognitive Development Summit. Speech delivered at Cincinnati, Ohio, 3 October. www.whitehouse.gov/firstlady/news-speeches/, accessed 15 October 2001.

———. 2001u. Laura Bush Welcomes Recipients of the United Negro College Fund Liberty Scholarship. Speech delivered in Washington, D.C., 26 October. www.whitehouse.gov/firstlady/news-speeches/, accessed 14 March 2002.

———. 2001v. Remarks by Mrs. Bush at Women's Day Awards Luncheon. Speech given in New York City, 30 October. www.whitehouse.gov/firstlady/news-speeches/, accessed 14 March 2002.

———. 2001w. Remarks for Mrs. Bush to Best Friends "For Our Children" Event. Speech delivered in Washington, D.C., 7 November. www.whitehouse.gov/firstlady/news-speeches/, accessed 14 March 2002.

———. 2001x. Remarks by Mrs. Bush at the National Press Club. Speech delivered in Washington, D.C., 8 November. www.whitehouse.gov/firstlady/news-speeches/, accessed 14 March 2002.

———. 2001y. Radio Address by Laura Bush to the Nation. Speech delivered from Crawford, Tex., 17 November. www.whitehouse.gov/firstlady/news-speeches/, accessed 14 March 2002.

———. 2002a. Remarks for Mrs. Bush at Topeka Public Library Gala. Speech delivered in Topeka, Kans., 9 January www.whitehouse.gov/firstlady/news-speeches/, accessed 14 March 2002.

———. 2002b. Speech by the First Lady for Martin Luther King Jr. Day at Ebenezer Baptist Church. Speech given in Atlanta, Ga., 21 January. www.whitehouse.gov/firstlady/news-speeches/, accessed 14 March 2002.

———. 2002c. Mrs. Bush's Remarks before the Senate Committee on Health, Education, Labor and Pensions. Testimony delivered in Washington, D.C., 24 January. www.whitehouse.gov/firstlady/news-speeches/, accessed 14 March 2002.

———. 2002d. Remarks of Mrs. Laura Bush at USAID Event with Interim Chairman of the Afghan Authority Hamid Karzai. Speech delivered at the Ronald Reagan Building in Washington, D.C., 29 January. www.whitehouse.gov/firstlady/news-speeches/, accessed 14 March 2002.

———. 2002e. Remarks by Mrs. Bush—Transition to Teaching/New Teacher Project. Speech delivered at Powell Elementary School in Washington, D.C., 26 February. www.whitehouse.gov/firstlady/news-speeches/, accessed 3 March 2002.

———. 2002f. Opening Remarks by Mrs. Bush at White House Conference on Preparing Tomorrow's Teachers. Speech delivered at the White House in Washington, D.C., 5 March. www.whitehouse.gov/firstlady/news-speeches/, accessed 14 March 2002.

———. 2002g. Remarks by Mrs. Bush to the United Nations. Speech delivered for International Women's Day in New York City, 8 March. www.whitehouse.gov/firstlady/news-speeches/, accessed 14 March 2002.

———. 2002h. Remarks by Mrs. Bush to House Education and Workforce Committee. Testimony delivered in Washington, D.C., 14 March. www.whitehouse.gov/firstlady/news-speeches/, accessed 28 March 2002.

———. 2002i. Remarks of Mrs. Laura Bush to Back-to-School Project for Afghan Girls. Speech delivered at the Samuel W. Tucker Elementary School, 20 March. www.whitehouse.gov/firstlady/news-speeches/, accessed 28 March 2002.

———. 2002j. Remarks by Mrs. Laura Bush on Early Education to Eradicate Poverty and Promote Social Integration. Speech delivered in Peru, 23 March. www.whitehouse.gov/firstlady/news-speeches/, accessed 23 April 2002.

———. 2002k. Mrs. Laura Bush to Lead Presidential Delegation to the Ceremonial Funeral of the Queen Mother of England. Press release, Office of Mrs. Bush. 4 April. www.whitehouse.gov/firstlady/news-speeches/, accessed 23 April 2002.

———. 2002l. Statement by Mrs. Laura Bush Regarding Today's Services for the Queen Mother. Statement read in London, England, 9 April. www.whitehouse.gov/firstlady/news-speeches/, accessed 13 June 2002.

———. 2002m. Remarks by Mrs. Laura Bush at Organization for Economic Cooperation and Development (OECD) Forum Speech delivered in Paris, France, 14 May. www.whitehouse.gov/firstlady/news-speeches/, accessed 21 May 2002.

———. 2002n. Radio Address of First Lady Laura Bush to Radio Free Afghanistan. Speech delivered in Prague, Czech Republic, 21 May. www.whitehouse.gov/firstlady/news-speeches/, accessed 31 May 2002.

———. 2002o. Closing Remarks by Mrs. Bush at the White House Conference on School Libraries. Speech delivered at the White House in Washington, D.C., 4 June. www.whitehouse.gov/firstlady/news-speeches/, accessed 13 June 2002.

———. 2003. National First Ladies Library Dedication of the Education and Research Center. Remarks delivered at the First Ladies Library in Canton, Ohio, 4 September. http://www.whitehouse.gov/news/releases/2003/09/print/20030904-12.html, accessed 5 May 2004.

Copp, Tara. 2001. Laura Bush as First Lady: More Low-Key. *Chicago Sun-Times*, final ed., 21 April, 17.

Duke, Lynne. 2002. In Laura Bush, World's Women Gain Powerful Rights Advocate. *Washington Post*, final ed., 9 March, C01.

Felix, Antonia. 2002. *Laura: America's First Lady, First Mother*. Avon, Mass.: Adams Media Corporation.

Fiore, Faye. 2001. Laura Bush Has Role Changed from Seldom Heard Wife to the Nation's Comforter. *Los Angeles Times*, home ed. 10 October, part 5, 1.

Gamerman, Ellen. 2001. First Lady Makes Education "Her Issue." *Baltimore Sun*, final ed., 27 February, A3.

Gamerman, Ellen, and Gerard Shields. 2000. Laura Bush Is Hailed as Her Husband's New Secret Weapon. *Baltimore Sun*, 1 August, A6.

Gerhart, Ann. 2002a. The First Lady's Reading, Stopped by 9–11, Laura Bush Resumes Her Senate Testimony on Early Childhood Education. *Washington Post*, 25 January, C01.

———. 2002b. Laura Bush's Before-School Conference. *Washington Post*, 6 March, C01.

———. 2002c. At the Wheel, Laura Bush Shows She Can Shift Gears; First Lady Reworks Script on First Leg of Europe Trip. *Washington Post*, final ed., 15 May, C01.

———. 2002d. Laura Bush, Standing by Her Husband While Far Away. *Washington Post*, 18 May, C01.

———. 2002e. Mrs. Bush's Prague Pilgrimage; The First Lady Takes a Grand—and Sometimes Grim—Tour. *Washington Post*, final ed., 21 May, C01.

———. 2004. *The Perfect Wife: The Life and Choices of Laura Bush*. New York: Simon and Shuster.

Givhan, Robin. 2000. Taking Sensible First Footsteps; Laura Bush Is Arriving Well Heeled for Washington. *Washington Post*, final ed., 29 December, C01.

Harnden, Toby. 2000. Bush Women Take to the Road to Win Over Female Vote. *Daily Telegraph* (London), 17 October, 19.

Hillary Watch. 2002. *Human Events*, 58:9, 16.

Himes, Cragg. 2001. Starring in the East Wing (and Beyond). *Houston Chronicle*, 3 star ed., 9 November, A46.

Jayson, Sharon. 2001. Laura Bush Shares Love of Books. *The Atlantic Constitution*, 20 January, A6.

Jones, Jeffrey M., and Joseph Carroll. 2001. George W. and Laura Bush Top List of Most Admired. *Gallup Poll Monthly*, December, 52–55.

King, Larry. 2001. Interview with Laura Bush. CNN, aired 18 December.

Lange, John. 2000. Expect a Lady of First Regardless of Who Wins. *Pittsburgh Post-Gazette*, two star ed., 5 March, A8.

Leavitt, Paul. 2001. Laura Bush Urges Kids to Read and Be Tolerant. *USA Today*, 12 October, A11.

Leonard, Mary. 2000a. Behind the Scenes, Mrs. Bush Has a Pivotal Role. *Boston Globe*, third edition, 31 July, A1.

———. 2000b. Campaign 2000 . . . Convention Rhetoric Targets Women. *Boston Globe*, third ed., 3 August, A8.

———. 2001. War Gives Laura Bush Her Own Cause. *Boston Globe*, 29 November, A15.

MacPherson, Karen. 2001. Laura Bush Celebrates Authors, Reading. *Pittsburgh Post-Gazette*, sooner ed., 20 January, A6.

McQuillan, Laurence. 2001. Bush Dominates Most-Admired Opinion Poll. *USA Today*, 27 December, A3.

———. 2002. First Lady Quietly Making a Statement Abroad. *USA Today*, 17 May, 5A.

Milbank, Dana. 2001. *Smashmouth: Two Years in the Gutter with Al Gore and George W. Bush—Notes from the 2000 Campaign Trail*. New York: Basic Books.

Minutaglio, Bill. 1999. *First Son: George W. Bush and the Bush Family Dynasty*. New York: Random House.

Mitchell, Alison. 2000. Reluctance Aside, Mrs. Bush Shows Savvy in Campaign, *Plain Dealer* (Cleveland), 21 September, final ed. 16A.

Muir, Kate. 2000. Stand by My Man. *Times* (London), 30 October, n.p.

Neuffer, Elizabeth. 2002. The Task: Educating a Generation of Women, and Quickly. *Boston Globe*, 17 March, E1.

Ritsch, Massie. 2001. First Lady, Mexican Leader Praise Valley School. *Los Angeles Times*, 23 March, B1.

Romano, Lois. 2000. Laura Bush: A Twist on Traditional; Reluctant Celebrity Took Unconventional Route. *Washington Post*, final ed., 14 May, A01.

Rose, Hillary. 2000. Tipper v Laura. *Times* (London), features, 24 June, n.p.

Saunders, Debra J. 2002. A Real-Life Mrs. Cleaver. *San Francisco Chronicle*, 13 June, A29.

Simon, Roger. 2001. *Divided We Stand: How Al Gore Beat George Bush and Lost the Presidency*. New York: Crown Publishers.

Smith, Lynne. 2000. The Republican Convention. *Los Angeles Times*, 31 July, 16.

Stone, Tanya Lee. 2001. *Laura Welch Bush: First Lady*. Brookfield, Conn.: Millbrook Press.

Thomma, Stephen. 2001. The First Lady Makes Her Presence Felt. *Milwaukee Journal Sentinel*, 18 September, A10.

Walters, Barbara, and Diane Sawyer. 2001. Interview with President George W. Bush and Laura Bush. *20/20* (ABC), 5 December.

Wax, Emily. 2002. VA Students Help Bush Launch Outreach to Afghan Children. *Washington Post*, 21 March, B04.

Wertheimer, Molly Meijer, 2003. Laura Bush: A First Lady in Time of War. Unpublished paper, National Communication Association Conference, New Orleans, 21 November.

Index

Bush, Pauline Pierce ("Robin"), 189–90, 191–92
Butt, Archibald ("Archie"), 8
Byran, Helen, xi

Caddell, Patrick, 146
Campbell, David, 2
Campbell, Karlyn Kohrs, xi, xii, xvii–xviii, xix, 72, 80, 91, 224, 227, 230
Caputo, Lisa, 218
Carlson, Margaret, 4
Caroli, Betty Boyd, xii, xvi, 4, 6, 8, 10, 93n1, 99–100, 116, 120n6, 124, 211, 236
Carpenter, Liz, 77, 78, 80, 155, 242
Carson, Johnny, 222
Carson, Rachael, 85
Carter, Jimmy: administration of, 140–41, 151, 152, 153, 154, 156, 159, 196; as a campaigner, 142; and Gerald M. Ford, 195; image of, 144, 152, 155; interview of, 142, 145, 152; and the Iran hostage crises, 155, 157; political career of, 143
Carter, Rosalynn: as an advocate, xvii, 140–41, 143, 144, 145, 147–52, 159; autobiography of, 152, 159; biography of, 141–44, 160; as a business partner, 143, 151; and cabinet meetings, 140, 144; as a campaigner, 141, 143–44, 152, 154–58; criticism of, 148, 153, 155–56; as a diplomat, 62, 140–41, 145, 146, 147, 152, 153, 159–60; education of, 142; and the elderly, 148, 149–50, 152, 159; and the Equal Rights Amendment, 144, 148, 150, 151, 159; as first lady, 140, 144, 145, 146, 152; as first lady of Georgia, 143, 148; as a helpmate, 145; as a hostess, 152; and husband's presidency, 152–58; and husband's speeches, 145, 147; image of, 145; influence of, 146, 159; and interviews, 143, 144, 147, 159; and Jackie Kennedy, 46; legacy of, 158–60; and letters, 150; and the media, 141, 145, 148, 149, 153–54, 156; and mental health, 144, 147, 148,

149, 153, 159, 160; as a mother, 142, 151; parents of, 141–42; as a political partner, 4, 140–41,144–47, 151, 152, 159; and the press, 143, 159; and public speaking, 143, 145, 150, 151, 153–54, 155, 156, 157–58, 161n2; and religion, 141, 146; rhetorical activities of, 141, 144–58; and social reform, 141, 144, 147–52, 157; as a surrogate, xvii, 141, 144, 152, 159; and testimony before congress, 149, 159, 254; and volunteerism, 144, 148, 150, 152; and the White House, 144, 174; as a wife, 142, 151; and women's rights, 146, 148, 152, 156
Carter, Ruth, 142
Casals, Pablo, 53
Cassini, Oleg, 45, 46–47, 52
Cater, Douglass, 81
Checkers Speech, 101–2, 118, 120n4
Chirac, Jacques, 260
Cheney, Lynn, 244
Civil Rights Act of 1964, 81, 91
Cleveland, Francis, 133
Clift, Eleanor, 228
Clinton, Chelsea Victoria, 222
Clinton, Hillary Rodham: as an advocate, 217, 220–21, 224, 226, 232, 253, 254; as an author, 221, 226, 232; biography of, 218–24; and the bully pulpit, 225; as a campaigner, 1, 221; and children, 217, 220–21, 222, 226, 228, 232; and conservatism, 220; criticism of, 1, 3, 5, 230; and democracy, 228–31; as a diplomat, 62; education of, 218–21; and Eleanor Roosevelt, 16; and femininity, xviii; as a feminist, 223, 232; as first lady, 72, 217, 223–25, 226, 231–32; as first lady of Arkansas, 1, 221–22; and health care reform, 5, 11, 224–26; as a hostess, 225; and husband's infidelity, 222–23, 226, 231; image of, 217, 218; and interviews, 223, 225; and Laura Bush, 236, 242, 245; as a lawyer, 221, 222, 227; legacy of, 231–32; marriage of, 222; and the media, 218, 224, 226, 232; and the

About the Contributors

Karrin Vasby Anderson is assistant professor of speech communication at Colorado State University where she teaches courses in political communication, women and communication, and public speaking. Her research interests include gender and political leadership, and media coverage of political candidates. She has published articles on Hillary Rodham Clinton and Elizabeth Dole in *Rhetoric and Public Affairs* and *Women's Studies in Communication*.

Lisa R. Barry has taught courses on persuasion and rhetoric as well as media studies. Presently, she teaches English at Montgomery County Public Schools. She has received teaching and research awards, including top papers in visual communication and in the Feminist and Women's Studies Divisions of the National Communication Association. She has published her work in *Communication Teacher* and elsewhere.

Diane M. Blair is assistant professor in the Department of Communication at California State University, Fresno, where she teaches courses in rhetorical theory, rhetorical criticism, and American public address. Her research interests include political rhetoric and feminist criticism, and her scholarship has appeared in journals such as *Rhetoric and Public Affairs* and *Communication Quarterly*. She is a contributor to *The Eleanor Roosevelt Encyclopedia*.

Diana B. Carlin is dean of the Graduate School and International Programs and a professor of communication studies at the University of Kansas where she teaches courses in political communication and communication and gender studies. Her research focuses on women in politics, political debates, and speech writing. She has published extensively on political communication in *Argumentation and Advocacy*, *American Behavioral Scientist*, *Political Communication*, and *Rhetoric and Public Affairs*.

Nichola D. Gutgold is assistant professor of speech communication at the Pennsylvania State University, Berks-Lehigh Valley College, where she teaches courses in public speaking, speech writing, and organizational communication. She has published articles on pedagogy, organizational communication, and political rhetoric.

Linda B. Hobgood is the director of the Speech Center at the University of Richmond and instructor in the Department of Rhetoric and Communication Studies. She teaches a variety of courses such as the rhetoric of first ladies, political rhetoric, and speech writing. She has published articles on group communication, speaking centers, and applied theory and pedagogy.

Anne F. Mattina is an associate professor of communication as Stonehill College in Easton, Massachusetts. Her research interests include women's labor reform rhetoric and antislavery activism. Her work has appeared in such publications as *Communication Quarterly*, *The McNeese Review*, and the *Women Studies Annual*.

Mary Mooney practices corporate communications for a Texas-based healthcare conglomerate. Ms. Mooney has taught at George Mason University, Boston College, and Emerson College. Her women's studies research includes an FDA-sponsored historical analysis of contraceptives in the American news media, an examination of women and corporate success, and related issues in gender and politics.

Janette Kenner Muir is associate dean of New Century College, an interactive and interdisciplinary program at George Mason University. Dr. Muir has taught courses in rhetorical criticism and political communication, and published research on subjects such as Clinton's presidential campaigns, Hillary Clinton, and the Hill/Thomas hearings. She also has edited a book on how to use C-SPAN in communication classes.

Elizabeth J. Natalle is associate professor of communication and women's studies at the University of North Carolina at Greensboro. In addition to her course in gender and communication theory, she teaches a seminar on feminist rhetorical criticism. Dr. Natalle is the author of *Feminist Theatre: A Study in Persuasion* and the coauthor of *The Woman's Public Speaking Handbook*.

Shawn J. Parry-Giles is assistant professor of communication, director of the Center for Political Communication and Civic Leadership, and affiliate assistant professor of women's studies at the University of Maryland. Her courses focus on political communication, as well as rhetorical, feminist, and media criticism. Her research has appeared in the *Quarterly Journal of Speech, Political Communication, Presidential Studies Quarterly,* and *Critical Studies in Media Communication.* She is author of *The Rhetorical Presidency, Propaganda, and the Cold War, 1945–1955* and coauthor of *Constructing Clinton: Hyperreality and Presidential Image-Making in Postmodern Politics.*

Molly Meijer Wertheimer is professor of speech communication and affiliate associate professor of women's studies at the Pennsylvania State University, Hazleton campus. She teaches courses on public speaking and on women, the humanities, and the arts. She is editor of *Inventing a Voice: The Rhetoric of American First Ladies of the Twentieth Century* and *Listening to Their Voices: The Rhetorical Activities of Historical Women* and coauthor of *Public Speaking as a Liberal Art,* 6th ed. Her research and reviews have appeared in journals such as *Philosophy and Rhetoric,* the *Quarterly Journal of Speech,* and *Rhetorica.*